杭州

统计年鉴 2017

HANGZHOU STATISTICAL YEARBOOK

杭州统计年鉴 2017

HANGZHOU STATISTICAL YEARBOOK

杭州市统计局
国家统计局杭州调查队
杭州市社会经济调查局

中国统计出版社
China Statistics Press

图书在版编目（CIP）数据

杭州统计年鉴. 2017 / 杭州市统计局, 国家统计局杭州调查队, 杭州市社会经济调查局编. -- 北京 : 中国统计出版社, 2017.9
ISBN 978-7-5037-8068-4

Ⅰ. ①杭… Ⅱ. ①杭… ②国… ③杭… Ⅲ. ①统计资料－杭州－2017－年鉴 Ⅳ. ①C832.551-54

中国版本图书馆CIP数据核字(2017)第200646号

杭州统计年鉴2017

作　　者/ 杭州市统计局
　　　　　国家统计局杭州调查队
　　　　　杭州市社会经济调查局
责任编辑/ 陈越月
装帧设计/ 张子杰
出版发行/ 中国统计出版社
地　　址/ 北京市丰台区西三环南路甲6号　邮政编码/100073
电　　话/ 邮购（010）63376909　书店（010）68783171
网　　址/ http://csp.stats.gov.cn
印　　刷/ 浙江新中商务印刷有限公司
经　　销/ 新华书店
开　　本/ 890mm×1240mm　1/16
字　　数/ 991千字
印　　张/ 28.75
版　　别/ 2017年9月第1版
版　　次/ 2017年9月第1次印刷

ISBN 978-7-5037-8068-4

定价：300.00元

如有印装差错，由本社发行部调换

HANGZHOU STATISTICAL YEARBOOK
杭州统计年鉴
2017 编委会和编辑人员

HANGZHOU STATISTICAL YEARBOOK

杭州统计年鉴

2017 Editorial Board and Staff

编者说明

一、《杭州统计年鉴—2017》是一部信息密集的资料性年刊。本年鉴系统收集了全市和各区、县（市）2016年经济和社会各方面的统计数据，以及多个重要历史年份和近年全市主要统计数据。

二、本年鉴分为13个篇章：综合；人口和就业人员；农业；工业、能源；建筑业；交通运输、邮电；固定资产投资；国内贸易；对外经济、旅游；财政、金融、保险；城市建设、环境保护；科技、教育、文化、卫生、体育；人民生活、物价、民政。为便于读者使用，各篇章附有简要说明和主要统计指标解释。

三、本年鉴辑中涉及到历史数据，均以最新版本为准；本年鉴中部分数据合计数或相对数由于单位取舍不同而产生的计算误差，均未做机械调整。

四、2001年起，萧山、余杭撤市建区，市区数据含萧山、余杭区；2014年起富阳撤市建区，市区数据包括富阳区。

五、本年鉴表中符号使用说明："－"表示这一栏没有数字；"…"表示该数字不足本表最小计量单位；"#"表示其中的主要项；"空格"表示该项统计数据不详或无该项数据；"*"表示表下有注解。

六、本年鉴所使用的度量衡单位均采用国际统一标准计量单位，金额除特别标明外，均以人民币计量。

七、与2016年版《杭州统计年鉴》相比较，本年鉴在篇章结构和内容上主要做了以下修订：第一篇增加了主要年份分地区生产总值发展指数、2011－2015年十大产业主要指标、2015－2016年信息经济主要指标、2016年"1＋6"产业集群主要指标、主要年份分地区建筑业增加值、2015－2016年分机构类型和登记注册类型法人单位数、2016年分行业法人单位数统计表式；第二篇增加2016年末分行业非私营单位职工素质情况；第四篇增加2016年分行业规模以上工业企业主要经济效益指标、2000－2016年分地区规上工业增加值发展指数、2013－2016年规上工业三大新兴产业发展情况、2016年规模以下工业主要指标统计表式；第七篇增加2011－2016年全市固定资产投资发展指数、2011－2016年分地区固定资产投资发展指数、2010－2016年分行业基础设施投资统计表式；第八篇增加2011－2016年规模以上服务企业主要经济指标、2016年分行业和类型规模以上服务业主要经济指标、2011－2016年规模以上服务业非企业单位主要经济指标、2016年分行业规模以上服务业非企业单位主要经济指标统计表式；第十篇增加2011－2016年金融机构人民币信贷收支表、2011－2016年金融机构人民币信贷收支表；第十二篇增加2011－2016年R&D经费投入情况、2011－2016年规模以上工业R&D经费投入情况、2015－2016年图书出版数量统计表式。根据最新统计报表制度对个别专业内容及相关统计指标进行了调整。

八、《杭州统计年鉴》公开出版以来，受到了社会各界的关心和支持，对此我们深表谢意。限于我们的水平，欢迎广大读者继续对年鉴的不足之处给予批评和指正，帮助我们进一步提高统计年鉴的编辑工作，更好地为广大读者服务（网址：http：//www. hzstats. gov. cn/）。

Editorial Note

Ⅰ. *Hangzhou Statistical Yearbook 2017* is an informative annuals that covers comprehensive data series of Hangzhou's social and economic development. Which contains very comprehensive statistics of Hangzhou's social and economic development in 2016. It covers Hangzhou's data in recent years and some historically important years.

Ⅱ. The Yearbook contains 13 chapters: 1. General Survey; 2. Population and Employment; 3. Agriculture; 4. Industry and Energy; 5. Construction; 6. Transportation, Post and Telecommunications; 7. Investment in Fixed Assets; 8. Domestic Trade; 9. Foreign Economic Cooperation and Tourism; 10. Finance, Banking and Insurance; 11. Urban Construction and Environmental Protection; 12. Science and Technology, Education, Culture, Public Health and Sports; 13. People's Livelihood, Price Indices and Civil Administration. To facilitate readers, each chaper provides brief introduction and explanatory notes on main statistical indicators.

Ⅲ. Please refer to the newly published version of the Yearbook for updated historical data. Statistical discrepancies on totals and relative figures due to rounding are not adjusted in the Yearbook.

Ⅳ. Because of the change of urban administrative division, the data of Xiaoshan District and Yuhang District have been included into the urban districts since 2001, and it is the same with Fuyang District since 2014.

Ⅴ. Notations used in this book:"—" indicates that the column has no figure;"…" indicates that the figure is not large enough to be measured with the smallest unit in the table;"blank space" indicates that the date are unknown, or are not available;"#" indicates the major items of the total;" * " indicates"see footnotes below".

Ⅵ. The international standard unit of measurement is applied in this book, all amounts are denominated in RMB, except those with special notes.

Ⅶ. In comparison with Hangzhou Statistical Yearbook 2016, following revisions have been made in this new version in terms of the statistical contents and editing : The 1 chapter added seven statistical tables , such as Indices of Gross Domestic Product by Region (Main Year), Ten Major Industries (2011 – 2015), Information Economy (2015 – 2016)," 1 + 6" Industrial Cluster (2016), Value Added of Construction by Region (Main Years), Number of Corporation Units by Types of Organization and Registration (2015 – 2016), Number of Corporation Units by Sector (2016). The 2 chapter added one statistical tables , such as The Education Level of the Staff and Workers in Non – private Units by Sector (End of 2016). The 4 chapter added four statistical tables , such as Main Economic Indicators of Industrial Enterprises Above Designated Size by Sector (2016), Index of Added Valve of Industrial Enterprises Above Designated Size by Region (2000 – 2016), Development of the Three Recently Emerging Industries Above Designated Size (2013 – 2016), Main Indicators of Industrial Enterprises Below Designated Size (2016). The 7 chapter added three statistical tables , such as Indices of Investment in Fixed Assets (1979 – 2016) , Indices of Investment in Fixed Assets by Region (2011 – 2016), Investment in Infrastructure by Sector (2011 – 2016). The 8 chapter added five statistical tables , such as Indices of Total Retail Sale of Consumer Goods (2001 – 2016), Main Indicators of Service Enterprises Above Designated Size (2011 – 2016), Main Indicators of Service Enterprises Above Designated Size by Sector and Type (2016), Main Indicators of Service Non – Enterprises Units Above Designated Size (2011 – 2016), Main Indicators of Service Non – Enterprises Units Above Designated Size by Sector (2016). The 10 chapter added two statistical tables , such as Gredit Funds Balance Sheet of Financial Institution (RMB, Sources of Funds, 2011 – 2016), Gredit Funds Balance Sheet of Financial Institution (RMB, Use of Funds, 2011 – 2016). The 12 chapter added three statistical tables , such as Basic Statistics on R&D Activities Funds (2011 – 2016), Basic Statistics on R&D Activities of Industrial Enterprises above Designated Size (2011 – 2016), Number of Books Pulished (2015 – 2016). According to the new statistical report system, a few contents and indicators are adjusted.

Ⅷ. Since published openly, Previous Editions of Hangzhou Statistics Yearbook have enjoyed wide concern and support; and we express heartfelt thanks. In order to get further improvement in the yearbook editing, we welcome all candid comments and criticism from our readers (website: http: //www. hzstats. gov. cn/).

目　录
Contents

一、综合
Ⅰ. General Survey

二、人口和就业人员

Ⅱ. Population and Employment

三、农业

Ⅲ. Agriculture

四、工业、能源
Ⅳ. Industry and Energy

五、建筑业

Ⅴ. Construction

六、交通运输、邮电

Ⅵ. Transportation, Post and Telecommunications

七、固定资产投资

Ⅶ. Investment in Fixed Assets

八、国内贸易

Ⅷ. Domestic Trade

九、对外经济、旅游

Ⅸ. Foreign Economic Cooperation and Tourism

十、财政、金融、保险
X．Finance, Banking and Insurance

十一、城市建设、环境保护

Ⅺ. Urban Construction and Environmental Protection

十二、科技、教育、文化、卫生、体育

Ⅻ. Science and Technology, Education, Culture, Public Health and Sports

十三、人民生活、物价、民政

XIII. People's Livelihood, Price Indices and Civil Administration

2016 年杭州市国民经济和社会发展统计公报

杭 州 市 统 计 局
国家统计局杭州调查队
2017 年 3 月

2016 年，全市深入贯彻落实中央、省、市各项决策部署，以服务保障 G20 杭州峰会为圆心，主动把握和引领经济发展新常态，坚定不移打好转型升级系列组合拳，着力培育经济发展新动能，全市经济实现了持续稳定增长，发展质量效益同步提升，经济社会发展保持了稳中有进、稳中向好的良好态势，实现了“十三五”发展良好开局。

一、综　　合

（一）经济总量。

2016 年，全市实现生产总值 11313.72 亿元，比上年增长 9.6%。其中第一产业增加值 304.21 亿元，第二产业增加值 4120.93 亿元，第三产业增加值 6888.59 亿元，分别增长 1.8%、4.5% 和 13.5%。常住人口人均生产总值 124286 元，增长 7.8%。按国家公布的 2016 年平均汇率折算，为 18718 美元。三次产业结构由上年的 2.9∶38.9∶58.2 调整为 2.7∶36.4∶60.9（见图 1、图 2）。

图 1　2011 年 –2016 年全市生产总值及增速

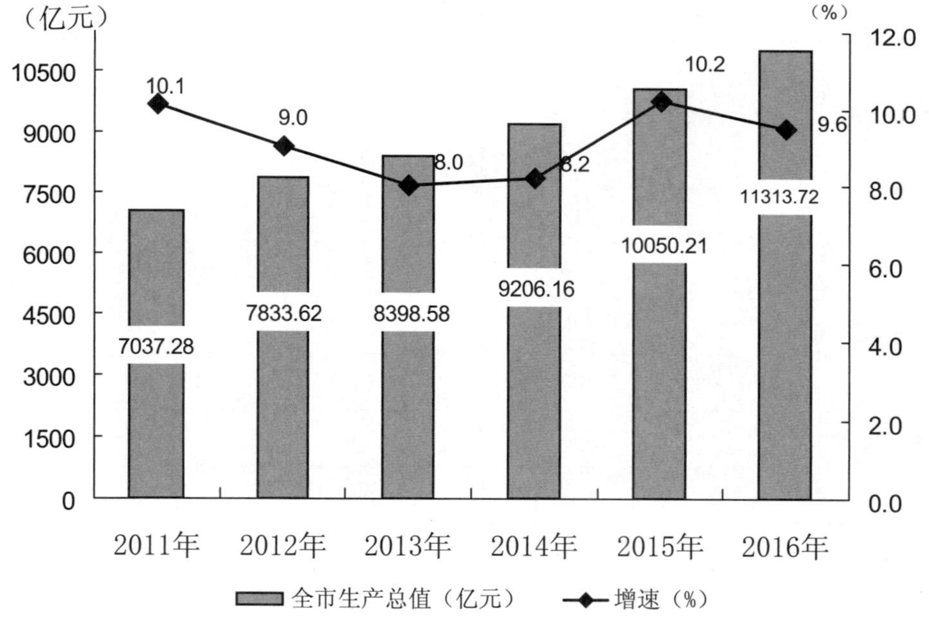

图 2　全市三次产业增加值占 GDP 比重(%)

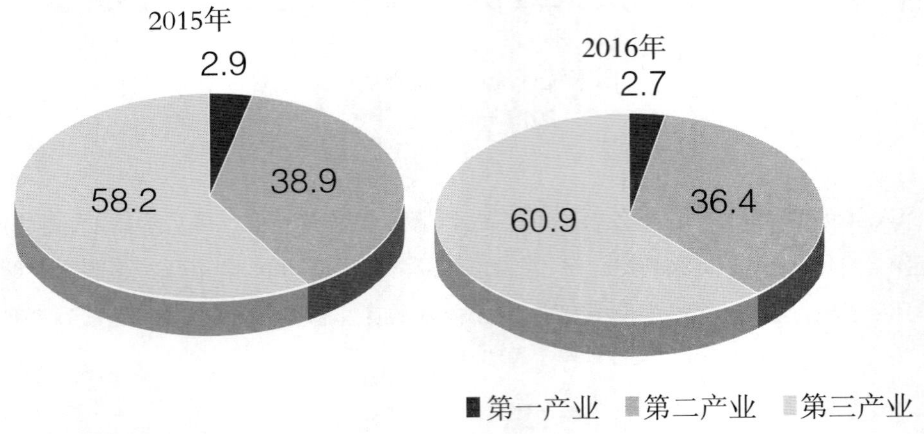

(二)民营经济。

全市民营经济实现增加值 6586.09 亿元,占 GDP 的 59.6%。年末,全市私营企业 40.06 万户,比上年末增长 19.7%;个体工商户 42.60 万户,增长 10.3%。私营企业和个体工商户从业人员分别为 281.70 万人、84.45 万人,增长 8.9% 和 6.3%。

(三)信息经济。

全市信息经济实现增加值 2688.00 亿元,增长 22.8%,占 GDP 的 24.3%,同比提高 1.3 个百分点。其中,电子商务产业、移动互联网产业、数字内容产业分别增长 45.2%、45.1% 和 35.0%(见表 1)。

表 1　全市信息经济分产业增加值

产业名称	2015 年		2016 年	
	绝对值(亿元)	增速(%)	绝对值(亿元)	增速(%)
合　计	2313.85	25.0	2688.00	22.8
电子商务	826.54	34.5	1026.73	45.2
云计算与大数据	828.96	29.6	960.58	28.2
物联网	307.21	12.7	335.45	8.8
互联网金融	326.17	33.5	230.40	7.0
智慧物流	58.07	8.4	96.45	18.5
数字内容	1234.45	35.5	1499.21	35.0
软件与信息服务	1596.45	29.4	1869.42	28.8
电子信息产品制造	557.83	12.5	620.73	11.0
移动互联网	844.71	37.5	1034.00	45.1
集成电路	42.54	8.6	53.23	21.5
信息安全	221.58	15.3	250.27	14.6
机器人	15.77	1.5	19.98	4.2

注:各产业内部有重复,合计为剔除重复数据。

（四）财政收支。

全市财政总收入2558.41亿元，一般公共预算收入1402.38亿元，分别增长14.0%和13.2%。一般公共预算支出1404.31亿元，增长16.4%，其中，民生类支出1084.40亿元，增长17.4%，民生支出占比77.2%（见图3）。

图3　2011年－2016年全市一般公共预算收入

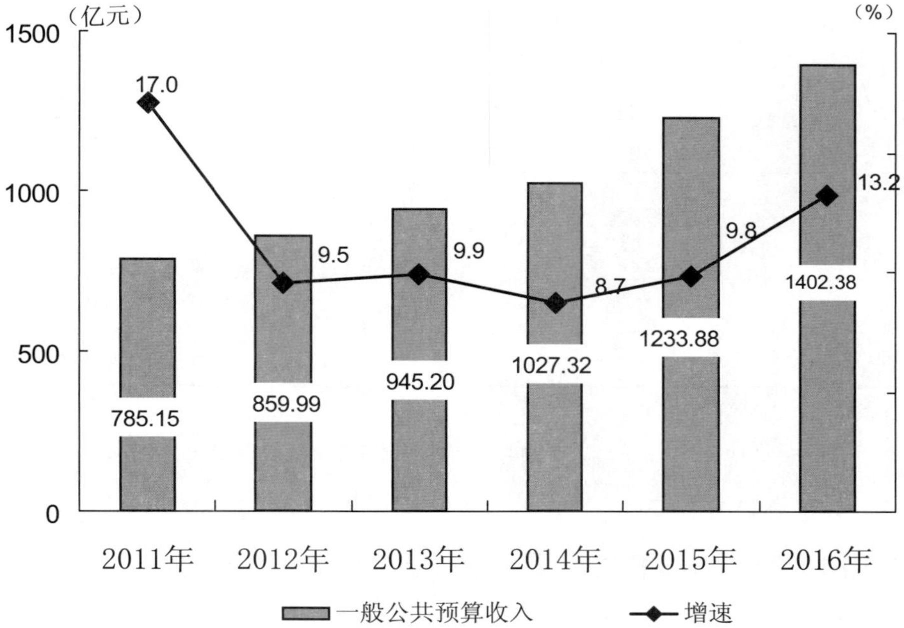

（五）市场价格。

市区居民消费价格比上年上涨2.6%，涨幅同比提高0.8个百分点。八大类商品和服务项目价格呈"六升二降"格局（见图4、表2）。

图4　2016年市区居民消费价格月度涨跌幅度

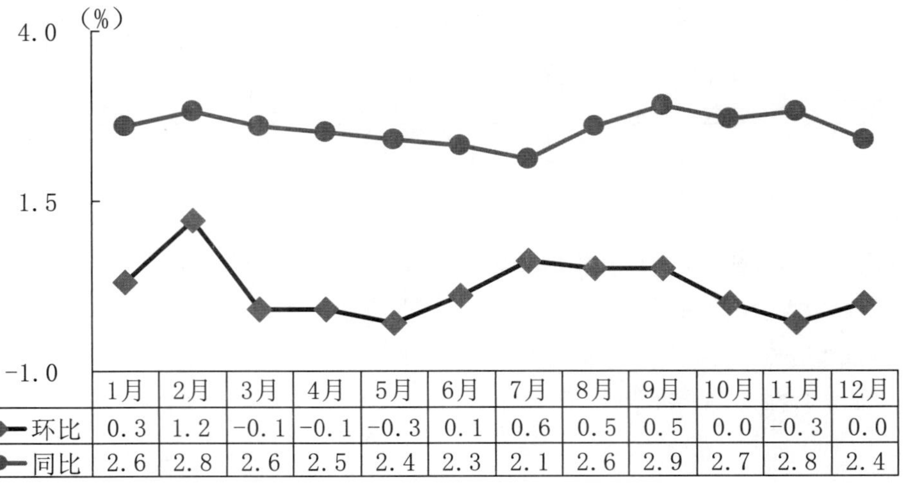

	1月	2月	3月	4月	5月	6月	7月	8月	9月	10月	11月	12月
环比	0.3	1.2	-0.1	-0.1	-0.3	0.1	0.6	0.5	0.5	0.0	-0.3	0.0
同比	2.6	2.8	2.6	2.5	2.4	2.3	2.1	2.6	2.9	2.7	2.8	2.4

表 2　市区居民消费价格比上年涨跌幅度

单位:%

项　　目	2016 年
市区居民消费价格	2.6
1. 食品烟酒	6.0
2. 衣着	0.3
3. 居住	2.2
4. 生活用品及服务	-0.4
5. 交通和通信	-1.0
6. 教育文化和娱乐	3.7
7. 医疗保健	0.8
8. 其他用品和服务	2.7

全市工业生产者出厂价格下降0.8%，工业生产者购进价格下降1.1%，降幅同比分别缩小2.7和6.0个百分点(见图5)。

图 5　2016 年全市工业生产者价格月度同比涨跌幅度

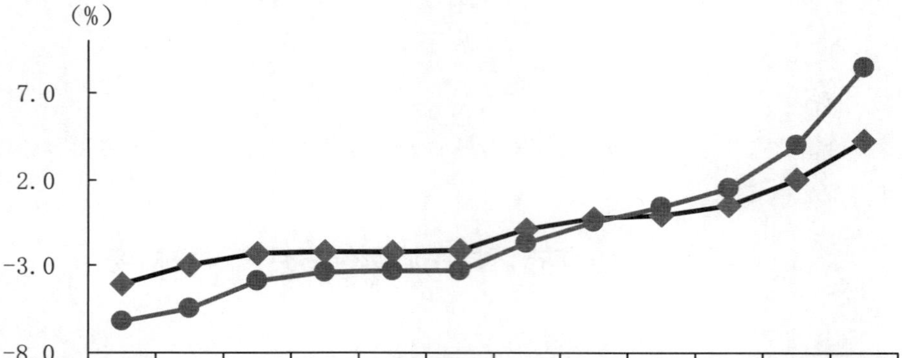

	1月	2月	3月	4月	5月	6月	7月	8月	9月	10月	11月	12月
出厂价格	-4.0	-3.0	-2.3	-2.2	-2.2	-2.1	-0.9	-0.2	-0.1	0.5	2.0	4.2
购进价格	-6.2	-5.4	-3.9	-3.4	-3.3	-3.3	-1.7	-0.5	0.4	1.5	4.0	8.4

(六)人口就业。

至年末，全市常住人口918.80万人，比上年末增加17.00万人，其中城镇人口700.13万人，占比76.2%，比2015年提高0.9个百分点；人口出生率为11.1‰，人口自然增长率为6.0‰。全市户籍人口736.00万人，人口出生率为13.21‰，人口自然增长率为7.16‰。全市新增城镇就业人员27.13万人，安置失业人员再就业11.48万人。年末城镇登记失业率1.72%(见图6)。

图6　2011 年－2016 年全市常住人口和户籍人口数量

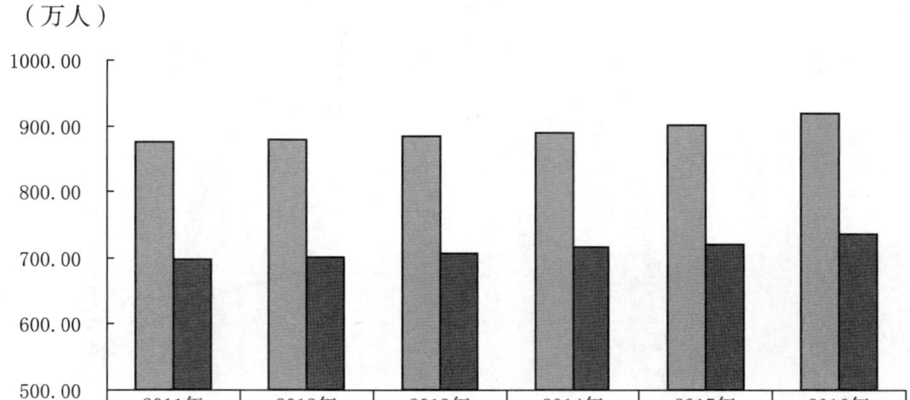

	2011年	2012年	2013年	2014年	2015年	2016年
常住人口	873.80	880.20	884.40	889.20	901.80	918.80
户籍人口	695.71	700.52	706.61	715.76	723.55	736.00

二、农　　业

全市实现农林牧渔业增加值 309.26 亿元，增长 5.8%。其中，农业 193.38 亿元，林业 41.67 亿元，牧业 41.58 亿元，分别增长 7.1%、5.9% 和 5.1%；渔业 27.57 亿元，下降 3.1%；农林牧渔服务业 5.05 亿元，增长 13.5%。全市粮食总产量 63.60 万吨，增长 0.3%；蔬菜产量 335.34 万吨，增长 5.2%；水果产量 76.41 万吨，肉类产量 26.27 万吨，水产品产量 19.48 万吨，分别下降 3.2%、5.6% 和 7.2%。新建市级“菜篮子”基地 35 个，各级粮食生产功能区 152 个。

三、工业和建筑业

（一）工业生产。

全市实现工业增加值 3726.20 亿元，增长 5.2%，其中规模以上工业增加值 2990.34 亿元，增长 5.6%。规模以上工业中，战略性新兴产业、装备制造业、高新技术产业分别实现增加值 812.07 亿元、1249.59 亿元和 1372.92 亿元，增长 11.6%、14.6% 和 12.5%。新产品产值率由上年 35.4% 提高到 37.4%。工业产品产销率为 99.4%。

（二）工业效益。

全市规模以上工业企业实现利税 1655.64 亿元，增长 6.8%，其中利润 946.06 亿元，增长 6.7%。企业亏损面 17.0%。

（三）建筑业。

全市实现建筑业增加值 396.12 亿元，下降 1.8%。具有总承包和专业承包资格的建筑企业 1474 家，完成施工产值 4105.30 亿元，增长 0.2%；房屋建筑施工面积 27220.71 万平方米，下降 3.2%；房屋建筑竣工面积 9754.11 万平方米，下降 3.8%。

四、固定资产投资和房地产业

（一）固定资产投资。

全市完成固定资产投资 5842.42 亿元，增长 5.1%。非国有投资 3561.16 亿元，增长 0.6%，占固定资产投资的 61.0%，其中民间投资 3006.78 亿元，增长 1.0%，占固定资产投资的 51.5%。从产业投向看，第一产业 39.36

亿元，增长25.1%；第二产业886.90亿元，下降4.8%，其中工业883.95亿元，下降5.0%；第三产业4916.16亿元，增长7.0%（见图7）。

图7　2011年－2016年全市固定资产投资及增速

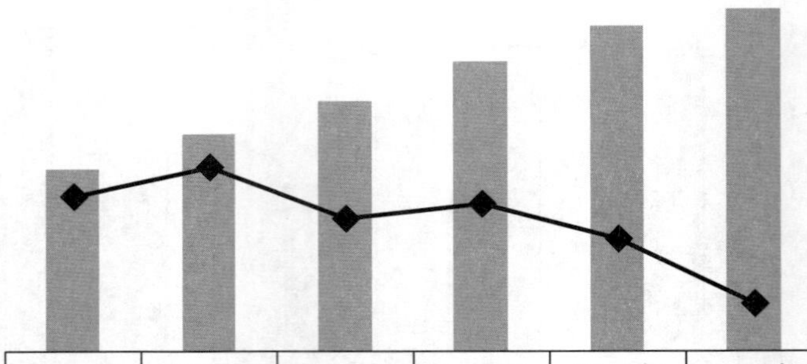

	2011年	2012年	2013年	2014年	2015年	2016年
投资（亿元）	3100.02	3722.75	4263.87	4952.70	5556.32	5842.42
增速（%）	16.9	20.1	14.5	16.2	12.2	5.1

（二）房地产业。

全市完成房地产开发投资2606.41亿元，增长5.4%，其中住宅投资1559.98亿元，增长8.2%。房屋施工面积11562.96万平方米，增长3.8%；竣工面积1922.99万平方米，增长15.5%。全年商品房销售面积2326.69万平方米，增长57.1%，其中住宅销售1887.11万平方米，增长46.1%。保障性安居工程项目开工76161套，竣工58664套。

五、国内贸易

全市实现批发和零售业增加值883.72亿元，增长6.8%；住宿餐饮业增加值175.26亿元，下降1.4%。

全市实现社会消费品零售总额5176.20亿元，增长10.5%，扣除价格因素，实际增长8.9%。其中商品零售额4637.58亿元，增长10.7%，餐饮收入538.62亿元，增长8.7%。城镇消费品零售额4904.61亿元，增长10.4%；乡村消费品零售额271.59亿元，增长10.9%（见图8）。

在限额以上批发零售贸易业零售额中，文化办公用品类、五金电料类商品分别增长40.1%和29.9%，粮油食品类、服装鞋帽针纺织品类商品分别增长16.7%和14.8%，汽车类、通讯器材类商品分别增长10.7%和7.4%；金银珠宝类、石油及制品类商品分别下降12.6%和5.4%。

全市实现网络零售额3445.65亿元，增长28.6%，居民网络消费额1499.98亿元，增长34.0%。

图8　2011年－2016年全市社会消费品零售总额及增速

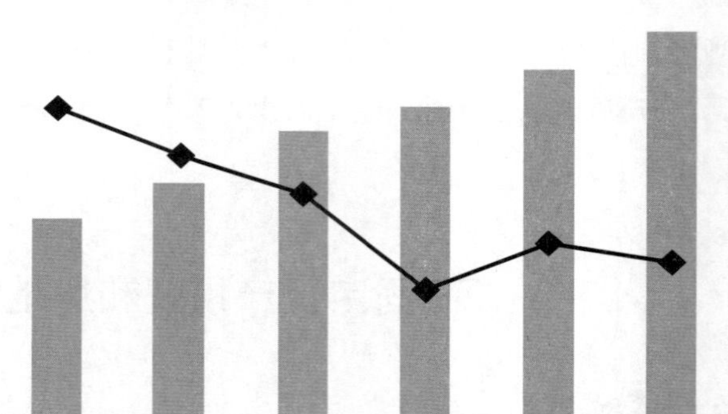

	2011年	2012年	2013年	2014年	2015年	2016年
零售总额（亿元）	2690.22	3165.19	3864.84	4201.46	4697.23	5176.20
增速（%）	20.9	17.7	15.1	8.7	11.8	10.5

六、对外经济

(一)对外贸易。

全市实现货物进出口总额4485.97亿元,增长8.7%。其中,进口总额1172.17亿元,增长14.6%;出口总额3313.80亿元,增长6.7%。(不含省属企业,出口3019.05亿元,增长9.5%)。出口总额中,机电产品出口1357.20亿元,高新技术产品出口424.23亿元,分别增长8.3%和7.6%。按贸易方式分,一般贸易出口2922.94亿元,增长8.7%;进料加工贸易出口347.38亿元,下降8.1%。出口市场中,亚洲、欧洲市场分别增长8.0%和8.3%(见表3)。

全市服务贸易进出口总额1399.64亿元,增长18.0%。其中,出口总额945.67亿元,增长19.0%。

表3 2016年全市货物进出口总额及增速

指　　标	总额(亿元)	增长(%)
货物进出口总额	4485.97	8.7
货物出口额	3313.80	6.7
一般贸易	2922.94	8.7
进料加工贸易	347.38	-8.1
机电产品	1357.20	8.3
高新技术产品	424.23	7.6
货物进口额	1172.17	14.6

(二)对外合作。

至年末,全市设立各类境外投资企业(机构)1586个,其中非贸易企业624个。境外合同投资52.18亿美元,其中非贸易性投资41.92亿美元,增长185.0%。对外承包工程和劳务合作营业额19.26亿美元,增长8.9%。离岸服务外包合同执行额58.72亿美元,增长13.1%。

(三)利用外资。

全市批准外商直接投资462项,实际利用外资72.09亿美元,增长1.4%。新批总投资3000万美元以上项目145个,总投资141.27亿美元,占新批外商项目总投资的94.0%。引进世界500强投资项目10个,至2016年末,有117家世界500强企业来杭投资198个项目。

(四)跨境电子商务。

全市实现跨境电商进出口总额81.12亿美元,增长134.2%。其中,出口60.60亿美元,进口20.52亿美元,分别增长166.7%和72.3%。

(五)浙商回归。

全市共引进内资项目2733个,到位资金1397.07亿元,增长11.8%。其中浙商回归项目到位资金709.96亿元,增长7.5%。

(六)开发区建设。

杭州经济技术开发区、杭州高新技术产业开发区、萧山经济技术开发区、杭州之江国家旅游度假区、余杭经济技术开发区、富阳经济技术开发区、临江国家高新区等7个国家级开发区实现规模以上工业主营业务收入6719.15亿元,利润总额609.65亿元,分别增长9.6%和18.5%;规模以上服务业主营业务收入2251.06亿元,利润总额309.58亿元,分别增长14.7%和17.8%。

七、交通、邮电和旅游

(一)交通邮电。

全市实现交通运输、仓储和邮政业增加值325.46亿元,增长9.2%。

全社会货物运输总量3.02亿吨,增长2.7%。旅客运输量2.05亿人次,下降11.1%。至年末,萧山国际机场已开通航线240条,其中国际航线38条,港澳台航线7条。内地航线进出港旅客2741.43万人次,增长11.0%;国际及地区航线进出港旅客418.06万人次,增长14.5%。境内公路总里程达到16306.07公里,其中高速公路632.04公里。

全市民用机动车拥有量达263.35万辆,下降3.7%。民用汽车拥有量234.15万辆,增长4.3%,其中,私人汽车192.27万辆,增长4.0%。

全市邮政企业和规模以上快递服务企业实现业务收入215.17亿元,增长34.8%。规模以上快递服务企业业务量18.05亿件,增长43.6%。实现电信业务收入190.7亿元,增长5.9%。年末固定电话用户265.70万户,下降9.5%;移动电话用户1734.41万户,宽带用户443.55万户,分别增长0.4%和15.9%。

(二)旅游业。

全市实现旅游产业增加值808.89亿元,增长13.3%。

全市实现旅游总收入2571.84亿元,增长16.9%,其中旅游外汇收入31.49亿美元,增长7.5%。接待入境旅游者363.23万人次,增长6.3%;接待国内游客1.37亿人次,增长13.8%(见表4)。

至年末,全市各类旅行社达717家,增长4.7%;星级宾馆173家,其中五星级24家,四星级46家;A级景区70个,其中5A级3个,4A级34个。

表4　2011年-2016年全市国际国内旅游人数

年　　份	入境旅游者(万人次)	国内旅游者(亿人次)
2011年	306.31	0.72
2012年	331.12	0.82
2013年	316.01	0.94
2014年	326.13	1.06
2015年	342.00	1.20
2016年	363.23	1.37

八、金　　融

全市实现金融业增加值982.02亿元,增长5.8%。

年末全市金融机构459家,当年新增50家。全市金融机构本外币存款余额33386.04亿元,增长11.8%;贷款余额26169.00亿元,增长12.2%,其中住户贷款7800.77亿元,增长33.1%,非金融企业及机关团体贷款18124.97亿元,增长5.1%(见表5)。

表 5 2016 年全市金融机构本外币存贷款余额及增速

指　　标	年末数(亿元)	比上年末增长(%)
各项存款余额	33386.04	11.8
其中:住户存款	8493.27	11.5
非金融企业存款	14476.29	10.3
各项贷款余额	26169.00	12.2
其中:住户贷款	7800.77	33.1
非金融企业及机关团体贷款	18124.97	5.1

全年新增上市公司 17 家,募集资金 297.41 亿元。至年末,全市上市公司累计 135 家,实现上市融资 3806.97 亿元。新三版挂牌企业 347 家。

全市保费收入 518.40 亿元,增长 38.5%,其中,财产险保费收入 172.49 亿元,增长 9.9%,人身险保费收入 345.91 亿元,增长 59.1%。支付各类保险赔款 158.88 亿元,增长 13.7%,其中财产险 100.04 亿元,增长 6.7%,人身险 58.85 亿元,增长 28.1%。

九、教育和科技

(一)教育。

全市共有小学 447 所,在校学生 54.30 万人;初中 249 所,在校学生 21.58 万人;普通高中 77 所,在校学生 11.04 万人。学前三年幼儿入园率为 98.8%,初中毕业生升入各类高中比例为 99.7%。优质高中招生比例由上年的 86.4% 提高到 86.7%。普通高等院校 39 所,在校学生 48.10 万人,其中在校研究生 5.30 万人,分别比上年增长 1.1% 和 5.6%;毕业生 12.84 万人,其中毕业研究生 1.37 万人,分别增长 2.7% 和 3.8%。高等教育毛入学率由上年的 60.4% 提高到 62.2%。全市累计解决义务教育阶段外来务工人员子女入学 27.77 万人。

(二)科技。

全市发明专利申请量 24951 件,发明专利授权量 8647 件,增长 40.4% 和 4.2%。新认定国家重点扶持高新技术企业 515 家,累计达 3035 家。年内新增 11 个中国驰名商标,累计 157 个。年末培育认定研发中心 1765 家,其中省级研发中心 662 家。技术市场共吸纳科技成果 6597 项,实现交易额 84.22 亿元。科技企业孵化器 105 家、其中国家级 30 家,孵化总面积 289.00 万平方米。纳入国家科技孵化器体系的众创空间达到 35 家。全市研究和试验发展(R&D)经费支出与地区生产总值之比为 3.06%。

十、文化、卫生和体育

(一)文化。

全市实现文化创意产业增加值 2541.68 亿元,增长 21.2%。

全市有各类专业艺术表演团体 20 个、文化馆 15 个、公共图书馆 15 个,图书馆藏书 2137 万册。全市有线电视接入户 332.13 万户,其中数字电视 320.99 万户,分别增长 2.8% 和 3.4%。全年拍摄电视剧 30 部,共 1342 集。生产原创动画片 7197 分钟。摄制完成 20 部电影。全市拥有非物质文化遗产保护项目 368 个,比上年增加 34 个。

(二)卫生。

年末,全市拥有各类医疗卫生机构 4691 个,其中医院 277 个,比上年末分别增加 263 个和 33 个。拥有床位 6.95 万张,其中医院床位 6.40 万张,分别增长 9.1% 和 9.6%。有各类专业卫生技术人员 10.12 万人,其中执业

(助理)医师3.82万人,注册护士4.20万人,分别增长8.7%、9.8%和9.9%。全市医疗机构完成诊疗人数12170.06万人次,增长3.7%。全市婴儿死亡率和5岁以下儿童死亡率分别为2.10‰和2.99‰。每十万孕产妇死亡率为1.34人。

(三)体育。

在巴西里约奥运会上,杭州入选中国体育代表团的体育健儿共获得1金1银1铜佳绩。成功举办国际(杭州)毅行大会、国际钱塘江冲浪对抗赛、杭州马拉松等大型品牌体育赛事活动,吸引近50个国家(地区)、1000余人次国际友人参加。全市现有体育场地面积1658.22万平方米,全市体育锻炼人口占比由上年的40.2%提高至40.5%。

十一、人民生活和社会保障

(一)人民生活。

全年全体居民人均可支配收入46116元,增长8.1%,扣除价格因素,实际增长5.4%。其中,城镇常住居民人均可支配收入52185元,增长8.0%,农村常住居民人均可支配收入27908元,增长8.5%,扣除价格因素,实际分别增长5.3%和5.8%。全体居民人均消费支出31905元,增长5.7%。其中,城镇常住居民人均消费支出35686元,农村常住居民人均消费支出20563元,分别增长5.5%和6.4%(见表6、表7)。

表6　2016年全市常住居民人均可支配收入

指标名称	城镇居民		农村居民	
	收入(元)	增幅(%)	收入(元)	增幅(%)
可支配收入	52185	8.0	27908	8.5
(一)工资性收入	30090	4.2	17059	7.6
(二)经营净收入	4607	2.3	7108	7.2
(三)财产净收入	7906	15.4	1137	15.8
(四)转移净收入	9582	18.7	2604	15.8

表7　2016年全市常住居民人均消费支出

指标名称	城镇居民		农村居民	
	支出(元)	增幅(%)	支出(元)	增幅(%)
人均生活消费支出	35686	5.5	20563	6.4
(一)食品烟酒	9945	8.4	5957	11.2
(二)衣着	2302	6.7	1228	6.1
(三)居住	9685	6.3	5297	6.2
(四)生活用品及服务	1841	13.5	1062	5.4
(五)交通通讯	5050	-11.5	3735	-4.3
(六)教育文化娱乐	3815	21.5	1762	16.9
(七)医疗保健	2143	7.0	1163	10.2
(八)其他用品和服务	905	-0.2	359	1.1

年末，城镇居民人均现住房建筑面积35.8平方米，每百户居民家庭拥有家用汽车52.3辆、空调226.6台、家用电脑112台；农村居民人均现住房建筑面积69.9平方米，每百户农村居民家庭拥有家用汽车42.4辆、空调168.2台、家用电脑75台。

（二）社会保障。

年末全市参加基本养老保险671.49万人，比上年末增加2.84万人；参加基本医疗保险897.53万人，增加26.82万人；参加职工失业、工伤、生育保险人数分别达374.16、428.41和349.33万人，比上年末净增24.74、1024和22.68万人。城乡基本医疗保险参保率为99.1%。全年推出公共租赁住房配租房源7492套，新增货币补贴保障家庭1169户。市区城乡居民最低生活保障标准由每人每月744元调整为819元，各县（市）最低生活保障标准同步提高。全市城镇享受最低生活保障人数2.19万人，农村享受最低生活保障9.94万人。

（三）社会福利。

年末全市拥有老年食堂979家，城乡社区居家养老服务照料中心2970家，比上年增加641家。拥有各类福利院、敬老院341所，比上年增加25所，床位6.73万张，增长8.7%，收养人员2.29万人。开展第十六次“春风行动”，共募集社会帮扶资金5535万元。

十二、城市建设

（一）城市基础设施建设。

全市完成基础设施投资1630.53亿元，增长20.3%。市政府驻地顺利迁址。建成杭长、萧山机场高速。地铁2号线西北段、4号线南段等加快建设，三期建设规划获批。杭富、杭临城际铁路试验段开工。东湖快速路、紫之快速路等建成通车。深入推进“三改一拆”，全面深化“无违建县（市、区）”创建，推进主城区城中村改造五年攻坚行动和“两路两侧”、“四边三化”专项整治。打造钱江新城、西湖、武林广场、运河“四大亮灯”工程为代表的标志性文化景观。

（二）公用事业。

全年杭州电网建设投入44.91亿元。新开工110千伏及以上输电工程20项，容量198万千伏安，线路179.76公里。全市用电量678.29亿千瓦时，增长4.9%，其中城乡居民生活用电107.30亿千瓦时，增长18.9%。

市区自来水日供水能力达到384万立方米，最高日供水量338.17万立方米。

年末市区公共交通运营线路703条，其中，主城区356条。市区新增公共交通运营线路15条，其中，主城区12条。

全市新增停车泊位64734个，其中，公共泊位12667个。

全年地铁客运量达到2.69亿人次，增长20.3%。

十三、环境保护和安全生产

（一）环境保护。

实施美丽杭州、生态文明先行示范区建设“三年行动计划”，扎实推进国家生态文明先行示范区建设。持续推动河道综保、湘湖综保工程和“三江两岸”生态景观保护与建设，三江沿线生态廊道基本成型。市区空气质量优良天数为260天，优良率71.0%，PM2.5年平均浓度为48.8$\mu g/m^3$，下降14.5%。至年末，人均公园绿地面积达14.25平方米，建成区绿化覆盖率为40.7%。全年规模以上工业单位增加值能耗下降6.3%，单位GDP能耗下降6.9%。

（二）安全生产。

全年共发生各类事故1176起、死亡558人、受伤182人。亿元GDP安全生产事故死亡率由上年的0.069人降至0.051人。

公报注释：

1.2016年起研究与开发支出计入地区生产总值。

2.全市生产总值和各产业增加值绝对数按现行价格计算，增长速度按不变价格计算；三次产业划分执行国家统计局2012年制定的《三次产业划分规定》。

资料来源：

本公报中城镇新增就业、登记失业率、社会保障数据来自市人力社保局；财政数据来自市财政局；农业园区、粮食功能区数据来自市农业局；教育数据来自市教育局；货物进出口数据来自杭州海关；低保、社会服务和救助、福利彩票数据来自市民政局；公路里程、公路货运量、水运货运量、公路客运量、水运客运量数据来自市交通局；货物出港量、客运出港量、通航线路数据来自萧山机场；地铁客运量来自市地铁集团；春风行动捐款数据来自市总工会；截污纳管项目、垃圾分类小区数据来自市城管委；停车泊位、人均公园绿地面积数据来自市建委；生态建设、环境监测数据来自市环保局；各类事故发生起数、死亡人数、直接经济损失数据来自市安监局；网络零售额数据来自省商务厅；实际利用外资、对外承包工程、对外劳务合作、服务贸易数据来自市商务委；邮政业务数据来自市邮政管理局；旅游数据来自市旅委；货币金融数据来自人民银行杭州中心支行；保险业数据来自中国保监会浙江监管局；高新技术企业、研发中心、专利数据来自市科委；艺术表演团体、公共图书馆、文化馆、公共电子阅览室数据来自市文广新局；上市公司数据来自市金融办；卫生数据来自市卫生计生委；体育数据来自市体育局；价格、城乡居民收支、人均住房面积、百户居民耐用品数据来自国家统计局杭州调查队；其它数据均来自于市统计局。

Statistical Communiqué of Hangzhou on the 2016 National Economic and Social Development

Hangzhou Municipal Bureau of Statistics
Hangzhou Survey Office of National Bureau of Statistics
March, 2017

In 2016, Hangzhou implement the deployment of the central decision – making thoroughly, to service the G20 summit in Hangzhou as the center, to lead and to seize the initiative on the new normal economic development, to lay upgrade series of combination punches unswervingly, to cultivate new energy for economic development. The city's economy achieved a sustained and stable growth, with the synchronous lifting of the quality and efficiency. The economic and social development has maintained a good momentum of steady and better progress, to achieve the "13th Five – Year Plan" development of a good start.

I. General Outlook

Economic Aggregate

The gross domestic product (GDP) of the year was 1131.372 billion yuan, up by 9.6 percent over the previous year. Of this total, the value added of the primary industry was 30.421 billion yuan with an annual increase of 1.8%, that of the secondary industry was 412.093 billion yuan with an annual increase of 4.5%, and the tertiary industry was 688.859 billion yuan with an annual increase of 13.5%. The city's per capita GDP was 124,286 yuan, or 18.718 U.S dollars using the average exchange rate in 2016 which published by the Central Bank, up by 7.8%. The proportions of the three industries changed from 2.9:38.9:58.2 in 2015 to 2.7:36.4:60.9 in 2016.

Hangzhou GDP and Growth, 2011 – 2016

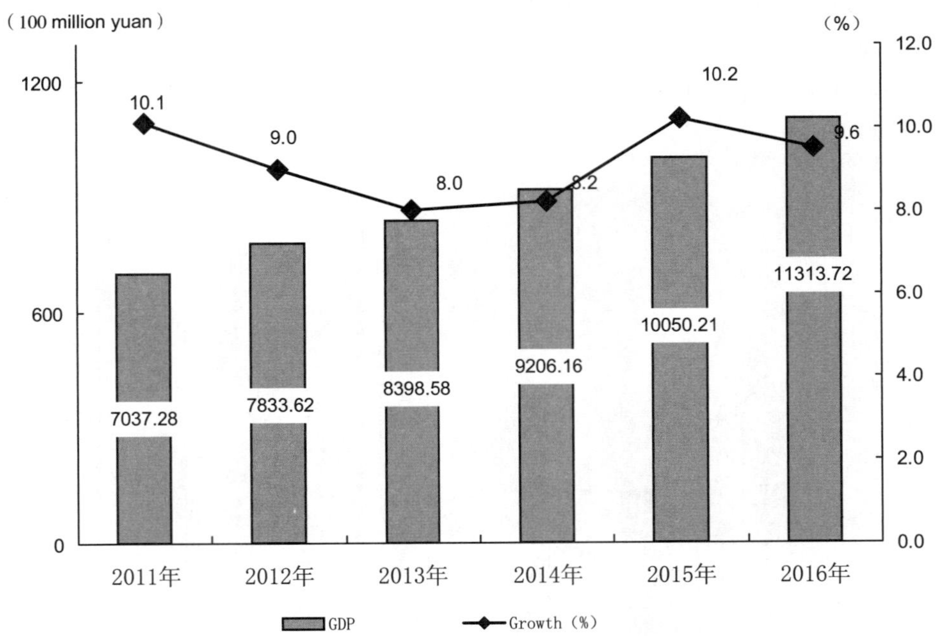

Proportion of Hangzhou's Three Industries in 2015 and 2016

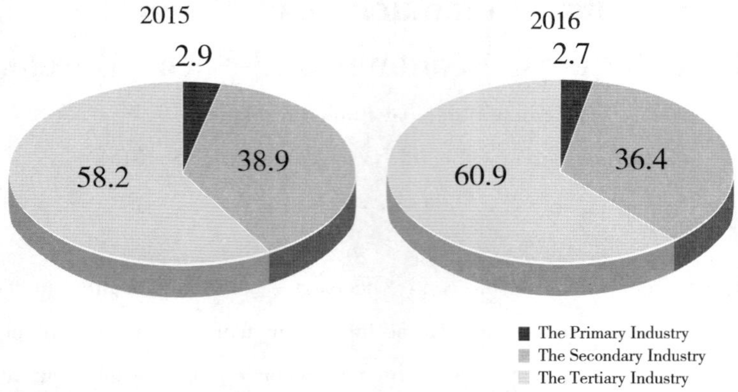

Non - State - Owned Economy

The value added of the non - state - owned economy was 658.609 billion yuan, accounting for 59.6% of Hangzhou's GDP. At the end of the year, there were 400.6 thousand private enterprises and 426.0 thousand individual businesses, up by 19.7% and 10.3% respectively. The employees of private enterprises reached 2,817.0 thousand with an annual increase of 8.9%, and that of individual businesses reached 844.5 thousand with an annual increase of 6.3%.

Information Economy

The value added of the information economy was 268.8 billion yuan, a 22.8% increase, and accounting for 24.3% of Hangzhou's GDP with an increase of 1.3 percentages over the previous year. E - commerce sectors, Mobile Internet industry, Digital content grow respectively by 45.2%, 45.1%, 35.0%.

Fiscal Revenue and Expenditure

The general fiscal revenue of the city reached 255.841 billion yuan, up by 14.0%, of this total, the general budgetary revenue of the local government was 140.238 billion yuan, up by 13.2%. The fiscal expenditure of the local government was 140.431 billion yuan, up by 16.4%, of this total, the fiscal expenditure for promoting people's livelihood reached 108.44 billion yuan, up by 17.4%, accounting for 77.2%.

The General Budgetary Revenue of The Local Government from 2011 to 2016

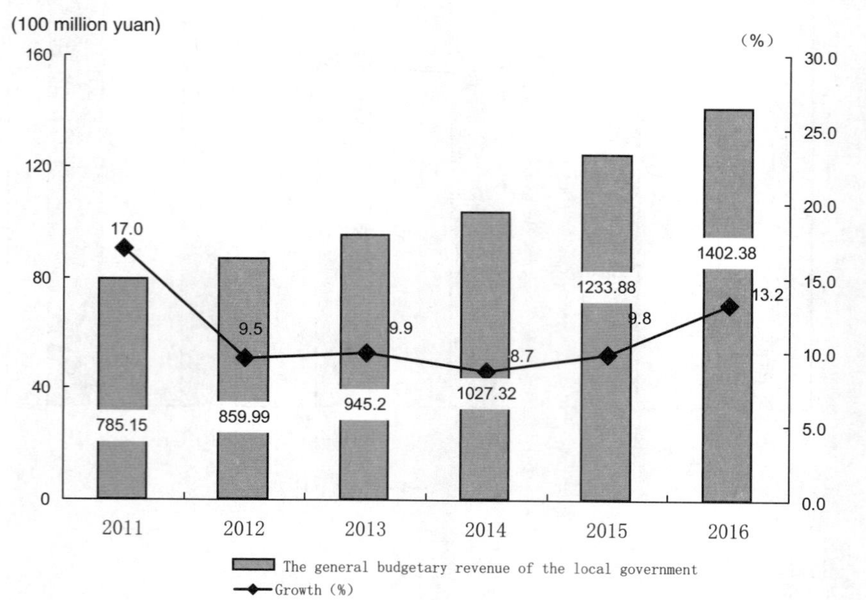

Commodity Price

The consumer prices in urban area went up by 2.6% over the previous year, up by 0.8 percentages compared with the previous year. The prices of 8 major kinds of commodity and service items presented the layout of '6 rising and 2 reducing'.

Monthly Changes in Urban Consumer Price in 2016

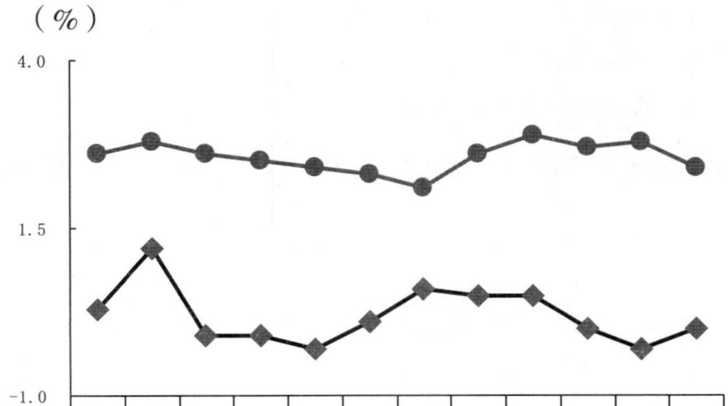

	Jan.	Feb.	Mar.	Apr.	May	Jun.	Jul.	Aug.	Sept.	Oct.	Nov.	Dec.
last month	0.3	1.2	-0.1	-0.1	-0.3	0.1	0.6	0.5	0.5	0.0	-0.3	0.0
previous month	2.6	2.8	2.6	2.5	2.4	2.3	2.1	2.6	2.9	2.7	2.8	2.4

Urban Consumer Price Rise (%)

Item	2016
The general level of CPI in urban district	2.6
1. Food and Tobacco	6.0
2. Clothing	0.3
3. Residence	2.2
4. Daily necessities and Services	-0.4
5. Transportation and Communication	-1.0
6. Education, Culture and Entertainment	3.7
7. Health Care	0.8
8. Other supplies and Services	2.7

The producer prices for manufactured goods and the producer purchasing prices fell by 0.8% and 1.1% respectively. The decline was reduced by 2.7 and 6.0 percentage points respectively

Monthly Changes in producer prices in 2016

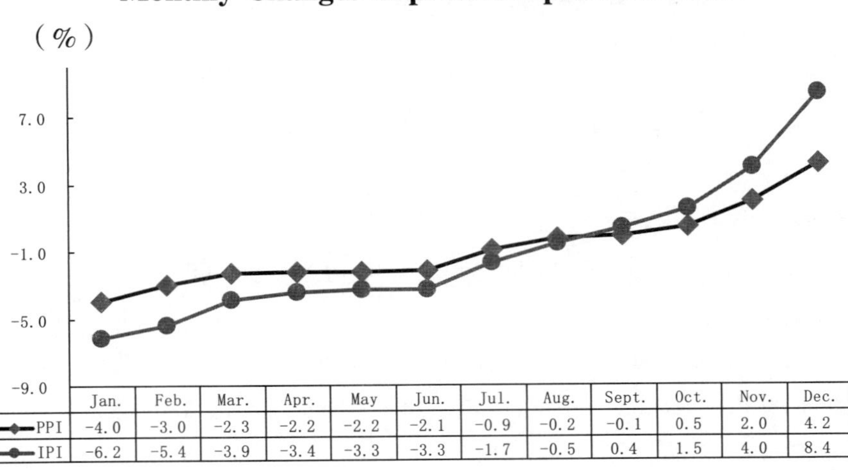

	Jan.	Feb.	Mar.	Apr.	May	Jun.	Jul.	Aug.	Sept.	Oct.	Nov.	Dec.
PPI	-4.0	-3.0	-2.3	-2.2	-2.2	-2.1	-0.9	-0.2	-0.1	0.5	2.0	4.2
IPI	-6.2	-5.4	-3.9	-3.4	-3.3	-3.3	-1.7	-0.5	0.4	1.5	4.0	8.4

Population and Employment

By the end of the year, the total number of permanent residents in Hangzhou reached 9.188 million according to sample survey on population changing, an increase of 170 thousand over that at the end of the previous year. Of this total, urban population reached 7.0013 million, and the proportion increased to 76.2% from 75.3% of that at the end of the previous year; the crude birth rate was 11.1‰, and the natural growth rate of population was 6.04‰. The population of household registration reached 7.36 million, the crude birth rate was 13.21‰, and the natural growth rate of population was 7.16‰. The newly increased employed people in urban areas numbered 271.3 thousand, and 114.8 thousand unemployed people were re – employed. The registered urban unemployment rate was 1.72% at the year end.

The Number of Permanent Residents and The Population of Household Registration from 2011 to 2016

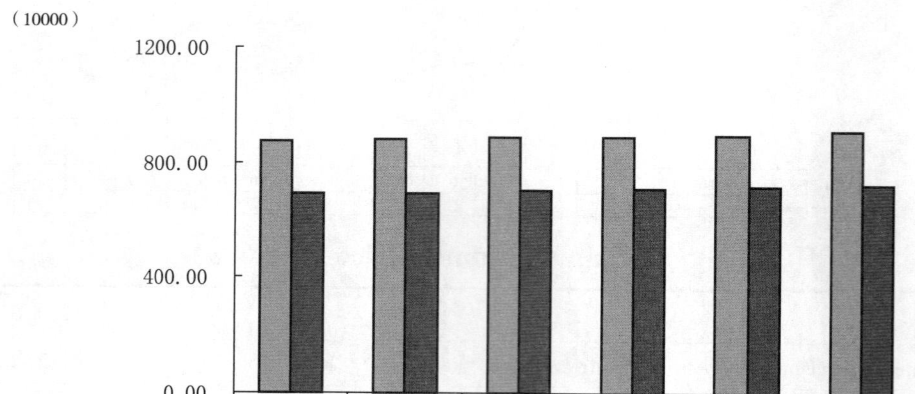

	2011	2012	2013	2014	2015	2016
permanent residents	873.80	880.20	884.40	889.20	901.80	918.80
household registration	695.71	700.52	706.61	715.76	723.55	736.00

II. Agriculture

The value added of agriculture, forestry, animal husbandry and fishery achieved 30.926 billion yuan, up by 5.8%. Of this total, the value added of agriculture, forestry animal husbandry was 19.338 billion yuan, 4.167 billion yuan, 4.158 billion yuan. up by 7.1%、5.9% and 5.1% respectively. The value added of fishery was 2.757 billion yuan, down by 3.1%. The value added of service industry for agriculture was 0.505 billion yuan, up by 13.5%. The total output of grain was 0.636 million tons, up by 0.3%; the output of vegetable was 3.3534 million tons, up by 5.2%; the output of fruit was 0.7641 million tons, down by 3.2%; the output of meat was 0.2627 million tons, down by 5.6%; and that of aquatic products was 0.1948 million tons, down by 7.2%. In 2016, Hangzhou had newly built 35 municipal vegetable bases, and 152 grain production functional zones.

III. Industry and Construction

Industry Production

The value added of the industrial sector was 372.62 billion yuan, up by 5.2%. Of this total, the value added of industrial enterprises above the designated size was 299.034 billion yuan, up by 5.6%. The value added of strategic emerging industries, equipment manufacturing industries and high – tech industries reached 81.207 billion yuan, 124.959 billion yuan and 137.292 billion yuan respectively, up by 11.6%, 14.6% and 12.5%. The output value ratio of new products went up to 37.4% from 35.4% of the previous year. The sales – output ratio of industrial products reached 99.4%.

Industrial Efficiency

The profits & taxes of the industrial enterprises above designated size were 165.564 billion, up by 6.8%, of this total, the profits reached 94.606 billion yuan, up by 6.7%. The number of loss – making enterprises accounted for the entire enterprise was 17.0%.

Construction

The value added of construction enterprises was 39.612 billion yuan, down by 1.8% over the previous year. There were 1,474 construction enterprises with the qualification of general contract and special contract, and the construction output value amounted to 410.53 billion yuan, up by 0.2%; the floor space of buildings under construction was 272.2071 million square meters, down by 3.2%, the floor space of buildings completed was 97.5411 million square meters, down by 3.5%.

IV. Investment in Fixed Assets and Real Estate

Investment in Fixed Assets

The completed investment in fixed assets was 584.242 billion yuan, up by 5.1% over the previous year. The non – state – owned investment 356.116 billion, up by 0.6%, accounting for 61.0%. The nongovernment investment was 300.678 billion yuan, up by 1.0%, accounting for 51.5% of nongovernment investment. Grouped by sectors, the investment in the primary industry was 3.936 billion yuan, up by 25.1%; the investment in the secondary industry was 88.69 billion yuan, down by 4.8%, of which the industrial investment was 88.395 billion yuan, down by 5.0%; the investment in the tertiary industry was 491.616 billion yuan, up by 7.0%.

Investment in Fixed Assets and the Growth Rates from 2011 to 2016

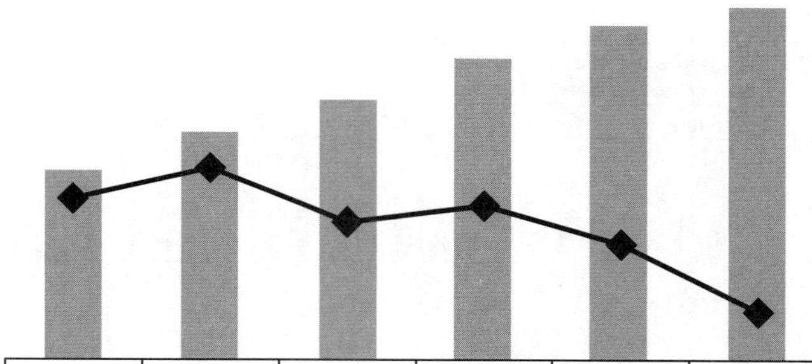

	2011	2012	2013	2014	2015	2016
Investment in fixed assets(100 million yuan)	3100.02	3722.75	4263.87	4952.70	5556.32	5842.42
Growth rate over the last year(%)	16.9	20.1	14.5	16.2	12.2	5.1

Investment in Real Estate

The completed investment in real estate development was 260.641 billion yuan, up by 5.4% over the previous year. Of which, residential investment was 155.998 billion yuan, an increase of 8.2%. The floor space under construction was 115.6296 million square meters, up by 3.8%; the completed floor space was 19.2299 million square meters, up by 15.5%. The sold floor space of commercial buildings was 23.2669 million square meters, up by 57.1%, of this total, the sold floor space of commercial residential buildings was 18.8711 million square meters, up by 46.1%. A total of 76,161 sets of security housing were newly started to construct, and 58,664 units had been completed.

V. Domestic Trade

The value added of wholesale and retail trades was 88.372 billion yuan, up by 6.8% over the previous year, that of the hotels and catering services was 17.526 billion yuan, down by 1.4%.

The total retail sales of consumer goods reached 517.62 billion yuan, a growth of 10.5% over the previous year, or a real growth of 8.9% after deducting price factors. Of this total, the retail sales was 463.758 billion yuan, up by 10.7%, the revenue of repast was 53.862 billion yuan, up by 8.7%. The retail sales of consumer goods in urban areas was 490.461 billion yuan, up by 10.4%; and that in rural areas was 27.159 billion yuan, up by 10.9%.

Of the total retail sales of commodities by wholesale and retail enterprises above designated size, the year on year growth of sales for cultural office supplies 40.1%, for hardware 29.9%, or grain, oil and food 16.7%, for clothes, shoes, hats and textiles 14.8%, for motor vehicles 10.7%, for communication equipment 7.4%, and that for gold and silver jewelry, petroleum and petroleum products was down by 12.6% and 5.4% respectively.

The online retail in Hangzhou reached 344.565 billion yuan, a growth of 28.6% over the previous year. The residents network spending reached 149.998 billion yuan, up by 34.0%.

Total Retail Sales of Consumer Goods and Growth Rates from 2011 to 2016

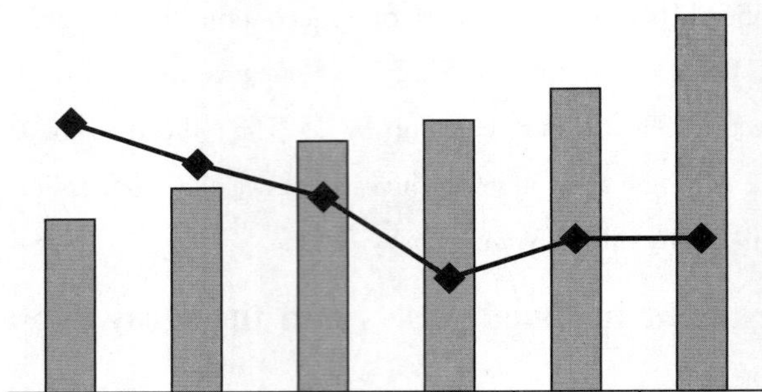

	2011	2012	2013	2014	2015	2016
Total retail sales of consumer goods(100 million yuan)	2690.22	3165.19	3864.84	4201.46	4697.23	5842.42
Growth rate over the last year(%)	20.9	17.7	15.1	8.7	11.8	11.8

VI. Foreign Economic Relations

International Trade

The total value of import and export of goods in 2016 was 448.597 billion yuan, up by 14.6% over the previous year. Of this total, the value of goods imported was 117.217 billion yuan, up by 14.6%; that of exported was 331.38 billion yuan, up by 6.7% (the value of goods exported excluding the province – owned enterprises was 301.905 billion yuan, up by 9.5%). Of the total value of export, the value of electromechanical products exported was 135.72 billion yuan, and that of high – tech products exported was 42.423 billion yuan, up by 8.3% and 7.6% respectively. Grouped by trading modes, the general trade of exports was 292.294 billion yuan, up by 8.7%; the processing trade of exports was 34.738 billion yuan, down by 8.1%. Grouped by exporting markets, the value of exports to Europe and Asia increased by 8.0% and 8.3%.

The total value of import and export of service trade was 139.964 billion yuan, up by 18.0% over the previous year. Of this total, the value of import and export of service trade was 139.964 billion yuan, up by 19.0%.

The total value of import and export of goods in Hangzhou in 2016

Item	Total value (100 million yuan)	Increase over the previous year (%)
Total Value of Import and Export of goods	4485.97	8.7
Export	3313.80	6.7
General Trade of Exports	2922.94	8.7
Processing Imported Materials	347.38	-8.1
Electromechanical Products exported	1357.20	8.3
High - techPproducts Exported	424.23	7.6
Import	1172.17	14.6

International Cooperation

By the end of 2016, the total number of overseas enterprises (institutions) invested by Hangzhou investors was 1,586, of which the non - trading enterprises was 624. The contracted overseas investment reached 5.218 billion US dollars, of which the non - trading investment was 4.192 billion US dollars, up by 185.0%. The accomplished business revenue through contracted overseas engineering projects and labor cooperation was 1.926 billion US dollars, up by 8.9%. The executed value of offshore service outsourcing was 5.872 billion US dollars, up by 13.1%.

Utilization of Foreign Capital

The year 2016 witnessed the authorizing of 462 projects with 7.209 billion US dollars of actually utilized foreign direct investment, up by 1.4% over the previous year. The investment of 145 newly authorized projects which of each over 30 million US dollars amounted 14.127 billion US dollars, accounting for 94.0% of the total newly approved foreign investment. There were 10 newly introduced investment projects which funded by companies of Fortune Global 500. By the end of 2016, 117 projects had been settled in Hangzhou that invested by 198 companies of Fortune Global 500.

Cross - border E - Commerce

The total value of import and export of Cross - border E - Commerce in Hangzhou was 8.112 billion US dollars, up by 134.2% over the previous year. Of this total, the value of Cross - border E - Commerce imported 6.06 billion US dollars, up by 166.7%; that of exported was 2.052 billion US dollars, up by 72.3%.

Return of Zhejiang Merchants

In 2016, 2733 projects of domestic investment were introduced with 139.707 billion yuan of actually utilized investment, up by 11.8%. Of this total, the return capital of Zhejiang Merchants reached 70.996 billion yuan, up by 7.5%.

Construction of Development Zones

There were 7 national - level development zones in Hangzhou including Hangzhou Economic and Technological Development Zone, Hangzhou High - Tech Development Zone, Xiaoshan Economic & Technological Development Zone, Hangzhou Zhijiang National Holiday Resort Zone, Hangzhou Yuhang Economic and Technological Development Zone, Fuyang Economic, Technological Development Zone and Linjiang National High - Tech Zone. The main business revenue of industrial enterprises above designated size was 671.915 billion yuan with an increase of 9.6%, and the total profits reached 60.965 billion yuan with an increase of 18.5%. The main business revenue of service industry above designated size was 225.106 billion yuan with an increase of 14.7%, and the total profits reached 30.958 billion yuan with an increase of 17.8%.

VII. Transportation, Post, Telecommunications and Tourism

Transportation and Post

The value added of transportation, storage and post achieved 325.46 billion yuan, up by 9.2%.

The annual total freight traffic was 0.302 billion tons, up by 2.7% over the previous year. The total passenger traffic was 0.205 billion persons, down by 11.1%. By the end of 2016, 240 air routes had been opened, including 38 international routes and 7 routes to Hongkong, Macao and Taiwan. 27.4143 million passengers made arrivals and departure there in mainland routes ,up by 11.0%. 4.1806 million passengers made arrivals and departure there in international and regional routes,up by 14.5%. The total length of highways within Hangzhou reached 16,306.07km, including 632.04km expressways.

The total possession of motor vehicles reached 2.6335 million, down by 3.7%. The total possession of civil vehicles reached 2.3415 million , of which private – owned cars numbered 1.9227 million up by 4.3% and 4.0% over the previous year respectively.

The business income of postal enterprises and express delivery enterprises above designated size totaled 21.517 billion yuan, an annual increase of 34.8%. The express delivery enterprises above designated size reached 1.805 billion, up by 43.6%. The business income of telecommunication services totaled 19.07 billion yuan, up by 5.9%. At the end of 2016, there were 2.657 million fixed – line telephone subscribers and 17.3441 million mobile phone users, down by 9.5% and up by 0.4% respectively. The broadband subscribers amounted to 4.4355 million, up by 15.9%.

Tourism

The value added of tourism industry achieved 80.889 billion yuan, up by 13.3%.

The annual earnings from tourism reached 257.184 billion yuan, up by 16.9% over the previous year, of which the foreign exchange earnings from international tourism was 3.149 billion US dollars, up by 7.5%. The number of overseas visitor arrivals was 3.6323 million person – times, up by 6.3%; that of domestic visitors was 0.137 billion person – times, up by 13.8%.

At the end of 2016, there were 717 travel agencies, up by 4.7%; 173 star – rated hotels, including 24 5 – star hotels and 46 4 – star hotels; 70 A – rated scenic spots, including 3 AAAAA scenic spots and 34 AAAA scenic spots.

Overseas Visitor Arrivals and Domestic Visitors in Hangzhou from 2011 to 2016

year	Overseas visitor arrivals (million person – times)	Domestic visitors (billion person – times)
2011	3.0631	0.072
2012	3.3112	0.082
2013	3.1601	0.094
2014	3.2613	0.106
2015	3.42	0.12
2016	3.6323	0.137

VIII. Financial Intermediation

The value added of financial intermediation achieved 98.202 billion yuan, up by 5.8%.

There were 459 financial institutions in Hangzhou at year – end, 50 added. The saving deposits of RMB and foreign exchange from all of the financial institutions in Hangzhou was 3338.604 billion yuan, up by 11.8%; and the loans balance was 2616.9 billion yuan, up by 12.2%, of this total, the loan balance of household was 780.077 billion yuan, up by 33.1%; the loan balance of non – financial enterprise was 1812.497 billion yuan, up by 5.1%.

Deposit and Loan Balance in RMB and Foreign Exchange from all of The Financial Institutions at the End of 2016

Item	Year – end Figure (100 million yuan)	Increase/Decrease of the Increased Amount
Total Deposit Balance	33386.04	11.8
Of which: Household Deposit	8493.27	11.5
Non – financial Enterprise Deposit	14476.29	10.3
Total Loan Balance	26169.00	12.2
Of which: Household Loans	7800.77	33.1
Non – financial Enterprise Loans	18124.97	5.1

In 2016, there were 17 newly authorized listed companies in Hangzhou, and raised a total of 29.741 billion yuan. By the end of the year, the number of listed companies in Hangzhou accumulated to 135, and funds raised through stock markets amounted to 380.697 billion yuan. 347 companies were listed on the New Third Board.

The premiums received by the insurance companies totaled 51.84 billion yuan with an annual increase of 38.5%, of this total, the premiums of property insurance was 17.249 billion yuan, up by 9.9%, that of life insurance was 34.591 billion yuan, up by 59.1%. The payments of insurance indemnity of various kinds totaled 15.888 billion yuan, up by 13.7%, of this total, the payments of property insurance was 10.004 billion yuan, up by 6.7%, that of life insurance was 5.885 billion yuan, up by 28.1%.

IX. Education, Science & Technology

Education

There were 447 primary schools with 543 thousand students, 249 junior secondary schools with 215.8 thousand students, and 77 regular senior secondary schools with 110.4 thousand students in Hangzhou. The ratio of enrollment to kindergartens of those who 3 years younger than the school age reached 98.8%, the enrollment rate to senior schools from junior secondary schools was 99.7%. The coverage ratio of high quality senior secondary schools was 86.7%, an increase of 0.3 percentages. There were 39 regular institutions of higher education with 481 thousand students, of which 53 thousand were graduate students, up by 1.1% and 5.6%. 128.4 thousand were graduates, of which 13.7 thousand were graduate students, up by 2.7% and 3.8%. The gross enrollment rate to general colleges and universities rose to 62.2% from 60.4% of the previous year. 277.7 thousand children of migrant workers were enrolling in the stage of compulsory education.

Science & Technology

In 2016, 24,951 patents for invention were applied and 8,647 were authorized, up by 40.4% and 4.2% over the previous year respectively. There were accumulated 3,035 national – level supported high – tech enterprises, an annual increase of 515. There were 157 China's well – known trademarks, an annual increase of 11. At the year – end, there were 1,765 foster recognized research and development center,662 provincial level research and development center. A total of 6,597 scientific and technological achievements with 8.422 billion trading volume were received by technology market. A total of 105 high – tech business incubators with 289 square meters were built, of which 30 were national – level. There were 35 maker spaces into the national science and technology incubator system. The expenditures on research and development activities (R&D) accounted for 3.06% of Hangzhou's GDP.

X. Culture, Public Health and sports

Culture

The value added of culture creation industry achieved 254.168 billion yuan, up by 21.2%.

By the end of 2016, there were 20 professional arts performing organizations, 15 cultural centers, and 15 public libraries with 21.37 million books. The city's cable TV households received 332.13 million, of which 320.99 million digital TV, up by 2.8% and 3.4% over the previous year respectively. During the whole year, a total of 1,342 episodes in 30 TV dramas and 20 films were produced; also created and produced were 7,197 – minute – long animation film. Hangzhou was listed with 368 intangible cultural heritage protection project, an annual increase of 34.

Public Health

At the year – end, there were 4,691 medical and health institutions in Hangzhou, including 277 hospitals, increasing 263 and 33 over the previous year respectively. The number of beds was 69,500, of which 64,000 were hospital beds, up by 9.1% and 9.6% respectively. There were 101,200 professional medical personnel, of whom the licensed (assistant) doctors were 38,200 and registered nurses were 42,000, up by 8.7%, 9.8% and 9.9% respectively. A total of 12170.06 million patients receive diagnosis and treatment in medical institutions, up 3.7%. The infant mortality rate and mortality rate of children under five – year old were 2.1‰ and 2.99‰. The mortality per 100,000 pregnant women was 1.34 persons.

Sports

In Brazil Rio Olympic Games, Chinese sports delegation athletes selected from Hangzhou won a total of 1 gold, 1 silver, 1 bronze medals. The success of International (Hangzhou) International Conference, walk Qiantang River surfing tournament, the Hangzhou marathon and other large brand sporting events, attractied nearly 50 countries (regions), and more than 1000 foreign friends. Zangzhou has an existing sports areo of 16 million 582 thousand and 200 square meters. Compared with last year, the proportion of physical exercise population increased from 40.2% to 40.5%.

XI. Living Conditions and Social Security

Living Conditions

The annual per capita disposable income in Hangzhou was 46,116 yuan, an increase of 8.1% or a real increase of 5.4% after deducting price factors. In terms of resident areas, the annual per capita disposable income of urban households reached 52,185 yuan, up by 8.0% or a real increase of 5.3% after deducting price factors, and the annual per capita disposable income of rural households was 27,908 yuan, up by 8.5% or 5.8% after deducting price factor. The per capita consumption expenditure in Hangzhou was 31,905 yuan, an increase of 5.7%。The per capita consumption expenditure of urban households was 35,686 yuan, and that of rural households was 20,563 yuan, up by 5.5% and 6.4% respectively.

Per Capita Disposable Income in Hangzhou in 2016

Item	Urban Residents		Rural Residents	
	Income (yuan)	Increase over the previous year (%)	Income (yuan)	Increase over the previous year (%)
Disposable Income	52,185	8.0	27,908	8.5
(一) Income from Wages	30,090	4.2	17,059	7.6
(二) Income of Staff & workers in Other - owned Units	4,607	2.3	7,108	7.2
(三) Property Income	7,906	15.4	1,137	15.8
(四) Transfer Income	9,582	18.7	2,604	15.8

Per Capita Consumption Expenditure of Urban Households and Rural Households in Hangzhou in 2016

Item	Urban Residents		Rural Residents	
	Consumption Expenditure (yuan)	Increase over the previous year (%)	Consumption Expenditure (yuan)	Increase over the previous year (%)
Expenditure	35,686	5.5	20,563	6.4
(一) Food alcohol and tobacco	9,945	8.4	5,957	11.2
(二) Clothing	2,302	6.7	1,228	6.1
(三) Residence	9,685	6.3	5,297	6.2
(四) Daily necessities and services	1,841	13.5	1,062	5.4
(五) Transportation and Communication	5,050	-11.5	3,735	-4.3
(六) Education, cultural and Recreation	3,815	21.5	1,762	16.9
(七) Medicine and Medical Service	2,143	7.0	1,163	10.2
(八) Other Supplies and Services	905	-0.2	359	1.1

By the end of the year, the per capita floor space of residential building in urban areas reached 35. 8 square meters, and every 100 urban households had 52. 3 family cars, 226. 6 air conditioners, 112 home computers, ;the per capita floor space of residential building in rural areas reached 69. 9 square meters, and every 100 rural households had 42. 4 family cars, 168. 2 air conditioners, 75 home computers.

Social Security

By the end of the year, a total of 6. 7149 million people participated in the basic social pension insurance, a year – on – year increase of 28. 4 thousand; a total of 8. 9753 million people participated in the basic medical insurance program, an increase of 268. 2 thousand; a total of 3. 7416 million people participated in the unemployment insurance, 4. 2841 million people participated in the work accident insurances, 3. 4933 million people participated in the maternity insurance, a year – on – year increase of 247. 4 thousand, 102. 4 thousand and 226. 8 thousand respectively. The enrollment rates to basic medical insurance program reached 99. 1%. 1,169 households were newly added as low – rent housing security families, and 7,492 units of public rental housing were available. The minimum subsistence guarantee for residents in urban areas increased to 819 yuan from 744 yuan, and that for residents in rural areas increased by the same percentage. 21,900 urban residents receive the basic cost of living allowance, and 99,400 rural residents receive the rural equivalent.

Social Welfare

There were 979 canteens for the aged,for the rural aged in Hangzhou and 2,970 home – based care service stations with a year – on – year increase of 770. By the end of the year, there were all together 341 welfare institutions and nursing homes for the aged, an increase of 25 over the previous year, providing 67,300 beds , up by 8. 7% , accommodating 22,900 inmates. A total of 55. 35 million yuan of social funds was raised by the 16th ‘Spring Breeze Action’.

XII. Urban Construction

Urban Infrastructure Construction

In 2016, the investment in infrastructure amounted to 163. 053 billion yuan, up by 20. 3%. Municipal government successfully relocated. Hangchang and Xiaoshan Airport expressway has been biult. Accelerating the construction of metro Line 2 northwest section,and line 4, south section . The three phase of the construction plan has been approved. Hangfu and Hanglin Intercity Railway test section have already started. East Lake expressway, purple road have opened to traffic. To further promote the three changes of a split, to deepen the create of "no illegally built county (city and district)", to promote the urban transformation of villages for five year plan and Four sides of the three special rectification . To create a iconic cultural landscape of Qianjiang New Town, West Lake, Wulin Square and canal "four lights up" project.

Public Utilities

The annual investment in construction of power grids amounted to 4. 491 billion yuan. A total of 20 transmission projects, each of which was above 110 KV, were newly under construction, the transmission capacity and the electrical wiring amounted to 1. 98million KVA and 179. 76 km respectively. The electricity consumption of the whole city was 67. 829 billion KWH, up by 4. 9% , of this total, the consumption of residents in urban and rural areas was 10. 73 billion KWH, up by 18. 9%.

The daily capacity of water supply in urban areas reached 3. 84 million cubic meters. The highest daily water supply of 3. 3817 million cubic meters.

At the end of the year, there were 703 urban public transport routes, of which 356 were the main urban areas. There were 15 new public transport routes in the urban area, of which 12 were the main urban areas.

50,156 parking spaces were newly completed, of which 12,667 public berths.

The annual passenger capacity of metro reached 0.269 billion, up by 20.3%.

XIII. Environment Protection and Work Safety

Environment Protection

To implement the "beautiful Hangzhou, and the three year action plan of the ecological civilization first demonstration zone construction ". To promote the national ecological civilization first demonstration area construction firmly. To promote the river comprehensive protection , Xianghu comprehensive protection project and the "Sanjiang two sides" ecological landscape protection and construction continuly. The ecological corridor along Sanjiang was basically shaped. The air quality in urban areas was 260 days, the excellent rate was 71%, and the average concentration in PM2.5 was 48.8 g/m^3, down by 14.5%. By the end of the year, the per capita green space reached 14.25 square meters, and the green coverage rate in built - up areas was 40.7%. Over the year, the added value of industrial units above designated size has decreased by 6.3%, and the energy consumption per unit GDP is expected to decrease by more than 6.9%.

Work Safety

The number of accidents, the death doll, and the number of injure due to various work accidents were 1,176, 558, and 182. The death toll due to work accidents for every 100 million yuan worth of GDP was decreased to 0.051 people from 0.069 people of the previous year.

Notes:

1. From 2016, research and test development expenditure was included in the GDP.
2. GDP and absolute added value of various industries are calculated based on current price, whereas the growth rate is calculated based on constant price in 2010; the classification on primary, secondary and tertiary industries is subject to the Classification on Primary, Secondary and Tertiary Industries which is made by National Statistics Office in 2012.

Source of Statistics:

Statistics on newly increased employed people in urban areas, registered urban unemployment rate and social security are from Hangzhou Municipal Bureau of Human Resources and Social Security; fiscal statistics are from Hangzhou Bureau of Finance; statistics on agricultural park and grain production functional zone are from Hangzhou Agriculture Bureau; statistics on education are from Hangzhou Municipal Commission of Education; statistics on import and export are from Hangzhou Customs; statistics on subsistence allwance, social services and assistance, elfare lottery are from Hangzhou Municipal Bureau of Civil Affairs; statistics on highway mileage, freight traffic and passenger traffic are form Hangzhou Traffic Management Bureau; statistics on passengers made arrivals and departure, Route are form Xiaoshan International Airport; statistics on passenger capacity of metro are form Hangzhou Metro Group; statistics on 'Spring Breeze Action' are from Federation of trade Unions; statistics on garbage classification area are from Hangzhou Urban Management Committee; statistics on parking space, centralized disposal rate of urban sewage and per capita green land of parks are Hangzhou Municipal Commission of Housing and Urban - Rural Development; statistics on ecological construction and environmental monitoring are from Hangzhou Municipal Bureau of Environmental Protection; statistics on safety production are from Hangzhou Administration of Work Safety; statistics on online retail are from Zhejiang Provincial Department of

Commerce; statistics on actually utilized foreign direct investment are from Hangzhou Municipal Commission of Commerce; statistics on tourism are from Hangzhou Municipal Commission of Tourism Development; statistics on money and finance People's Bank of Hangzhou Center Branch; statistics on insurance are from Zhejiang Bureau of China Insurance Regulatory Commission; statistics on patent are from Hangzhou Municipal Science and Technology Commission; statistics on public library are from Hangzhou Municipal Administration of Press, Publication, Radio, Film and Telecision; statistics on newly authorized listed company are from Hangzhou Finance Office; statistics on healthcare are from Hangzhou Municipal Commission of Health and Family Planning; statistics on sports are from Hangzhou Municipal Bureau of Sports; statistics on price are from Hangzhou Survey Office of National Bureau of Statistics; other statistics are from Hangzhou Municipal Bureau of Statistics.

一、综合

GENERAL SURVEY

1 综　　合 General Survey

主要统计指标 Major Statistical Indicators

全市生产总值	Gross Domestic Product	11313.72	亿元	(100 million yuan)
为上年	As Compared with the Preceding Year	109.6	%	(%)
第一产业	Primary Industry	304.21	亿元	(100 million yuan)
为上年	As Compared with the Preceding Year	101.8	%	(%)
第二产业	Secondary Industry	4120.93	亿元	(100 million yuan)
为上年	As Compared with the Preceding Year	104.5	%	(%)
第三产业	Tertiary Industry	6888.59	亿元	(100 million yuan)
为上年	As Compared with the Preceding Year	113.5	%	(%)
常住居民人均生产总值	Per Capita GDP (Long-term Residents)	124286	元	(yuan)
为上年	As Compared with the Preceding Year	107.8	%	(%)
生产总值构成	Composition of Gross Domestic Product	100	%	(%)
第一产业	Primary Industry	2.7	%	(%)
第二产业	Secondary Industry	36.4	%	(%)
第三产业	Tertiary Industry	60.9	%	(%)

1-01 行政区划(2016年末)

Administrative Division(End of 2016)

单位:个 (unit)

地　区	Region	街　道 Subdistrict Offices	乡(镇) Towns and Townships	镇 Towns	村、社区 Villages and Communities	村 Villages
全　市	**Whole City**	**92**	**98**	**75**	**3115**	**2043**
市　区	Urban District	80	39	33	1918	919
上城区	Shangcheng	6	-	-	54	-
下城区	Xiacheng	8	-	-	74	-
江干区	Jianggan	10	-	-	182	4
拱墅区	Gongshu	10	-	-	108	-
西湖区	Xihu	10	2	2	204	45
高新(滨江)区	Hi-Tech(Binjiang)	3	-	-	59	-
萧山区	Xiaoshan	14	12	12	587	411
余杭区	Yuhang	14	6	6	346	183
富阳区	Fuyang	5	19	13	304	276
桐庐县	Tonglu	4	10	6	201	183
淳安县	Chun'an	-	23	11	437	425
建德市	Jiande	3	13	12	256	229
临安市	Lin'an	5	13	13	303	287

注:萧山区含大江东产业集聚区、江干区含经济技术开发区、西湖区含风景名胜区。

a) Figures of Xiaoshan include Dajiangdong, figures of Jianggan include Economic and Technological Development Zone, figures of Xihu include the West Lake Scenic Zone.

1－02　土地面积和人口密度(2016 年末)
Land Area and Population Density(End of 2016)

地　　区	Region	土地面积 (平方千米) Land Area (sq. km)	年末总人口 (万人) Population (10000 persons)	人口密度 (人/平方千米) Population Density (person/sq. km)
全　　市	**Whole City**	**16596**	**918.80**	**554**
市　区	Urban District	4876	737.99	1514
上城区	Shangcheng	18	35.32	19622
下城区	Xiacheng	31	53.60	17290
江干区	Jianggan	210	106.15	5055
拱墅区	Gongshu	88	58.20	6614
西湖区	Xihu	263	84.42	3210
高新(滨江)区	Hi－Tech(Binjiang)	73	33.56	4597
萧山区	Xiaoshan	1163	157.20	1352
余杭区	Yuhang	1222	135.90	1112
富阳区	Fuyang	1808	73.64	407
桐庐县	Tonglu	1780	42.30	238
淳安县	Chun'an	4452	34.96	79
建德市	Jiande	2364	44.70	189
临安市	Lin'an	3124	58.85	188

注:萧山区含大江东产业集聚区、江干区含经济技术开发区、西湖区含风景名胜区。

a) Figures of Xiaoshan include Dajiangdong, figures of Jianggan include Economic and Technological Development Zone, figures of Xihu include the West Lake Scenic Zone.

1－03 平均每天主要社会经济活动(主要年份)

Selected Indicators on Average Daily Social and Economic Activities(Main Years)

指 标 Item	2005	2010	2011	2012	2013	2014	2015	2016
全市生产总值 (万元) Gross Domestic Product (10,000 yuan)	80621	163444	192802	214620	230098	252224	275349	309118
工业增加值 (万元) Value－Added of Industry (10,000 yuan)	36427	67212	79181	84749	86477	93559	95831	101809
规模以上工业企业利税总额 (万元) Total Pre－tax Profits of Industrial Enterprises above Designated Size (10,000 yuan)	12347	33324	36452	36711	39748	42139	42731	45236
农林牧渔业总产值 (万元) Gross Output Value of Farming,Forestry, Animal Husbandry and Fishery (10,000 yuan)	6013	8667	9783	10530	10942	11468	12066	12768
固定资产投资 (万元) Investment in Fixed Assets (10,000 yuan)	35008	72654	84932	101993	116818	135690	152228	159629
住宅竣工面积 (平方米) Floor Space of Residential Buildings Completed (sq. m)	19327	21981	23038	18466	23154	25425	29323	30419
社会消费品零售总额 (万元) Total Retail Sales of Consumer Goods (10,000 yuan)	26724	60959	73705	86718	105886	115108	128691	141426
住户存款新增额 (万元) The Increased Amount of Household Deposits (10,000 yuan)	9767	19289	15247	14863	8729	9825	8739	23921
财政总收入 (万元) Total Financial Revenue (10,000 yuan)	14268	34121	40792	44600	47534	52606	61335	69902

1－04 国民经济

Major Indicators of

指　　标		Item	
年末常住人口	（万人）	Long－term Residents(End of 2016)	(10,000 persons)
年末户籍人口	（万人）	Honsehold Registration Population(End of 2016)	(10,000 persons)
#城镇人口	（万人）	Urban Population	(10,000 persons)
年末从业人员数	（万人）	Total Number of Employed Persons(End of 2016)	(10,000 persons)
全市生产总值	（亿元）	Gross Domestic Product	(100 million yuan)
第一产业	（亿元）	Primary Industry	(100 million yuan)
第二产业	（亿元）	Secondary Industry	(100 million yuan)
第三产业	（亿元）	Tertiary Industry	(100 million yuan)
人均生产总值(户籍)	（元）	Per Capita GDP(Household)	(yuan)
人均生产总值(常住)	（元）	Per Capita GDP(Long－term)	(yuan)
主要农产品产量		Output of Major Farm Products	
粮食	（万吨）	Grain	(10,000 tons)
棉花	（吨）	Cotton	(ton)
油菜籽	（吨）	Rapeseeds	(ton)
茶叶	（吨）	Tea	(ton)
蚕茧	（吨）	Silk－worm Cocoons	(ton)
生猪年末存栏	（万头）	Hogs in Stock at Year End	(10,000 heads)
肉类产量	（万吨）	Output of Meat	(10,000 tons)
淡水产品产量	（吨）	Freshwater Aquatic Products	(ton)
全部工业总产值	（亿元）	The Total Output Value of Industrial Enterprises	(100 million yuan)
规模以上工业总产值	（亿元）	The Output Valne of Industrial Enterprises Above Designated Size	(100 million yuan)
规模以上工业企业利税总额	（亿元）	Total Pre－tax Profits of Industrial Enterprises Above Designated Size	(100 million yuan)
客运量	（万人次）	Total Passenger Traffic	(10,000 person－times)
货运量	（万吨）	Total Freight Traffic	(10,000 tons)
固定资产投资	（亿元）	Investment in Fixed Assets	(100 million yuan)
社会消费品零售总额	（亿元）	Total Retail Sales of Consumer Goods	(100 million yuan)

注:1. 规模以上工业的计算口径,1997 年以前为乡及乡以上,1998 年－2010 年为主营业务收入 500 万元及以上,2011 年起为 2000 万元及以上。

2. 从 2014 年起,粮食数据按粮食生产统计监测抽样调查口径。

3. 2016 年全市户籍城镇人口尚未核定。

主要指标（主要年份）

National Economy(Main Years)

1985	1990	1995	2000	2005	2010	2011	2012	2013	2014	2015	2016
	583.21		701.70	771.30	870.54	873.80	880.20	884.40	889.20	901.80	918.80
543.05	574.78	597.96	621.58	660.45	689.12	695.71	700.52	706.61	715.76	723.55	736.00
153.46	169.00	191.43	226.99	297.54	365.24	376.03	384.09	393.88	404.27	447.24	
330.37	363.49	422.55	408.11	481.10	626.33	637.77	644.43	650.51	654.92	663.03	676.95
90.49	189.62	762.01	1382.56	2943.84	5965.71	7037.28	7833.62	8398.58	9206.16	10050.21	11313.72
15.97	30.94	69.25	103.96	148.21	208.41	236.77	255.11	261.60	274.35	287.95	304.21
52.08	96.17	410.80	709.32	1494.36	2819.81	3280.52	3500.13	3574.25	3845.58	3909.01	4120.93
22.44	62.51	282.76	569.28	1301.27	2937.49	3519.99	4078.37	4562.73	5086.24	5853.25	6888.59
1675	3310	12797	22342	44871	86932	101634	112211	119372	129448	139653	155030
				38542	70024	80689	89323	95190	103813	112230	124286
180.00	189.56	174.50	153.08	103.50	100.25	97.81	96.88	95.92	62.54	63.38	63.60
6704	6693	8038	2112	1038	929	828	876	825	742	705	599
51849	60683	61446	80436	70733	76676	79815	76589	79826	63580	66227	57515
22742	26429	19824	24810	25551	30500	31385	32283	28503	26548	28139	28150
7980	11085	13240	9308	16339	15637	16127	15514	14502	12294	10426	8146
166.10	159.00	147.58	172.16	165.28	192.53	203.23	210.76	219.23	173.46	156.82	126.91
11.16	14.93	19.21	25.24	30.74	31.79	32.5	33.49	34.04	29.67	27.84	26.27
30400	47588	63294	91626	147800	208945	212277	210527	197992	186026	178880	173447
				6589.51	12810.52	14881.98	15595.28	15211.78	15851.40	15018.77	15054.78
128.59	292.26	1020.03	1543.57	5441.13	11081.04	12352.92	12959.68	12418	12853.05	12415.68	12420.96
24.81	31.54	63.05	161.61	450.68	1224.48	1330.48	1339.94	1450.55	1538.07	1559.68	1655.64
6724	8119	16620	18607	24124	33772	34778	35819	36409	24070	23942	20541
2488	6522	10347	11459	19909	25915	28831	30089	30734	29335	29384	30170
14.19	22.92	156.63	376.65	1277.8	2651.88	3100.02	3722.75	4263.87	4952.70	5556.32	5842.42
47.81	98.17	299.35	514.68	978.43	2225.00	2690.22	3165.19	3864.84	4201.46	4697.23	5176.20

a) The standard for above designated size of industry, before 1997, it was above the sub - district level; 1998 - 2010, it was the annual sales income over 5 million yuan; since 2011, it was the annual sales income over 20 million yuan.

b) The data of grain was obtained from the sampling survey of grain production in 2014.

c) In 2016, the population of registered urban residents has not been approved.

1-04 续表

指 标		Item	
境外旅游者人数	(万人次)	Number of Foreign Tourists	(10,000 person-times)
财政总收入	(亿元)	Total Financial Revenue	(100 million yuan)
一般公共预算支出	(亿元)	General Public Budget Revenue	(100 million yuan)
金融机构存款余额(本外币)	(亿元)	Deposits of Financial Institutions	(100 million yuan)
金融机构贷款余额(本外币)	(亿元)	Loans of Financial Institutions	(100 million yuan)
住户存款余额	(亿元)	Household Deposits	(100 million yuan)
非私营单位就业人员工资总额	(亿元)	Total Wages of Employed Persons in Non-private Units	(100 million yuan)
非私营单位就业人员平均工资	(元)	Average Wage of Employed Persons in Non-private Units	(yuan)
市区居民消费价格指数	(以1978年为100)	Consumer Price Index in Urban District	(Year of 1978 = 100)
市区商品零售价格指数	(以1978年为100)	Retail Price Index in Urban District	(Year of 1978 = 100)
全体居民人均可支配收入	(元)	Per Capita Annual Disposable Income of Urban and Rural Residents	(yuan)
城镇居民人均可支配收入	(元)	Per Capita Annual Disposable Income of Urban Residents	(yuan)
农村居民人均可支配收入	(元)	Per Capita Annual Net Income of Rural Residents	(yuan)
高等学校在校学生数	(人)	Student Enrollment in Institutions of Higher Education	(person)
中等专业学校在校学生数	(人)	Student Enrollment in Secondary Specialized Schools	(person)
普通中学在校学生数	(人)	Student Enrollment in Secondary Schools	(person)
小学在校学生数	(人)	Student Enrollment in Primary Schools	(person)
卫生机构数	(个)	Number of Health Institutions	(unit)
#医院	(个)	Number of Hospitals	(unit)
卫生技术人员	(人)	Number of Medical Technical Personnel	(person)
#执业(助理)医师	(人)	Number of Certified Doctors(Include Assistant Doctors)	(person)
床位数	(张)	Number of Beds in Health Institutions	(unit)
#医院	(张)	Beds in Hospital	(unit)

continued

1985	1990	1995	2000	2005	2010	2011	2012	2013	2014	2015	2016
23.84	38.83	44.13	70.71	151.36	275.71	306.31	331.12	316.01	326.13	341.56	363.23
18.65	25.25	55.13	142.85	520.79	1245.43	1488.92	1627.89	1734.98	1920.11	2238.75	2558.41
5.77	11.82	24.91	73.43	238.33	616.58	747.50	786.28	855.74	961.18	1205.48	1404.31
48.50	133.77	707.97	2088.47	6748.72	17084.35	18396.57	20148.77	22174.71	24450.51	29863.83	33386.04
58.01	162.27	567.20	1686.64	5545.30	15078.73	16573.74	18090.90	19350.46	21316.83	23327.95	26169.00
15.96	69.75	342.34	788.56	2191.66	4990.97	5547.48	6089.98	6408.59	6767.20	7617.75	8493.27
13.01	27.79	89.05	126.75	297.02	933.06	1122.28	1483.90	1758.23	1982.27	2152.40	2417.60
1266	2382	7156	14257	31069	48772	54408	56417	63664	69209	76073	85022
140.21	246.68	503.06	611.07	623.07	701.33	734.99	753.36	772.19	787.63	801.81	822.66
142.61	256.45	476.99	504.42	470.47	526.76	549.94	560.39	568.80	573.35	574.50	583.12
–	–	–	–	–	–	–	–	35763	39237	42642	46116
1026	1985	6301	9668	16601	30035	34065	37511	40925	44632	48316	52185
624	1171	3012	4894	7655	13186	15245	17017	21208	23555	25719	27908
36996	39866	63124	122386	351918	434811	446721	459181	471820	474652	475558	480953
16527	23564	42784	45238	20344	3999	4100	3909	3656	3974	3968	4402
244399	199940	257071	342533	362257	352997	340634	331353	327346	324414	321306	326187
414839	460514	513988	485679	458942	453897	465289	472613	483489	502688	524513	543038
1582	1738	1712	1599	2196	2819	2958	3017	4139	4198	4428	4691
404	440	414	396	127	151	167	198	208	218	244	277
25593	30990	34245	35487	42353	61117	65869	71618	78340	85614	93036	101194
11503	14483	16465	16317	17833	24345	25773	27369	29686	31977	34832	38172
19637	24121	26684	27166	33251	42828	45291	49471	52056	55779	63632	69452
15010	18879	21360	23303	25907	33611	39363	44019	46636	50805	58400	63994

1－05 全市生产总值及发展指数(1978－2016年)

Gross Domestic Product and its Indices(1978－2016)

单位:万元　　　　(10000 yuan)

年份 Year	地区生产总值(当年价格) Gross Domestic Product (Current Price)	第一产业 Primary Industry	第二产业 Secondary Industry	第三产业 Tertiary Industry	人均生产总值(元)(按户籍) Per Capita GDP (Household Registered)	人均生产总值(元)(按常住) Per Capita GDP (Long－term Registered)	地区生产总值指数(%) Indices of Gross Domestic product(%) (1978＝100)	第一产业 Primary Industry	第二产业 Secondary Industry	第三产业 Tertiary Industry
1978	284046	63372	169344	51330	565	－	100	100	100	100
1979	335285	83852	194132	57301	659	－	113.3	114.2	114.0	110.0
1980	406508	81524	253545	71439	791	－	135.7	105.6	151.1	130.7
1981	468206	90955	287632	89619	904	－	154.0	108.7	172.2	162.3
1982	501854	108769	294725	98360	957	－	165.1	129.8	177.7	176.3
1983	558947	101106	334413	123428	1054	－	183.6	115.6	203.1	219.9
1984	694690	126443	405535	162712	1298	－	225.3	140.1	245.4	283.7
1985	904897	159684	520853	224360	1675	－	268.9	139.9	300.8	352.8
1986	1053589	177589	601277	274723	1917	－	299.9	145.0	335.3	409.9
1987	1260162	204366	718892	336904	2276	－	338.4	148.7	382.2	471.6
1988	1525427	256838	855305	413284	2717	－	363.3	145.5	419.8	497.2
1989	1662945	282746	896736	483463	2928	－	352.1	145.1	396.5	509.0
1990	1896216	309404	961673	625139	3310	－	372.4	154.4	422.2	528.0
1991	2279545	334024	1131088	814433	3952	－	439.8	161.1	492.4	669.5
1992	2900690	349033	1487838	1063819	4996	－	540.5	161.6	637.5	814.8
1993	4247094	419364	2264440	1563290	7263	－	703.2	171.2	878.7	1004.7
1994	5855239	575131	3143430	2136678	9924	－	888.1	185.0	1161.6	1225.7
1995	7620055	692510	4100008	2827537	12797	－	1064.8	198.2	1434.6	1445.1
1996	9066133	839985	4776225	3449923	15095	－	1203.3	208.9	1644.0	1621.4
1997	10363299	913611	5415017	4034671	17113	－	1360.9	223.1	1852.8	1861.3
1998	11348899	960558	5879589	4508752	18611	－	1513.3	244.0	2071.4	2060.5
1999	12252795	975821	6307510	4969464	19961	－	1667.7	257.4	2280.6	2287.1
2000	13825616	1039641	7093233	5692742	22342	－	1867.8	272.1	2565.7	2563.9
2001	15680138	1114569	7935809	6629760	25074	－	2095.7	292.3	2891.6	2884.4
2002	17818302	1146388	9018225	7653689	28150	－	2372.3	304.2	3276.2	3308.4
2003	20997744	1265890	10757812	8974042	32819	－	2732.9	322.5	3885.6	3725.3
2004	25431796	1322341	13182254	10927201	39293	－	3142.8	338.9	4534.4	4258.0
2005	29438430	1482145	14943581	13012704	44871	－	3551.4	350.5	5037.8	4956.3
2006	34434972	1548594	17283905	15602473	51908	44128	4059.5	364.7	5672.8	5820.3
2007	41040117	1634719	20458811	18946588	61315	51416	4651.7	372.8	6483.5	6761.1
2008	47889748	1798300	23725807	22365641	70948	58862	5165.2	386.7	7062.8	7705.1
2009	51114007	1905093	23657646	25551268	75111	61821	5680.2	398.7	7486.6	8822.4
2010	59657106	2084144	28198060	29374902	86932	70024	6361.8	408.7	8332.6	9995.8
2011	70372782	2367708	32805209	35199865	101634	80689	7004.3	418.9	9057.5	11195.2
2012	78336168	2551127	35001330	40783711	112211	89323	7634.7	429.4	9709.6	12449.1
2013	83985753	2615974	35742503	45627276	119372	95190	8245.5	435.4	10389.3	13606.9
2014	92061634	2743492	38455759	50862382	129448	103813	8921.6	443.3	11220.4	14777.1
2015	100502079	2879492	39090099	58532488	139653	112230	9831.6	450.8	11837.6	16934.5
2016	113137223	3042063	41209307	68885853	155030	124286	10775.4	458.9	12370.2	19220.7

注:2016年起研究与试验发展支出计入地区生产总值。

a) From 2016, research and test development expenditure was included in the GDP.

1－06 市区生产总值及发展指数(1978－2016年)

Gross Domestic Product and its Indices of Urban District (1978－2016)

单位:万元 (10000 yuan)

年份 Year	地区生产总值(当年价格) Gross Domestic Product (Current Price)	第一产业 Primary Industry	第二产业 Secondary Industry	第三产业 Tertiary Industry	人均生产总值(元)(按户籍) Per Capita GDP (Household Registered)	人均生产总值(元)(按常住) Per Capita GDP (Long－term Registered)	地区生产总值指数(%)(1978＝100) Indices of Gross Domestic product(%) (1978＝100)	第一产业 Primary Industry	第二产业 Secondary Industry	第三产业 Tertiary Industry
1978	141995	5215	106663	30117	1389	–	100	100	100	100
1979	167206	6527	126517	34162	1555	–	116.4	109.4	118.1	111.6
1980	208220	5943	159161	43116	1863	–	145.3	94.0	150.9	133.9
1981	229243	6165	171946	51132	2005	–	159.9	90.3	163.9	157.2
1982	248297	7327	183284	57686	2125	–	173.7	107.3	176.0	175.6
1983	282171	5938	200334	75899	2369	–	197.9	83.1	193.8	229.5
1984	353781	8469	244445	100867	2919	–	245.4	114.9	235.5	298.4
1985	448574	11233	293579	143762	3633	–	289.9	120.7	270.1	382.2
1986	513639	12245	324585	176809	4042	–	317.3	122.6	287.7	445.1
1987	605234	15408	370668	219158	4724	–	353.2	137.1	313.8	517.4
1988	708474	19602	425319	263553	5441	–	370.8	136.0	332.7	534.0
1989	772208	23869	435847	312492	5848	–	347.0	146.7	296.7	545.2
1990	896496	23919	470844	401733	6722	–	366.5	147.6	314.6	573.6
1991	1096628	25767	547949	522912	8158	–	426.0	151.4	356.3	691.1
1992	1413278	27611	712697	672969	10420	–	535.3	153.1	447.4	877.8
1993	2086571	36208	1052187	998176	15196	–	687.6	157.7	583.7	1117.4
1994	2788314	48257	1395127	1344931	19945	–	870.9	172.3	779.6	1335.3
1995	3697794	57784	1866784	1773226	25969	–	1041.6	183.5	945.7	1574.3
1996	4727377	110881	2356408	2260088	28552	–	1194.9	194.7	1103.6	1769.5
1997	5414265	130062	2630349	2653853	32227	–	1354.9	214.2	1230.3	2052.6
1998	5905726	134320	2786159	2985247	34620	–	1482.5	230.7	1337.2	2266.1
1999	6317335	145242	2915614	3256479	36394	–	1599.3	254.5	1431.1	2467.8
2000	7111586	145715	3278310	3687561	40127	–	1785.5	255.5	1596.7	2763.9
2001	12260891	582492	6026353	5652046	32607	–	2017.2	275.7	1805.3	3126.0
2002	14042278	605433	6901224	6535621	36640	–	2300.8	290.0	2038.6	3607.4
2003	16647332	665083	8343138	7639111	42675	–	2664.8	302.2	2448.4	4058.3
2004	20362738	664676	10368453	9329609	51241	–	3077.4	313.1	2873.9	4630.5
2005	23495459	732463	11582930	11180067	57934	–	3461.2	318.2	3141.5	5406.6
2006	27483121	755663	13254773	13472684	66731	51073	3955.9	320.5	3493.9	6399.6
2007	32738842	773208	15546960	16418675	78541	58907	4525.3	322.7	3948.4	7455.8
2008	38139834	830741	17926048	19383045	90400	66808	5018.5	324.8	4266.5	8505.2
2009	41086525	874987	17987776	22223762	96251	70418	5539.5	334.6	4539.5	9704.4
2010	47768030	941591	21358545	25467894	110541	78665	6198.7	339.3	5029.8	10975.7
2011	56297165	1054368	24746674	30496123	128656	89967	6818.5	345.7	5437.2	12281.8
2012	62711287	1128362	26276722	35306203	141597	99616	7432.2	353.0	5796.0	13657.4
2013	67258795	1123778	26756092	39378925	150089	105497	8011.9	350.8	6196.0	14845.6
2014	79773702	1563084	32020016	46190602	153152	112322	8668.9	353.7	6697.8	16107.5
2015	87219983	1628558	32394494	53196931	164886	121681	9570.5	358.2	7052.8	18475.2
2016	98354845	1704347	34069866	62580632	182554	134798	10498.8	360.8	7334.9	20987.9

1－07 全市生产总值指数(1978－2016 年)
Indices of Gross Domestic Product (1978－2016)

(上年＝100) (Preceding Year＝100)

年 份 Year	地区生产总值 Gross Domestic Product	第一产业 Primary Industry	第二产业 Secondary Industry	第三产业 Tertiary Industry	人均生产总值(元)(按户籍) Per Capita GDP(yuan) (Household Registered)	人均生产总值(元)(按常住) Per Capita GDP(yuan) (Long－term Registered)
1978	120.2	119.1	123.7	111.6	119.0	
1979	113.3	114.2	114.0	110.0	112.1	
1980	119.7	92.5	132.5	118.8	118.4	
1981	113.6	102.9	114.0	124.2	112.6	
1982	107.2	119.4	103.2	108.6	105.9	
1983	111.2	89.1	114.3	124.7	109.9	
1984	122.7	121.2	120.8	129.0	121.6	
1985	119.4	99.9	122.6	124.4	118.2	
1986	111.5	103.7	111.5	116.2	110.3	
1987	112.8	102.5	114.0	115.1	111.3	
1988	107.4	97.8	109.8	105.4	105.8	
1989	96.9	99.8	94.4	102.4	95.8	
1990	105.8	106.4	106.5	103.7	104.9	
1991	118.1	104.4	116.6	126.8	117.3	
1992	122.9	100.3	129.5	121.7	122.1	
1993	130.1	105.9	137.8	123.3	129.1	
1994	126.3	108.1	132.2	122.0	125.2	
1995	119.9	107.1	123.5	117.9	118.8	
1996	113.0	105.4	114.6	112.2	112.0	
1997	113.1	106.8	112.7	114.8	112.1	
1998	111.2	109.4	111.8	110.7	110.5	
1999	110.2	105.5	110.1	111.0	109.4	
2000	112.0	105.7	112.5	112.1	111.1	
2001	112.2	107.4	112.7	112.5	111.1	
2002	113.2	104.1	113.3	114.7	111.8	
2003	115.2	106.0	118.6	112.6	114.0	
2004	115.0	105.1	116.7	114.3	113.7	
2005	113.0	103.4	111.1	116.4	111.5	
2006	114.3	104.1	112.6	117.4	113.0	
2007	114.6	102.2	114.3	116.2	113.6	112.0
2008	111.0	103.7	108.9	114.0	110.1	108.9
2009	110.0	103.1	106.0	114.5	109.1	108.2
2010	112.0	102.5	111.3	113.3	111.0	108.7
2011	110.1	102.5	108.7	112.0	109.1	107.6
2012	109.0	102.5	107.2	111.2	108.2	108.4
2013	108.0	101.4	107.0	109.3	107.1	107.3
2014	108.2	101.8	108.0	108.6	107.0	107.6
2015	110.2	101.7	105.5	114.6	108.9	109.1
2016	109.6	101.8	104.5	113.5	108.1	107.8

注:本表按可比价格计算。

a) The indices in this table are calculated at comparable prices.

1－08　市区生产总值指数(1978－2016年)

Indices of Gross Domestic Product of Urban District (1978－2016)

(上年=100)　　(Preceding Year=100)

年份 Year	地区生产总值 Gross Domestic Product	第一产业 Primary Industry	第二产业 Secondary Industry	第三产业 Tertiary Industry	人均生产总值(元)(按户籍) Per Capita GDP(yuan)(Household Registered)	人均生产总值(元)(按常住) Per Capita GDP(yuan)(Long－term Registered)
1978	120.1	118.8	122.3	113.6	118.0	
1979	116.4	109.4	118.1	111.6	111.4	
1980	124.8	85.9	127.8	120.0	119.7	
1981	110.1	96.1	108.6	117.4	107.6	
1982	108.6	118.8	107.4	111.7	106.3	
1983	113.9	77.5	110.1	130.7	111.7	
1984	124.0	138.2	121.5	130.0	121.8	
1985	118.2	105.0	114.7	128.1	116.0	
1986	109.4	101.6	106.5	116.7	107.4	
1987	111.3	111.8	109.1	116.0	109.4	
1988	105.0	99.2	106.0	103.2	103.3	
1989	93.6	107.9	89.2	102.1	92.2	
1990	105.6	100.6	106.0	105.2	104.6	
1991	116.2	102.6	113.3	120.5	115.3	
1992	125.7	101.1	125.6	127.3	124.5	
1993	128.5	103.0	130.5	127.3	126.9	
1994	126.6	109.3	133.6	119.5	124.4	
1995	119.6	106.5	121.3	117.9	117.4	
1996	114.7	106.1	116.7	112.4	105.3	
1997	113.4	110.0	111.5	116.0	104.7	
1998	109.4	107.7	108.7	110.4	107.8	
1999	107.9	110.3	107.0	108.9	106.0	
2000	111.6	100.4	111.6	112.0	109.3	
2001	113.0	107.9	113.1	113.1	111.2	
2002	114.1	105.2	112.9	115.4	111.9	
2003	115.8	104.2	120.1	112.5	113.8	
2004	115.5	103.6	117.4	114.1	113.4	
2005	112.5	101.6	109.3	116.8	110.2	
2006	114.3	100.7	111.2	118.4	112.5	
2007	114.4	100.7	113.0	116.5	113.0	110.8
2008	110.9	100.7	108.1	114.1	109.5	108.0
2009	110.4	103.0	106.4	114.1	109.1	108.0
2010	111.9	101.4	110.8	113.1	110.5	107.5
2011	110.0	101.9	108.1	111.9	108.6	106.7
2012	109.0	102.1	106.6	111.2	107.7	108.4
2013	107.8	99.4	106.9	108.7	106.8	106.7
2014	108.2	100.8	108.1	108.5	106.7	107.6
2015	110.4	101.3	105.3	114.7	108.7	109.3
2016	109.7	100.7	104.0	113.6	107.7	107.8

1－09 全市分行业

Composition of

单位:万元

行　　业	Sector	全 Whole	
		2016	为上年(%) As Compared with the Preceding Year(%)
全市生产总值	Gross Domestic Product	113137223	109.6
按行业分	Grouped by Sector		
#农、林、牧、渔业	Farming, Forestry, Animal Husbandry & Fishery	3092579	102.0
工业	Industry	37262023	105.2
建筑业	Construction	3961195	98.2
批发和零售业	Wholesale and Retail Trade	8837232	106.8
交通运输、仓储和邮政业	Transportation, Storage and, Post	3254572	109.2
住宿和餐饮业	Hotels and Catering Services	1752556	98.6
信息传输、软件和信息技术服务业	Information Transmission, Software and Information Technology Services	17317584	132.6
金融业	Financial Intermediation	9820185	105.8
房地产业	Real Estate	6901134	102.9
租赁和商务服务业	Leasing and Busyness Service	4004168	125.1
科学研究、技术服务业	Scientific Research, Technical Service	3098796	108.3
水利环境和公共设施管理业	Management of Water Conservancy, Enviroment and Public Facilities	838858	109.5
居民服务、修理和其他服务业	Service for the Residents, Repair and Others	1394628	108.1
教育	Education	3905886	109.6
卫生和社会工作	Health Care and Social Work	2399941	110.2
文化、体育和娱乐业	Culture, Sports and Entertainment	1392865	110.9
公共管理、社会保障和社会组织	Public Administration ,Social Security and Social Organization	3903020	110.6
第一产业	Primary Industry	3042063	101.8
第二产业	Secondary Industry	41209307	104.5
第三产业	Tertiary Industry	68885853	113.5
按构成分	by Structure		
#劳动者报酬	Labourer's Remuneration	50930990	–
生产税净额	Net Taxes on Production	18881439	–
固定资产折旧	Depreciation of Fixed Assets	12910038	–
营业盈余	Operating Surplus	30414756	–

生产总值构成(2016 年)

Gross Domestic Product(2016)

(10000 yuan)

市 City		#市 区 Urban District			
比 重 (%) Proportion(%)		2016	为上年(%) As Compared with the Preceding Year(%)	比 重 (%) Proportion(%)	
2016	2015			2016	2015
		98354845	109.7		
2.7	2.9	1739165	101.0	1.8	1.9
32.9	34.8	30816388	104.8	31.3	33.2
3.5	4.1	3262155	96.7	3.3	4.0
7.8	8.1	7775441	108.4	7.9	8.1
2.9	3.0	2592629	108.2	2.6	2.7
1.5	1.6	1421610	98.1	1.4	1.5
15.3	12.7	16562348	132.1	16.8	14.1
8.7	9.4	9148729	106.0	9.3	10.0
6.1	6.1	6237430	103.0	6.3	6.4
3.5	3.1	3714669	125.0	3.8	3.3
2.7	2.5	3002684	107.5	3.1	2.8
0.7	0.7	749300	110.1	0.8	0.7
1.2	1.3	1173715	110.0	1.2	1.2
3.5	3.1	3385502	107.0	3.4	3.1
2.1	2.0	2173623	109.4	2.2	2.1
1.2	1.3	1329870	111.6	1.4	1.4
3.4	3.3	3269587	106.8	3.3	3.3
2.7	2.9	1704347	100.7	1.7	1.9
36.4	38.9	34069866	104.0	34.6	37.1
60.9	58.2	62580632	113.6	63.6	61.0
45.0	45.1	43444422	–	44.2	45.1
16.7	17.7	16631639	–	16.9	17.7
11.4	10.2	11166378	–	11.4	10.2
26.9	27.0	27112405	–	27.6	27.0

1-10 全市分地区和产业生产总值构成(2016年)

Gross Domestic Product by Region and Industry(2016)

单位:万元 (10000 yuan)

地　区	Region	地区生产总值 Gross Domestic Product	第一产业 Primary Industry	第二产业 Secondary Industry	工　业 Industry	建筑业 Construction	第三产业 Tertiary Industry	户籍人口人均GDP(元) Per Capita GDP (yuan)(Household Registered)	常住人口人均GDP(元) Per Capita GDP (Long-term Registered)
全　市	**Whole City**	**113137223**	**3042063**	**41209307**	**37262023**	**3961195**	**68885853**	**155030**	**124286**
市　区	Urban District	98354845	1704347	34069866	30816388	3262155	62580632	182554	134798
#上城区	Shangcheng	9283452	-	3712527	3527193	185336	5570924	283539	262913
下城区	Xiacheng	8307155	-	355467	125415	230107	7951688	206321	155129
江干区	Jianggan	5588494	4638	1219150	553120	666215	4364706	135812	76982
拱墅区	Gongshu	4727021	-	874092	725890	148260	3852929	139203	81995
西湖区	Xihu	9769868	39557	995753	696409	299616	8734558	147223	120452
高新(滨江)区	Hi-Tech (Binjiang)	9585774	13770	5054400	4888001	166494	4517604	450057	287688
萧山区	Xiaoshan	19541783	676342	9279201	8596183	685760	9586240	153919	124748
大江东产业集聚区	Dajiangdong Industry Cluster District	2885569	133724	2410589	2284676	125913	341256	191088	168994
余杭区	Yuhang	14478402	497084	4930729	4535372	397465	9050589	149612	110611
富阳区	Fuyang	7126504	447873	3299958	2993778	309230	3378673	106406	96966
经济技术开发区	Economic and Technological Development Zone	7388461	3872	5645371	5570633	74849	1739219		
西湖风景名胜区	The West Lake Scenic Zone	363217	7550	13496	5206	8290	342171	180665	118893
桐庐县	Tonglu	3733996	244840	1962825	1798211	166493	1526331	90982	88379
淳安县	Chun'an	2356512	342939	810805	659890	151683	1202768	51224	67454
建德市	Jiande	3504257	327496	1760048	1576097	185257	1416713	68831	78439
临安市	Lin'an	5187612	422441	2605763	2411437	195608	2159409	97789	88232

1－11　分地区生产总值(主要年份)
Gross Domestic Product by Region (Main Years)

单位:万元　　(10000 yuan)

地　区	Region	2005	2010	2011	2012	2013	2014	2015	2016
全　市	**Whole City**	**29438430**	**59657106**	**70372782**	**78336168**	**83985753**	**92061634**	**100502079**	**113137223**
市　区	Urban District	23495459	47768030	56297165	62711287	67258795	79773702	87219983	98354845
#上城区	Shangcheng	2564579	5258963	6133492	6644749	7389318	8005940	8482025	9283452
下城区	Xiacheng	1981140	4515546	5319752	5873718	6400548	6898798	7619880	8307155
江干区	Jianggan	1155829	2970781	3478363	3957866	4289933	4566848	4938851	5588494
拱墅区	Gongshu	1607349	2942067	3467376	3894365	3764825	3939940	4244220	4727021
西湖区	Xihu	2084152	4758469	5677027	6372300	7008109	8020086	8878113	9769868
高新(滨江)区	Hi－Tech (Binjiang)	1376799	3439684	4246699	4880188	6073310	6930324	7735050	9585774
萧山区	Xiaoshan	5904071	12155961	14413914	16090498	16592205	17276336	18127888	19541784
大江东产业集聚区	Dajiangdong Industry Cluster District							2553889	2885569
余杭区	Yuhang	2883710	6562136	7689302	8718372	9800819	11012328	12397057	14478402
富阳区	Fuyang	2006472	4121151	4878795	5377572	5668246	6014722	6451465	7126504
经济技术开发区	Economic and Technological Development Zone		3606570	4261972	4522917	4717483	5308744	6203217	7388461
西湖风景名胜区	The West Lake Scenic Zone		204276	232108	252472	259287	275951	315391	363217
桐庐县	Tonglu	1027441	1952611	2308431	2549395	2742048	3061292	3344754	3733996
淳安县	Chun'an	584804	1178678	1407623	1603247	1736807	1920615	2074215	2356512
建德市	Jiande	982458	1871486	2214747	2448213	2677482	2989338	3187469	3504257
临安市	Lin'an	1341795	2765150	3266021	3646455	3902375	4316686	4675658	5187612

1-12 分地区生产总值指数(主要年份)

Indices of Gross Domestic Product by Region(Main Years)

(上年=100) (Preceding Year=100)

地 区	Region	2000	2005	2010	2011	2012	2013	2014	2015	2016
全 市	**Whole City**	**112.0**	**113.0**	**112.0**	**110.1**	**109.0**	**108.0**	**108.2**	**110.2**	**109.6**
市 区	Urban District	111.6	112.5	111.9	110.0	109.0	107.8	108.2	110.4	109.7
上城区	Shangcheng		111.8	108.7	109.5	107.0	106.5	107.8	109.1	106.2
下城区	Xiacheng		111.4	111.8	109.6	107.7	107.8	106.6	111.1	107.4
江干区	Jianggan		115.7	110.8	109.3	110.6	107.1	106.5	110.9	110.3
拱墅区	Gongshu		104.7	112.3	110.5	110.5	107.9	107.6	108.5	108.1
西湖区	Xihu		114.0	112.1	111.2	109.4	108.3	108.3	111.7	110.3
高新(滨江)区	Hi-Tech (Binjiang)		116.2	113.1	113.1	111.5	110.5	111.5	113.8	114.9
萧山区	Xiaoshan	116.1	114.5	112.2	111.0	110.1	108.3	107.9	108.2	108.2
大江东产业集聚区	Dajiangdong Industry Cluster District								117.0	112.1
余杭区	Yuhang	112.5	116.2	113.7	109.6	110.1	110.2	109.5	111.3	112.2
富阳区	Fuyang	111.4	114.8	112.3	110.5	108.7	109.1	108.3	109.3	108.6
经济技术开发区	Economic and Technological Development Zone		113.2	110.9	110.1	107.5	107.2	108.2	109.5	110.6
西湖风景名胜区	The West Lake Scenic Zone		122.4	113.9	109.0	105.9	101.5	105.1	111.3	109.1
桐庐县	Tonglu	110.9	115.2	112.6	110.3	108.6	108.1	108.5	109.5	108.8
淳安县	Chun'an	110.2	113.5	111.0	111.0	111.6	110.3	108.3	108.2	110.7
建德市	Jiande	108.6	112.5	111.5	110.3	108.5	107.8	107.8	108.5	108.4
临安市	Lin'an	110.8	117.1	114.0	110.6	109.8	109.0	108.2	108.9	108.5

1－13 分地区第一产业增加值(主要年份)

Value Added of Primary Industry by Region(Main Years)

单位:万元 (10000 yuan)

地　区	Region	2005	2010	2011	2012	2013	2014	2015	2016
全　市	**Whole City**	**1482145**	**2084144**	**2367708**	**2551127**	**2615974**	**2743492**	**2879492**	**3042063**
市　区	Urban District	732463	941591	1054368	1128362	1123778	1563084	1628558	1704347
#上城区	Shangcheng	－	－	－	－	－	－	－	－
下城区	Xiacheng	4902	－	－	－	－	－	－	－
江干区	Jianggan	25293	9556	8593	7327	6303	5573	4869	4638
拱墅区	Gongshu	7019	2912	2004	614	－	－	－	－
西湖区	Xihu	40555	38686	42528	44853	43185	42407	43005	39557
高新(滨江)区	Hi－Tech (Binjiang)	19785	16945	18236	18343	17320	17074	14402	13770
萧山区	Xiaoshan	335323	472211	528775	567823	584638	615991	638480	676342
大江东产业集聚区	Dajiangdong Industry Cluster District							128257	133724
余杭区	Yuhang	267280	384518	436754	471892	455379	455424	469595	497084
富阳区	Fuyang	182959	286661	331636	359913	379042	399288	423572	447873
经济技术开发区	Economic and Technological Development Zone		12470	13026	12398	11121	9400	9058	3872
西湖风景名胜区	The West Lake Scenic Zone		4293	4452	5112	5832	6500	7077	7550
桐庐县	Tonglu	107813	160028	183348	197441	206463	217828	228557	244840
淳安县	Chun'an	132422	218432	248773	270778	283787	301077	320370	342939
建德市	Jiande	157794	207552	238574	258136	270044	286495	304848	327496
临安市	Lin'an	168694	269880	311009	336497	352860	375008	397159	422441

1-14 分地区第二产业增加值(主要年份)

Value Added of Secondary Industry by Region(Main Years)

单位:万元 (10000 yuan)

地 区	Region	2005	2010	2011	2012	2013	2014	2015	2016
全 市	**Whole City**	**14943581**	**28198060**	**32805209**	**35001330**	**35742503**	**38455759**	**39090099**	**41209307**
市 区	Urban District	11582930	21358545	24746674	26276722	26756092	32020016	32394494	34069866
#上城区	Shangcheng	1383279	2328599	2748958	2920974	3323176	3555001	3541784	3712527
下城区	Xiacheng	457613	503515	528663	548891	519853	507846	424128	355467
江干区	Jianggan	530387	1023232	1165033	1232278	1282251	1333886	1273302	1219150
拱墅区	Gongshu	1010185	1195898	1379983	1483426	1082440	989683	868875	874092
西湖区	Xihu	597190	927948	1034458	1016631	1038356	1058316	1025825	995753
高新(滨江)区	Hi-Tech (Binjiang)	816751	1633267	1961196	2188350	2990393	3680504	3973170	5054400
萧山区	Xiaoshan	3833572	7399022	8708660	9559330	9352948	9282655	9200966	9279201
大江东产业集聚区	Dajiangdong Industry Cluster District							2124255	2410589
余杭区	Yuhang	1637762	3347711	3774134	4003780	4179815	4412453	4611442	4930729
富阳区	Fuyang	1208899	2487569	2927977	3155766	3159057	3165902	3199297	3299958
经济技术开发区	Economic and Technological Development Zone		2824206	3355219	3443715	3545701	4042887	4755845	5645371
西湖风景名胜区	The West Lake Scenic Zone		10056	11347	9808	10639	8663	14366	13496
桐庐县	Tonglu	635743	1190528	1388187	1485433	1549978	1721284	1817277	1962825
淳安县	Chun'an	220748	509526	612506	685730	711833	762658	770033	810805
建德市	Jiande	546726	1048611	1240160	1332896	1438668	1612988	1660233	1760048
临安市	Lin'an	748535	1603281	1889706	2064784	2126875	2338814	2448061	2605763

1－15　分地区工业增加值(主要年份)
Value Added of Industry by Region(Main Years)

单位:万元　(10000 yuan)

地　区	Region	2005	2010	2011	2012	2013	2014	2015	2016
全　市	**Whole City**	**13263991**	**24532551**	**28900944**	**30933324**	**31564031**	**34148954**	**34978318**	**37262023**
市　区	Urban District	10221817	18363679	21599838	22997710	23420616	28375206	28952807	30816388
#上城区	Shangcheng	1251279	2138350	2567662	2723855	3135606	3369525	3372607	3527193
下城区	Xiacheng	352252	244306	264258	266569	257694	204456	188912	125415
江干区	Jianggan	389088	461192	545880	563358	611014	636701	618002	553120
拱墅区	Gongshu	923082	1059215	1232797	1326480	911180	806021	693832	725890
西湖区	Xihu	366200	490551	563256	592165	599273	624695	630961	696409
高新(滨江)区	Hi－Tech (Binjiang)	702955	1429247	1730844	1921883	2737768	3499731	3812540	4888001
萧山区	Xiaoshan	3578182	6821499	8076434	8889277	8685228	8526903	8473528	8596183
大江东产业集聚区	Dajiangdong Industry Cluster District							1978159	2284676
余杭区	Yuhang	1445060	2995855	3397253	3595182	3754685	4008284	4196522	4535372
富阳区	Fuyang	1121971	2298470	2711715	2931055	2921956	2917814	2934656	2993778
经济技术开发区	Economic and Technological Development Zone		2744584	3273392	3329678	3413608	3927967	4642686	5570633
西湖风景名胜区	The West Lake Scenic Zone		5692	7122	5826	6654	4043	7785	5206
桐庐县	Tonglu	584116	1057999	1244325	1336037	1388339	1556780	1654178	1798211
淳安县	Chun′an	171216	388588	471183	534696	551863	582588	608312	659890
建德市	Jiande	485699	956561	1137197	1226161	1322121	1471828	1510862	1576097
临安市	Lin′an	679171	1467252	1736687	1907666	1959136	2162550	2252159	2411437

1－16 分地区建筑业增加值(主要年份)

Value Added of Construction by Region(Main Years)

单位:万元　　(10000 yuan)

地 区	Region	2005	2010	2011	2012	2013	2014	2015	2016
全 市	**Whole City**	**1679589**	**3665510**	**3904265**	**4068006**	**4190741**	**4320080**	**4125377**	**3961195**
市 区	Urban District	1361112	2994866	3146836	3279012	3340439	3653089	3450168	3262155
#上城区	Shangcheng	132000	190249	181296	197119	187572	185477	169179	185336
下城区	Xiacheng	105362	259209	264405	282322	262207	303442	235269	230107
江干区	Jianggan	141298	562041	619154	668919	671400	697362	655481	666215
拱墅区	Gongshu	87104	136683	147186	156946	171312	183717	175100	148260
西湖区	Xihu	230990	437397	471202	424466	439323	433881	395130	299616
高新(滨江)区	Hi－Tech (Binjiang)	113796	204020	230352	266467	252708	180863	160722	166494
萧山区	Xiaoshan	255390	577523	632225	670052	670139	758368	730118	685760
大江东产业集聚区	Dajiangdong Industry Cluster District							146096	125913
余杭区	Yuhang	192701	351856	376881	408597	426988	406179	416980	397465
富阳区	Fuyang	86928	189099	216261	224712	239792	250999	267622	309230
经济技术开发区	Economic and Technological Development Zone		79621	81827	114038	132191	115026	113268	74849
西湖风景名胜区	The West Lake Scenic Zone		4364	4224	3983	3986	4620	6581	8290
桐庐县	Tonglu	51627	132528	143862	149396	163295	166296	164934	166493
淳安县	Chun'an	49531	120938	141324	151034	160648	180802	162471	151683
建德市	Jiande	61027	92049	102963	106735	117698	142406	150648	185257
临安市	Lin'an	69364	136029	153019	157118	168870	177487	197156	195608

1－17　分地区第三产业增加值(主要年份)

Value Added of Tertiary Industry by Region(Main Years)

单位:万元　　(10000 yuan)

地　区	Region	2005	2010	2011	2012	2013	2014	2015	2016
全　市	**Whole City**	**13012704**	**29374902**	**35199865**	**40783711**	**45627276**	**50862382**	**58532488**	**68885853**
市　区	Urban District	11180067	25467894	30496123	35306203	39378925	46190602	53196931	62580632
#上城区	Shangcheng	1181299	2930364	3384534	3723775	4066142	4450938	4940241	5570924
下城区	Xiacheng	1518625	4012031	4791089	5324827	5880696	6390952	7195753	7951688
江干区	Jianggan	600150	1937993	2304736	2718262	3001379	3227389	3660680	4364706
拱墅区	Gongshu	590144	1743257	2085389	2410325	2682385	2950257	3375345	3852929
西湖区	Xihu	1446406	3791835	4600041	5310815	5926567	6919363	7809284	8734558
高新(滨江)区	Hi－Tech (Binjiang)	540263	1789472	2267267	2673495	3065597	3232746	3747479	4517604
萧山区	Xiaoshan	1735176	4284727	5176479	5963345	6654619	7377691	8288442	9586240
大江东产业集聚区	Dajiangdong Industry Cluster District							301378	341256
余杭区	Yuhang	978669	2829907	3478414	4242701	5165626	6144452	7316020	9050589
富阳区	Fuyang	614613	1346921	1619182	1861893	2130147	2449532	2828596	3378673
经济技术开发区	Economic and Technological Development Zone		769894	893727	1066804	1160661	1256457	1438314	1739219
西湖风景名胜区	The West Lake Scenic Zone		189927	216309	237552	242816	260788	293947	342171
桐庐县	Tonglu	283885	602055	736897	866521	985608	1122181	1298920	1526331
淳安县	Chun'an	231634	450720	546344	646739	741187	856881	983813	1202768
建德市	Jiande	277938	615323	736013	857181	968770	1089854	1222388	1416713
临安市	Lin'an	424566	891989	1065305	1245174	1422640	1602864	1830438	2159409

1－18　主要指标占全省比重(2016 年)

Proportion of Main Indicators in Whole Province(2016)

指　标 Item		全　省 Zhejiang Province	杭州市 Hangzhou City	杭州市占全省(%) Proportion of Hangzhou in Zhejiang(%)
年末常住人口 Long－term Residents(End of 2013)	(万人) (10000 persons)	5590.00	918.80	16.4
年末户籍人口 Household Registration Population(End of 2013)	(万人) (10000 persons)	4910.85	736.00	15.0
年末就业人员数 Total Number of Employed Persons	(万人) (10000 persons)	3760.00	676.95	18.0
地区生产总值 Gross Domestic Product	(亿元) (100 million yuan)	47251.36	11313.72	24.0
第一产业 Primary Industry	(亿元) (100 million yuan)	1965.18	304.21	15.5
第二产业 Secondary Industry	(亿元) (100 million yuan)	21194.61	4120.93	19.5
第三产业 Tertiary Industry	(亿元) (100 million yuan)	24091.57	6888.59	28.6
常住人口人均生产总值 Per Capita GDP of Long－term Residents	(元) (yuan)	84916	124286	－
农林牧渔业总产值 Gross Output Value of Farming, Forestry, Animal Husbandry and Fishery	(亿元) (100 million yuan)	3146.06	467.30	14.9
主要农产品产量 Output of Major Farm Products				
#粮食 Grain	(万吨) (10000 tons)	752.17	63.60	8.5
蚕茧 Silk－worm Cocoons	(万吨) (10000 tons)	3.31	0.81	24.6
生猪年末存栏 Hogs in Stock at Year End	(万头) (10000 heads)	573.83	126.91	22.1
肉类产量 Output of Meat	(万吨) (10000 tons)	93.92	26.27	28.0
淡水产品总产量 Freshwater Aquatic products	(万吨) (10000 tons)	114.28	17.34	15.2

1－18　续表1　continued 1

指　标 Item	全　省 Zhejiang Province	杭州市 Hangzhou City	杭州市占全省(％) Proportion of Hangzhou in Zhejiang(％)
规模以上工业增加值 (亿元) Value－added of Industrial Enterprises above Designated Size (100 million yuan)	14008.82	2990.34	21.3
规模以上工业企业利税总额 (亿元) Total Pre－tax Profits of Industrial Enterprises above Designed Size (100 million yuan)	7343.63	1655.64	22.5
主要工业产品产量 Output of Major Industrial Products			
#发电量 (亿千瓦时) Electricity (100 million kwh)	3089.11	179.10	5.8
氢氧化钠(烧碱)(折100％) (万吨) Caustic Soda(100％ discount) (10000 tons)	159.92	19.41	12.1
碳酸钠(纯碱) (万吨) Soda Ash (10000 tons)	30.71	30.71	100.0
合成氨 (万吨) Synthetic Ammonia (10000 tons)	68.89	21.01	30.5
水泥 (万吨) Cement (10000 tons)	10796.54	1609.45	14.9
钢材 (万吨) Steels (10000 tons)	3760.90	442.48	11.8
化学纤维 (万吨) Chemical Fiber (10000 tons)	2106.42	623.15	29.6
纱 (万吨) Yarn (10000 tons)	215.80	61.40	28.5
自行车 (万辆) Bicycles (10000 units)	958.24	170.75	17.8
彩色电视机 (万台) Colour TV Sets (10000 units)	658.22	0.55	0.1
电冰箱 (万台) Household Refrigerator (10000 units)	797.74	111.20	13.9
洗衣机 (万台) Washing Machine (10000 units)	1396.80	298.49	21.4
客运量 (万人次) Volume of Passenger Transport (10000 person－times)	107377	20541	19.1

1－18　续表2　continued 2

指　　标 Item		全　省 Zhejiang Province	杭州市 Hangzhou City	杭州市占全省(%) Proportion of Hangzhou in Zhejiang(%)
货运量 Volume of Goods Transport	(万吨) (10000 tons)	215018	30170	14.0
固定资产投资 Investment in Fixed Assets	(亿元) (100 million yuan)	29571.00	5842.42	19.8
社会消费品零售总额 Total Retail Sales of Consumer Goods	(亿元) (100 million yuan)	21970.79	5176.20	23.6
出口额 Total Exports	(亿美元) (100 million USD)	2678.60	502.59	18.8
实际利用外资 Foreign Capital Actually Used	(亿美元) (100 million USD)	175.77	72.09	41.0
境外旅游者人数 Number of International Tourists	(万人次) (10000 person－times)	1120.30	363.23	32.4
财政总收入 Total Financial Revenue	(亿元) (100 million yuan)	9224.90	2558.41	27.7
#一般公共预算收入 General Public Budget Revenue	(亿元) (100 million yuan)	5301.81	1402.38	26.5
一般公共预算支出 Financial Expenditure	(亿元) (100 million yuan)	6976.33	1404.31	20.1
金融机构存款余额(本外币) Deposits of Financial Institutions	(亿元) (100 million yuan)	99530.29	33386.04	33.5
金融机构贷款余额(本外币) Loans of Financial Institutions	(亿元) (100 million yuan)	81804.50	26169.00	32.0
住户存款余额 Household Deposit	(亿元) (100 million yuan)	38755.05	8493.27	21.9
非私营单位就业人员平均工资 Average Wage of Employed Persons of Non－private Units	(元) (yuan)	73326	85022	－
全体居民人均可支配收入 Per Capita Annual Disposable Income of Urban and Rural Residents	(元) (yuan)	38529	46116	－
城镇居民人均可支配收入 Per Capita Annual Disposable Income of Urban Residents	(元) (yuan)	47237	52185	－
农村居民人均可支配收入 Per Capita Annual Disposable Income of Rural Residents	(元) (yuan)	22866	27908	－
高等学校在校学生数 Number of Institutions of Higher Education	(万人) (10000 persons)	106.34	48.10	45.2
普通中学在校学生数 Number of Secondary Schools	(万人) (10000 persons)	226.87	32.62	14.4
小学在校学生数 Number of Primary Schools	(万人) (10000 persons)	355.02	54.30	15.3

1－19 国民经济主要指标人均水平(主要年份)
Major Per Capita Indicators of National Economy(Main Years)

指 标 Item	2000	2005	2010	2011	2012	2013	2014	2015	2016
全市生产总值 (元) Gross Domestic Product (yuan)	22342	44871	70024	80689	89323	95190	103813	112230	124286
规模以上工业总产值 (元) Gross Industrial Output Value above Designatted Size (yuan)	24943	82936	130064	141634	147773	106639	144937	138645	136449
农林牧渔业总产值 (元) Gross Output Value of Farming, Forestry, Animal Husbandry and Fishery (yuan)	2467	3345	3713	4094	4382	4526	4720	4918	5133
社会消费品零售总额 (元) Total Retail Sales of Consumer Goods (yuan)	8317	14869	26117	30845	36091	43804	47378	52454	56863
财政总收入 (元) Financial Revenue (yuan)	2308	7938	14618	17071	18562	19664	21652	25000	28105
#一般公共预算收入 (元) General Public Budget Revenue (yuan)	1118	3818	7880	9002	9806	10713	11585	13779	15406
一般公共预算支出 (元) General Public Budgetary Expenditure (yuan)	1187	3633	7237	8571	8966	9699	10839	13462	15427
全体居民可支配收入 (元) Annual Disposable Income of Urban and Rural Residents (yuan)	–	–	–	–	–	35763	39237	42642	46116
全体居民消费性支出 (元) Annual Living Expendituer of Urban and Ruarual Residents (yuan)	–	–	–	–	–	26827	28492	30181	31905
城镇居民可支配收入 (元) Annual Disposable Income of Urban Residents (yuan)	9668	16601	30035	34065	37511	40925	44632	48316	52185
城镇居民消费性支出 (元) Annual Living Expenditure of Urban Residents (yuan)	7790	13438	20219	22642	22800	30659	32165	33818	35686
农村居民可支配收入 (元) Annual Disposable Income of Rural Residents (yuan)	4894	7655	13186	15245	17017	21208	23555	25719	27908
农村居民消费性支出 (元) Annual Living Expenditure of Rural Residents (yuan)	3393	6004	10267	12125	13612	16021	17816	19334	20563

1－20 全市十大产业
Ten Major

指标 Item	监测指标 Monitoring Index	2011			
		监测指标绝对值（亿元）Absolute Value (100 million yuan)	增速（%）Growth（%）	增加值（亿元）Added Value (100 million yuan)	增速（%）Growth（%）
剔重合计 Total(eliminate repetition)	－	－	－	3010	13.6
文化创意 Cultural and Creative Industry	主营业务收入（限上企业）Revenne from Principal Business (Above Designated Size)	1692	24.1	843	14.3
旅游休闲 Tourism and Leisure	总收入（全部）Total Revenue (Total)	1191	16.1	418	10.9
金融服务 Financial Services	增加值（全部）Added value (Total)	－	－	731	11.3
电子商务 E－commerce	服务收入 Service Income	181	63.9	127	47.2
信息软件 Information Software	主营业务收入（限上）Revenne from Principal Business (Above Designated Size)	872	26.1	342	16.3
先进装备制造 Advanced Equipment Manufacturing Industry	销售产值（规上工业）Sales Value (Industry above Designated Size)	4263	14.1	841	14.9
物联网 The Internet of Things	主营业务收入（限上企业）Revenne from Principal Business (Above Designated Size)	395	27.7	134	24.2
生物医药 Biomedicine	销售产值（规上工业）Sales Value (Industry above Designated Size)	364	15.5	120	16.2
节能环保 Energy Saving	销售产值（规上工业）Sales Value (Industry above Designated Size)	487	16.2	126	9.2
新能源 New Energy	销售产值（规上工业）Sales Value (Industry above Designated Size)	220	38.3	49	12.0

主要指标(2011 -2015 年)

Industries(2011 -2015)

2012				2013				2014				2015			
监测指标绝对值(亿元) Absolute Value (100 million yuan)	增速(%) Growth(%)	增加值(亿元) Added Value (100 million yuan)	增速(%) Growth(%)	监测指标绝对值(亿元) Absolute Value (100 million yuan)	增速(%) Growth(%)	增加值(亿元) Added Value (100 million yuan)	增速(%) Growth(%)	监测指标绝对值(亿元) Absolute Value (100 million yuan)	增速(%) Growth(%)	增加值(亿元) Added Value (100 million yuan)	增速(%) Growth(%)	监测指标绝对值(亿元) Absolute Value (100 million yuan)	增速(%) Growth(%)	增加值(亿元) Added Value (100 million yuan)	增速(%) Growth(%)
-	-	3512	13.6	-	-	3909	12.1	-	-	4472	12.3	-	-	5222	15.3
2028	19.3	1061	15.6	2506	22.1	1360	18.0	2842	15.6	1607	15.9	3948	33.1	2232	20.4
1392	16.9	481	11.8	1604	15.2	538	11.3	1886	17.6	626	12.0	2201	16.7	720	12.8
-	-	820	10.1	-	-	879	10.0	-	-	962	9.8	-	-	978	15.2
312	72.4	233	55.1	501	59.4	394	55.7	740	48.4	560	30.1	1262	44.2	827	34.5
1092	26.4	478	18.5	1412	26.9	679	23.5	1751	22.9	912	18.2	3108	41.3	1596	29.4
4116	7.6	900	9.3	4412	5.9	970	8.8	3703	7.5	986	9.1	3867	4.2	1082	11.2
438	12.2	157	15.3	524	17.2	194	15.8	569	10.2	242	15.9	892	19.4	307	12.7
374	16.2	160	18.8	424	10.0	175	3.0	418	8.9	205	17.8	442	4.9	220	4.5
520	7.9	144	8.5	584	6.3	144	7.2	589	2.6	148	5.0	617	-1.7	156	3.5
187	-7.0	44	-3.5	192	-2.3	43	-1.8	186	3.8	40	7.3	210	13.1	43	18.5

1－21 信息经济主要指标(2015－2016 年)
Information Economy(2015－2016)

指　标 Item	2015				2016			
	主营业务收入(亿元) Revenne from Principal Business (100 million yuan)	增速(%) Growth (%)	增加值(亿元) Added Value (100 million yuan)	增速(%) Growth (%)	主营业务收入(亿元) Revenne from Principal Business (100 million yuan)	增速(%) Growth (%)	增加值(亿元) Added Value (100 million yuan)	增速(%) Growth (%)
剔重合计 **Total(eliminate repetition)**	**5247**	**25.2**	**2314**	**25.0**	**6814**	**26.8**	**2688**	**22.8**
分产业 **By Sector**								
电子商务产业 E－commerce	1262	44.2	827	34.5	1574	44.4	1027	45.2
云计算与大数据产业 Cloud Computing and Big Data	1262	24.6	829	29.6	1588	26.1	961	28.2
物联网产业 Internet of Things	892	19.4	307	12.7	1105	23.6	335	8.8
互联网金融产业 Internet Finance	－	－	326	33.5	－	－	230	7.0
智慧物流产业 Wisdom Logistics	290	7.1	58	8.4	532	27.6	96	18.5
数字内容产业 Digital Content	2308	57.7	1234	35.5	3207	42.2	1499	35.0
软件与信息服务产业 Soft－ware and Information Service	3108	41.3	1596	29.4	4116	34.5	1869	28.8
电子信息产品制造产业 Electronic Information Products Manufacturing Industry	1967	10.5	558	12.5	2284	12.7	621	11.0
移动互联网产业 Mobile Internet	1159	37.1	845	37.5	1450	42.5	1034	45.1
集成电路产业 Integrate Circuit Industry	117	6.0	43	8.6	140	20.0	53	21.5
信息安全产业 Information Security Industry	427	16.1	222	15.3	529	23.9	250	14.6
机器人产业 Robot Industry	50	5.9	16	1.5	60	3.6	20	4.2

1－22 按机构类型和登记注册类型分组的法人单位数(2016 年)

Number of Corporation Units by Types of Organization and Registration(2016)

单位:个 (unit)

指标名称	Item	法人单位数 Number of Corporation Units 合计 Total	单产业法人单位 Containing Single Industrial Activity	多产业法人单位 Containing Multiple Industrial Activity
合计	**Total**	**371518**	**361182**	**10336**
按机构类型分组	**By Type of Organization**	**371518**	**361182**	**10336**
企业	Enterprises	349567	339997	9570
事业单位	Publlic Institution	5116	4680	436
机关	Office	1219	1020	199
社会团体	Social Group	3682	3634	48
民办非企业单位	Private Non－enterprise Unit	2680	2656	24
基金会	Foundation	108	107	1
居委会	Neighborhood Committees	1071	1058	13
村委会	Villagers Committees	2018	1998	20
农民专业合作社	Specialty Cooperative of Peasants	4130	4119	11
其他组织机构	Other	1927	1913	14
按登记注册类型分组	**Grouped By Registered Type**	**371518**	**361182**	**10336**
内资	Domestic－funded	366571	356623	9948
国有	State－owned	8266	7468	798
集体	Collective－owned	2338	2252	86
股份合作	Cooperative	409	386	23
联营	Joint Ownership	142	140	2
国有联营	State Joint Ownership	11	10	1
集体联营	Collective Joint	60	60	0
国有与集体联营	Joint State－collective	20	20	0
其他联营	Other Joint Ownership	51	50	1
有限责任公司	Limited Liability Corporations	19423	17675	1748

单位:个　　　　1－22　续表　continued　　　　(unit)

指标名称	Item	法人单位数 Number of Corporation Units		
		合计 Total	单产业法人单位 Containing Single Industrial Activity	多产业法人单位 Containing Multiple Industrial Activity
国有独资公司	State－funded Corporations	595	479	116
其他有限责任公司	Other Limited Liability Corporations	18828	17196	1632
股份有限公司	Share－holding Corporations Ltd.	1554	1258	296
私营	Private	320780	313888	6892
私营独资	Private－funded	31483	31099	384
私营合伙	Private Partnership	4326	4300	26
私营有限责任公司	Private Limited Liability Corporations	283964	277552	6412
私营股份有限公司	Private Share－holding Corporations Ltd.	1007	937	70
其他内资	Other Domestic－funded	13659	13556	103
港澳台商投资	Enterprises With Investment from Hong Kong,Macao and Taiwan	2344	2159	185
与港澳台商合资经营	Joint－venture Enterprises with funds from Hong Kong,Macao and Taiwan	899	822	77
与港澳台商合作经营	Cooperative Enterprises with funds from Hong Kong,Macao and Taiwan	33	30	3
港澳台商独资	Enterprises With Sole Investment from Hong Kong,Macao and Taiwan	1355	1259	96
港澳台商投资股份有限公司	Share－holding Corporations Ltd. With Investment from Hong Kong,Macao and Taiwan	30	24	6
其他港、澳、台商投资	Other Enterprises With Investment from Hong Kong,Macao and Taiwan	27	24	3
外商投资	With Foreign Investment	2603	2400	203
中外合资经营	Joint－venture	1082	993	89
中外合作经营	Cooperation Enterprises	45	43	2
外资企业	With Sole Foreign Investment	1407	1298	109
外商投资股份有限公司	Share－holding Corporations Ltd. With Foreign Investment	39	38	1
其他外商投资	Other Enterprises With Foreign Investment	30	28	2

1－23 按行业和地区分组的法人单位数(2016 年)

Number of Corporation Units by Sector and Region(2016)

单位:个 (unit)

指标名称 Item	法人单位数 Number of Corporation Units		
	合计 Total	单产业法人单位 Containing Single Industrial Activity	多产业法人单位 Containing Multiple Industrial Activity
合计 Total	**371518**	**361182**	**10336**
一、按国民经济行业分组 Grouped by Sector	**371518**	**361182**	**10336**
农、林、牧、渔业 Farming, Forestry, Animal Husbandry and Fishery	7249	7195	54
农业 Agriculture	3836	3809	27
林业 Forestry	1073	1067	6
畜牧业 Animal Husbandry	817	807	10
渔业 Fishery	983	973	10
农、林、牧、渔服务业 Services for Farming, Forestry, Animal Husbandry and Fishery	540	539	1
采矿业 Mining and Quarrying	268	263	5
煤炭开采和洗选业 Coal Mining and Dressing	4	3	1
黑色金属矿采选业 Ferrous Metals Mining and Dressing	8	8	0
有色金属矿采选业 Nonferrous Metals Mining and Dressing	16	14	2
非金属矿采选业 Nonmetal Minerals Mining and Dressing	233	231	2
开采辅助活动 Supplementary Activities for Mining	3	3	0
其他采矿业 Other Minerals Mining and Dressing	4	4	0
制造业 Manufacturing Industry	55691	54578	1113
农副食品加工业 Agricultural Products Processing	992	936	56
食品制造业 Food Manufacturing	773	723	50
酒、饮料和精制茶制造业 Wine, Beverage and Tea Manufacturing	569	541	28
烟草制品业 Tobacco Processing	4	3	1
纺织业 Textile Industry	4652	4564	88

指标名称 Item	法人单位数 Number of Corporation Units		
	合计 Total	单产业法人单位 Containing Single Industrial Activity	多产业法人单位 Containing Multiple Industrial Activity
纺织服装、服饰业 Textile Products and Costune Indnstry	5066	4997	69
皮革、毛皮、羽毛及其制品和制鞋业 Leather. Furs. Downand Related and Shoes Products	1238	1223	15
木材加工和木、竹、藤、棕、草制品业 Timber Processing, Bamboo, Cane, Palm Fiber and Straw Products	1100	1086	14
家具制造业 Furniture Manufacturing	1057	1033	24
造纸和纸制品业 Paper Making and Paper Products	2483	2465	18
印刷和记录媒介复制业 Printing and Record Media	1426	1403	23
文教、工美、体育和娱乐用品制造业 Cultural, Educational. Industrial Arts. Sports and Entertainment Goods	2417	2391	26
石油加工、炼焦和核燃料加工业 Petroleum Processing, Coking and Nuclear Fuel Processing	93	90	3
化学原料和化学制品制造业 Raw Chemical Materials and Chemical Products	2162	2107	55
医药制造业 Medical and Pharmaceutical Products	312	293	19
化学纤维制造业 Chemical Fiber	250	246	4
橡胶和塑料制品业 Rubber and Plastic Products	3681	3633	48
非金属矿物制品业 Nonmetal Minerals Products	2816	2765	51
黑色金属冶炼和压延加工业 Smelting and Processing of Ferrous Metal	550	541	9
有色金属冶炼和压延加工业 Smelting and Processing of Nonferrous Metals	401	392	9
金属制品业 Metals Products	5822	5746	76
通用设备制造业 Ordinary Machinery	5866	5753	113
专用设备制造业 For Special Purpose Equipment Manufacturing	2700	2645	55
汽车制造业 Automobile Manufacturing	1654	1620	34
铁路、船舶、航空航天和其他运输设备制造业 Railway. watercraft. Avigation spaceflight and other Equipment Manufacturing	551	538	13
电气机械和器材制造业 Electric Equipment and Machinery	3634	3537	97

指标名称　Item	法人单位数　Number of Corporation Units		
	合计 Total	单产业法人单位 Containing Single Industrial Activity	多产业法人单位 Containing Multiple Industrial Activity
计算机、通信和其他电子设备制造业 Computers. Telecommunications and Other Electronic Equipment Manufacturing	1793	1735	58
仪器仪表制造业 Instruments and Meters Manufacturing	915	875	40
其他制造业 Other Manufacturing	327	321	6
废弃资源综合利用业 Multiple Utilization of Waste Resouces	201	193	8
金属制品、机械和设备修理业 Metal Products, Machinery and Equipment Repair	186	183	3
电力、热力、燃气及水生产和供应业 Produotion and supply of electricity, gas & water	616	575	41
电力、热力生产和供应业 Production and Supply of Electric Power and Hot Water	382	362	20
燃气生产和供应业 Production and Supply of Gas	64	51	13
水的生产和供应业 Production and Supply of Tap Water	170	162	8
建筑业 Construction	15335	14553	782
房屋建筑业 Housing	1878	1643	235
土木工程建筑业 Civil Engineering	3053	2822	231
建筑安装业 Installation	2009	1890	119
建筑装饰和其他建筑业 Building Decoration and Others	8395	8198	197
批发和零售业 Wholesale and Retail Trade	122847	120138	2709
批发业 Wholesale	79802	78376	1426
零售业 Retail Trade	43045	41762	1283
交通运输、仓储和邮政业 Transportation, Storage and Post	5957	5646	311
铁路运输业 Railway Transport	10	10	0
道路运输业 Highway Transport	4023	3861	162
水上运输业 Water Transport	91	85	6

单位:个 1-23 续表3 continued 3 (unit)

指标名称 Item	法人单位数 Number of Corporation Units		
	合计 Total	单产业法人单位 Containing Single Industrial Activity	多产业法人单位 Containing Multiple Industrial Activity
航空运输业 Air Transport	39	32	7
管道运输业 Pipeline Transport	2	2	0
装卸搬运和运输代理业 Carrying and Transportation Agents	1103	1030	73
仓储业 Storage	305	293	12
邮政业 Postal Services	384	333	51
住宿和餐饮业 Hotels and Catering Services	6860	6298	562
住宿业 Hotels	2174	1989	185
餐饮业 Catering Services	4686	4309	377
信息传输、软件和信息技术服务业 Information Transmission , Software and Information Technology Services	30550	30086	464
电信、广播电视和卫星传输服务 Telecommunication, Radio and Television, Satellite Transmission Services	301	266	35
互联网和相关服务 Internet and Related Services	1667	1626	41
软件和信息技术服务业 Software and Information Technology Services	28582	28194	388
金融业 Banking and Insurance	2240	1992	248
货币金融服务 Monetary and Financial Services	285	205	80
资本市场服务 Capital Market Services	1034	990	44
保险业 Insurance	200	96	104
其他金融业 Others	721	701	20
房地产业 Real Estate	10067	9382	685
房地产业 Real Estate	10067	9382	685
租赁和商务服务业 Renting and Business Service	58396	56926	1470
租赁业 Renting	2452	2385	67

单位:个　　1-23　续表4　continued 4　　(unit)

指标名称 Item	法人单位数 Number of Corporation Units		
	合计 Total	单产业法人单位 Containing Single Industrial Activity	多产业法人单位 Containing Multiple Industrial Activity
商务服务业 Commercial Service	55944	54541	1403
科学研究和技术服务业 Scientific Research and Technical Service	25569	24905	664
研究和试验发展 Research and Experiment	2594	2557	37
专业技术服务业 Technical Services	11033	10541	492
科技推广和应用服务业 Promotion and Application of Service and Technology Services	11942	11807	135
水利、环境和公共设施管理业 Water Conservancy, Environment and Public Utility	1650	1556	94
水利管理业 Water Conservancy	118	109	9
生态保护和环境治理业 Ecological Protection and Environmental Management	201	185	16
公共设施管理业 Public Facilities	1331	1262	69
居民服务、修理和其他服务业 Service for the Residents ,Repair and Others	5644	5441	203
居民服务业 Resident Services	2401	2285	116
机动车、电子产品和日用产品修理业 Motor Vehicles , Electronics and Household Goods Repair Industry	2249	2184	65
其他服务业 Other Services	994	972	22
教育 Education	4536	4277	259
教育 Education	4536	4277	259
卫生和社会工作 Health Care, Sports & Social Welfare	2112	1865	247
卫生 Health Care	1410	1169	241
社会工作 Sports & Social Welfare	702	696	6
文化、体育和娱乐业 Culture, Sports and Entertainment	5835	5721	114
新闻和出版业 News and Publishing	176	174	2
广播、电视、电影和影视录音制作业 Television, Radio, Film and Television Sound Recording Production	775	757	18
文化艺术业 Culture and Arts	1591	1575	16
体育 Sports	855	809	46

指标名称　Item	法人单位数　Number of Corporation Units		
	合计 Total	单产业法人单位 Containing Single Industrial Activity	多产业法人单位 Containing Multiple Industrial Activity
娱乐业 Recreation	2438	2406	32
公共管理、社会保障和社会组织 Public Administration ,Social Security and Social Organization	10096	9785	311
中国共产党机关 Communist Party Agencies	161	153	8
国家机构 Government Agencies	2402	2184	218
人民政协、民主党派 The CPPCC, Democratic Parties	41	40	1
社会保障 Social Security	76	73	3
群众团体、社会团体和其他成员组织 Mass Organizations,Social Groups and Other Members of Organization	4327	4279	48
基层群众自治组织 Mass Grass－root Organization	3089	3056	33
二、按地区分组	**371518**	**361182**	**10336**
杭州市 HangZhou	371518	361182	10336
上城区 Shangcheng	18869	18032	838
下城区 Xiacheng	22802	21772	1029
江干区 Jianggan	42097	40995	1102
拱墅区 Gongshu	31711	30780	931
西湖区 Xihu	57754	55856	1898
高新(滨江区) Hi－Tech(Binjiang)	20403	19935	468
萧山区 Xiaoshan	62475	61194	1281
余杭区 Yuhang	49702	48478	1224
富阳区 Fuyang	22510	22045	465
桐庐县 Tonglu	12399	12153	246
淳安县 Chun′an	6835	6571	264
建德市 Jiande	8947	8710	237
临安市 Lin′an	15014	14661	353

1－24 “1＋6”产业集群主要指标(2016 年)
“1＋6” Industrial Cluster(2016)

产业分组	Industry Grouping	2016 增加值(亿元) Added Value (100 million yuan)	2016 增速(%) Growth (%)
信息经济产业	Information Economy Industry	2688	22.8
文化创意产业	Cultural and Creative Industry	2542	21.2
金融产业	Financial Industry	996	6.7
旅游休闲产业	Tourism Leisure Industry	809	13.3
健康产业	Health Industry	663	16.5
时尚产业(制造业)	Fashion Industry (Manufacturing)	298	11.7
高端装备产业(制造业)	High－end Equipment Industry (Manufacturing)	380	15.2

1－25 气　　象
Meteorological

指　　标		Item		市　区 Urban District	萧山区 Xiaoshan
一、气　温		**The Atmospheric Temperature**			
全年平均气温	（度）	Annual Average Temperature	（℃）	18.2	17.9
极端最高气温	（度）	The Highest Temperature of the Year	（℃）	40.3	39.6
出现日期	（日/月）	Date	（d/m）	24/7	26/7
极端最低气温	（度）	The Lowest Temperature of the Year	（℃）	－8.2	－8.4
出现日期	（日/月）	Date	（d/m）	25/1	25/1
二、降　雨		**Rainfall**			
本年降雨日数	（日）	Total Rainy Days	（day）	170	172
全年降雨总量	（毫米）	Annual Rainfall	（millimeters）	1797.3	1808.8
最长连续降雨日数	（日）	Longest Consecutive Days of Rain	（day）	7（三次）	10
最长连续降雨总量	（毫米）	Rainfall	（millimeters）	124.4、142.7、71.8	81
最长连续降雨起止日期	（日/月）	Start/End	（d/m）	20－26/4、10－16/9、17－23/10	14－23/10
日最大降雨量	（毫米）	Maximum Daily Rainfall	（millimeters）	70.5	67.7
出现日期	（日/月）	Date	（d/m）	15/9	12/6
三、全年日照总时数	**（小时）**	**Total Sunshine Hours**	**（hours）**	**1522.4**	**1783.9**
四、降　霜		**Frost**			
全年降霜日数	（日）	Annual Frost Days	（day）	18	23
初霜日期	（日/月）	Start Date	（d/m）	27/11	27/11
终霜日期	（日/月）	End Date	（d/m）	26/3	12/3
五、降　雪		**Snow**			
全年降雪日数	（日）	Annual Frost Days	（day）	9	9
初雪日期	（日/月）	Start Date	（d/m）	5/12	5/12
终雪日期	（日/月）	End Date	（d/m）	10/3	10/3

概　　况(2016 年)
Conditions by Region(2016)

余杭区 Yuhang	富阳区 Fuyang	桐庐县 Tonglu	淳安县 Chun'an	建德市 Jiande	临安市 Lin'an
17.3	18.0	18.1	18.3	18.1	17.1
39.8	39.4	40.3	39.3	40.2	39
27/7	27 - 28/7	27/7	25/7、29/7、19/8	19/8	24/7
-8.0	-9.1	-10.0	-7.1	-8.4	-11.3
25/1	25/1	25/1	25/1	25/1	25/1
183	180	177	208	181	184
1769.1	1741.7	1853.3	1953.7	1909.8	2107.0
10	10	15	20	15	11
141.7	60.7	195.5	191.4	325.8	151.2
20 - 29/5、14 - 20/8	14 - 23/10	20/5 - 3/6	30/3 - 18/4	20/5 - 3/6	19 - 29/6
63.3	87.1	88.6	77.8	122.3	190.4
29/5	15/9	25/6	1/6	28/5	28/9
-	**1662.3**	**1403.4**	**1683.3**	**1498.1**	**1656.7**
-	14	18	9	22	24
28/12	27/11	26/11	17/12	27/11	7/12
15/2	11/3	21/2	16/2	28/3	12/3
	7	8	9	8	8
	5/12	5/12	6/12	20/1	/
	10/3	10/3	16/2	10/3	10/3

1－26　市区分月气象概况(2016 年)
Monthly Meteorological Conditions in Urban District(2016)

月　份	Month	平均气温(度) Average Temperature(℃)	日照时数(小时) Sunshine Hours(hours)	降雨天数(天) Rainfall Days (day)	降水量(毫米) Precipitation(mm)
全　年	**Whole Year**	**18.2**	**1522.4**	**170**	**1797.3**
1　月	January	4.9	67.8	19	135.5
2　月	February	8.2	143.6	6	30.6
3　月	March	12.3	128.1	10	62.5
4　月	April	17.6	106.7	19	250.6
5　月	May	21.3	126.6	17	251.7
6　月	June	25.1	105.9	20	282.4
7　月	July	30.5	214.1	14	79.5
8　月	August	30.2	256.9	8	154.9
9　月	September	24.6	120.8	15	247.5
10　月	October	20.4	33.7	19	145.9
11　月	November	13.3	80.3	14	93.9
12　月	December	9.5	137.9	9	62.3

主要统计指标解释

地区生产总值(GDP)　指一个国家(或地区)所有常住单位在一定时期内生产活动的最终成果。地区生产总值有三种表现形态,即价值形态、收入形态和产品形态。从价值形态看,它是所有常住单位在一定时期内生产的全部货物和服务价值超过同期投入的全部非固定资产货物和服务价值的差额,即所有常住单位的增加值之和;从收入形态看,它是所有常住单位在一定时期内创造并分配给常住单位和非常住单位的初次收入分配之和;从产品形态看,它是所有常住单位在一定时期内最终使用的货物和服务价值与货物减去进出口货物和服务。在实际核算中,生产总值有三种计算方法,即生产法、收入法和支出法。三种方法分别从不同的方面反映生产总值及其构成。

三次产业　是根据社会生产活动历史发展的顺序对产业结构的划分,产品直接取自自然界的部门称为第一产业,对初级产品进行再加工的部门称为第二产业,为生产和消费提供各种服务的部门称为第三产业。它是世界上较为通用的产业结构分类,但各国的划分不尽一致。2012 年前的三次产业划分标准按照当年《统计年鉴》,从 2013 年起,三次产业划分调整为:

第一产业是指农、林、牧、渔业(不含农、林、牧、渔服务业)。

第二产业是指工业[采矿业(不含开采辅助活动),制造业(不含金属制品、机械和设备修理业),电力、热力、燃气及水生产和供应业]和建筑业。

第三产业即服务业,是指除第一产业、第二产业以外的其他行业。

最终消费　指常住单位在一定时期内对于货物和服务的全部消费支出,也就是常住单位为满足物质文化和精神生活的需要,从本国经济领土和国外购买的货物和服务的支出;不包括非常住单位在本国经济领土内的消费支出。最终消费分为居民消费和政府消费。

居民消费　指常住住户对货物和服务的全部最终消费支出。居民消费按市场价格计算,既按居民支付的购买者价格计算。购买者价格是购买者取得货物所支付的价格包括购买者支付的运输和商业费用。居民消费除了直接以货币形式购买货物和服务的消费之外,还包括以其他方式获得的货物和服务的消费支出,既所谓的虚拟消费支出。居民虚拟消费支出包括以下几个类型:单位以实物报酬及实物转移的形式提供给劳动者的货物和服务;住户生产并由本住户消费了的货物和服务,其中的服务仅指住户的自由住房服务;金融机构提供的金融媒介服务;保险公司提供的保险服务。

政府消费　指政府部门为全社会提供公共服务的消费支出和免费或以较低价格向住户提供的货物和服务的净支出。前者等于政府服务的产出价值减去政府单位所获得的经营收入的价值,政府服务的产出价值等于它的经常性业务支出加上固定资产折旧;后者等于政府部门免费或以较低价格向住户提供的货物和服务的市场减去向住户收取的价值。

资本形成总额　指常住单位在一定时期内获得的减去处置的固定资产加存货的变动,包括固定资本形成总额和存货增加。

固定资产形成总额　指常住单位购置、转入和自产自用的固定资产,扣除固定资产的销售和转让,分有形资产形成总额和无形资产形成总额。有形资产形成总额包括一定时期内完成的建筑工程、安装工程和设备工器具(减处置)价值,以及土地改良、新增役种奶毛娱乐用牲畜和新增林木价值。无形固定资产总额包括矿藏的勘探、计算机软件、娱乐和文学艺术品原件等获得减处置。

存货增加　指常住认为存货实物量变动的市场价值,即期末价值减期初价值的差额。存货量增加可以是正值,也可以是负值;正值表示存货上升,负值表示存货下降。它包括生产单位购进的原材料燃料和储备物资等存货,以及生产单位生产的产成品在制品等存货等。

货物和服务净出口　指货物和服务出口减货物和服务进口的差额。出口包括常住单位从非常住单位出售或无偿转让的各种货物和服务的价值;进口包括常住单位从非常住单位购买或无常得到的各种货物和服务的价值。由于服务活动的提供与使用同时发生,因此服务的进出口业务并不发生出入境现象,一般把常住单位从国外得到的服务作为进口,非常住单位从本国得到的服务作为出口。货物的进口和出口都按离岸价格计算。

劳动者报酬　指劳动者因从事生产活动所获得的全部报酬。包括劳动者获得的各种形式的工资、奖金和津贴,既包括货币形式,也包括实物形式的;还包括劳动者所享受的公费医疗和医药卫生费上下班交通补贴和单位支付的社会保险费等。对于个体经济来说其所有者所获得的劳动报酬和经营利润不易区分,这两部分统一作为劳动报酬处理。

生产税净额　指生产税减生产补贴后的余额。生产税指政府对生产单位生产销售和从事经营活动以及因从事生产活动使用某些生产要素(如固定资产土地劳动力)所征收的各种税、附加费和规费。生产补贴和生产税相反,指政府对生产单位的单方面收入转移,因此视为负生产税,包括政策亏损补贴、粮食系统价格补贴、外贸企业出口退税收入等。

固定资产折旧 在一定时期内为弥补固定资产损耗按照核定的固定资产损耗率提取的固定资产折旧,或按国民经济核算统一规定的折旧率虚拟计算的固定资产折旧。它反映了固定资产在当期生产中的转移价值。各类企业和企业化管理的事业单位的固定资产折旧是指实际计提并计入成本费中的折旧费;不计提折旧的政府机关非企业化管理的事业单位和居民住房的固定资产折旧是按照统一固定的折旧率和固定资产原值计算的虚拟折旧。原则上,固定资产折旧应按照固定资产的重置价值计算,但是目前我国尚不具备对全社会固定资产进行重估价的基础,所以暂时只能采用上述方法。

营业盈余 指常住单位创造的增加值扣除劳动者报酬生产税净额和固定资产折旧后的余额。它相当于企业的营业利润加上生产补贴,但要扣除从利润中开支的工资和福利等。

可比价格 指在不同时期的价值指标对比时,扣除了价格变动的因素,以确切反映物量的变化。按可比价格计算有两种方法:一种是直接用产品产量乘每一年的不变价格计算;另一种使用价格指数换算。

不变价格 指用同类产品的年平均价格作为固定价格,来计算各年产品价值。按不变价格计算的产品价值消除了价格变动因素,不同时期对比可反映出生产的发展速度。新中国成立后,随着工农业产品价格的变化,国家统计局先后五次制定了全国统一的工业产品不变价格和农业产品不变价格,从 1949 年到 1957 年使用 1952 工(农)业产品不变价格,从 1957 年到 1971 年使用 1957 年不变价格,从 1981 年到 1990 年使用 1980 年不变价格,从 1990 年开始使用 1990 年不变价格。

十大产业 2011 年,杭州在国民经济和社会发展第“十二个”五年发展规划纲要中,提出:着力在现代服务业和战略性新兴产业中培育产业基础强、发展潜力大的十大产业。包括:文化创意、旅游休闲、金融服务、电子商务、信息软件、先进装备制造、物联网、生物医药、节能环保、新能源产业。

信息经济 2014 年,杭州发布了关于加快发展信息经济的若干意见,发展目标是到 2020 年,率先成为特色鲜明、全国领先的信息经济强市和智慧经济创新城市。确立发展电子商务、云计算与大数据、物联网、互联网金融、智慧物流、数字内容等六大核心产业以及软件与信息服务、电子信息产品制造、移动互联网、集成电路、信息安全、机器人等六大重点领域。

“1 +6 产业集群” 2016 年,杭州在国民经济和社会发展第“十三个”五年规划纲要中,提出:构建以信息经济为引领、现代服务业为主导、先进制造业为支撑、都市现代农业为基础的现代产业新体系,推进产业迈向中高端。确立发展万亿信息产业集群以及文化创意、旅游休闲、金融服务、健康、时尚、高端装备制造等六大千亿产业集群的目标。

降水量 从天空降落到地面的液态或固态(经融化后)降水,未经蒸发、渗透、流失而在水平面上积聚的深度。降水量以毫米为单位。

空气的温度(简称气温) 表示空气冷热程度的物理量。

日照时数 太阳在一地实际照射地面的时数。

Explanatory Notes on Main Statistical Indicators

Gross Domestic Product (GDP) refers to the final products of all resident units in a country (or a region) during a certain period of time. Gross domestic product is expressed in three different forms, i. e. value, income, and products respectively. The form of value refers to the total value of all products and services produced by all resident units during a certain period of time minus total value of intermediate input of materials and services of the nature of non – fixed assets or the summation of the value – added of all resident units; the form of income includes all the income created by all resident units and distributed primarily to all resident and non – resident units; the form of products refers to the value of all final goods and services for final use by all resident units minus imports of goods and services during a given period of time. In the practice of national accounting, gross domestic product is calculated with three approaches, i. e. production approach, income approach, and expenditure approach, which reflect gross domestic product and its composition from different aspects.

Three Industries Industry structure has been classified according to the historical sequence of development. Primary industry refers to extraction of natural resources; secondary industry involves processing of primary products; and tertiary industry provides services of various kinds for production and consumption. The above classification is universal although it varies to someextent from country to country. The explanatory notes on Three Industries were available on Hangzhou Statistical Yearbook of the year before 2012, and the indicators of Three Industry have been revised according to the national standards since 2013.

Primary Industry refers to argriculture, forestry, animal husbandry and fishery industries (excluding their service activities).

Second Industry refers to industry [mining and quarrying (excluding its support activities), manufacturing (excluding the repair services of metal product, machine and equipment), production and supply of electricity, heat, water and gas] and construction.

Tertiary Industry is the service industry, refers to all other economic acitivities not included in the primary or secondary industries.

Final Consumption refers to the total expenditure of resident units on final consumption of goods and services in a certain period, namely the expenditure of the resident units for perchases of good and services from domestic economic territory and abroad to meet the requirements of meterial, cultural and spritual life. It excludes the expenditure of non – resident units on consumption in the economic territory of the country. The final consumption is classified into household consumption and government consumption.

Households Consumption refers to the total expenditure of resident households on the final consumption of goods and services. The households consumption is calculated at market prices, namely the purchaser's prices which the households pay; the purchaser's prices of goods are the prices the households pay when they obtain the goods including the transport and commercial expenses paid by the households. In addition to the consumption of goods and services bought by the households directly with money, the expenditure on goods and services obtained by the households in other ways, i. e. the so – called imputed expenditure on consumption, is also included in the households consumption. The imputation expenditure of the households on consumption includes the following types: (a) the goods and services privided to the households by the units in the form of payment in kind and transfer in kind; (b) the goods and services produced and consumed by the households themselves, in which the services refer only to the services provided by the residential buildings owned by the households; (c) the services of financial intermediary provided by the financial institution; (d) the insurance services provided by the insurance companies.

Government Consumption refers to the expenditure on the consumption of the public services provided by the government to the whole society and the net expenditure on the goods and services provided by the government to the households at free charge or lower prices. The former equals to the output value of the government services minus the value of operating income obtained by the government departments. (The output value of the government services equals to its current operating expenditure plus depreciation of fixed assets). The latter equals to the market value of the goods and services provided by the government free of charge or at low prices to the households minus the value received by the government from the households.

Total Capital Formation refers to the fixed assets acquired minus those disposed and the change in inventory including the total fixed assets formation and the increase in inventory.

Total Fixed Capital Formation refers to the value of fixed assets purchased, transferred in by the resident units and those produced and used by themselves deducting the value of fixed assets sold and transferred out. It can be classfied into total tangible assets formation and total intangible asset formation. The total tangible assets formation and total intangible assets formation. The total tangible assets formation include the value of construction projects, installation projects completed and the equipment apparatus and instruments purchasedas well as the value of land improved, the value of draught animals, breeding stock, milk, wool and recreational animals and the newly increased economic forest in a certain period. The total ingangible assets formation includesthe prospecting of minerals, the acquisition of computer software, the orginals of recreational works and works of literature and arts minus the disposal of them.

Increase in Inventory refers to the market value of the change in inventory, i. e. the difference of value between the beginning and the end of the period. The increase in inventory can be positive or negative. A positive value indicates the increase in inventory while a negative value indicates the decrease in stock. The inventory includes the raw materials, fuels, and reserve materials purchased by the production units as well as the inventory of finished products, semifinished products work – in – progress, ect.

Net Export of Goods and Services refers to the difference of the exports of goods and services minus the imports of goods and services. The imports include the value of various goods and services sold or gratuitously transferred by the resident units to the non – resident units. The imports include the value of various goods and services purchased or gratuitously acquired by the resident units from the non – resident units. Because the provision of services and the use of them happen simultaneously, the import and export of services do not appear to have the phenomena of crossing the border of the country. The acquisition of services by the resident units from abroad is uaually treated as import while the acquisition of services by non – resident units in this country is uaually treated as export. The export and import of goods are calculated at FOB.

Labourer's Remuneration refers to the whole payment of various forms earned by the labourers from the productive activities they are engaged in. It includes wages, bonuses and allowances the labourers earned in monetary form and in kind. It also includes the free medical services provided to the labourers and the medicine expenses, traffic subsidies and social insurance free paid by the labourers' working units for them. As the individual economy is concerned, since the labourers' remuneration is not easily distingushed from the operating profit, both are treated as labourers remuneration.

Net Taxes on Production refers to the residual of the taxes on production minus the subsidies on production. The taxes on production refer to the various taxes, extra charges and fees levied on the production units on their production, sail and business activities as well as on some factors of production, such as fixed assets, land and labour force, used in the production activities they are engaged in. In contrast to the taxes on production, the subsidies on production refer to the unilateral transfer of part of the government's revenue to the production units and is therefore regarded as negative taxes on production. They include sunsidies on the loss due to implementation of government policies, price subsidies to the grain institutions, foreign trade corporations' receipts from drawback, ect.

Depreciation of Fixed Assets refers to the depreciation of fixed assets of a given period, drawn in accordance with the stipulated depreciation rate for purpose of compensating the wear loss of the fixed assets of the depreciation of fixed assets calculated in a fictitious way in accordance with the stipulated unified depreciation rate in the national economic accounting system. It reflects the value of transfer of the fixed assets in the production of the current period. The depreciation of fixed assets in various enterprises and institutions managed as enterprises refers to the depreciation expenses actually drawnand calculated as part of the cost. In government agencies and institutions not managed as enterprises which do not draw the depreciation expenses, as well as for the house of residents, the depreciation of fixed assets is the imputed depreciation, which is calculated in accordance with the stipulated unified depreciation rate. In principle, the depreciation of fixed assets should bs calculated on the basis of the repurchased value of the fixed assets. However, there is no actual condition to reevaluated all the fixed assets in China. Therefore, the abovementioned methods are temporarily adopted at present.

Operating Surplus refers to the balance of the value added created by the resident units deducting the laboures' remuneration, net taxes on production and the depreciation of fixed assets. It is equivalent to the business profit of the enterprises plus subsidies on production, but the wages and welfare expenses paid from the profits should be deducted.

Comparable Price is applied when comparing value indicators of different periods to reflect accurately the changes in physical value. The price is not considered here. Two methods are used for calculating comparable prices: 1. Multipling the output of products by their constant price of a certain year; 2. Conversion of the data in current prices by relevant price index.

Constant Prices refer to the average price of a given produce in a certain year, which is used to calculate the output value over time. As the output value at constant prices removes the factor of price changes, it reflects the trend of production development over time. Since 1949, with the changes in general price level, the State Statistical Bureau has issued nationally unified constant prices for five times, the 1952 constant prices for 1949 – 1957; the 1957 constant prices for 1958 – 1970; the 1970 constant prices for 1971 – 1981; the 1980 constant prices for 1981 – 1990; the 1990 constant prices have been used since 1991.

Ten Major Industries In 2011, in the outline of the 12th five – year development plan for the national economy and social development, Hangzhou proposed to develop ten well – founded and potential industries, in modern service industry and strategic emerging industries, Including: Cultural and Creative Industry, Tourism and Leisure, Financial Services, E – commerce, Information Software, Advanced Equipment Manufacturing Industry, Internet of Things, Biomedicine, Energy Saving, New Energy.

Information Economy In 2014, Hangzhou issued a document on speeding up the development of the information economy. By 2020, Hangzhou will be a national – leading information economy city with distinctive features and an innovative smart economy city. Hangzhou will promote the development of six key industries of E – commerce, Cloud Computing and Big Data, Internet of Things, Internet Finance, Wisdom Logistics, Digital Content, as well as six key areas of Soft – ware and Information Service, Electronic Information Products Manufacturing, Mobile Internet, Integrate Circuits, Information Security, Robot.

"1 +6" Industrial Cluster In 2016, in the outline of the 13th five – year plan for national economic and social development, hangzhou will quicken the establishment of a new system of modern industry based on the information economy as the lead, the modern service industry as the predominance, the advanced manufacturing industry as the support, the urban modern agriculture as the foundation, and promote the development of industries toward the medium – high end. We will build a series of large – scale industrial clusters, including a trillion scale information industry clusters, and six hundred billion scale industry clusters of Cultural and Creative Industry, Tourism Leisure Industry, Financial Industry, Health Industry, Fashion Industry (Manufacturing) and High – end Equipment Industry (Manufacturing).

Precipitation refers to the depth of rainfall onto the ground (as well as liquefied from solid forms) from above the air prior to its vaporization, seepage, running off.

It is calculated in the unit of millimeter (mm).

Air Temperature refers to the physical quantity reflecting the extent of coldness and hotness of the air.

Duration of sunshine refers to the real time for the ground to receive sunshine at a certain place.

二、人口和就业人员

POPULATION AND EMPLOYMENT

2 人口和就业人员 Population and Employment

主要统计指标
Major Statistical Indicators

年末常住人口	Long-term Residents	918.80	万人	(10, 000 persons)
为上年	As Compared with the Preceding Year	101.9	%	(%)
#城镇人口	Urban Population	700.13	万人	(10, 000 persons)
年末户籍登记户数	Total Registration Households(year-end)	229.57	万户	(10, 000 Subscribers)
为上年	As Compared with the Preceding Year	101.7	%	(%)
年末户籍登记人口	Total Registration Population(year-end)	736.00	万人	(10, 000 persons)
为上年	As Compared with the Preceding Year	101.7	%	(%)
#男性	Male	366.47	万人	(10, 000 persons)
为上年	As Compared with the Preceding Year	101.6	%	(%)
户籍人口自然增长率	Natural Growth Rate of Registered Population	7.58	‰	(‰)
年末就业人员	Number of Employed Persons(year-end)	676.95	万人	(10, 000 persons)
为上年	As Compared with the Preceding Year	102.1	%	(%)

2-01 历次普查常住人口情况

Long-term Residents in the Past Population Census

单位:万人 (10000 person)

地区	Region	第一次人口普查 1953.7.1 the First Population Census (1953.7.1)	第二次人口普查 1964.7.1 the Second Population Census (1964.7.1)	第三次人口普查 1982.7.1 the Third Population Census (1982.7.1)	第四次人口普查 1990.7.1 the Fourth Population Census (1990.7.1)	第五次人口普查 2000.11.1 the Fifth Population Census (2000.11.1)	第六次人口普查 2010.11.1 the Sixth Population Census (2010.11.1)
杭州市	**Hangzhou**	**301.13**	**421.90**	**526.05**	**583.21**	**687.87**	**870.04**
市区	Urban District	201.48	283.31	359.90	404.83	513.09	695.97
#上城区	Shangcheng				21.10	33.51	34.46
下城区	Xiacheng				25.66	41.24	52.61
江干区	Jianggan				36.12	56.54	99.88
拱墅区	Gongshu				29.34	42.93	55.19
西湖区	Xihu				35.40	59.33	82.00
高新(滨江)区	Hi-Tech(Binjiang)					11.59	31.90
萧山区	Xiaoshan	56.32	82.34	106.11	113.06	123.33	151.13
余杭区	Yuhang	52.28	64.96	80.50	86.08	81.77	117.03
富阳区	Fuyang	29.22	39.66	54.13	58.07	62.86	71.77
桐庐县	Tonglu	19.73	26.20	34.83	37.66	37.81	40.64
淳安县	Chun'an	27.49	38.66	42.03	43.55	38.23	33.68
建德市	Jiande	26.42	38.15	43.64	47.63	47.31	43.08
临安市	Lin'an	26.01	35.57	45.65	49.55	51.42	56.67

注:历年普查市区口径均已按现行行政辖区调整。

a) The data of the past population censuses in urban district were adjusted according to the current administrative division.

2-02 全市户籍人口和总户数(1978-2016年)
Registered Population and Households(1978-2016)

年份 Year	总户数(万户) Total Households (10000 households)	总人口数(万人) Total Population (10000 persons)	城镇人口(万人) Urban Population (10000 persons)	按性别分 By Sex 男(万人) Male (10000 persons)	女(万人) Female (10000 persons)
1978	117.89	505.55	116.06	260.74	244.81
1979	116.61	511.83	124.60	263.97	247.86
1980	119.11	515.53	128.88	266.02	249.51
1981	125.96	520.73	134.56	268.69	252.04
1982	131.53	528.06	139.94	272.72	255.34
1983	135.55	533.06	143.34	275.64	257.41
1984	139.24	537.49	147.46	278.04	259.45
1985	145.23	543.05	153.46	281.11	261.94
1986	151.59	549.53	157.19	284.57	264.96
1987	157.66	557.63	161.12	288.70	268.93
1988	164.41	565.04	164.87	292.21	272.83
1989	169.09	570.98	167.28	295.15	275.83
1990	171.94	574.78	169.00	297.02	277.76
1991	174.78	578.73	171.25	298.85	279.88
1992	177.68	582.40	174.03	300.63	281.77
1993	179.17	587.10	179.11	303.03	284.07
1994	180.65	592.93	186.50	306.00	286.93
1995	182.55	597.96	191.43	308.25	289.71
1996	184.33	603.22	196.68	310.76	292.46
1997	186.28	607.96	204.39	313.02	294.94
1998	187.80	611.64	210.52	314.69	296.95
1999	191.60	616.05	219.05	316.63	299.42
2000	193.48	621.58	227.00	319.09	302.49
2001	195.56	629.14	237.77	322.78	306.36
2002	198.27	636.81	252.02	326.62	310.19
2003	201.12	642.78	263.67	329.04	313.74
2004	204.52	651.68	282.58	332.62	319.06
2005	207.42	660.45	297.54	336.12	324.33
2006	209.91	666.31	309.78	338.23	328.08
2007	211.99	672.35	323.75	340.50	331.85
2008	213.74	677.64	340.76	342.45	335.19
2009	215.28	683.38	354.48	344.51	338.87
2010	216.51	689.12	365.24	346.56	342.56
2011	218.26	695.71	376.03	349.09	346.62
2012	218.95	700.52	384.09	350.90	349.62
2013	220.66	706.61	393.88	353.32	353.29
2014	222.35	715.76	404.27	357.26	358.50
2015	225.79	723.55	447.24	360.68	362.87
2016	229.57	736.00		366.47	369.53

注:1. 按公安户籍人口统计。
2. 城镇人口 2015 年前为非农业人口。
3. 2016 年全市户籍城镇人口尚未最终核定。

a) Figures in this table are based on the household registered statistics which published by Public Security Bureau.
b) Since 2015, the donotation of Non-agriculture Population has been adjusted to Urban Population.
c) In 2016, the population of registered urban residents has not been approved.

2-03 市区户籍人口和总户数(1978-2016年)

Registered Population and Households of Urban District(1978-2016)

年份 Year	总户数(万户) Total Households (10000 households)	总人口数(万人) Total Population (10000 persons)	城镇人口(万人) Urban Population (10000 persons)	按性别分 By Sex	
				男(万人) Male (10000 persons)	女(万人) Female (10000 persons)
1978	25.52	104.53	78.73	53.95	50.58
1979	26.23	110.50	85.05	57.09	53.41
1980	27.23	113.08	87.93	58.56	54.52
1981	29.88	115.59	90.53	59.96	55.63
1982	31.24	118.05	92.72	61.28	56.77
1983	32.69	120.13	94.94	62.43	57.70
1984	34.07	122.29	97.34	63.63	58.66
1985	35.36	124.67	100.01	64.96	59.71
1986	37.02	127.07	102.59	66.29	60.78
1987	38.70	129.16	104.09	67.38	61.78
1988	40.05	131.26	107.30	68.46	62.80
1989	41.19	132.84	108.88	69.28	63.56
1990	42.26	133.89	109.97	69.75	64.14
1991	42.98	134.97	111.20	70.33	64.64
1992	43.63	136.30	112.70	71.08	65.22
1993	44.55	138.33	115.13	72.22	66.11
1994	45.04	141.27	118.48	73.82	67.45
1995	46.06	143.52	121.38	74.91	68.61
1996	52.39	166.73	128.76	87.15	79.58
1997	53.14	169.29	131.76	88.53	80.76
1998	53.92	171.89	134.62	89.86	82.03
1999	54.64	175.27	139.29	91.65	83.62
2000	55.34	179.18	143.69	93.64	85.54
2001	115.81	379.49	193.26	194.59	184.90
2002	117.11	387.01	205.98	198.47	188.54
2003	119.01	393.19	216.13	201.14	192.05
2004	120.56	401.59	233.08	204.43	197.16
2005	122.02	409.52	245.56	207.70	201.82
2006	123.31	414.18	256.42	209.45	204.73
2007	124.40	419.50	269.30	211.59	207.91
2008	125.56	424.30	285.11	213.54	210.76
2009	126.92	429.44	297.83	215.56	213.88
2010	128.43	434.82	307.52	217.65	217.16
2011	130.14	440.34	317.63	219.86	220.48
2012	131.48	445.43	325.50	221.99	223.43
2013	133.27	450.82	334.38	224.24	226.58
2014	157.11	525.07	358.56	261.17	263.90
2015	160.47	532.86	389.14	264.71	268.15
2016	164.22	544.68		270.31	274.38

注:1. 城镇人口2015年前为非农业人口。
2. 2016年市区户籍城镇人口尚未最终核定。
a) Since 2015, the donotation of Non-agriculture Population has been adjusted to Urban Population.
b) In 2016, the population of registered urban residents has not been approved.

2-04 分地区户籍人口和总户数(2016年末)

Registered Population and Households by Region(End of 2016)

地　区 Region	总户数 (户) Total Households (household)	总人口数 (人) Total Population (person)	按性别分 By Sex	
			男(人) Male (person)	女(人) Female (person)
全　市 Whole City	**2295666**	**7359994**	**3664712**	**3695282**
市　区 Urban District	1642184	5446803	2703052	2743751
#上城区 Shangcheng	113708	326903	163356	163547
下城区 Xiacheng	130065	402738	201042	201696
江干区 Jianggan	158930	527403	262561	264842
经济技术开发区 Economic and Technological Development Zone	29282	106327	54642	51685
拱墅区 Gongshu	119639	345564	172493	173071
西湖区 Xihu	192846	690935	347836	343099
西湖风景名胜区 The West Lake Scenic Zone	6438	20082	9416	10666
高新(滨江)区 Hi-Tech(Binjiang)	61984	221116	112170	108946
萧山区 Xiaoshan	375777	1275928	625440	650488
大江东产业集聚区 Dajiangdong Industry Cluster District	42046	151905	74047	77858
余杭区 Yuhang	273866	984581	481208	503373
富阳区 Fuyang	215369	671635	336946	334689
桐庐县 Tonglu	147688	411439	205068	206371
淳安县 Chun'an	146838	460664	233401	227263
建德市 Jiande	171631	509552	258847	250705
临安市 Lin'an	187325	531536	264344	267192

2-05 分地区户籍人口年龄构成(2016年末)

Age Structure of Household Registered Population by Region(End of 2016)

地区 Region	0-17岁 0~17 years old		18-34岁 18~34 years old		35-59岁 35~59 years old		60岁以上 over 60 years old	
	人数(人) Number of people (person)	占总人口% of the total population	人数(人) Number of people (person)	占总人口% of the total population	人数(人) Number of people (person)	占总人口% of the total population	人数(人) Number of people (person)	占总人口% of the total population
全市 Whole City	**1177531**	**16.0**	**1695632**	**23.0**	**2892353**	**39.3**	**1594478**	**21.7**
市区 Urban District	904981	16.6	1270723	23.3	2094241	38.4	1176858	21.6
#上城区 Shangcheng	36885	11.3	71922	22.0	119369	36.5	98727	30.2
下城区 Xiacheng	51731	12.8	99428	24.7	146409	36.4	105170	26.1
江干区 Jianggan	101798	19.3	133188	25.3	191963	36.4	100454	19.0
经济技术开发区 Economic and Technological Development Zone	23997	22.6	44416	41.8	30285	28.5	7629	7.2
拱墅区 Gongshu	52698	15.2	75821	21.9	130958	37.9	86087	24.9
西湖区 Xihu	124034	18.0	186935	27.1	257841	37.3	122125	17.7
西湖风景名胜区 The West Lake Scenic Zone	2469	12.3	4073	20.3	7920	39.4	5620	28.0
高新(滨江)区 Hi-Tech(Binjiang)	48050	21.7	66699	30.2	76577	34.6	29790	13.5
萧山区 Xiaoshan	206732	16.2	270663	21.2	502953	39.4	295580	23.2
大江东产业集聚区 Dajiangdong Industry Cluster District	24245	16.0	32586	21.5	59270	39.0	35804	23.6
余杭区 Yuhang	178126	18.1	217191	22.1	388099	39.4	201165	20.4
富阳区 Fuyang	104927	15.6	148876	22.2	280072	41.7	137760	20.5
桐庐县 Tonglu	60585	14.7	92569	22.5	166738	40.5	91547	22.3
淳安县 Chun'an	68078	14.8	99260	21.5	198690	43.1	94636	20.5
建德市 Jiande	69932	13.7	117703	23.1	209103	41.0	112814	22.1
临安市 Lin'an	73955	13.9	115377	21.7	223581	42.1	118623	22.3

2－06 全市户籍人口自然变动情况(1978－2016年)
Natural Changes of Registered Population(1978－2016)

年份 Year	出生 Birth		死亡 Death		自然增长 Natural Growth	
	人数(人) Birth Population (person)	出生率(‰) Birth Rate(‰)	人数(人) Death Population (person)	死亡率(‰) Death Rate(‰)	人数(人) Natural Growth Population (person)	自然增长率(‰) Natural Growth Rate(‰)
1978	73550	14.63	29928	2.95	43622	8.68
1979	71442	14.04	29500	5.80	41942	8.24
1980	52145	10.15	30727	5.98	21418	4.17
1981	73015	14.09	31352	6.05	41663	8.04
1982	82910	15.81	30805	5.87	52105	9.94
1983	69940	13.18	33598	6.33	36342	6.85
1984	60091	11.23	33070	6.18	27021	5.05
1985	66757	12.36	33715	6.24	33042	6.12
1986	84702	15.50	33576	6.15	51126	9.35
1987	94127	17.00	33238	6.00	60889	11.00
1988	85472	15.23	35356	6.30	50116	8.93
1989	81048	14.27	34031	5.99	47017	8.28
1990	76579	13.37	34977	6.11	41602	7.26
1991	66144	11.47	33534	5.81	32610	5.66
1992	61708	10.63	34681	5.97	27027	4.66
1993	62465	10.68	34127	5.84	28338	4.84
1994	63580	10.78	35099	5.95	28481	4.83
1995	62586	10.51	36186	6.08	26400	4.43
1996	63680	10.60	25417	5.90	28263	4.70
1997	58471	9.65	34663	5.72	23808	3.93
1998	53951	8.85	38302	6.28	15649	2.57
1999	59085	9.63	36866	6.01	22219	3.62
2000	62300	10.07	40218	6.50	22082	3.57
2001	52088	8.33	33827	5.41	18261	2.92
2002	53064	8.38	35867	5.67	17197	2.72
2003	51420	8.04	36662	5.73	14758	2.31
2004	59940	9.26	34078	5.27	25862	3.99
2005	57233	8.72	35417	5.39	21816	3.33
2006	57790	8.71	38892	5.86	18898	2.85
2007	60296	9.01	37833	5.65	22463	3.36
2008	61332	9.09	42648	6.32	18684	2.77
2009	62441	9.18	39159	5.76	23282	3.42
2010	69606	10.14	46193	6.73	23413	3.41
2011	70337	10.16	38225	5.52	32112	4.64
2012	77349	11.08	49789	7.13	27560	3.95
2013	70850	10.07	37544	5.34	33306	4.73
2014	89743	12.62	40415	5.68	49328	6.94
2015	70617	9.81	40326	5.60	30291	4.21
2016	90896	12.46	35614	4.88	55282	7.58

注:本表按公安部门统计。

a) Figures in this table are based on the Public Security Bureau.

2－07 市区户籍人口自然变动情况(1978－2016年)
Natural Changes of Registered Population of Urban District(1978－2016)

年份 Year	出生 Birth		死亡 Death		自然增长 Natural Growth	
	人数(人) Birth Population (person)	出生率(‰) Birth Rate(‰)	人数(人) Death Population (person)	死亡率(‰) Death Rate(‰)	人数(人) Natural Growth Population (person)	自然增长率(‰) Natural Growth Rate(‰)
1978	11923	11.56	6449	6.25	5474	5.31
1979	13184	12.26	5808	5.40	7376	6.86
1980	9708	8.68	6511	5.82	3197	2.86
1981	14938	13.06	6599	5.77	8339	7.29
1982	18092	15.49	6494	5.56	11598	9.93
1983	17107	14.36	6949	5.84	10158	8.52
1984	16257	13.41	6892	5.69	9365	7.72
1985	15824	12.81	7403	6.84	8421	6.82
1986	17120	13.60	6865	5.45	10255	8.15
1987	18701	14.60	7070	5.52	11631	9.08
1988	18503	14.21	7503	5.76	11000	8.45
1989	15868	12.02	6985	5.29	8883	6.73
1990	14085	10.56	7490	5.62	6595	4.94
1991	10195	7.58	7025	5.22	3170	2.36
1992	9994	7.37	7259	5.35	2735	2.02
1993	10099	7.35	7196	5.24	2903	2.11
1994	9918	7.09	7082	5.06	2836	2.03
1995	9806	6.89	7367	5.17	2439	1.72
1996	12098	7.80	8221	5.30	3877	2.50
1997	12304	7.32	8630	5.13	3674	2.19
1998	11714	6.87	9060	5.31	2654	1.56
1999	13694	7.89	8148	4.69	5546	3.20
2000	15058	8.50	10996	6.20	4062	2.30
2001	30902	8.22	19439	5.17	11463	3.05
2002	33156	8.65	19922	5.20	13234	3.45
2003	29019	7.44	21176	5.43	7843	2.01
2004	34858	8.77	19445	4.89	15413	3.88
2005	34056	8.39	21310	5.25	12746	3.14
2006	33260	8.08	21156	5.14	12104	2.94
2007	37029	8.88	20051	4.81	16978	4.07
2008	38703	9.17	21428	5.08	17275	4.09
2009	40293	9.44	22178	5.20	18115	4.24
2010	47052	10.89	25404	5.88	21648	5.01
2011	47256	10.80	22140	5.06	25116	5.74
2012	51892	11.72	27271	6.16	24621	5.56
2013	48107	10.74	21332	4.76	26775	5.97
2014	69577	13.36	27249	5.23	42328	8.13
2015	55275	10.45	26492	5.01	28783	5.44
2016	71427	13.26	23544	4.37	47883	8.89

2-08 分地区户籍人口自然变动情况(2016年)

Natural Changes of Registered Population by Region(2016)

地 区 Region	出 生 Birth		死 亡 Death		自然增长 Natural Growth	
	人数(人) Birth Population (person)	出生率(‰) Birth Rate(‰)	人数(人) Death Population (person)	死亡率(‰) Death Rate(‰)	人数(人) Natural Growth Population (person)	自然增长率(‰) Natural Growth Rate(‰)
全 市 Whole City	**90896**	**12.46**	**35614**	**4.88**	**55282**	**7.58**
市 区 Urban District	71427	13.26	23544	4.37	47883	8.89
#上城区 Shangcheng	3023	9.23	1529	4.67	1494	4.56
下城区 Xiacheng	4387	10.90	1431	3.55	2956	7.34
江干区 Jianggan	8656	16.83	1403	2.73	7253	14.10
经济技术开发区 Economic and Technological Development Zone	2470	24.02	134	1.30	2336	22.72
拱墅区 Gongshu	4545	13.38	2030	5.98	2515	7.41
西湖区 Xihu	9380	13.72	1808	2.64	7572	11.07
西湖风景名胜区 The West Lake Scenic Zone	186	9.25	79	3.93	107	5.32
高新(滨江)区 Hi-Tech(Binjiang)	4857	22.80	650	3.05	4207	19.75
萧山区 Xiaoshan	14968	11.79	6795	5.35	8173	6.44
大江东产业集聚区 Dajiangdong Industry Cluster District	1932	12.79	804	5.32	1128	7.47
余杭区 Yuhang	14702	15.19	4413	4.56	10289	10.63
富阳区 Fuyang	6909	10.32	3485	5.20	3424	5.11
桐庐县 Tonglu	4172	10.17	2430	5.92	1742	4.24
淳安县 Chun'an	4765	10.36	2935	6.38	1830	3.98
建德市 Jiande	5370	10.55	3559	6.99	1811	3.56
临安市 Lin'an	5162	9.73	3146	5.93	2016	3.80

2－09　分地区户籍人口机械变动情况(2016年)
Mechanical Changes of Registered Population by Region(2016)

单位:人　　(person)

地　区 Region	本年迁入人数 Number of the Persons Moved in(person)		本年迁出人数 Number of the Persons Moved Out(person)		本年净迁入人数 Net Persons Moved in
	省　内 From Zhejiang Province	省　外 From Other Provinces	省　内 To Zhejiang Province	省　外 To Other Provinces	
全　市 Whole City	**37077**	**62554**	**13053**	**16489**	**70089**
市　区 Urban District	34862	57538	7132	14268	71000
#上城区 Shangcheng	1891	2723	280	666	3948
下城区 Xiacheng	3046	4171	722	1435	5060
江干区 Jianggan	7548	10595	1717	3144	13282
经济技术开发区 Economic and Technological Development Zone	3508	6169	1489	2709	5479
拱墅区 Gongshu	3589	3152	508	498	5735
西湖区 Xihu	6782	10565	2225	5185	9937
西湖风景名胜区 The West Lake Scenic Zone	66	114	15	42	123
高新(滨江)区 Hi－Tech(Binjiang)	3693	4894	544	761	7282
萧山区 Xiaoshan	1538	3923	406	974	4081
大江东产业集聚区 Dajiangdong Industry Cluster District	154	422	18	107	451
余杭区 Yuhang	6270	16077	447	936	20964
富阳区 Fuyang	505	1438	283	669	991
桐庐县 Tonglu	622	1225	1047	449	351
淳安县 Chun'an	409	1016	1614	400	－589
建德市 Jiande	528	1265	1996	712	－915
临安市 Lin'an	656	1510	1264	660	242

2-10 婚姻登记情况(2015-2016年)
Marriage Registration Situations(2015-2016)

地 区 Region	2016			2015		
	准予登记结婚对数(对) Marriages Legally Registered(couples)	再婚人数(人) Re-married (person)	离婚对数(对) Divorces (couples)	准予登记结婚对数(对) Marriages Legally Registered(couples)	再婚人数(人) Re-married (person)	离婚对数(对) Divorces (couples)
全 市 Whole City	**63260**	**29963**	**21033**	**67657**	**28037**	**19073**
市 区 Urban District	47806	22174	15369	51400	20647	13750
#萧山区 Xiaoshan	9488	3395	2180	9492	3219	2096
余杭区 Yuhang	7262	3542	2755	7629	3400	2374
富阳区 Fuyang	4939	2194	1773	5081	2205	1674
桐庐县 Tonglu	3318	1847	1303	3470	1581	1191
淳安县 Chun'an	3780	1711	1250	3895	1674	1168
建德市 Jiande	4155	1870	1448	4394	1833	1355
临安市 Lin'an	4201	2361	1663	4498	2302	1609

2－11　三次产业就业人员及构成（2010－2016年）

Number of Employed Persons by Three Industries（2010－2016）

单位：万人　　（10000 persons）

指标名称	Item	2010	2011	2012	2013	2014	2015	2016
全市总计	**Total**	**626.33**	**637.77**	**644.43**	**650.51**	**654.92**	**663.03**	**676.95**
第一产业	Primary Industry	75.70	72.21	70.39	70.07	66.39	67.01	66.11
第二产业	Secondary Industry	286.26	289.12	290.01	291.51	286.99	271.90	261.78
第三产业	Tertiary Industry	264.37	276.44	284.03	288.93	301.54	324.12	349.06
全市构成（以合计为100）	**Composition（Total＝100）**	**100**	**100**	**100**	**100**	**100**	**100**	**100**
第一产业	Primary Industry	12.1	11.3	10.9	10.8	10.1	10.1	9.8
第二产业	Secondary Industry	45.7	45.4	45.0	44.8	43.9	41.0	38.7
第三产业	Tertiary Industry	42.2	43.3	44.1	44.4	46.0	48.9	51.5

2-12 全市非私营及规上

Number of Employed Persons of the Whole City

单位:人

地区、行业	Region, Sector	就业人员合计 Number of Employed Persons	非私营单位 Non-private
全市	**Total**	**4504600**	**2901347**
市区	Urban District	4093898	2692081
#上城区	Shangcheng District	244433	181654
下城区	Xiacheng District	274799	231795
江干区	Jianggan District	467883	234837
拱墅区	Gongshu District	318445	154263
西湖区	Xihu District	668181	546841
高新(滨江)区	Hi-Tech(Binjiang) District	332044	260008
萧山区	Xiaoshan District	867779	524869
大江东产业集聚区	Dajiangdong Industry Cluster District	116569	72918
余杭区	Yuhang District	466596	249756
富阳区	Fuyang District	228544	120193
经济技术开发区	Economic and Technological Development Zone	195661	161194
西湖风景名胜区	The West Lake Scenic Zone	29533	26671
桐庐县	Tonglu County	109946	46326
淳安县	Chun'an County	69797	36830
建德市	Jiande City	79012	42516
临安市	Lin'an City	151947	83594
按国民经济行业分组	**Grouped by Sector**		
农、林、牧、渔业	Farming, Forestry, Animal Husbandry & Fishery	928	922
采矿业	Mining	2452	1014
制造业	Manufacturing	1077951	651937
电力、热力、燃气及水生产和供应业	Production & Supply of Electricity, Heat, Gas & Water	19904	18391
建筑业	Construction	1602423	795319
批发和零售业	Wholesale & Retail Trades	272430	172625
交通运输、仓储和邮政业	Transportation, Storage and Posts	148262	113833
住宿和餐饮业	Hotels and Catering Services	99539	66701
信息传输、软件和信息技术服务业	Information Transmission, Software and Information Technology	175489	128899
金融业	Financial Intermediation	120637	120029
房地产业	Real Estate	137157	109619
租赁和商务服务业	Leasing and Business Services	159714	114689
科学研究、技术服务业	Scientific Research, Technical Services	139376	115027
水利、环境和公共设施管理业	Management of Water Conservancy, Environment and Public Facilities	54208	25946
居民服务、修理和其他服务业	Service to Households, Repair and Other Services	25114	10828
教育	Education	186071	181376
卫生和社会工业	Health Care and Social Work	118518	112846
文化、体育和娱乐业	Culture, Sports and Entertainment	27488	24407
公共管理、社会保障和社会组织	Public Management, Social Security and Social Organizations	136939	136939

私营单位就业人员数(2016年末)

Including Private Units Above Designated Size(End of 2016)

(person)

女性 Female	非私营单位 Non – private	在岗职工 Staff and Workers	非私营单位 Non – private	其他就业人员 Other Employed Persons	非私营单位 Non – private
1401801	**969908**	**4166585**	**2721116**	**338015**	**180231**
1251213	888585	3778191	2523931	315707	168150
94670	78181	219585	169129	24848	12525
112791	96136	249725	214715	25074	17080
110811	71921	359216	203913	108667	30924
73674	50027	293725	134960	24720	19303
187759	155014	614164	507255	54017	39586
107504	88966	327129	256789	4915	3219
243828	142211	838703	510073	29076	14796
29378	16895	114403	71653	2166	1265
165509	95822	447984	237786	18612	11970
74197	40433	215956	112989	12588	7204
72254	62612	190565	157721	5096	3473
8216	7262	21439	18601	8094	8070
40179	21350	105379	43910	4567	2416
28996	14285	63592	34323	6205	2507
28776	16237	72578	39406	6434	3110
52637	29451	146845	79546	5102	4048
274	272	862	856	66	66
426	199	2335	936	117	78
436909	244342	1063393	643067	14558	8870
5297	4932	19539	18049	365	342
145051	63457	1403127	732334	199296	62985
141828	88306	261865	164251	10565	8374
36611	28124	143275	111559	4987	2274
55309	36899	88445	56888	11094	9813
64097	47778	174185	128011	1304	888
71222	70956	93721	93251	26916	26778
51697	40440	127008	100587	10149	9032
58992	40767	148075	106476	11639	8213
48785	42050	133418	110697	5958	4330
18028	10203	51862	24136	2346	1810
14647	5868	23418	10574	1696	254
115039	113081	173420	168845	12651	12531
81467	77511	108138	103056	10380	9790
14192	12793	21784	18828	5704	5579
41930	41930	128715	128715	8224	8224

2－13　全市非私营及规上

Everage Number of Employed Persons

单位：人

地区、行业	Region，Sector	就业人员年平均人数 Annual Average Number of Staff and Workers	非私营单位 Non－private
全市	**Total**	**4410678**	**2843503**
市区	Urban District	4011096	2637063
上城区	Shangcheng District	244548	182152
下城区	Xiacheng District	266545	224212
江干区	Jianggan District	467509	235270
拱墅区	Gongshu District	321478	159141
西湖区	Xihu District	641563	535302
高新（滨江）区	Hi－Tech（Binjiang） District	325160	254564
萧山区	Xiaoshan District	836486	494447
大江东产业集聚区	Dajiangdong Industry Cluster District	112462	66878
余杭区	Yuhang District	457126	245519
富阳区	Fuyang District	224891	117099
经济技术开发区	Economic and Technological Development Zone	196193	162213
西湖风景名胜区	The West Lake Scenic Zone	29597	27144
桐庐县	Tonglu County	106639	45292
淳安县	Chun'an County	65054	36011
建德市	Jiande City	77231	42324
临安市	Lin'an City	150658	82813
按国民经济行业分组	**Grouped by Sector**		
农、林、牧、渔业	Farming，Forestry，Animal Husbandry & Fishery	842	836
采矿业	Mining	2455	1050
制造业	Manufacturing	1075708	653963
电力、热力、燃气及水生产和供应业	Production & Supply of Electricity，Heat，Gas & Water	19843	18357
建筑业	Construction	1557636	758999
批发和零售业	Wholesale & Retail Trades	273052	175071
交通运输、仓储和邮政业	Transportation，Storage and Posts	142602	112374
住宿和餐饮业	Hotels and Catering Services	98708	65790
信息传输、软件和信息技术服务业	Information Transmission，Software and Information Technology	164661	123879
金融业	Financial Intermediation	115113	114527
房地产业	Real Estate	132661	105675
租赁和商务服务业	Leasing and Business Services	159574	111490
科学研究、技术服务业	Scientific Research，Technical Services	136214	112745
水利、环境和公共设施管理业	Management of Water Conservancy，Environment and Public Facilities	41835	26640
居民服务、修理和其他服务业	Service to Households，Repair and Other Services	24961	10728
教育	Education	185152	180383
卫生和社会工作	Health Care and Social Work	115694	110215
文化、体育和娱乐业	Culture，Sports and Entertainment	27417	24231
公共管理、社会保障和社会组织	Public Management，Social Security and Social Organizations	136550	136550

私营单位平均人员数(2016 年)

Including Private Units Above Designated Size(2016)

(person)

在岗职工年平均人数 Staff and Workers	非私营单位 Non - private	其他就业人员年平均人数 Average Number of Other Employed Persons	非私营单位 Non - private
4072220	**2660219**	**338458**	**183284**
3694399	2465556	316697	171507
219744	169242	24804	12910
243338	208773	23207	15439
362409	205320	105100	29950
296492	139389	24986	19752
586043	495129	55520	40173
319498	250952	5662	3612
806149	478235	30337	16212
108165	64185	4297	2693
438707	233597	18419	11922
212066	109812	12825	7287
189579	157159	6614	5054
20374	17948	9223	9196
101877	42680	4762	2612
59211	33822	5843	2189
71153	39381	6078	2943
145580	78780	5078	4033
776	770	66	66
2339	973	116	77
1060395	644590	15313	9373
19478	18013	365	344
1356760	691956	200876	67043
261983	166232	11069	8839
138207	109962	4395	2412
87572	55890	11136	9900
163335	122987	1326	892
92027	91565	23086	22962
123105	97252	9556	8423
148070	103384	11504	8106
129766	108262	6448	4483
39396	24789	2439	1851
23314	10470	1647	258
170653	165988	14499	14395
105158	100271	10536	9944
21766	18745	5651	5486
128120	128120	8430	8430

2－14 分行业非私营单位

The Education Level of the Staff and Workers in

单位：人

行　业	Sector	单位就业人员 The Education Level 大学本科及以上 Bachelor's Degree of above
总　计	**Total**	**792648**
农、林、牧、渔业	Farming, Forestry, Animal Husbandry & Fishery	136
采矿业	Mining	29
制造业	Manufacturing	121480
电力、热力、燃气及水生产和供应业	Production & Supply of Electricity, Heat, Gas & Water	6725
建筑业	Construction	41102
批发和零售业	Wholesale & Retail Trades	43324
交通运输、仓储及邮政业	Transportation, Storage and Posts	19406
住宿和餐饮业	Hotels and Catering Services	6622
信息传输、软件和信息技术服务业	Information Transmission, Software and Information Technology	92316
金融业	Financial Intermediation	72903
房地产业	Real Estate	19463
租赁和商务服务业	Leasing and Business Services	24746
科学研究和技术服务业	Scientific Research, Technical Services	54728
水利、环境和公共设施管理业	Management of Water Conservancy, Environment and Public Facilities	4768
居民服务、修理和其他服务业	Service to Households, Repair and Other Services	1526
教育	Education	126006
卫生和社会工作	Health Care and Social Work	65604
文化、体育和娱乐业	Culture, Sports and Entertainment	14086
公共管理、社会保障和社会组织	Public Management, Social Security and Social Organizations	77678

职工素质情况(2016 年末)

Non - private Units by Sector(End of 2016)

(persons)

文化程度 of the Employed Persons in Onits			单位就业人员中专业技术人员 Professional and Technical Personnel	单位就业人员中技术工人 Skilled Workers
大专 College Degree	中专及高中 Technical Secondary School and High School	初中及以下 Junior High School and Below		
474089	**668711**	**965899**	**693564**	**821352**
141	216	429	97	334
92	221	672	71	416
104040	187581	238836	118948	252129
4807	4661	2198	3113	9547
71230	198869	484118	101148	407333
45326	51155	32820	20685	20390
29021	40894	24512	8284	60342
11565	27084	21430	3170	7002
27045	7697	1841	75355	4497
24864	19893	2369	43097	3873
21948	31553	36655	14923	18585
22183	28450	39310	12794	8698
19721	11037	29541	55913	4765
4478	5331	11369	3663	4767
1363	2633	5306	1013	2738
23030	16535	15805	120413	6708
24665	13418	9159	86915	4652
5892	3109	1320	13555	936
32678	18374	8209	10407	3640

主要统计指标解释

人口数　指一定时点、一定地区范围内的有生命的个人的总和。

年度统计的年末人口数是指每年12月31日24时的人口数。

出生率(又称粗出生率)　指一定时期内(通常为一年)平均每千人所出生的人数的比率,一般用千分率表示。计算公式:

$$出生率=\frac{年出生人数}{年平均人数}\times 1000‰$$

出生人数是指活产婴儿,即胎儿脱离母体时(不管怀孕月数),有过呼吸或其他生命现象。

年平均人数是年初、年底人口数的平均数,也可用年中人口数代替。

死亡率(又称粗死亡率)　指一定时期内(通常为一年)一定地区的死亡人数与同期平均人数(或期中人数)之比,一般用千分率表示。计算公式:

$$死亡率=\frac{年死亡人数}{年平均人数}\times 1000‰$$

人口自然增长率　指一定时期内(通常为一年)人口自然增加数(出生人数减死亡人数)与该时期内平均人数(或期中人数)之比,一般用千分率表示。计算公式:

$$人口自然增长率=\frac{本年出生人数-本年死亡人数}{年平均人数}\times 1000‰$$

人口自然增长率=人口出生率-人口死亡率

就业人员　指从事一定社会劳动并取得劳动报酬或经营收入人员,包括各级机关企事业单位就业人员、个体户主、个体就业人员、农村就业人员及其他未包括的就业人员(包括宗教职业者、现役军人等)。

单位就业人员　是指在各级国家机关、政党机关、社会团体及企业、事业单位中工作,并取得劳动报酬的全部人员。包括在岗职工、再就业的离退休人员、民办教师、在各单位中工作的外方人员和港、澳、台方人员以及聘用的外单位下岗职工、兼职人员、从事第二职业人员、使用的劳务派遣人员。各单位的就业人员反映了实际参加生产或工作的全部劳动力。

在岗职工　指在本单位工作并由单位支付劳动报酬的人员,以及在本单位有工作岗位,但由于学习、病伤产假等原因暂未工作,仍由单位支付劳动报酬的人,包括本单位临时性用工并支付劳动报酬的人员。2012年开始在岗职工包含劳务派遣人员。

非私营单位　包括独立核算的机关、事业单位和国有、集体、股份制、港澳台投资及外商投资企业等。

非私营单位及规上私营单位　包括独立核算的非私营单位、规模以上私营工业企业、限额以上私营批发零售住宿餐饮企业、私营房地产开发经营企业、具有资质的私营建筑企业、规模以上私营服务企业、100人及以上的规模以下私营企业。

Explanatory Notes on Main Statistical Indicators

Total Population refers to the total number of people alive at a certain point of time within a given area. The annual statistics on total population is taken at midnight, the 31st of December.

Birth Rate (or Crude Birth Rate) refers to the ratio of the number of births to the average population during a certain period of time (usually a year), which is often expressed in ‰. The following formula is used:

$$\text{Birth Rate} = \frac{\text{Number of Births}}{\text{Average Number of Population}} \times 1000‰$$

Number of births refers to live births, i. e. the births when babies had showed any vital phenomena regardless of the length of pregnancy.

Annual Average Number of Population is the average of the number of population at the beginning of the year and that at the end of the year. Sometimes it is substituted for with the mid - year population.

Death Rate (or Crude Death Rate) refers to the ratio of the number of deaths to the average population (or mid - year population) during a certain period of time (usually a year), which is often expressed in ‰. The following formula is used:

$$\text{Death Rate} = \frac{\text{Number of Deaths}}{\text{Annual Average Number of Population}} \times 1000‰$$

Natural Growth Rate of Population refers to the ratio of natural increase in population (number of births minus number of deaths) in a certain period of time (usually a year) to the average population (or mid - year population) of the same period, which is often expressed in ‰. The following formulas are applied:

$$\text{Natural Growth Rate of Population} = \frac{\text{Number of Births} - \text{Number of Deaths}}{\text{Average Number of Population}} \times 1000‰$$

Natural Growth Rate of Population = Birth Rate - Death Rate

Employed Persons refer to persons who are engaged in social labour and receive remuneration payment or earn business income, including all employees of government, enterprises and institutions, self - employed workers, employed persons in the rural areas and other employed workers (including religious professionals, servicemen, etc.).

Persons Employed in Various Units refer to all the persons who are working in government agencies of various levels, political and party organizations, social organizations, enterprises, institutions, and receiving wages or other forms of payment. Including fully employed staff and works, re - employed retirees, teachers in schools run by the local people, foreigners and Chinese compatriots from Hong Kong, Macao, and Taiwan working in various units, part - time employees, employees of other units working temporarily, employees holding the second job, dispatch personnels. Persons Employed in various units reflect the actual total labor force which are engaged in the production or work.

Fully Employed Staff and Workers refer to persons who work in, and receive wages from their working units, as well as persons who have their work posts, but are temporarily absent from work for reasons of study or on sick, injury or maternal leave and still receive wages from their working units. including persons who are engaged in temporary employment and receive remuneration payment. Since 2012, the number of fully employed staff included the labor dispatch personnel.

Non - private Units include independent accounting units of government organizations and institutions, state - owned enterprises, collective - owned enterprises, and enterprises with funds from Hongkong, Macao and Taiwan.

Including Units above Designated Size include independent accounting units of non - private, private industrial enterprises above designated size, private enterprises above designated size of wholesale & retail trades, hotels, catering serrices, private enterprises for real estate development, private construction enterprises with qualification grade, private enterprises of service industry above designated size, private enterprises below designated size with at least 100 employed persons.

三、农业

AGRICULTURE

3 农　　业 Agriculture

主要统计指标 Major Statistical Indicators

农村机械总动力	Total Power of Agricultural Machinery	283.72	万千瓦	(10, 000 kw)
为上年	As Compared with the Preceding Year	94.7	%	(%)
农村就业人员数	Total Employed Persons in Rural Areas	281.76	万人	(10, 000 persons)
为上年	As Compared with the Preceding Year	99.0	%	(%)
农林牧渔业增加值	Value-added of Farming,Forestry,Animal Husbandry and Fishery	309.26	亿元	(100 million yuan)
为上年	As Compared with the Preceding Year	105.8	%	(%)
粮食总产量	Total Output of Grain Crops	63.60	万吨	(10, 000 tons)
为上年	As Compared with the Preceding Year	100.3	%	(%)
肉类产量	Total Output of Meat	26.27	万吨	(10, 000 tons)
为上年	As Compared with the Preceding Year	94.4	%	(%)

3－01 全市分地区农林牧渔业增加值(2016 年)

Value－added of Agriculture, Forestry, Animal Husbandry and Fishery(2016)

单位:万元 (10000 yuan)

地区 Region	农林牧渔业增加值合计 Total	为上年%	农业 Agriculture	为上年%	林业 Forestry	为上年%	牧业 Animal Husbandry	为上年%	渔业 Fishery	为上年%	服务业 Service	为上年%
全 市 Whole City	**3092579**	**105.8**	**1933812**	**107.1**	**416734**	**105.9**	**415814**	**105.1**	**275703**	**96.9**	**50516**	**113.5**
市区 Urban District	1739165	104.9	1108075	106.7	156705	109.9	218654	101.7	220913	94.9	34818	115.6
#江干区 Jianggan	4675	95.3	3458	98.7	15	100	966	82.1	199	114.4	37	100
西湖区 Xihu	40382	93.2	20749	112.4	308	60.9	95	5.3	18405	82.8	825	247.8
高新(滨江)区 Hi－Tech(Binjiang)	13770	95.6	12575	102.9	–	–	–	–	299	39.0	–	–
萧山区 Xiaoshan	691954	106.0	473758	107.0	8006	116.7	117152	110.0	77426	95.0	15612	108.1
大江东产业集聚区 Dajiangdong Industry Cluster District	136029	104.4	86113	107.9	146	102.1	27917	112.2	19548	83.5	2305	112.2
余杭区 Yuhang	513124	106.2	319764	106.3	61307	111.9	24167	96.4	91846	103.4	16040	119.3
富阳区 Fuyang	450177	105.8	268532	107.0	87029	108.3	74322	100.1	17990	100.0	2304	123.3
经济技术开发区 Economic and Technological Development Zone	3872	42.7	1729	112.5	–	–	1952	41.3	191	6.8	–	–
西湖风景名胜区 The West Lake Scenic Zone	7550	106.7	7510	106.7	40.0	102.6	–	–	–	–	–	–
桐庐县 Tonglu	247953	107.1	149354	106.1	43991	105.6	35601	111.9	15894	111.5	3113	108.0
淳安县 Chun'an	346880	107.1	242651	106.2	48664	110.0	34761	108.2	16863	109.0	3941	115.8
建德市 Jiande	332343	107.4	222441	108.4	23609	105.0	64981	107.6	16465	97.9	4847	104.6
临安市 Lin'an	426238	106.4	211291	109.2	143765	101.0	61817	109.9	5568	108.3	3797	109.0

3-02 农林牧渔业总产值(1978-2016年)

Gross Output Value of Agriculture, Forestry, Animal Husbandry and Fishery (1978-2016)

单位:万元 (10000 yuan)

年份 Year	农林牧渔业总产值 Gross Output Value	#农业产值 Farming	种植业产值 Planting	林业产值 Forestry	牧业产值 Animal Husbandry	渔业产值 Fishery	服务业产值 Service
1978	85922	67365	64378	3430	14474	653	-
1979	115649	84727	81989	4629	25216	1077	-
1980	112377	79006	76059	7262	25015	1094	-
1981	120792	87354	81659	8309	23799	1330	-
1982	150606	107566	103346	8912	31801	2327	-
1983	148878	103685	96272	9800	32693	2700	-
1984	177029	122567	115286	14769	35922	3771	-
1985	212961	136893	126026	19095	50110	6863	-
1986	238285	150803	138254	19990	58197	9295	-
1987	281326	173080	155960	26427	70129	11690	-
1988	358500	208838	187648	31434	101013	17215	-
1989	386805	225969	201389	27857	113952	19027	-
1990	421045	260031	233055	26962	113424	20628	-
1991	463578	284275	254834	37763	117458	24082	-
1992	497915	300828	256833	35589	133867	27631	-
1993	600760	365124	300736	47476	154766	33394	-
1994	812473	496392	415366	58627	217217	40237	-
1995	996440	620057	526328	81321	244054	51008	-
1996	1173294	740202	617573	95740	271652	65700	-
1997	1287650	797812	665172	114510	294153	81175	-
1998	1367578	845106	701850	121197	289085	112190	-
1999	1414737	876685	737406	126000	293495	118557	-
2000	1526530	903322	754311	136848	331563	154797	-
2001	1649978	965005	816884	149264	362303	173406	-
2002	1685036	932995	886285	162227	391844	197970	-
2003	1890129	991556	949138	182595	417798	232599	65581
2004	1982683	1010947	972594	206787	457619	234080	73250
2005	2194799	1136559	1103981	233039	495900	270810	58491
2006	2253822	1224822	1191816	267748	490448	206082	64722
2007	2471427	1308047	1279758	294707	585536	222601	60536
2008	2737605	1408124	1374083	320212	636633	309270	63366
2009	2897371	1497362	1462791	362317	642892	325626	69174
2010	3163392	1698775	1673470	329278	705596	349011	80732
2011	3570744	1907895	1882876	348535	836532	389985	87797
2012	3843403	2077191	2041481	381802	868504	420006	95900
2013	3993712	2161055	2120540	408170	911324	407292	105871
2014	4185804	2333804	2291071	470164	828184	442023	111629
2015	4404121	2524163	2468981	498051	807001	452309	122597
2016	4672994	2715276	2652659	531855	857427	435224	133212

注:本表按当年价格计算;从2003年起农林牧渔总产值包括农林牧渔业服务业产值(下同)。

a) Data in this table are calculated at current prices. From 2003, Gross Output Value includes the value of service for the agriculture, forestry, animal husbandry and fishery sector (the same below).

3－03 农林牧渔业总产值构成(1978－2016年)

Composition of Gross Output Value of Agriculture, Forestry, Animal Husbandry and Fishery(1978－2016)

单位:%　　　　(%)

年份 Year	农林牧渔业总产值 Gross Output Value	#农业产值 Farming	种植业产值 Planting	林业产值 Forestry	牧业产值 Animal Husbandry	渔业产值 Fishery	服务业产值 Service
1978	100	78.4	74.9	4.0	16.8	0.8	–
1979	100	73.3	70.9	4.0	21.8	0.9	–
1980	100	70.3	67.7	6.5	22.2	1.0	–
1981	100	72.3	67.6	6.9	19.7	1.1	–
1982	100	71.4	68.6	5.9	21.1	1.6	–
1983	100	69.6	64.7	6.6	22.0	1.8	–
1984	100	69.2	65.1	8.3	20.3	2.2	–
1985	100	64.3	59.2	9.0	23.5	3.2	–
1986	100	63.3	58.0	8.4	24.4	3.9	–
1987	100	61.5	55.4	9.4	24.9	4.2	–
1988	100	58.2	52.3	8.8	28.2	4.8	–
1989	100	58.4	52.1	7.2	29.5	4.9	–
1990	100	61.8	55.4	6.4	26.9	4.9	–
1991	100	61.3	55.0	8.2	25.3	5.2	–
1992	100	60.4	51.6	7.2	26.9	5.5	–
1993	100	60.8	50.1	7.9	25.8	5.5	–
1994	100	61.1	51.1	7.2	26.7	5.0	–
1995	100	62.2	52.8	8.2	24.5	5.1	–
1996	100	63.1	52.6	8.2	23.1	5.6	–
1997	100	62.0	51.7	8.9	22.8	6.3	–
1998	100	61.8	51.3	8.9	21.1	8.2	–
1999	100	62.0	52.1	8.9	20.7	8.4	–
2000	100	59.2	49.4	9.0	21.7	10.1	–
2001	100	58.5	52.2	9.0	22.0	10.5	–
2002	100	55.4	52.6	9.6	23.3	11.7	–
2003	100	52.5	50.2	9.7	22.1	12.3	3.4
2004	100	51.0	49.1	10.4	23.1	11.8	3.7
2005	100	51.8	50.3	10.6	22.6	12.3	2.7
2006	100	54.3	52.9	11.9	21.8	9.1	2.9
2007	100	52.9	51.8	11.9	23.7	9.0	2.5
2008	100	51.4	50.2	11.7	23.3	11.3	2.3
2009	100	51.7	50.5	12.5	22.2	11.2	2.4
2010	100	53.7	52.9	10.4	22.3	11.0	2.6
2011	100	53.4	52.7	9.8	23.4	10.9	2.5
2012	100	54.0	53.1	9.9	22.6	10.9	2.6
2013	100	54.1	53.1	10.2	22.8	10.2	2.7
2014	100	55.8	54.7	11.2	19.8	10.6	2.6
2015	100	57.3	56.1	11.3	18.3	10.3	2.8
2016	100	58.1	56.8	11.4	18.3	9.3	2.9

3-04 农林牧渔业分项产值(主要年份)

Gross Output Value of Agriculture, Forestry, Animal Husbandry and Fishery by Branch (Main Years)

单位:万元 (10000 yuan)

指标	Item	2000	2005	2010	2011	2012	2013	2014	2015	2016
农林牧渔业总产值(现价)	**Gross Output Value (Current Price)**	**1526530**	**2194799**	**3163392**	**3570744**	**3843403**	**3993712**	**4185804**	**4404121**	**4672994**
一、农业产值	**Farming**	**903322**	**1136559**	**1698775**	**1907895**	**2077191**	**2161055**	**2333804**	**2524163**	**2715276**
1. 种植业产值	Planting	754311	1103981	1673470	1882876	2041481	2120540	2291071	2468981	2652659
粮食	Grain	208546	178981	215990	230246	241471	248550	224164	228341	237016
油料	Oil-bearing Crops	19583	21608	31137	35245	35482	37649	37530	48373	48757
棉花	Cotton	2205	1146	1255	1155	1424	1571	1152	1094	929
麻类	Fiber Crops	384	176	42	21	16	25	8	6	5
甘蔗	Sugarcane	23815	19075	18756	20067	18417	18496	17347	16322	16393
烟叶	Tobacco	5	7	1	2	2	1	1	1	1
药材类	Crude Drugs	6005	15800	42927	50530	60454	67623	75180	86538	98927
蔬菜	Vegetables	303583	357734	535623	607469	664937	665429	686995	748644	835341
茶、桑、果、坚果	Tea, Mulberry & Fruits	106727	254379	484261	565641	605200	630899	749516	802647	834532
其他	Others	83458	255075	343478	372500	414078	450297	499178	537015	580758
2. 其他农业产值	Other Farming	149011	32578	25305	25019	35710	40515	42733	55182	62617
二、林业产值	**Forestry**	**136848**	**233039**	**329278**	**348535**	**381802**	**408170**	**470164**	**498051**	**531855**
人造林木生长	Artificial Forestry	18226	23140	27964	23828	32802	33734	31640	32574	32100
林产品	Forest Products	89914	168348	184740	197815	214198	227962	267839	294806	328623
竹木采伐	Lumbering	28708	41551	82063	90806	93552	103425	130794	127670	125116
采集野生植物	Wild Plant collected			34511	36086	41250	43049	39891	43001	46016
三、牧业产值	**Animal Husbandry**	**331563**	**495900**	**705596**	**836532**	**868504**	**911324**	**828184**	**807001**	**857427**
牲畜	Livestock Raising	175732	292025	430193	534840	556742	589952	522674	522001	587803
家禽饲养	Poultry Raising	65548	68631	70201	69653	82132	77869	72333	72394	65491
活的畜禽产品	Livestock Products	44098	68143	109625	124024	125886	132151	127075	112964	105500
捕猎野兽野禽	Hunting Wild Beast and Wild Fowl	2102	2856	4455	4698	5454	5126	6260	5256	6032
其他动物饲养	Other Animals Raising	44083	64245	91122	103317	98290	106226	99842	94386	92601
四、渔业产值	**Fishery**	**154797**	**270810**	**349011**	**389985**	**420006**	**407292**	**442023**	**452309**	**435224**
五、服务业产值	**Service**	**-**	**58491**	**80732**	**87797**	**95900**	**105871**	**111629**	**122597**	**133212**

3－05 农林牧渔业分项产值构成(主要年份)

Composition of Gross Output Value of Agriculture, Forestry, Animal Husbandry and Fishery by Branch (Main Years)

单位:% (%)

指标	Item	2000	2005	2010	2011	2012	2013	2014	2015	2016
农林牧渔业总产值(现价)	**Gross Output Value (Current Price)**	**100**	**100**	**100**	**100**	**100**	**100**	**100**	**100**	**100**
一、农业产值	**Farming**	**59.2**	**51.8**	**53.7**	**53.4**	**54.0**	**54.1**	**55.8**	**57.3**	**58.1**
1. 种植业产值	Planting	49.4	50.3	52.9	52.7	53.1	53.1	54.7	56.1	56.8
粮食	Grain	13.7	8.2	6.8	6.4	6.3	6.2	5.4	5.2	5.1
油料	Oil Plants	1.3	1.0	1.0	1.0	0.9	0.9	0.9	1.1	1
棉花	Cotton	0.1	0.1	–	–	–	–	–	–	–
麻类	Fiber Crops	–	–	–	–	–	–	–	–	–
甘蔗	Sugarcane	1.6	0.9	0.6	0.6	0.6	0.5	0.4	0.4	0.4
烟叶	Tobacco	–	–	–	–	–	–	–	–	–
药材类	Crude Drugs	0.4	0.7	1.4	1.4	1.6	1.7	1.8	2.0	2.1
蔬菜	Vegetables	19.9	16.3	16.9	17.0	17.3	16.7	16.4	16.9	17.9
茶、桑、果、坚果	Tea, Mulberry & Fruits	7.0	11.6	15.3	15.8	15.7	15.8	17.9	18.2	17.9
其他	Others	5.4	11.5	10.9	10.5	10.7	11.3	11.9	12.2	12.4
2. 其他农业产值	Other Farming	9.8	1.5	0.8	0.7	0.9	1.0	1.0	1.3	1.3
二、林业产值	**Forestry**	**9.0**	**10.6**	**10.4**	**9.8**	**9.9**	**10.2**	**11.2**	**11.3**	**11.4**
人造林木生长	Artificial Forestry	1.2	1.1	0.9	0.7	0.8	0.8	0.8	0.7	0.7
林产品	Forest Products	5.9	7.6	5.8	5.5	5.6	5.7	6.4	6.7	7
竹木采伐	Lumbering	1.9	1.9	2.6	2.5	2.4	2.6	3.1	2.9	2.7
采集野生植物	Wild Plant collected			1.1	1.1	1.1	1.1	0.9	1.0	1
三、牧业产值	**Animal Husbandry**	**21.7**	**22.6**	**22.3**	**23.4**	**22.6**	**22.8**	**19.8**	**18.3**	**18.3**
牲畜	Livestock Raising	11.5	13.3	13.6	15.0	14.5	14.8	12.5	11.9	12.6
家禽饲养	Poultry Raising	4.3	3.1	2.2	2.0	2.1	1.9	1.7	1.6	1.4
活的畜禽产品	Livestock Products	2.9	3.2	3.5	3.5	3.3	3.3	3.0	2.6	2.3
捕猎野兽野禽	Hunting Wild Beast and Wild Fowl	0.1	0.1	0.1	0.1	0.1	0.1	0.1	0.1	0.1
其他动物饲养	Other Animals Raising	2.9	2.9	2.9	2.8	2.6	2.7	2.4	2.1	2
四、渔业产值	**Fishery**	**10.1**	**12.3**	**11.0**	**10.9**	**10.9**	**10.2**	**10.6**	**10.3**	**9.3**
五、服务业产值	**Service**	**–**	**2.7**	**3.4**	**2.5**	**2.6**	**2.7**	**2.6**	**2.8**	**2.9**

3－06 分地区农林牧

Gross Output Value of Agriculture, Forestry,

单位:万元

指　标	Item	全　市 Whole City	市　区 Urban District	江干区 Jianggan	西湖区 Xihu	高新(滨江)区 Hi－Tech(Binjiang)
合　计	**Gross Output Value**	**4672994**	**2679422**	**7335**	**62975**	**19238**
一、农业产值	**Farming**	**2715276**	**1554596**	**5886**	**29480**	**16828**
(一)种植业产值	Planting	2652659	1534915	5886	29333	16828
#副产品产值	By－products	12421	6636	－	25	16
1.粮食作物	Grain	237016	129962	－	294	365
谷　物	Cereal	176504	106489	－	224	363
豆　类	Beans	22438	14790	－	42	2
薯　类	Tubers	38074	8683	－	28	－
2.油　料	Oil Plants	48757	19889	－	19	－
3.棉　花	Cotton	929	452	－	－	－
4.麻　类	Fiber Crops	5	2	－	－	－
5.甘　蔗	Sugarcane	16393	12340	－	202	－
6.烟　叶	Tobacco	1	－	－	－	－
7.药材类	Crude Drugs	98927	21830	－	55	－
8.蔬　菜	Vegetables	835341	577544	3376	10808	4351
9.茶、桑、果、坚果	Tea, Mulberry & Fruits	834532	303763	130	6072	564
10.其　他	Others	580758	469133	2380	11883	11548
(二)其他农业产值	Other Farming	62617	19681	－	147	－
二、林业产值	**Forestry**	**531855**	**199435**	**17**	**388**	**－**
1.人造林木生长	Artificial Forestry	32100	18780	17	386	－
2.林产品	Forest Products	328623	116102	－	－	－
3.村及村以下竹木采伐	Lumbering	125116	46912	－	－	－
4.采集野生植物	Wild Plant collected	46016	17641	－	－	－
三、牧业产值	**Animal Husbandry**	**857427**	**473174**	**1127**	**432**	**－**
1.牲畜	Livestock	587803	364636	1127	－	－
2.家禽饲养	Poultry Raising	65491	44323	－	24	－
3.活的畜禽产品	Livestock Products	105500	25100	－	48	－
4.捕猎野兽野禽	Hunting Wild Beast and Wild Fowl	6032	3256	－	－	－
5.其他动物饲养	Other Animals Raising	92601	35859	－	360	－
四、渔业产值	**Fishery**	**435224**	**357514**	**224**	**31124**	**2410**
五、服务业产值	**Service**	**133212**	**94703**	**81**	**1551**	**－**

渔业总产值(2016 年)

Animal Husbandry and Fishery by Region(2016)

(10000 yuan)

萧山区 Xiaoshan	大江东产业集聚区 Dajiangdong Industry Cluster Distr	余杭区 Yuhang	富阳区 Fuyang	经济技术开发区 Economic and Technological Development Zone	西湖风景名胜区 The West Lake Scenic Zone	桐庐县 Tonglu	淳安县 Chun'an	建德市 Jiande	临安市 Lin'an
1111942	**212783**	**785108**	**642331**	**7945**	**11986**	**365044**	**487716**	**524199**	**616613**
665018	**122087**	**450865**	**371241**	**3360**	**11918**	**215661**	**322228**	**324200**	**298591**
664967	122076	446001	356622	3360	11918	210610	321140	294119	291875
2580	860	1765	2220	30	–	1114	1955	1753	963
43985	12426	41378	43171	769	–	21007	27645	32042	26360
31582	7504	37597	35964	759	–	16209	15397	24494	13915
10194	4809	2275	2271	6	–	1468	3240	2463	477
2209	113	1506	4936	4	–	3330	9008	5085	11968
6160	2207	1330	12377	3	–	8383	9929	7381	3175
317	40	135	–	–	–	–	321	156	–
2	–	–	–	–	–	–	3	–	–
9187	2565	1589	1362	–	–	1975	404	1640	34
–	–	–	–	–	–	–	1	–	–
4942	3	7223	9610	–	–	6935	31532	29741	8889
304841	79433	164264	88121	1783	–	64331	63518	68921	61027
47136	8154	124918	112220	805	11918	82716	163601	134821	149631
248397	17248	105164	89761	–	–	25263	24186	19417	42759
51	11	4864	14619	–	–	5051	1088	30081	6716
15891	**188**	**82365**	**100706**	**–**	**68**	**53474**	**66163**	**29182**	**183601**
5576	106	12307	426	–	68	2344	8208	1808	960
7873	81	49634	58595	–	–	37123	36570	16068	122760
2204	1	17220	27486	–	–	6986	13906	7745	49567
238	–	3204	14199	–	–	7021	7479	3561	10314
270601	**57231**	**57288**	**140688**	**3038**	**–**	**63951**	**66728**	**137260**	**116314**
240885	53915	35525	86182	917	–	32411	42492	58044	90220
13819	1658	14732	15742	6	–	3034	1855	13164	3115
7322	369	4883	11732	1115	–	6002	5918	58863	9617
381	381	514	2361	–	–	1085	133	566	992
8194	908	1634	24671	1000	–	21419	16330	6623	12370
118018	**28427**	**149990**	**23639**	**1547**	**–**	**23455**	**25101**	**20960**	**8194**
42414	**4850**	**44600**	**6057**	**–**	**–**	**8503**	**7496**	**12597**	**9913**

3－07　主要农作物播种面积及产量(2015－2016年)

Sown Areas and Yield of Major Farm Crops(2015－2016)

指　标	Item	2016			2015		
		播种面积(千公顷) Sown Area (1000 hectares)	总产量(吨) Total Output (ton)	公顷产量(公斤) Yield per Hectare (kg/hectare)	播种面积(千公顷) Sown Area (1000 hectares)	总产量(吨) Total Output (ton)	公顷产量(公斤) Yield per Hectare (kg/hectare)
农作物总计	**Total Farm Crops**	**300.59**	**－**	**－**	**297.69**	**－**	**－**
一、粮　食	**Grain Crops**	**107.99**	**635975**	**5889**	**106.02**	**633820**	**5978**
#春粮	#Spring Grain	16.69	59001	5047	14.73	58863	3996
秋粮	Autumn Grain	62.5	443823	7101	60.49	430125	7111
(一)谷　物	Cereals	77.37	514767	6654	76.64	517941	6758
1. 稻谷	Rice	44.58	365029	8188	46.78	376011	8039
①早稻及早中稻	Early Rice & Semi－late Rice	1.78	11059	6202	2.26	14906	6598
②晚稻及迟中稻	Late Rice & Semi－late Rice	42.8	353970	8271	44.52	361106	8112
#单季稻	#Single－crop Rice	41.35	342964	8294	43.27	352011	8135
2. 小麦	Wheat	11.44	40074	3503	10.40	42473	4082
3. 大麦	Barley	0.56	2296	4064	0.54	2147	4006
4. 玉米	Corn	20.35	105697	5193	18.11	93546	5166
5. 其他谷物	Other Cereals	0.43	1671	3877	0.82	3764	4607
(二)豆　类	Beans	19.35	60748	3140	18.16	57830	3184
1. 大豆	Soybeans	16.92	54182	3203	16.22	52196	3217
2. 蚕(豌)豆	Broad Beans	1.85	4843	2621	1.58	4494	2852
3. 杂豆	Other Beans	0.58	1723	2966	0.36	1139	3138
(三)薯　类	Tubers	11.27	60460	5363	11.22	58050	5176

3－07 续表 continued

指　标	Item	2016			2015		
		播种面积（千公顷）Sown Area（1000 hectares）	总产量（吨）Total Output（ton）	公顷产量（公斤）Yield per Hectare（kg/hectare）	播种面积（千公顷）Sown Area（1000 hectares）	总产量（吨）Total Output（ton）	公顷产量（公斤）Yield per Hectare（kg/hectare）
二、油料	**Oil Plants**	**30.09**	**69706**	**2316**	**32.42**	**78264**	**2414**
1. 油菜籽	Rapeseeds	26.16	57515	2199	28.50	66227	2324
2. 花生	Peanuts	2.57	9706	3784	2.60	9656	3718
3. 芝麻	Sesame	1.3	2326	1784	1.26	2232	1766
4. 其他	Others	0.06	159	2524	0.06	150	2727
三、棉花（皮棉）	**Cotton**	**0.38**	**599**	**1572**	**0.45**	**705**	**1563**
四、麻类	**Fiber Cropers**	**0.006**	**15**	**2500**	**0.01**	**21**	**3500**
五、糖类	**Sugar Crops**	**1.62**	**96693**	**59872**	**1.65**	**97999**	**59465**
六、烟叶	**Tobacco**	**–**	**1**	**–**	**–**	**1**	**–**
七、药材	**Crude Drugs**	**5.24**	**31755**	**6064**	**4.92**	**30256**	**6148**
八、蔬菜	**Vegetables**	**96.9**	**3353377**	**34607**	**94.17**	**3188439**	**33859**
九、果用瓜	**Melon as Fruit**	**11.54**	**369905**	**32049**	**11.30**	**361735**	**32000**
#西瓜	Watermelon	8.2	279223	34023	8.19	280909	34291
草莓	Strawberry	1.29	38326	29595	1.21	37812	31327
十、花卉苗木	**Flower Gardening**	**35.36**	**–**	**–**	**34.97**	**–**	**–**
十一、其他作物	**Others**	**11.47**	**–**	**–**	**11.79**	**–**	**–**
#绿肥	Green Manure	1.51	–	–	1.54	–	–

3－08 分地区粮食

Sown Areas and Yield of

指 标		Item		全市 Whole City	市区 Urban District	江干区 Jianggan	西湖区 Xihu	高新(滨江)区 Hi－Tech (Binjiang)
一、播种面积总计	**(公顷)**	**Sown Area of Grain Crops**	**(hectare)**	**107986**	**57980**	**－**	**236**	**221**
春粮	(公顷)	Spring Grain	(hectare)	16690	10332	－	20.7	95
早稻	(公顷)	Early Rice	(hectare)	1783	1390	－	－	63
晚稻	(公顷)	Late Rice	(hectare)	42797	28100	－	126	63
薯类	(公顷)	Tubers	(hectare)	11274	2709	－	20	－
玉米	(公顷)	Corn	(hectare)	20352	6389	－	24	－
大豆	(公顷)	Soybeans	(hectare)	16916	9757	－	28	－
杂豆	(公顷)	Other Beans	(hectare)	581	264	－	9	－
其他谷物	(公顷)	Other Cereals	(hectare)	431	93	－	12	－
二、总产量	**(吨)**	**Yield of Grain Crops**	**(ton)**	**635975**	**364780**	**－**	**1536**	**1071**
春粮	(吨)	Spring Grain	(ton)	59001	37666	－	64.48	272
早稻	(吨)	Early Rice	(ton)	11059	8540	－	－	312
晚稻	(吨)	Late Rice	(ton)	353970	234958	－	1049	487
薯类	(吨)	Tubers	(ton)	60460	15927	－	151	－
玉米	(吨)	Corn	(ton)	105697	33967	－	115	－
大豆	(吨)	Soybeans	(ton)	54182	36431	－	85	－
杂豆	(吨)	Other Beans	(ton)	1723	936	－	27	－
其他谷物	(吨)	Other Cereals	(ton)	1671	487	－	63	－
三、公顷产量	**(公斤)**	**Yield per Hectare**	**(kg)**	**5889**	**6291**	**－**	**6504**	**4846**
春粮	(公斤)	Spring Grain	(kg)	5047	3646	－	3115	2863
早稻	(公斤)	Early Rice	(kg)	6202	6144	－	－	4952
晚稻	(公斤)	Late Rice	(kg)	8271	8361	－	8325	7725
薯类	(公斤)	Tubers	(kg)	5363	5879	－	7947	－
玉米	(公斤)	Corn	(kg)	5193	5316	－	3375	－
大豆	(公斤)	Soybeans	(kg)	3203	3734	－	3075	－

播种面积及产量(2016 年)

Grain Crops by Region(2016)

萧山区 Xiaoshan	大江东产业集聚区 Dajiangdong Industry Cluster Distr	余杭区 Yuhang	富阳区 Fuyang	经济技术开发区 Economic and Technological Development Zone	西湖风景名胜区 The West Lake Scenic Zone	桐庐县 Tonglu	淳安县 Chun'an	建德市 Jiande	临安市 Lin'an
23372	**7775**	**15917**	**17837**	**396**	**–**	**9147**	**16851**	**14904**	**9104**
4036	835	2409	3436	134.4	–	1235	979	2019	2125
790	654	358	79	100	–	47	–	346	–
7240	1476	10178	10355	138	–	3972	1210	5871	3644
631	33	443	1612	3	–	1072	3763	1587	2143
3240	793	1278	1832	15	–	1802	7480	3203	1478
7430	3929	1351	941	6	–	1073	3751	2045	290
146	61	39	70	–	–	17	70	208	22
13	4	2	66	–	–	58	184	53	43
127900	**39560**	**112419**	**119605**	**2249**	**–**	**54527**	**73425**	**88765**	**54478**
15020	4046	8621	13146	541.2	–	3670	3384	6754	7527
4908	3910	2400	485	435	–	282	–	2237	–
60198	12493	87430	84652	1142	–	31813	9220	48845	29134
4104	237	2787	8874	11	–	6181	17726	8636	11990
16964	4297	6593	10192	103	–	9389	36995	18016	7330
26994	14401	5181	4153	18	–	3277	8057	5511	906
495	235	136	278	–	–	50	145	518	74
65	20	8	351	–	–	311	456	188	229
5472	**5088**	**7063**	**6705**	**5674**	**–**	**5961**	**4357**	**5956**	**5984**
3722	4846	3579	3826	4027	–	2972	3457	3345	3542
6213	5978	6704	6135	4350	–	6000	–	6465	–
8315	8464	8590	8175	8275	–	8009	7620	8320	7995
6504	7182	6291	5505	3666	–	5760	4711	5442	5595
5236	5419	5159	5563	6867	–	5205	4946	5625	4959
3633	3665	3835	4413	2991	–	3045	2148	2695	3120

3－09 分地区油、菜、茶、

Statistics on Rapeseeds, Vegetables, Tea,

指标		Item		全市 Whole City	市区 Urban District	江干区 Jianggan	西湖区 Xihu	高新(滨江)区 Hi－Tech (Binjiang)
一、油料		**Oil Plants**						
播种面积	(公顷)	Sown Area	(hectare)	30092	12412	－	44	－
每公顷产量	(公斤)	Yield per Hectare	(kg)	2316	2585	－	1950	－
总产量	(吨)	Total Output	(ton)	69706	32090	－	86	－
二、蔬菜		**Vegetables**						
播种面积	(公顷)	Sown Area	(hectare)	96898	65085	1131	2129	554
总产量	(吨)	Total Output	(ton)	3353377	2430467	28804	41078	22902
三、茶叶		**Tea**						
(一)茶园面积	(公顷)	Tea Garden Area	(hectare)	34795	10619	22	1124	49
(二)总产量	(吨)	Output of Tea	(ton)	28150	15662	8	410	8
春　茶	(吨)	Spring Tea	(ton)	19422	10962	8	254	8
夏　茶	(吨)	Summer Tea	(ton)	5791	3399	－	37	－
秋　茶	(吨)	Autumn Tea	(ton)	2937	1301	－	119	－
四、桑蚕		**Silkworm Cocoons & Mulberry**						
(一)桑园总面积	(公顷)	Mulberry Garden Area	(hectare)	11353	1731	－	－	－
(二)蚕茧总产量	(吨)	Output of Silkworm Cocoons	(ton)	8146	1675	－	－	－
春　茧	(吨)	Spring Silkworm Cocoons	(ton)	3848	645	－	－	－
夏　茧	(吨)	Summer Silkworm Cocoons	(ton)	699	305	－	－	－
秋　茧	(吨)	Autumn Silkworm Cocoons	(ton)	3599	725	－	－	－

蚕、果生产情况(2016 年)

Silkworm Cocoons and Fruits Production by Region(2016)

萧山区 Xiaoshan	大江东产业集聚区 Dajiangdong Industry Cluster Distr	余杭区 Yuhang	富阳区 Fuyang	经济技术开发区 Economic and Technological Development Zone	西湖风景名胜区 The West Lake Scenic Zone	桐庐县 Tonglu	淳安县 Chun'an	建德市 Jiande	临安市 Lin'an
4231	1393	948	7167	22	–	3943	7487	4451	1799
2511	2856	2301	2670	2909	–	2040	1892	2436	2521
10626	3979	2181	19133	64	–	8023	14168	10889	4536
27457	7895	22855	10329	630	–	6560	9147	8415	7691
1278330	378250	684433	363033	11887	–	210782	254202	265081	192845
1239	–	3796	4027	–	362	3927	12668	4140	3441
585	–	8056	6469	–	126	3096	4366	2617	2409
468	–	5649	4474	–	101	1408	3445	1793	1814
46	–	1343	1964	–	9	900	468	594	430
71	–	1064	31	–	16	788	453	230	165
19	–	802	910	–	–	1080	6164	1367	1011
–	–	138	1537	–	–	1743	2649	891	1188
–	–	119	526	–	–	1129	1165	320	589
–	–	5	300	–	–	4	363	14	13
–	–	14	711	–	–	610	1121	557	586

3－09 续表

指标		Item		全市 Whole City	市区 Urban District	江干区 Jianggan	西湖区 Xihu	高新(滨江)区 Hi－Tech (Binjiang)
五、水果生产		**Fruits**						
(一)果园面积合计	(公顷)	Area of Orchards	(hectare)	29393	8852	–	51	85
柑桔园	(公顷)	Citrus	(hectare)	8202	353	–	9	5
梨 园	(公顷)	Pears	(hectare)	4189	1630	–	12	30
桃 园	(公顷)	Peaches	(hectare)	4305	1440	–	6	–
杨梅园	(公顷)	Red Bayberry	(hectare)	3141	1345	–	1	47
枇杷园	(公顷)	Loquat	(hectare)	2437	841	–	–	–
柿子园	(公顷)	Persimmons	(hectare)	815	212	–	1	–
葡萄园	(公顷)	Grapes	(hectare)	1364	950	–	20	3
其他果园	(公顷)	Others	(hectare)	3824	1865	–	2	–
(二)水果总产量	(吨)	Yield of Fruits	(ton)	764081	316898	–	2166	1388
柑 桔	(吨)	Citrus	(ton)	154580	4338	–	182	8
梨 头	(吨)	Pears	(ton)	63766	29212	–	392	295
桃 子	(吨)	Peaches	(ton)	73171	39001	–	114	–
杨 梅	(吨)	Red Bayberry	(ton)	14183	6003	–	18	14
枇 杷	(吨)	Loquat	(ton)	5899	2683	–	–	–
柿 子	(吨)	Persimmons	(ton)	8027	2307	–	5	–
葡 萄	(吨)	Grapes	(ton)	25374	17211	–	567	20
果用瓜	(吨)	Melon as Fruit	(ton)	369905	203975	–	853	1051
其他水果	(吨)	Others	(ton)	36184	9819	–	35	–

continued

萧山区 Xiaoshan	大江东产业集聚区 Dajiangdong Industry Cluster Distr	余杭区 Yuhang	富阳区 Fuyang	经济技术开发区 Economic and Technological Development Zone	西湖风景名胜区 The West Lake Scenic Zone	桐庐县 Tonglu	淳安县 Chun'an	建德市 Jiande	临安市 Lin'an
2474	126	3356	2889	–	–	3759	8417	6381	1984
33	6	44	262	–	–	131	4547	3087	84
152	4	869	567	–	–	1385	558	352	264
178	4	486	770	–	–	853	982	716	314
656	–	239	402	–	–	538	431	609	218
3	–	771	67	–	–	123	859	601	13
75	–	29	107	–	–	38	448	85	32
215	102	375	337	–	–	126	83	45	160
1118	6	448	297	–	–	354	327	653	625
117384	33701	77121	115853	2986	–	86529	107734	199157	53763
439	121	626	3083	–	–	2579	55739	91704	220
1343	166	14274	12908	–	–	19492	5544	6163	3355
1574	91	8204	29109	–	–	9542	10012	9213	5403
2804	–	1304	1863	–	–	1809	1554	3375	1442
34	23	2522	127	–	–	344	1360	1400	112
831	14	520	951	–	–	387	3585	1338	410
4994	2154	7295	4335	–	–	1643	908	2424	3188
101019	30989	38148	59918	2986	–	46389	23085	71438	25018
3491	124	3321	2972	–	–	2648	3718	8355	11644

3－10 分地区畜牧业

Statistics on Animal Husbanday

指 标		Item		全市 Whole City	市区 Urban District	江干区 Jianggan	西湖区 Xihu
一、生猪		**Hogs**					
生猪年末存栏	（万头）	Being Raised at Year－end	（10000 heads）	126.91	81.76	－	－
#能繁殖的母猪	（万头）	#Reproducible	（10000 heads）	10.9	8.11	－	－
年内肥猪出栏	（万头）	Slaughtered Hogs of the Year	（10000 heads）	280.43	180.11	－	－
全年饲养量	（万头）	Number of Hogs Raised in the year	（10000 heads）	407.34	261.87	－	－
二、牛		**Cattle & Buffaloes**					
牛年末存栏	（头）	Being Raised at Year－end	（head）	14720	6113	－	－
#良种及改良种乳牛	（头）	#Improved Milk Cows	（head）	6435	3956	－	－
牛年内出栏	（头）	Slaughtered Cattle & Buffaloes of the Year	（head）	11806	5778	－	－
三、羊		**Sheep & Goats**					
羊年末存栏	（万只）	Being Raised at Year－end	（10000 heads）	26.21	18.57	5.78	－
羊年内出栏	（万只）	Slaughtered Sheep & Goats of the Year	（10000 heads）	37.5	28.34	2.38	－
四、兔		**Rabbits**					
兔年末存栏	（万只）	Being Raised at Year－end	（10000 heads）	15.69	7.34	－	－
兔年内出栏	（万只）	Slaughtered Rabbits of the Year	（10000 heads）	73.84	20.56	－	－
五、家禽		**Poultry**					
家禽年末存栏	（万只）	Being Raised at Year－end	（10000 heads）	983.76	443.58	－	0.89
家禽内出栏	（万只）	Slaughtered Poultry of the Year	（10000 heads）	2535.87	1751.62	－	1.66
六、年末养蜂箱数	**（箱）**	**Beehives**	**（case）**	**183152**	**54164**	**－**	**－**
七、畜禽产品产量		**Output of Livestock Products**					
1.肉类产量	（吨）	Output of Meat	（ton）	262696	167918	731	22
#猪 肉	（吨）	Pork	（ton）	211752	133086	－	－

渔业生产(2016 年)

and Fishery by Region(2016)

高新(滨江)区 Hi-Tech(Binjiang)	萧山区 Xiaoshan	大江东产业集聚区 Dajiangdong Industry Cluster Distr	余杭区 Yuhang	富阳区 Fuyang	经济技术开发区 Economic and Technological Development Zone	西湖风景名胜区 The West Lake Scenic Zone	桐庐县 Tonglu	淳安县 Chun'an	建德市 Jiande	临安市 Lin'an
-	65.89	10.21	4.09	11.77	0.01	-	7.09	13.84	7.58	16.64
-	6.92	0.9	0.41	0.78	-	-	0.35	0.44	0.79	1.21
-	125.91	31.48	12.19	41.76	0.25	-	15.47	22.16	22.34	40.35
-	191.8	41.69	16.28	53.53	0.26	-	22.56	36	29.92	56.99
-	2844	-	380	1673	1216	-	1707	1459	1903	3538
-	2740	-	-	-	1216	-	-	-	439	2040
-	196	-	335	4572	673	-	1615	797	854	2762
-	5.56	1.37	4.35	2.84	0.04	-	1.16	0.6	2.05	3.83
-	10.83	2.51	7.5	7.59	0.04	-	1.59	0.49	1.49	5.59
-	0.99	0.66	5.17	1.18	-	-	2.54	0.13	0.56	5.12
-	2.47	2.09	5.61	12.48	-	-	7.26	0.17	3.52	42.33
-	187.37	34.33	94.87	160.42	0.03	-	55.63	53.66	375.59	55.3
-	544.74	66.17	508.29	696.61	0.32	-	114.35	67.66	475.6	126.64
-	**19946**	**10290**	**2771**	**31447**	**-**	**-**	**65418**	**32452**	**18000**	**13118**
-	103799	23937	19080	43887	399	-	14170	18236	26722	35650
-	93016	22360	8439	31364	267	-	11584	16991	18924	31167

3－10 续表

指 标		Item		全市 Whole City	市区 Urban District	江干区 Jianggan	西湖区 Xihu
牛 肉	（吨）	Beef	(ton)	1886	916	–	–
羊 肉	（吨）	Mutton	(ton)	7485	5647	731	–
兔 肉	（吨）	Rabbit Meat	(ton)	1245	351	–	–
禽 肉	（吨）	Poultry Meat	(ton)	39945	27875	–	22
2. 禽蛋产量	（吨）	Poultry Eggs	(ton)	103768	18466	–	–
3. 蜂蜜产量	（吨）	Honey	(ton)	33281	21256	–	–
4. 蜂皇浆产量	（公斤）	Honey Tonic	(kg)	502188	134478	–	–
5. 牛奶产量	（吨）	Milk	(ton)	28648	18041	–	–
6. 兔毛产量	（吨）	Rabbit Wool	(ton)	35	12	–	–
八、渔业生产		**Fishery**					
（一）淡水产品产量总计	（吨）	Total Output of Freshwater Aquatic Products	(ton)	173447	135508	187	18450
其中：养殖产量	（吨）	Artificially Cultured	(ton)	164038	132825	107	17915
1. 鱼 类	（吨）	Fish	(ton)	111852	79986	187	13802
#鲫 鱼	（吨）	#Crucians	(ton)	14011	9494	10	2420
鳊 鱼	（吨）	Breams	(ton)	7029	3796	–	783
黑 鱼	（吨）	Snake Heads	(ton)	8064	8054	–	1233
2. 虾蟹类	（吨）	Shrimps, Prawns & Crabs	(ton)	25624	24991	–	726
3. 贝 类	（吨）	Shellfish	(ton)	2889	1605	–	47
4. 其 他	（吨）	Others	(ton)	33082	28926	–	3875
#甲 鱼	（吨）	Turtles	(ton)	31006	27448	–	3868
（二）淡水养殖面积合计	（公顷）	Freshwater Aquiculture Area	(hectare)	58729	11634	20	1793

continued

高新(滨江)区 Hi－Tech(Binjiang)	萧山区 Xiaoshan	大江东产业集聚区 Dajiangdong Industry Cluster Distr	余杭区 Yuhang	富阳区 Fuyang	经济技术开发区 Economic and Technological Development Zone	西湖风景名胜区 The West Lake Scenic Zone	桐庐县 Tonglu	淳安县 Chun'an	建德市 Jiande	临安市 Lin'an
–	37	–	74	686	119	–	301	118	137	414
–	1912	481	1860	1139	5	–	316	72	297	1153
–	39	31	124	188	–	–	139	4	44	707
–	8795	1065	8583	10467	8	–	1771	1051	7292	1956
–	1826	199	4806	11732	7	–	4781	6005	68125	6391
–	2020	579	303	18933	–	–	6102	3491	1466	966
–	63205	13801	6955	64318	–	–	255854	44508	13883	53465
–	10651	–	–	–	7390	–	–	–	3481	7126
–	–	–	12	–	–	–	–	–	1	22
1040	43468	9676	58311	13166	886	–	13231	8922	10735	5051
680	42692	9626	58111	12445	875	–	10377	8621	7776	4439
675	16532	3692	36419	12078	293	–	12664	5479	9455	4268
200	–	–	2860	3947	57	–	1579	1181	1041	716
25	–	–	1741	1247	–	–	1263	103	1589	278
1	1295	–	5474	51	–	–	–	10	–	–
180	22156	5101	967	372	590	–	198	164	205	66
–	–	–	1350	208	–	–	213	–	893	178
185	4780	883	19575	508	3	–	156	3279	182	539
185	4705	883	18374	316	–	–	156	2978	63	361
60	3676	765	4329	1503	253	–	41041	1420	1918	2716

3－11 分地区林业

Statistics on Forestry

指 标	Item	全市 Whole City	市区 Urban District
一、营林情况	**Afforestation**		
1. 当年造林面积 （公顷）	Afforested Areas (hectare)	2084.73	881.00
2. 迹地更新面积 （公顷）	Area of Forest Updating (hectare)	2724.87	226.67
3. 封山育林面积 （公顷）	Area of Afforestation in Enclosed Mountain (hectare)	92439	37534
4. 零星(四旁)植树 （万株）	Planting Trees (10000 plant)	424.91	209.31
5. 中、幼龄林抚育面积(公顷)	Area of Grown Forest Cultivated (hectare)	17388.60	3380.00
二、林产品产量	**Output of Forest Products**		
1. 油茶籽 （吨）	Camellia Seeds (ton)	10432	10
2. 竹笋干 （吨）	Dried Bamboo Shoots (ton)	61658	22845
3. 核 桃 （吨）	Walnuts (ton)	20172	223
4. 板 栗 （吨）	Chestnuts (ton)	13188	1840
三、竹木采伐量	**Lumbering**		
1. 木 材 （万立方米）	Timber Cut (10000 cu. m)	20.59	2.35
2. 竹 材 （万支）	Bamboo Cut (10000 pieces)	3596	2147

生产（2016 年）
by Region（2016）

萧山区 Xiaoshan	余杭区 Yuhang	富阳区 Fuyang	桐庐县 Tonglu	淳安县 Chun'an	建德市 Jiande	临安市 Lin'an
350.67	6.67	523.67	444.47	199.27	560.00	-
-	26.67	200.00	665.60	499.07	733.53	600.00
13339		23133	40846	7387	3339	3333
30.00	179.31		62.00	72.60	40.00	41.00
833.33	713.33	1700.00	1933.07	3695.53	6000.00	2380.00
		10	985	7717	1600	120
1930	10720	10195	7856	6951	2006	22000
	23	200	1325	6407	96	12121
400	150	1290	2986	4550	2850	962
0.27	0.42	1.66	1.45	5.31	6.24	5.24
138	786	1223	110	569	220	550

3-12 分地区主要农
Possession of Major Agricultural

指 标		Item		全市 Whole City	市区 Urban District
一、农业机械总动力	**(千瓦)**	**Total Power of Agricultural Machinery**	**(kw)**	**2837185**	**1674001**
耕作机械动力	(千瓦)	Cultivation Machinery	(kw)	222293	138029
收获机械动力	(千瓦)	Harvest Machinery	(kw)	46994	35718
植保机械动力	(千瓦)	Plant Protection Machinery	(kw)	50987	11803
排灌机械动力	(千瓦)	Drainage & Irrigation Machinery	(kw)	407656	245354
农副产品加工机械动力	(千瓦)	Processing Machinery of Agricultural Products	(kw)	157106	46958
运输机械动力	(千瓦)	Transport Machinery	(kw)	432762	282787
渔业机械动力	(千瓦)	Fishery Machinery	(kw)	117980	101832
其他机械动力	(千瓦)	Other Machinery	(kw)	1401407	811520
二、主要农机具		**Agricultural Machinery and Machinery For Processing Farm Products**			
大中型拖拉机	(台)	Large & Medium Tractors	(unit)	1247	1058
机引农具	(台)	Mechanized Farm Implement	(unit)	2723	2494
农用小型拖拉机	(台)	Mini - tractors	(unit)	12162	7043
联合收获机	(台)	Combine Harvesters	(unit)	905	710
机动割晒机	(台)	Motorized Harvesters	(unit)	7	6
机动脱粒机	(台)	Motorized Thresher	(unit)	74253	58429
谷物烘干机	(台)	Cereal Dryer	(unit)	508	284
机动喷雾(粉)器	(架)	Motorized Sprayer	(unit)	31442	7496
农用水泵	(台)	Water Pump for Agricultural Use	(unit)	134617	49435
节水喷灌机械	(套)	Saving Water and Sprinkling Machinery	(set)	4246	628
粮食加工机械	(台)	Grain Processing Machinery	(unit)	19597	3612
棉花加工机械	(台)	Cotton Processing Machinery	(unit)	297	194
油料加工机械	(台)	Oil Processing Machinery	(unit)	1676	310
农用运输机械	(台)	Vehicles for Agricultural Use	(unit)	20115	12308

机具年末拥有量(2016 年)
Machinery at the Year – end by Region(2016)

萧山区 Xiaoshan	大江东产业集聚区 Dajiangdong Industry Cluster Distr	余杭区 Yuhang	富阳区 Fuyang	桐庐县 Tonglu	淳安县 Chun'an	建德市 Jiande	临安市 Lin'an
607687	**105981**	**431911**	**377085**	**174614**	**307059**	**289629**	**391882**
57001	13322	44184	35029	11802	13546	26210	32706
11549	2859	8312	13031	5569	1159	3201	1347
4590	572	3126	3721	1546	2865	4769	30004
86845	8677	81646	55774	31739	22023	47056	61485
24045	4221	15161	11013	11619	48356	23137	27036
127742	10938	68662	50023	29362	50018	50295	20300
78901	16300	8940	2144	1452	12328	2221	147
217014	49092	201880	206350	81525	156765	132741	218857
609	244	266	181	72	21	57	39
1771	651	537	185	74	23	82	50
1729	104	2680	2468	964	1239	2348	568
340	63	122	229	69	27	71	28
		4	2		1		
7105	624	28233	14198	11022	2150	2112	540
129	49	89	66	65	23	88	48
3289	338	1642	1665	720	2212	2112	18902
16936	1025	14739	15009	12830	4799	25398	42155
206	23	405	9	53	527	2980	58
1351	176	1056	1106	1277	7115	2083	5510
135	83	8	51	21	60	16	6
172	88	45	84	242	610	316	198
5660	66	3035	2676	1662	1893	2264	1988

3－13 农业物资
Agricultural Material

指　　标		Item		全市 Whole City	市区 Urban District
一、农村用电量	**（万千瓦时）**	**Electricity Consumed in Rural Area（10000 kwh）**		**1099435**	**881181**
二、农业化肥施用量		**Consumption of Chemical Fertilizer**			
（一）按实物量计算	（吨）	Physical Quantity Consumption	（ton）	464935	258708
1. 氮　肥	（吨）	Nitrogenous Fertilizer	（ton）	195016	108848
2. 磷　肥	（吨）	Phosphate Fertilizer	（ton）	73048	46201
3. 钾　肥	（吨）	Potash Fertilizer	（ton）	38458	18148
4. 复合肥	（吨）	Compound Fertilizer	（ton）	158413	85565
（二）按折纯法计算	（吨）	Pure Consumption	（ton）	94408	45816
1. 氮　肥	（吨）	Nitrogenous Fertilizer	（ton）	41904	21091
2. 磷　肥	（吨）	Phosphate Fertilizer	（ton）	11083	5524
3. 钾　肥	（吨）	Potash Fertilizer	（ton）	7392	3003
4. 复合肥	（吨）	Compound Fertilizer	（ton）	34029	16198
三、农用塑料薄膜使用量	**（吨）**	**Use of Plastic Film**	**（ton）**	**10671**	**2904**
四、农用柴油使用量	**（吨）**	**Consumption of Diesel Oil**	**（ton）**	**26165**	**9238**
五、农药使用量	**（吨）**	**Consumption of Pesticide**	**（ton）**	**6776**	**3391**

消耗情况(2016年)
Consumption(2016)

萧山区 Xiaoshan	大江东产业集聚区 Dajiangdong Industry Cluster Distr	余杭区 Yuhang	富阳区 Fuyang	桐庐县 Tonglu	淳安县 Chun'an	建德市 Jiande	临安市 Lin'an
178354	**23583**	**211843**	**420605**	**62425**	**13945**	**21943**	**119941**
175855	33526	52113	24037	35917	56939	49251	64120
67595	14071	26184	12316	16792	30417	21475	17484
35007	6661	7717	2576	7465	6535	6496	6351
11941	862	5174	584	3889	6126	5236	5059
61312	11932	13038	8561	7771	13807	16044	35226
20735	3930	12619	10159	10193	7152	17874	13373
9492	1998	5499	5173	4036	2943	8239	5595
3158	608	1158	927	1465	754	2260	1080
1436	107	1138	292	1143	387	1797	1062
6649	1217	4824	3767	3549	3068	5578	5636
2071	**338**	**374**	**269**	**736**	**4091**	**1812**	**1128**
6256	**1317**	**2335**	**426**	**4812**	**1841**	**3648**	**6626**
1509	**275**	**949**	**794**	**687**	**620**	**1023**	**1055**

3-14 分地区农村

Basic Situations of

指标	Item	全市 Whole City	市区 Urban District	江干区 Jianggan	西湖区 Xihu
一、农村人口与从业人员	**Rural Population and Employed Persons**				
农村户数 (万户)	Rural Household (10000 households)	132	81.31	1.53	4.6
农村人口 (万人)	Rural Population (10000 persons)	482.94	326.41	6.82	17.87
男	Male	244.08	165.16	3.33	8.79
女	Female	238.86	161.25	3.49	9.08
农村劳动力资源数 (万人)	Rural Laboar Resources (10000 persons)	314.83	211.29	4.07	11
男	Male	164.54	110.48	2.14	5.71
女	Female	150.29	100.81	1.93	5.29
农村从业人员 (万人)	Jobholders in Rural Areas (10000 persons)	281.76	187.99	3.33	9.87
男	Male	149.68	99.76	1.74	5.2
#从事农业人员	Persons Involved in Agriculture	37.49	18.77	0.21	1
女	Female	132.08	88.23	1.59	4.67
#从事农业人员	Persons Involved in Agriculture	29.74	14.21	0.15	0.85
二、农村基础设施	**Public Facilities in Rural Areas**				
自来水受益村数	Number of Villages with Access to Tap Water	2053	926	4	36
通有线电视村数	Number of Villages Connecting to Cable TV	2053	926	4	36
通宽带村数	Number of Villages Connecting to Prroadband	2053	926	4	36

基本情况(2016 年末)

Rural Areas by Region(End of 2016)

高新(滨江)区 Hi - Tech(Binjiang)	萧山区 Xiaoshan	大江东产业集聚区 Dajiangdong Industry Cluster Distr	余杭区 Yuhang	富阳区 Fuyang	经济技术开发区 Economic and Technological Development Zone	西湖风景名胜区 The West Lake Scenic Zone	桐庐县 Tonglu	淳安县 Chun'an	建德市 Jiande	临安市 Lin'an
3.25	34.91	4.97	19.73	16.96	0.05	0.28	10.91	11.43	12.48	15.87
12.41	124.76	18.47	107.9	55.99	0.09	0.57	33.95	35.57	39.96	47.05
6.1	61.42	9.24	56.65	28.57	0.05	0.25	17.22	17.96	20.47	23.27
6.31	63.34	9.23	51.25	27.42	0.04	0.32	16.73	17.61	19.49	23.78
8.44	78.77	12.34	72.41	36.23	0.06	0.31	22.2	24.21	25.53	31.6
4.33	40.17	6.37	38.94	19.01	0.03	0.15	11.48	12.66	13.64	16.28
4.11	38.6	5.97	33.47	17.22	0.03	0.16	10.72	11.55	11.89	15.32
7.69	69.44	11.27	64.73	32.59	0.05	0.29	20.5	23.19	21.92	28.16
4	35.87	5.84	35.32	17.45	0.03	0.15	10.65	12.57	11.98	14.72
0.05	6.09	1.01	4.57	6.78	-	0.07	2.88	5.92	5.5	4.42
3.69	33.57	5.43	29.41	15.14	0.02	0.14	9.85	10.62	9.94	13.44
0.02	4.88	0.78	3.08	5.16	-	0.07	2.42	5.11	4.33	3.67
	411	59	187	279		9	183	425	232	287
	411	59	187	279		9	183	425	232	287
	411	59	187	279		9	183	425	232	287

3-15 农村基本情况(2010-2016年)
Basic Situations of Rural Areas(2010-2016)

指标 Item	2010	2011	2012	2013	2014	2015	2016
一、农村人口与从业人员 Rural Population and Employed Persons							
农村户数 (万户) Rural Household (10000 households)	131.82	132.94	129.29	132.18	131.96	132.15	132
农村人口 (万人) Rural Population (10000 persons)	431.34	434.23	425.49	469.90	480.04	482.63	482.94
男 Male		218.03	213.81	236.03	241.82	243.47	244.08
女 Female		216.20	211.68	233.87	238.22	239.16	238.86
农村劳动力资源数 (万人) Rural Laboar Resources (10000 persons)	280.05	281.16	276.62	304.14	314.45	313.79	314.83
男 Male		146.23	143.66	157.27	163.98	163.94	164.54
女 Female		134.93	132.96	146.87	150.47	149.85	150.29
农村从业人员 (万人) Jobholders in Rural Areas (10000 persons)	261.77	262.10	257.30	279.91	286.01	284.73	281.76
男 Male	138.18	137.33	134.85	145.70	151.05	151.21	149.68
#从事农业人员 Persons Involved in Agriculture					36.50	37.58	37.49
女 Female	123.59	124.77	122.45	134.21	134.96	133.52	132.08
#从事农业人员 Persons Involved in Agriculture					29.75	30.22	29.74
二、农村基础设施 Public Facilities in Rural Areas							
自来水受益村数 Number of Villages with Access to Tap Water	2097	2081	2078	2058	2054	2054	2053
通有线电视村数 Number of Villages Connecting to Cable TV	2098	2081	2078	2058	2054	2054	2053
通宽带村数 Number of Villages Connecting to Prroadband			2078	2058	2054	2054	2053
三、农林牧渔业增加值 Value-added of Agriculture, Forestry, Animal Husbandry and Fishery	**2084144**	**2367708**	**2551127**	**2654059**	**2783252**	**2924013**	**3092579**
农业 Farming	1219343	1386520	1510382	1571300	1685668	1806178	1933812
林业 Forestry	260287	277061	302796	324240	371932	393332	416734
牧业 Animal	351494	421453	435191	458201	405348	395476	415814
渔业 Fishery	226096	253456	270629	262233	280544	284506	275703
服务业 Service	26924	29218	32129	38085	39760	44521	50516

主要统计指标解释

农林牧渔业总产值 是以货币表现的农、林、牧、渔业全部产品的总量和对农林牧渔生产活动进行的各种支持性服务活动的价值。它反映一定时期内农林牧渔业生产的总规模和总成果。

农林牧渔业的统计范围是:

(1)农业 包括农作物种植业和其他农业。

农作物种植业 包括谷类、豆类、薯类、棉花、麻类、烟叶、蔬菜、药材、瓜类和其他农作物的种植以及茶园、桑园、果园的生产经营。

其他农业 包括采集野生植物的果实、纤维、树脂、油料以及柴草、野生药材、菌类等。

(2)林业 包括林木的栽培(不包括茶园、桑园和果园的栽培、管理和收获等活动)、林产品的采集、村及村以下合作经济组织和农户的竹木砍伐。

(3)牧业 包括除渔业养殖以外的一切动物饲养和放牧以及野生动物的捕猎和饲养。

(4)渔业 包括水生动物和海藻类植物的养殖和捕捞。

(5)农林牧渔服务业 包括对农林牧渔生产活动进行的各种支持性服务活动。

粮食产量 指全社会的产量,包括国营农场等全民所有制经营、集体统一经营和农民家庭经营的产量,还包括工矿企业家属办的农场和其他生产单位的产量。粮食除包括稻谷、小麦、大麦、玉米、高粱、谷子及其他杂粮外,还包括薯类和豆类。其产量计算方法,豆类按去豆荚后的干豆计算,薯类按5公斤鲜薯折1公斤粮食计算,其他粮食一律按脱粒后的原粮计算。

猪、牛、羊肉产量 指当年出栏并已屠宰的猪、牛、羊的肉产量,即屠宰后除去头蹄下水后带骨的(即胴体重)重量。

水产品产量 指人工养殖的水产品和天然生长的水产品的捕捞量。包括海水的鱼类、虾蟹类、贝类和藻类以及内陆水域的鱼类、虾蟹类和贝类,不包括淡水生植物。

有效灌溉面积 指具有一定水源,地块比较平整、灌溉工程或设备已经配套,在一般年景下当年能够进行正常灌溉的耕地面积。

农业机械总动力 指主要用于农、林、牧、渔业的各种动力机械的动力总和。包括耕作机械、排灌机械、收获机械、农用运输机械、植物保护机械、牧业机械、林业机械和其他农业机械[内燃机按引擎马力折成瓦(特)计算,电动机按功率折成瓦(特)计算]。不包括专门用于乡、镇、村、组办工业、基本建设、非农业运输、科学试验和教学等非农业方面的动力机械与作业机械。

农村用电量 指本年度内扣除在农村中的全民所有制工业、交通、基建单位的用电量以后的农村生产上和生活上的全年用电总度数(全年累计数),包括国家电网的供电量,也包括农村自办电站的供电量。

农用化肥施用量 指本年内实际用于农业生产的化肥数量。包括氮肥、磷肥、钾肥及复合肥。化肥施用量要求按折纯量计算数量。折纯量是指氮肥、磷肥、钾肥分别按含氮、含五氧化二磷、含氧化钾的百分之一百成分进行折算后的数量。复合肥按其所含主要成分折算。

Explanatory Notes on Main Statistical Indicators

Gross Output Value of Farming, Forestry, Animal Husbandry and Fishery refers to the total volume of products of farming, forestry, animal husbandry and fishery in value terms and output value of all kinds of service activities that support farming, forestry, animal husbandry and fishery production. It reflects the total scale and total result of agricultural production during a given period of time.

The statistical scopes for Farming, Forestry, Animal Husbandry and Fishery are:

(1) **Farming** include crop cultivation and other farming crop cultivation, include planting of grain, beans, tubers, cotton, oil – bearing crops, sugar crops, fiber crops, tobacco, vegetables, medicinal materials, melons and others, as well as tea, mulberry and fruit plantation.

Other farming include gathering of wild plant fruits, fiber, gum, oil, firewood, wild medicinal materials, fungi and commodity industry run by rural household.

(2) **Forestry** include planting of trees (not including planting, management & harvest of tea, mulberry and fruit plantation), collection of forest products, cutting and felling of bamboo and trees by villages and other cooperative organizations under villages.

(3) **Animal Husbandry** include raising and grazing of any kind of animal and hunting and raising of wild animal, excluding fish breeding.

(4) **Fishery** include cultivation and catches of aquatic animals and seaweed.

(5) **Service Industry for Farming, Forestry, Animal Husbandry and Fishery** refers to all kinds of service activities that support farming, forestry , animal husbandry and fishery production.

Grain Yield refers to the total yield including grains produced by state farms, collective units, industrial enterprises and mines. Grain includes rice, wheat, corn, sorghum, millet and other miscellaneous grains as well as tubers and beans. Output of beans refers to dry beans without pods. The output of tubers was converted into that of grain at the ratio 5:1. Output of all other grains refers to husked grain.

Output of Pork, Beef, and Mutton refers to the meat of slaughtered hogs, cattle, sheep and goats with head, feet and offal taken away.

Output of Aquatic Products refers to catches of both artificially cultured and naturally grown aquatic products, including fish, shrimps, crabs and shellfish in sea and inland water as well as seaweed. Freshwater plants are not included.

Irrigated Area refers to areas that are effectively irrigated, i. e. level land which has water source and complete sets of irrigation facilities to lift and move adequate water for irrigation purpose under normal conditions.

Total Power of Farm Machinery refers to total mechanical power of machinery used in farming, forestry, animal husbandry, and fishery, including ploughing, irrigation and drainage, harvesting, transport, plant protection, stock breeding, forestry and fishery. The power of internal combustion engines is required to convert horsepower into watts and the power of electric motors is required to be converted into watts. Machinery employed for non – agricultural purposes, such as the machines used in township – run and village – run industry, construction, non – agricultural transport, scientific experiments and teaching, is excluded.

Electricity Consumption in Rural Areas refers to the total degree of electricity consumption in rural production and living (annual aggregate) after discounting the ownership by the whole people in the rural areas of industrial, transport and infrastructure unit of electricity consumption, including the national grid power supply, and also including the power supply in rural areas on their own power station.

Consumption of Chemical Fertilizers in Agriculture refers to the quantity of chemical fertilizers applied in agriculture in the year, including nitrogenous fertilizer, phosphate fertilizer, potash fertilizer, and compound fertilizer. The consumption of chemical fertilizers is required in calculation to convert the gross weight into weight into weight containing 100% effective component (e. g. 100% nitrogen content in nitrogenous fertilizer, 100% phosphorous pentoxide contents in phosphate fertilizer, 100% potassium oxide contents in potash fertilizer). Compound fertilizer is converted with its major component.

四、工业、能源

INDUSTRY AND ENERGY

4 工业、能源

Industry and Energy

主要统计指标

Major Statistical Indicators

规模以上工业企业单位数	Number of Industrial Enterprises above Designated Size	5684	个	(unit)
为上年	As Compared with the Preceding Year	93.6	%	(%)
规模以上工业增加值	Value-added of Industrial Enterprises above Designated Size	2990.34	亿元	(100 million yuan)
为上年	As Compared with the Preceding Year	105.6	%	(%)
规模以上工业总产值	Gross Output Value of Industrial Enterprises above Designated Size	12420.96	亿元	(100 million yuan)
为上年	As Compared with the Preceding Year	100.0	%	(%)
轻工业	Light Industry	4693.99	亿元	(100 million yuan)
为上年	As Compared with the Preceding Year	97.4	%	(%)
重工业	Heavy Industry	7726.97	亿元	(100 million yuan)
为上年	As Compared with the Preceding Year	101.7	%	(%)

4－01　全市工业企业单位数(主要年份)

Number of Industrial Enterprises of the Whole City(Main Years)

单位:个　　(unit)

年　份 Year	合　计 Total	国有经济 State－owned Enterprises	集体经济 Collective－owned Enterprises	其他各种经济类型 Enterprises of Other Types of Ownership
1978	2868	680	2188	－
1980	3519	691	－	－
1985	5800	823	－	－
1990	6183	921	4966	11
1991	6234	933	5219	82
1992	6235	941	5162	132
1995	6744	1086	4722	936
1996	6148	1011	4268	869
1997	4980	760	3250	970
1998	2559	464	815	1280
1999	2474	396	689	1389
2000	2715	282	598	1835
2001	3580	237	252	3091
2002	4015	172	232	3611
2003	4689	144	219	4326
2004	7738	185	192	7361
2005	7359	124	169	7066
2006	7826	110	162	7554
2007	8674	71	131	8472
2008	9907	73	101	9733
2009	10032	71	84	9877
2010	10370	74	68	10228
2011	5868	52	25	5791
2012	5927	56	20	5851
2013	6284	25	11	6248
2014	6169	22	9	6138
2015	6073	17	5	6051
2016	5684	15	4	5665

注:1997年及以前为乡及以上工业;1998－2010年为主营业务收入500万及以上;2011年为主营业务收入2000万及以上(后同)。

a) Data after 2011 refer to all the industrial enterprises with annual Sales income of over 20 million yuan, data in 1998－2010 refer to all the industrial enterprises with annual sales income of over 5 million yuan, data in 1997 and before refer to enterprises at township and above level.

4-02 市区工业企业单位数(主要年份)

Number of Industrial Enterprises in Urban District(Main Years)

单位:个　　(unit)

年　份 Year	合　计 Total	国有经济 State - owned Enterprises	集体经济 Collective - owned Enterprises	其他各种经济类型 Enterprises of Other Types of Ownership
1978	787	313	414	-
1980	894	315	579	-
1985	1250	345	859	7
1990	1360	361	971	28
1991	1411	382	990	39
1992	1490	395	1024	71
1995	1998	440	1102	456
1996	2043	458	1109	476
1997	1733	372	951	410
1998	1019	315	315	389
1999	959	255	284	420
2000	1005	182	253	570
2001	2645	195	200	2250
2002	2838	140	178	2520
2003	3230	115	158	2957
2004	5527	156	122	5249
2005	4995	98	104	4793
2006	5195	85	91	5019
2007	5726	54	77	5595
2008	6530	55	64	6411
2009	6477	52	49	6376
2010	6478	51	37	6390
2011	3867	36	10	3821
2012	3862	37	7	3818
2013	4145	18	5	4122
2014	4716	17	5	4694
2015	4584	12	3	4569
2016	4235	11	2	4222

4－03　全市工业总产值（主要年份）
Gross Industrial Output Value of the Whole City(Main Years)

单位：万元　　　　(10000 yuan)

年　份 Year	规模以上工业 Industry above Designated Size	轻工业 Light Industry	重工业 Heavy Industry	国有经济 State－owned	集体经济 Collective－owned	其他经济 Other Types of Ownership
1978	429624	–	–	334799	94825	–
1980	617910	–	–	451349	166561	–
1985	1285888	793766	492122	726172	546642	13074
1990	2922600	1848911	1073689	1532900	1300900	88800
1991	3524900	2201757	1323143	1779400	1601400	144200
1992	4527400	2735168	1792232	2141000	2084000	302400
1995	10200259	5600664	4599595	3585284	3999638	2615337
1996	8831167	4606720	4224447	2905614	3320757	2604796
1997	9114651	4871887	4242764	3185886	2971634	2957131
1998	11099357	5726407	5372950	3422316	2824793	4852248
1999	12000796	6129963	5870833	3164602	2543981	6292213
2000	15435682	7623300	7812382	1860336	2698406	10876940
2001	19195133	9957027	9238106	1788783	1911315	15495035
2002	24002972	12435498	11567474	2147066	2151485	19704421
2003	32025226	15652463	16372763	2484171	2444002	27097053
2004	44865779	19761946	25103833	3419970	558890	40886919
2005	54411271	24059690	30351581	6054280	603438	47753553
2006	69754590	29093450	40661140	6776754	667615	62310221
2007	83514029	35878400	47635629	7688908	517878	75307243
2008	93795792	38735329	55060463	7440679	386111	85969002
2009	93907334	40115956	53791378	7576482	354714	85976138
2010	110810397	45764739	65045658	9050510	300262	101459625
2011	123529249	48660810	74868439	10220511	171901	113136837
2012	129596777	51377588	78219189	11507163	167343	117922271
2013	124180035	48663751	75516284	7140899	39776	116999360
2014	128530518	49979222	78551296	6922198	32246	121576073
2015	124156803	48207987	75948816	2309361	14146	121833295
2016	124209589	46939900	77269689	5534102	12292	118663195

4-04 市区工业总产值(主要年份)

Gross Industrial Output Value in Urban District(Main Years)

单位:万元 (10000 yuan)

年份 Year	规模以上工业 Industry above Designated Size	轻工业 Light Industry	重工业 Heavy Industry	国有经济 State - owned	集体经济 Collective - owned	其他经济 Other Types of Ownership
1978	304242	-	-	248534	55708	-
1980	433623	-	-	335789	97834	-
1985	812246	512767	301998	536498	267613	8135
1990	1533000	1026764	599899	1067400	416500	49100
1991	1814600	1140394	674072	1237600	496800	80200
1992	2291300	1379154	917085	1497400	601200	192700
1995	4760900	2507752	2753196	2252300	908900	1599700
1996	4599778	2460319	2139459	2018768	951432	1629578
1997	4997257	2889406	2609217	2537740	819984	1639533
1998	6110192	3068600	3041592	2989467	1123013	1997712
1999	6280838	3178286	3102552	2668519	979070	2633249
2000	7804302	3635578	4168724	1498595	968509	5337198
2001	16156245	8377563	7778681	1695132	1792228	12668885
2002	20252484	10431428	9821056	2036097	2045450	16170937
2003	26945006	13080771	13864235	2390424	2305431	22249151
2004	37564968	16361706	21203262	3097656	419720	34047592
2005	44775260	19601053	25174207	5592419	390555	38792286
2006	57255453	23722868	33532585	6305071	347788	50602594
2007	67565456	29452269	38113187	7123810	323842	60117804
2008	74564803	31236743	43328060	6812616	219140	67533047
2009	74059755	32178951	41880805	6880470	148937	67030348
2010	86653885	36440816	50213069	8155395	156026	78342464
2011	97800625	39467105	58333520	9253445	70299	88476881
2012	101396009	41428864	59967145	10452692	72743	90870574
2013	94197123	38407906	55789218	6332681	22398	87842044
2014	110230328	42840596	67389732	6463681	22354	103744292
2015	105641721	40775608	64866113	1841145	8633	103791944
2016	105688299	39331082	66357217	5061048	6629	100620622

4－05　规模以上工业企业主要经济效益指标(1998－2016 年)

Main Economic Indicators of Industrial Enterprises Above Designated Size(1998－2016)

单位:亿元　　(100 million yuan)

年份 Year	规模以上工业总产值 Output Value of Industrial Enterprises Above Designated Size	规模以上工业增加值 Added Value of Industrial Enterprises Above Designated Size	资产总计 Total Assets	流动资产合计 Total Current Assets	主营业务收入 Revenne from Principal Business	利润总额 Total Profits	利税总额 Total Profits and Tax
1998	1109.94	274.70	1486.02	732.72	1036.09	38.44	101.36
1999	1200.07	298.90	1620.93	800.60	1132.80	54.47	127.89
2000	1543.57	360.97	1828.35	946.32	1465.49	76.20	161.61
2001	1919.51	444.91	2148.96	1122.07	1828.28	107.56	208.54
2002	2400.30	597.01	2514.19	1313.92	2288.21	145.48	274.98
2003	3202.52	783.51	3258.93	1783.50	3117.46	194.16	359.54
2004	4486.58	1019.47	4118.31	2300.84	4363.27	226.74	427.23
2005	5441.13	1126.54	4781.34	2692.73	5282.80	234.99	450.68
2006	6975.46	1363.17	5564.68	3215.19	6807.64	314.49	576.51
2007	8351.40	1717.65	6573.12	3880.23	8057.03	414.55	730.50
2008	9379.58	1743.20	7506.26	4437.50	8976.46	453.92	802.13
2009	9390.73	1792.00	8405.62	4968.21	9026.32	510.97	882.62
2010	11081.04	2153.83	9937.41	6011.68	10843.24	764.47	1224.48
2011	12352.92	2369.00	10968.69	6709.76	12022.57	795.53	1330.48
2012	12959.68	2492.00	11983.52	7215.40	12525.39	771.68	1339.94
2013	12418.00	2664.13	12680.28	7609.51	12424.15	853.60	1450.55
2014	12853.05	2813.51	13376.72	7938.51	12833.70	904.60	1538.07
2015	12415.68	2875.05	14015.54	8306.78	12237.39	891.12	1559.68
2016	12420.96	2990.34	14467.36	8502.92	12367.54	946.06	1655.64

4－05　续表　continued

年份 Year	资产负债率(%) Ratio of Debts to Assets(%)	流动资产周转次数(次) Turnover of Current Assets(times)	成本费用利润率(%) Ratio of Profits to Costs(%)	全员劳动生产率(元/人) Overall Labor Productivity (Yuan/Person)	产品销售率(%) Rate of Production Sold (%)
1998	57.02	1.47	3.86	37976	95.91
1999	55.69	1.46	5.06	44307	98.07
2000	58.59	1.62	5.49	52713	97.19
2001	57.20	1.70	6.26	59518	97.40
2002	56.82	1.82	6.84	76402	97.76
2003	58.70	1.87	6.69	91284	97.68
2004	59.80	2.00	5.50	98809	98.10
2005	60.12	2.06	4.69	105786	98.25
2006	59.83	2.23	4.87	120289	98.36
2007	60.43	2.21	5.44	138016	98.17
2008	60.42	2.10	5.34	152070	98.14
2009	59.07	1.86	5.86	151002	98.63
2010	58.34	1.96	7.60	166516	98.83
2011	59.12	1.91	6.96	190110	98.61
2012	49.57	1.74	6.60	232587	98.63
2013	58.09	1.63	7.39	222570	99.18
2014	56.83	1.62	7.61	245726	98.48
2015	55.69	1.54	7.91	257020	98.50
2016	54.29	1.53	7.97	278384	99.43

4-06 分地区工业

Number of Industrial Enterprises

单位:个

项 目	Item	全 市 Whole City	市区 Urban District	上城区 Shangcheng	下城区 Xiacheng	江干区 Jianggan	拱墅区 Gongshu	西湖区 Xihu
规模以上工业合计	**Industrial above Designated Size**	**5684**	**4235**	**43**	**25**	**71**	**83**	**138**
一、按轻重工业分	**Grouped by Light & Heavy Industry**							
轻工业	Light Industry	2743	2025	17	7	31	31	49
重工业	Heavy Industry	2941	2210	26	18	40	52	89
二、按所有制分	**Grouped by Ownership**							
国有企业	State - owned Enterprises	15	11	2	-	-	-	1
集体企业	Collective - owned Enterprises	4	2	-	-	1	-	-
股份合作企业	Cooperative Enterprises	7	7	-	-	-	1	-
联营企业	Joint Ownership Enterprises	1	1	-	1	-	-	-
有限责任公司	Limited Liability Corporations	937	722	10	14	15	23	50
股份有限公司	Share - holding Corporations Ltd.	219	169	6	3	4	6	6
私营企业	Private Enterprises	3554	2492	15	4	38	43	62
外商及港澳台投资企业	Enterprises with Investment from Foreign、Hong Kong、Macao and Taiwan	946	831	10	3	13	10	19
其他企业	Other Enterprises	1	1	-	-	-	-	-
合计中:国有控股企业	Of the Total:Controlling Share Hold Enterprises	218	170	6	7	2	7	8
三、按企业规模分	**Grouped by Size of Enterprises**							
大型企业	Large	128	115	2	1	1	1	4
中型企业	Medium - sized	641	556	7	2	12	7	17
小微企业	Small	4915	3564	34	22	58	75	117

企业单位数（2016 年末）

by Region（End of 2016）

（unit）

高新（滨江）区 Hi－Tech（Binjiang）	萧山区 Xiaoshan	大江东产业集聚区 Dajiangdong Industry Cluster Distr	余杭区 Yuhang	富阳区 Fuyang	经济技术开发区 Economic and Technological Development Zone	西湖风景名胜区 The West Lake Scenic Zone	桐庐县 Tonglu	淳安县 Chun′an	建德市 Jiande	临安市 Lin′an
189	**1605**	**263**	**1152**	**641**	**316**	**2**	**379**	**121**	**344**	**605**
50	902	114	567	252	135	2	216	70	157	275
139	703	149	585	389	181	–	163	51	187	330
1	1	–	2	1	3	–	1	1	1	1
–	–	–	–	1	–	–	1	–	1	–
–	1	–	3	2	–	–	–	–	–	–
–	–	–	–	–	–	–	–	–	–	–
48	230	53	163	106	70	1	33	18	51	113
28	36	7	57	17	5	1	8	4	14	24
64	1028	142	756	442	47	–	275	89	266	432
48	309	61	171	72	191	–	61	9	11	34
–	–	–	–	–	–	–	–	–	–	–
21	34	12	34	23	29	1	11	4	14	19
18	41	11	14	6	29	–	3	–	2	8
33	202	47	143	59	81	–	22	14	15	34
138	1362	205	995	576	206	2	354	107	327	563

4－07 分地区工业

Gross Industrial

单位:万元

项 目	Item	全 市 Total	市 区 Urban District	上城区 Shangcheng
规模以上工业合计	**Industrial above Designated Size**	**124209589**	**105688299**	**7157725**
一、按轻重工业分	**Grouped by Light & Heavy Industry**			
轻工业	Light Industry	46939900	39331082	3464131
重工业	Heavy Industry	77269689	66357217	3693594
二、按所有制分	**Grouped by Ownership**			
国有企业	State－owned Enterprises	5534102	5061048	3314066
集体企业	Collective－owned Enterprises	12292	6629	－
股份合作企业	Cooperative Enterprises	46853	46853	－
联营企业	Joint Ownership Enterprises	4866	4866	－
有限责任公司	Limited Liability Corporations	37802068	33792529	3341996
股份有限公司	Share－holding Corporations Ltd.	11944766	9166962	289034
私营企业	Private Enterprises	36032209	26610626	102011
外商及港澳台投资企业	Enterprises with Investment from Foreign、Hong Kong、Macao and Taiwan	32828231	30998787	110619
其他企业	Other Enterprises	4202	4202	－
合计中:国有控股企业	Of the Total:Controlling Share Hold Enterprises	25281803	23690960	6528195
三、按企业规模分	**Grouped by Size of Enterprises**			
大型企业	Large	36510137	33568227	259759
中型企业	Medium－sized	35021956	30054055	229664
小微企业	Small	52677496	42066018	6668303

总产值(2016 年)
Output Value by Region(2016)

(10000 yuan)

下城区 Xiacheng	江干区 Jianggan	拱墅区 Gongshu	西湖区 Xihu	高新(滨江)区 Hi - Tech (Binjiang)	萧山区 Xiaoshan
516835	**1466385**	**1757644**	**2150363**	**13728664**	**37509136**
60214	207640	789945	797195	1495619	16614834
456621	1258745	967699	1353168	12233045	20894301
–	–	–	8965	7269	879508
–	4018	–	–	–	–
–	–	3168	–	–	15903
4866	–	–	–	–	–
263019	126100	1059365	699441	5852013	12668453
206293	47412	135108	58149	2778035	2612561
12539	292784	359620	579777	730901	12281144
30118	996071	200383	804030	4360447	9051567
–	–	–	–	–	–
270202	56856	912204	342548	6013610	6069217
198006	693109	551956	613605	8415211	11749796
45991	372369	568460	749574	2762071	12214715
272839	400907	637229	787184	2551382	13544624

单位:万元　　4－07　续表

项　目	Item	大江东产业集聚区 Dajiangdong Industry Cluster District	余杭区 Yuhang	富阳区 Fuyang
规模以上工业合计	**Industrial above Designated Size**	**11395498**	**14614942**	**11767415**
一、按轻重工业分	**Grouped by Light & Heavy Industry**			
轻工业	Light Industry	2831352	6055111	3197223
重工业	Heavy Industry	8564145	8559832	8570192
二、按所有制分	**Grouped by Ownership**			
国有企业	State－owned Enterprises	－	478058	344994
集体企业	Collective－owned Enterprises	－	－	2611
股份合作企业	Cooperative Enterprises	－	14123	13659
联营企业	Joint Ownership Enterprises	－	－	－
有限责任公司	Limited Liability Corporations	6052818	3531406	4131990
股份有限公司	Share－holding Corporations Ltd.	390718	2339309	610822
私营企业	Private Enterprises	2761211	5571259	5249787
外商及港澳台投资企业	Enterprises with Investment from Foreign、Hong Kong、Macao and Taiwan	2190751	2680788	1413552
其他企业	Other Enterprises	－	－	－
合计中:国有控股企业	Of the Total:Controlling Share Hold Enterprises	4332135	1278639	1625313
三、按企业规模分	**Grouped by Size of Enterprises**			
大型企业	Large	5898949	2547475	1567819
中型企业	Medium－sized	2923962	5129513	3294949
小微企业	Small	2572586	6937954	6904646

continued (10000 yuan)

经济技术开发区 Economic and Technological Development Zone	西湖风景名胜区 The West Lake Scenic Zone	桐庐县 Tonglu	淳安县 Chun'an	建德市 Jiande	临安市 Lin'an
19661835	**12266**	**4785360**	**2520175**	**4242487**	**6973267**
7127690	12266	2026105	1773688	1363355	2445670
12534145	–	2759255	746488	2879132	4527597
28188	–	99668	70426	122595	180366
–	–	2044	–	3619	–
–	–	–	–	–	–
–	–	–	–	–	–
6290188	8922	693717	324527	1260828	1730468
86895	3344	137777	141003	614144	1884880
1507941	–	2824077	1745045	2011183	2841279
11748622	–	1028079	239175	230118	332073
–	–	–	–	–	–
4389939	3344	565872	91417	452773	480781
10825972	–	510997	–	776198	1654715
5132613	–	1168643	1092743	940370	1766146
3703249	12266	3105721	1427432	2525919	3552406

4－08 分地区工业

Value of Industrial

单位:万元

项　目	Item	全　市 Total	市　区 Urban District	上城区 Shangcheng
规模以上工业合计	**Industrial above Designated Size**	**123496342**	**105191682**	**7457263**
一、按轻重工业分	**Grouped by Light & Heavy Industry**			
轻工业	Light Industry	46552044	39035484	3757508
重工业	Heavy Industry	76944298	66156197	3699755
二、按所有制分	**Grouped by Ownership**			
国有企业	State－owned Enterprises	5535519	5062465	3313892
集体企业	Collective－owned Enterprises	12280	6653	－
股份合作企业	Cooperative Enterprises	44509	44509	－
联营企业	Joint Ownership Enterprises	4866	4866	－
有限责任公司	Limited Liability Corporations	37771125	33791241	3635503
股份有限公司	Share－holding Corporations Ltd.	11905744	9175002	297426
私营企业	Private Enterprises	35559082	26252314	99298
外商及港澳台投资企业	Enterprises with Investment from Foreign、Hong Kong、Macao and Taiwan	32659115	30854631	111145
其他企业	Other Enterprises	4103	4103	－
合计中:国有控股企业	Of the Total:Controlling Share Hold Enterprises	25543291	23961377	6821993
三、按企业规模分	**Grouped by Size of Enterprises**			
大型企业	Large	36291930	33377117	262645
中型企业	Medium－sized	34701093	29770618	225949
小微企业	Small	52503320	42043947	6968669

销售产值(2016年)
Products Sales by Region(2016)

(10000 yuan)

下城区 Xiacheng	江干区 Jianggan	拱墅区 Gongshu	西湖区 Xihu	高新(滨江)区 Hi-Tech (Binjiang)	萧山区 Xiaoshan
501618	**1464919**	**1762340**	**2140459**	**13740053**	**36980467**
60988	219881	777558	799671	1441380	16283296
440630	1245038	984783	1340788	12298673	20697171
–	–	–	8604	7269	–
–	4043	–	–	–	–
–	–	3160	–	–	–
4866	–	–	–	–	–
239466	132610	1070137	711608	5898299	12435428
209855	51415	133674	55839	2757839	2619345
13329	294096	350178	569627	734939	12040267
34102	982755	205192	794781	4341708	8990711
–	–	–	–	–	–
273128	52412	924603	344246	5994733	6063066
200789	693109	542007	621927	8322038	11577562
45991	372239	587180	734898	2860596	11965285
254838	399572	633153	783633	2557419	13437620

项　目	Item	大江东产业集聚区 Dajiangdong Industry Cluster District	余杭区 Yuhang	富阳区 Fuyang
规模以上工业合计	**Industrial above Designated Size**	**11335530**	**14461903**	**11671791**
一、按轻重工业分	**Grouped by Light & Heavy Industry**			
轻工业	Light Industry	2788773	5955748	3174430
重工业	Heavy Industry	8546757	8506154	8497361
二、按所有制分	**Grouped by Ownership**			
国有企业	State－owned Enterprises	－	478119	344994
集体企业	Collective－owned Enterprises	－	－	2611
股份合作企业	Cooperative Enterprises	－	13428	12713
联营企业	Joint Ownership Enterprises	－	－	－
有限责任公司	Limited Liability Corporations	6020411	3483140	4088117
股份有限公司	Share－holding Corporations Ltd.	392186	2364370	605252
私营企业	Private Enterprises	2712038	5483051	5217282
外商及港澳台投资企业	Enterprises with Investment from Foreign、Hong Kong、Macao and Taiwan	2210894	2639795	1400822
其他企业	Other Enterprises	－	－	－
合计中:国有控股企业	Of the Total:Controlling Share Hold Enterprises	4354442	1313745	1604512
三、按企业规模分	**Grouped by Size of Enterprises**			
大型企业	Large	5864614	2542660	1562499
中型企业	Medium－sized	2857579	5065395	3259088
小微企业	Small	2613338	6853848	6850204

continued (10000 yuan)

经济技术开发区 Economic and Technological Development Zone	西湖风景名胜区 The West Lake Scenic Zone	桐庐县 Tonglu	淳安县 Chun'an	建德市 Jiande	临安市 Lin'an
19583201	**14911**	**4692450**	**2500396**	**4215587**	**6896228**
7033549	14911	1992237	1766578	1340179	2417567
12549652	–	2700213	733818	2875408	4478661
30079	–	99668	70426	122595	180366
–	–	2043	–	3584	–
–	–	–	–	–	–
–	–	–	–	–	–
6204842	11567	680948	321704	1260519	1716713
76643	3344	135095	125432	619128	1851088
1526826	–	2769488	1743496	1981550	2812235
11744812	–	1005208	239340	228212	331724
–	–	–	–	–	–
4313224	3344	556336	91417	453738	480424
10866756	–	494746	–	780528	1639539
5084954	–	1148444	1073527	940604	1767900
3631491	14911	3049261	1426869	2494455	3488789

4－09 全市规模以上工业

Main Economic Indicators of Industrial

单位:万元

项 目	Item	企业单位数(个) Number of Enterprises (unit)	亏损企业(个) Loss Making Enterprises (unit)	工业总产值(当年价格) Gross Industrial Output Value (current price)	新产品产值 Output of New Products
总 计	**Total**	**5684**	**831**	**124209589**	**46423002**
按隶属关系分	**Grouped by Subordination**				
中央属	Central	37	7	6108789	701156
省属	Provincial	46	8	7080860	628447
市属	Municipal	81	15	6245601	2170698
县(市)属	County and below	56	9	6630330	4495367
按所有制分	**Grouped by Ownership**				
国有企业	State－owned Enterprises	15		5534102	7358
集体企业	Collective－owned Enterprises	4		12292	
股份合作企业	Cooperative Enterprises	7	1	46853	5310
联营企业	Joint Ownership Enterprises	1		4866	
有限责任公司	Limited Liability Corporations	937	144	37802068	17735500
股份有限公司	Share－holding Corporations Ltd.	219	30	11944766	6260042
私营企业	Private Enterprises	3554	465	36032209	10393864
外商及港澳台投资企业	Enterprises with Investment from Foreign、Hong Kong、Macao and Taiwan	946	191	32828231	12020929
其他企业	Other Enterprises	1	－	4202	－
按企业规模分	**Grouped by Size of Enterprises**				
大型企业	Large	128	16	36510137	21251441
中型企业	Medium－sized	641	72	35021956	13936359
小微企业	Small	4915	743	52677496	11235202
按轻重工业分	**Grouped by Light & Heavy Industry**				
轻工业	Light Industry	2743	386	46939900	12176790
重工业	Heavy Industry	2941	445	77269689	34246212

企业主要经济指标(2016年)(一)
Enterprises Above Designated Size(2016)(Ⅰ)

(10000 yuan)

工业销售产值 Value of Industrial Products Sales	出口交货值 Export delivery value	实收资本 Total Capital Hold	国家资本 State Capital	个人资本 Personal Capital	港澳台资本 Hongkong, Macau and TaiWan Capital	外商资本 Foreign Capital	就业人员年平均人数(人) Annual Average Number of Staff and Workers (person)
123496342	**16866200**	**28398613**	**3495114**	**7259031**	**2411081**	**3649697**	**1074178**
6514458	13506	781252	386901	8531	139082	14495	12743
7057348	159333	1301712	604263	126710	106204	94613	21518
6294474	957423	1659674	743497	150786	40488	206551	49448
6511124	226412	1359287	891952	76786	41761	16189	21077
5535519		341365	333436				6378
12280		739					111
44509	7	9269		9142			1036
4866		100					65
37771125	3274708	7288517	1923798	1081126	185	28242	240826
11905744	1456695	5027132	580306	1822643	44059	35663	100875
35559082	4898749	6506021	7610	3900793	1619	4216	413046
32659115	7236041	9225452	649964	445309	2365218	3581576	311805
4103	–	18	–	18	–	–	36
36291930	5193277	8038968	1650848	1404590	777113	926528	263746
34701093	5372802	7928069	894821	1683414	606855	1095206	318916
52503320	6300121	12431576	949445	4171026	1027113	1627963	491516
46552044	7625299	9950821	761529	2649810	962120	1553030	501515
76944298	9240901	18447791	2733585	4609221	1448961	2096667	572663

项　目	Item	企业单位数(个) Number of Enterprises (unit)	亏损企业(个) Loss Making Enterprises (unit)	工业总产值(当年价格) Gross Industrial Output Value (current price)	新产品产值 Output of New Products
按市、县分	**Grouped by County**				
市　区	Urban District	4235	652	105688299	40304853
#萧山区	Xiaoshan	1605	213	37509136	14005227
余杭区	Yuhang	1152	194	14614942	5999995
富阳区	Fuyang	641	106	11767415	4196655
桐庐县	Tonglu	379	31	4785360	1882697
淳安县	Chun'an	121	7	2520175	484892
建德市	Jiande	344	20	4242487	1372892
临安市	Lin'an	605	121	6973267	2377667
按国民经济行业分	**Grouped by Economic Sector**				
采掘业	Mining and Quarrying	33	5	247898	38789
煤炭开采和洗选业	Coal Mining and Dressing	1		2065	
黑色金属矿采选业	Ferrous Metals Mining and Dressing	1	1		
有色金属矿采选业	Nonferrous Metals Mining and Dressing	5	1	53304	200
非金属矿采选业	Nonmetal Minerals Mining and Dressing	26	3	192529	38589
制造业	Manufacturing Industry	5565	813	114932841	46240446
农副食品加工业	Agricultural Products Processing	132	8	1340344	199080
食品制造业	Food Manufacturing	108	19	1862739	243807
酒、饮料和精制茶制造业	Wine, Beverage and Tea Manufacturing	53	3	2133012	323124
烟草制品业	Tobacco Processing	2		3111240	20951
纺织业	Textile Industry	708	79	8629586	1834376
纺织服装、服饰业	Textile Products and Costune Indnstry	313	62	2658900	550688
皮革、毛皮、羽毛及其制品和制鞋业	Leather. Furs. Downand Related and Shoes Products	134	25	1464462	256158
木材加工和木、竹、藤、棕、草制品业	Timber Processing, Bamboo, Cane, Palm Fiber and Straw Products	36	5	244931	67883
家具制造业	Furniture Manufacturing	80	10	1505087	790760

continued 1 (10000 yuan)

工业销售产值 Value of Industrial Products Sales	出口交货值 Export delivery value	实收资本 Total Capital Hold	国家资本 State Capital	个人资本 Personal Capital	港澳台资本 Hongkong, Macau and TaiWan Capital	外商资本 Foreign Capital	就业人员年平均人数(人) Annual Average Number of Staff and Workers (person)
105191682	13573351	24832109	3120873	6024556	2305112	3397480	898117
36980467	4036973	9953954	1518190	1891448	1124530	1173184	314251
14461903	2433633	3450704	195840	1217150	322343	305100	194098
11671791	709082	2759266	256702	937073	51630	199646	93341
4692450	1239679	851998	43603	289773	40571	73972	45814
2500396	165968	380273	49483	165847	17728	3405	17499
4215587	686523	768976	206925	227436	17837	36601	36590
6896228	1200679	1565256	74230	551420	29833	138238	76158
248916	–	93625	28799	29978	–	–	2381
2013		98		98			15
2201							5
52461		37580	24719	12861			658
192241		55947	4080	17019			1703
114234428	16866200	26367665	2288860	7200342	2338573	3587296	1051079
1362018	73291	210523		83624	29687	21367	10098
1827858	119273	650853	29807	120673	89433	191887	24360
2124299	27479	502532	18400	30633	60127	168826	15985
3412769	10872	69040		3630	1400		3061
8497114	1545845	1551664	7951	653632	159325	172225	115243
2654855	1320218	645138	3705	139358	282377	94521	60652
1451695	853711	240825	270	54397	29963	25607	24241
244577	40808	45611		21552	681	98	3513
1493641	604327	289388		67881	22366	84087	27468

单位:万元

4－09 续表2

项 目	Item	企业单位数(个) Number of Enterprises (unit)	亏损企业(个) Loss Making Enterprises (unit)	工业总产值(当年价格) Gross Industrial Output Value (current price)	新产品产值 Output of New Products
造纸和纸制品业	Paper Making and Paper Products	261	40	3453028	900598
印刷和记录媒介复制业	Printing and Record Media	84	22	572967	112264
文教、工美、体育和娱乐用品制造业	Cultural, Educational. Industrial Arts. Sports and Entertainment Goods	123	14	1742741	401484
石油加工、炼焦和核燃料加工业	Petroleum Processing, Coking and Nuclear Fuel Processing	12	3	74354	13514
化学原料和化学制品制造业	Raw Chemical Materials and Chemical Products	321	43	9323140	3127813
医药制造业	Medical and Pharmaceutical Products	88	10	4271423	1292015
化学纤维制造业	Chemical Fiber	110	12	4883759	1227639
橡胶和塑料制品业	Rubber and Plastic Products	284	31	5967579	1887035
非金属矿物制品业	Nonmetal Minerals Products	300	52	3948293	901207
黑色金属冶炼和压延加工业	Smelting and Processing of Ferrous Metals	87	17	1766703	309529
有色金属冶炼和压延加工业	Smelting and Processing of Nonferrous Metals	63	11	3441362	663261
金属制品业	Metals Products	333	53	4206338	1561834
通用设备制造业	Ordinary Machinery	491	69	8544425	4309836
专用设备制造业	For Special Purpose Equipment Manufacturing	223	37	1822282	708671
汽车制造业	Automobile Manufacturing	200	26	8668218	6637952
铁路、船舶、航空航天和其他运输设备制造业	Railway. watercraft. Avigation spaceflight and other Equipment Manufacturing	55	8	471474	130828
电气机械和器材制造业	Electric Equipment and Machinery	488	95	11372059	5834322
计算机、通信和其他电子设备制造业	Computers. Telecommunications and Other Electronic Equipment Manufacturing	296	40	14104825	10346989
仪器仪表制造业	Instruments and Meters Manufacturing	132	16	2371580	1214988
其他制造业	Other Manufacturing	22		263549	130798
废弃资源综合利用业	Multiple Utilization of Waste Resouces	25	2	709255	240522
金属制品、机械和设备修理业	Metal Products, Machinery and Equipment Repair	1	1	3189	522
电力、燃气及水的生产和供应业	Produotion and supply of electricity, gas & water	86	13	9028850	143767
电力、热力生产和供应业	Production and Supply of Electric Power and Hot Water	53	3	6702317	135454
燃气生产和供应业	Production and Supply of Gas	13	3	1946179	
水的生产和供应业	Production and Supply of Tap Water	20	7	380355	8313

continued 2 (10000 yuan)

工业销售产值 Value of Industrial Products Sales	出口交货值 Export delivery value	实收资本 Total Capital Hold	国家资本 State Capital	个人资本 Personal Capital	港澳台资本 Hongkong, Macau and TaiWan Capital	外商资本 Foreign Capital	就业人员年平均人数(人) Annual Average Number of Staff and Workers (person)
3431584	195088	749273	26073	362978	16877	25030	34897
564456	11239	196724	23339	50443	31137	2739	9116
1694208	375831	257348	396	54869	28983	92951	18619
73613	1269	12511		10715	334		538
9254677	999126	2134208	36066	305320	52276	238619	52198
4074680	366089	959422	174992	57679	20852	264130	35430
4745759	296166	1261873		375149	84989	82398	23713
5991858	827876	982227	91527	281092	36149	218804	52030
3915844	166664	870901	41435	361469	29222	137000	34332
1750300	27155	269298	5571	96262	22912	7172	8783
3431439	229728	373730	6875	79115	3026	21671	7631
4142437	598631	873408	32680	404486	129352	40334	44035
8388725	1321726	2214197	77171	649770	140148	336541	95475
1792231	439369	710485	40806	230024	107990	146983	31622
8629068	477277	2726261	1155726	279603	351660	290765	49312
453591	139464	155082	30020	42152	1000	10822	7221
11320110	1961337	3158849	139736	707501	223150	371705	98839
14164312	3428507	3521571	343961	1324790	367967	467578	122377
2377990	385442	640980	2352	289839	15192	66486	34121
276928	22382	23497		15845		5037	3865
688450		69247		45863		1615	2203
3345	10	1000				300	101
9012998	–	1937324	1177455	28710	72508	62401	20718
6703614		1056883	496730	19485	38700	9819	13258
1947662		435164	310993	1225	31308	52582	2341
361721		445277	369732	8000	2500		5119

4－10 全市规模以上工业

Main Economic Indicators of Industrial

单位：万元

项　目	Item	资产合计 Total Assets	流动资产合　计 Total Circulating Funds	应收账款 Receivables	存　货 Stock
总　　计	**Total**	**144673645**	**85029167**	**27731439**	**17305702**
按隶属关系分	**Grouped by Subordination**				
中　央　属	Central	6548893	3637448	834718	1891106
省　　属	Provincial	6123982	1653085	523781	286718
市　　属	Municipal	9522698	4903174	1289219	1330558
县(市)属	County and below	5887009	3756087	2065677	550929
按所有制分	**Grouped by Ownership**				
国有企业	State－owned Enterprises	2917443	174366	16453	23624
集体企业	Collective－owned Enterprises	13326	12287	1847	287
股份合作企业	Cooperative Enterprises	79138	64339	16357	5545
联营企业	Joint Ownership Enterprises	1044	980	364	527
有限责任公司	Limited Liability Corporations	44071078	24685528	9229749	5596092
股份有限公司	Share－holding Corporations Ltd.	26195650	13386117	4095735	2499387
私营企业	Private Enterprises	34624890	22522599	7150304	4798912
外商及港澳台投资企业	Enterprises with Investment from Foreign、Hong Kong、Macao and Taiwan	36768209	24181051	7219853	4380892
其他企业	Other Enterprises	2868	1899	777	437
按企业规模分	**Grouped by Size of Enterprises**				
大型企业	Large	44376862	26286593	10675549	4028095
中型企业	Medium－sized	40914091	24044783	6507024	4804457
小微企业	Small	59382693	34697791	10548866	8473151
按轻重工业分	**Grouped by Light & Heavy Industry**				
轻工业	Light Industry	52906218	31374041	7334958	7814560
重工业	Heavy Industry	91767427	53655126	20396481	9491142

企业主要经济指标(2016年)(二)
Enterprises Above Designated Size(2016)(Ⅱ)

(10000 yuan)

产成品 Finished Products	固定资产合计 Fixed Assets	累计折旧 Accumulated Depreciation	本年折旧 Depreciation of the year	负债合计 Total Liabilities	流动负债合计 Total Current Liabilities	非流动负债合计 Total Non－current Liabilities	所有者权益合计 Creditors´Equity
6826985	**30412722**	**24018492**	**3356665**	**78545323**	**67365455**	**10359573**	**65742928**
279507	1989196	1531132	195682	3418683	2428603	757492	3201006
130673	3277756	3327881	367863	3450763	1566334	1881668	2673219
713222	2301611	1712645	222301	5298071	4017519	1265760	4224627
206542	1609298	1076603	179484	4357816	3920894	436921	1529193
6901	2724159	2946537	324370	2058285	512853	1544917	859157
118	933	2430	215	6749	6734		6577
4242	6562	8445	863	44948	44889	60	34189
417	64	180	19	686	686		359
1815745	9504365	6743656	953203	27426095	22612933	4373380	16474049
1060792	3256185	2392387	315317	9817091	8047258	1713335	16372881
2091100	7395739	5412193	892429	21048819	19920770	865190	13400972
1847436	7523748	6512192	870193	18141354	16218038	1862691	18593173
235	969	473	57	1295	1295	-	1573
1618882	7320879	5276715	799674	22959238	19751175	3193837	21417622
1946194	9250618	7417477	1043769	21715449	18541114	2798535	18991194
3261909	13841225	11324300	1513221	33870636	29073166	4367201	25334112
2972197	11336678	9296993	1221646	26855896	24015493	2464385	25736717
3854787	19076044	14721499	2135019	51689427	43349962	7895188	40006211

单位:万元　　4－10　续表1

项　目	Item	资产合计 Total Assets	流动资产合　计 Total Circulating Funds	应收账款 Receivables	存　货 Stock
按市、县分	**Grouped by County**				
市　区	Urban District	127108552	75255365	24322366	15485009
#萧山区	Xiaoshan	47482582	24997809	7294221	5024977
余杭区	Yuhang	16736164	10230491	3565779	2245125
富阳区	Fuyang	15033432	8803004	2365934	1616369
桐庐县	Tonglu	4077110	2356919	802703	447737
淳安县	Chun′an	1478553	711434	229418	155701
建德市	Jiande	3626106	1616826	528448	296488
临安市	Lin′an	8383324	5088624	1848504	920768
按国民经济行业分	**Grouped by Economic Sector**				
采掘业	Mining and Quarrying	380963	207691	44440	13223
煤炭开采和洗选业	Coal Mining and Dressing	2301	726	299	134
黑色金属矿采选业	Ferrous Metals Mining and Dressing	2516	2436	1797	326
有色金属矿采选业	Nonferrous Metals Mining and Dressing	115135	44173	5223	3725
非金属矿采选业	Nonmetal Minerals Mining and Dressing	261012	160356	37121	9039
制造业	Manufacturing Industry	130918915	82743371	27436087	17220599
农副食品加工业	Agricultural Products Processing	929156	544597	184102	148424
食品制造业	Food Manufacturing	2700602	1599505	758623	226784
酒、饮料和精制茶制造业	Wine, Beverage and Tea Manufacturing	1752596	908279	254307	176096
烟草制品业	Tobacco Processing	3236095	2375615	390400	1711232
纺织业	Textile Industry	8415261	5035585	1028805	1184988
纺织服装、服饰业	Textile Products and Costune Indnstry	2527328	1615779	364560	407055
皮革、毛皮、羽毛及其制品和制鞋业	Leather. Furs. Downand Related and Shoes Products	1353392	985578	287688	256683
木材加工和木、竹、藤、棕、草制品业	Timber Processing, Bamboo, Cane, Palm Fiber and Straw Products	187477	106172	30858	25383
家具制造业	Furniture Manufacturing	1374150	988221	220553	153699

continued 1 (10000 yuan)

产成品 Finished Products	固定资产合计 Fixed Assets	累计折旧 Accumulated Depreciation	本年折旧 Depreciation of the year	负债合计 Total Liabilities	流动负债合计 Total Current Liabilities	非流动负债合计 Total Non - current Liabilities	所有者权益合计 Creditors´ Equity
6089969	26192005	20953534	2897595	69712477	59582636	9400379	57114795
2132965	10315681	7699836	1166697	27580919	23946116	3122963	19684593
931556	3906324	2560460	403025	9199411	8302073	852231	7514509
696539	3128494	2081944	336882	9401885	7934581	1392217	5593092
180325	1033088	716107	110043	2369159	2141248	204107	1636187
65253	475405	365633	56923	597412	485806	117843	856651
124976	1181483	952073	135981	1808760	1563985	228550	1809711
366462	1530741	1031145	156123	4057516	3591779	408694	4325584
6657	75146	46341	9419	205045	185970	18782	173401
117	689	312	110	849	849		1452
					2971		
2891	37389	6101	1086	40297	30729	7303	74838
3649	37069	39928	8223	163900	151422	11478	97111
6804363	24085134	18364658	2745112	70060280	63064841	6189119	60484485
59404	228949	109396	21762	541280	507079	31350	384065
114988	661114	387451	65656	1154776	1112725	38409	1545825
51802	686511	777982	91775	875882	830710	45107	876714
172695	461297	363102	47780	874107	873693	414	2361988
594488	2060564	2059213	273530	4965180	4679630	161484	3362987
215806	579793	392579	49475	1270080	1184173	58276	1257978
45196	184017	101706	15836	943963	919958	12593	404962
9869	40930	28079	4053	127822	125569	1957	59655
49725	232469	128644	20161	666303	663331	2130	706706

项 目	Item	资产合计 Total Assets	流动资产合计 Total Circulating Funds	应收账款 Receivables	存货 Stock
造纸和纸制品业	Paper Making and Paper Products	4696105	2774949	737994	428338
印刷和记录媒介复制业	Printing and Record Media	786222	428400	164038	82966
文教、工美、体育和娱乐用品制造业	Cultural,Educational. Industrial Arts. Sports and Entertainment Goods	888891	565545	112863	222400
石油加工、炼焦和核燃料加工业	Petroleum Processing, Coking and Nuclear Fuel Processing	67284	50430	18486	11916
化学原料和化学制品制造业	Raw Chemical Materials and Chemical Products	10508846	4927307	1021537	940001
医药制造业	Medical and Pharmaceutical Products	4869195	2829299	723183	707590
化学纤维制造业	Chemical Fiber	7188709	3517955	315114	663672
橡胶和塑料制品业	Rubber and Plastic Products	5322265	3040043	992292	671337
非金属矿物制品业	Nonmetal Minerals Products	5186646	3448726	1729855	410334
黑色金属冶炼和压延加工业	Smelting and Processing of Ferrous Metals	1504717	1024614	164645	286077
有色金属冶炼和压延加工业	Smelting and Processing of Nonferrous Metals	2540787	1793581	233509	426597
金属制品业	Metals Products	4117808	2729425	905380	824213
通用设备制造业	Ordinary Machinery	12022263	7741950	2597912	1642838
专用设备制造业	For Special Purpose Equipment Manufacturing	2711729	1830548	633664	441478
汽车制造业	Automobile Manufacturing	9552675	5951696	3369587	720699
铁路、船舶、航空航天和其他运输设备制造业	Railway. watercraft. Avigation spaceflight and other Equipment Manufacturing	542551	337342	108612	80144
电气机械和器材制造业	Electric Equipment and Machinery	13870272	9092297	3489220	1726029
计算机、通信和其他电子设备制造业	Computers. Telecommunications and Other Electronic Equipment Manufacturing	17310521	13030904	5514112	2071278
仪器仪表制造业	Instruments and Meters Manufacturing	3817849	2743769	989085	449568
其他制造业	Other Manufacturing	222141	177384	18953	32919
废弃资源综合利用业	Multiple Utilization of Waste Resouces	712714	545572	75645	88889
金属制品、机械和设备修理业	Metal Products, Machinery and Equipment Repair	2671	2307	504	972
电力、燃气及水的生产和供应业	Produotion and supply of electricity, gas & water	13373767	2078105	250912	71880
电力、热力生产和供应业	Production and Supply of Electric Power and Hot Water	9265095	1097788	173216	36294
燃气生产和供应业	Production and Supply of Gas	1375111	162989	37663	12649
水的生产和供应业	Production and Supply of Tap Water	2733561	817328	40034	22938

continued 2 (10000 yuan)

产成品 Finished Products	固定资产合计 Fixed Assets	累计折旧 Accumulated Depreciation	本年折旧 Depreciation of the year	负债合计 Total Liabilities	流动负债合计 Total Current Liabilities	非流动负债合计 Total Non－current Liabilities	所有者权益合计 Creditors´Equity
189336	981212	837187	127351	2940923	2813585	94288	1745175
37150	285873	285861	33087	450095	397160	51461	336125
57143	227012	189972	23180	465074	448398	16769	419529
5683	11098	11858	1517	39774	38874	900	27509
461161	2705891	1770612	289417	4977521	4310808	655362	5529412
259812	1050039	494107	87678	2193885	1777064	414894	2675309
341363	960615	1044017	113687	3695765	3175381	371572	3320789
384093	1421838	1414779	205235	2917091	2716346	191998	2402334
206854	1141815	1023881	134846	3415815	3220638	167194	1766557
117352	288647	313089	42653	858715	792197	64039	640722
109821	423608	295186	46233	1830332	1701992	110790	688380
265570	787790	537943	85909	2487985	2401207	65654	1617331
614734	1867231	1253602	203725	6155635	5506702	601816	5858377
133033	558800	409681	57678	1355058	1201849	139070	1343299
370817	2071475	1126893	261692	6937298	6087647	849339	2615375
29235	150437	80862	13870	317783	296918	15298	222902
873172	2138815	1396368	185637	6932241	5693537	1032186	6955206
853243	1448705	1151938	185413	8585194	7679868	848858	8725323
147997	324525	305008	41995	1445608	1364161	79293	2350664
13742	33386	25418	2984	98448	98448		123694
18933	70551	48130	11274	538306	442850	66617	159267
148	129	116	24	2344	2344		327
15964	6252442	5607494	602135	8279997	4114645	4151672	5085042
5965	4429863	4324563	465200	6029239	3082762	2936182	3227129
4262	791913	324431	57754	826689	447319	375986	548422
5738	1030666	958501	79180	1424070	584565	839505	1309491

4－11 全市规模以上工业

Main Economic Indicators of Industrial

单位:万元

项 目	Item	主营业务收入 Revenues in Main Business	主营业务成本 Costs in Main Business	主营业务税金及附加 Sales Taxes and Extra Charges in Main Business
总 计	**Total**	**123675449**	**98483041**	**2834976**
按隶属关系分	**Grouped by Subordination**			
中 央 属	Central	6344411	3652536	2035769
省 属	Provincial	7124624	6482799	23090
市 属	Municipal	6358042	4806194	39003
县(市)属	County and Below	5885430	4590802	221185
按所有制分	**Grouped by Ownership**			
国有企业	State－owned Enterprises	5543915	5286094	14749
集体企业	Collective－owned Enterprises	12280	10473	207
股份合作企业	Cooperative Enterprises	51169	43118	275
联营企业	Joint Ownership Enterprises	4866	4617	15
有限责任公司	Limited Liability Corporations	37455031	29244488	2351142
股份有限公司	Share－holding Corporations Ltd.	12581516	9492379	73092
私营企业	Private Enterprises	35373341	30282464	191382
外商及港澳台投资企业	Enterprises with Investment from Foreign、Hong Kong、Macao and Taiwan	32649228	24115760	204106
其他企业	Other Enterprises	4103	3648	8
按企业规模分	**Grouped by Size of Enterprises**			
大型企业	Large	36441169	27624830	397702
中型企业	Medium－sized	34652019	28089665	170675
小微企业	Small	52582262	42768546	2266598
按轻重工业分	**Grouped by Light & Heavy Industry**			
轻工业	Light Industry	46127502	34390418	2267424
重工业	Heavy Industry	77547947	64092623	567552

企业主要经济指标(2016 年)(三)
Enterprises Above Designated Size(2016)(Ⅲ)

(10000 yuan)

销售费用 Sales Expenses	管理费用 Management Expenses	财务费用 Financial Expenses	利息支出 Interest Expenditure	营业利润 Business Profits	利润总额 Total Profits	利税总额 Total Pre－tax Profits	本年应交增值税 Value Added Tax Payable
6003286	**7570830**	**1240878**	**1527342**	**8569266**	**9460607**	**16556419**	**4233991**
144951	198493	73539	71788	165829	160057	2703717	506629
70775	221618	12274	24271	313739	295722	496460	176696
669266	522091	83174	75559	248539	328040	585204	217296
58024	277361	64617	41769	701213	728479	1058064	108236
1843	61026	6637	7108	174451	132423	288998	139951
369	488	121	126	622	731	1202	263
774	4557	1599	625	893	2151	4246	1820
77	141	–		16	16	121	89
1412661	1953103	372824	444834	2513271	2704327	6352771	1294603
849575	1129037	111388	190437	1115317	1319431	1832773	439209
1015362	1879465	527484	561958	1674406	1824197	3061576	1043424
2722611	2542902	220756	322185	3090034	3477063	5014370	1314545
14	109	69	69	255	268	364	88
2661046	2474614	227234	313131	3350942	3799512	5396865	1181782
1659986	2227095	337710	473584	2478767	2755057	4084621	1156431
1682254	2869121	675934	740627	2739557	2906038	7074934	1895778
3437348	2659777	495866	664393	3202505	3519779	7919435	2126727
2565938	4911053	745013	862949	5366760	5940828	8636985	2107264

单位:万元　　4－11　续表1

项　目	Item	主营业务收　入 Revenues in Main Business	主营业务成　本 Costs in Main Business	主营业务税金及附加 Sales Taxes and Extra Charges in Main Business
按市、县分	**Grouped by County**			
市　区	Urban District	105877597	83593183	2736082
#萧山区	Xiaoshan	36699995	31384144	394430
余杭区	Yuhang	14466346	11698107	83630
富阳区	Fuyang	11528178	10060920	51269
桐庐县	Tonglu	4509390	3873347	18798
淳安县	Chun′an	2423511	2060715	15295
建德市	Jiande	4110558	3456103	25650
临安市	Lin′an	6754393	5499694	39152
按国民经济行业分	**Grouped by Economic Sector**			
采掘业	Mining and Quarrying	240603	177495	6423
煤炭开采和洗选业	Coal Mining and Dressing	2013	1527	156
黑色金属矿采选业	Ferrous Metals Mining and Dressing	2201	2204	
有色金属矿采选业	Nonferrous Metals Mining and Dressing	52974	39696	565
非金属矿采选业	Nonmetal Minerals Mining and Dressing	183416	134069	5702
制造业	Manufacturing Industry	114366467	89969668	2786614
农副食品加工业	Agricultural Products Processing	1398891	1229857	4407
食品制造业	Food Manufacturing	2128551	1605854	9699
酒、饮料和精制茶制造业	Wine, Beverage and Tea Manufacturing	2028869	1367168	36003
烟草制品业	Tobacco Processing	3146976	710276	2003494
纺织业	Textile Industry	8380404	7332812	39565
纺织服装、服饰业	Textile Products and Costune Indnstry	2567172	2168960	16139
皮革、毛皮、羽毛及其制品和制鞋业	Leather. Furs. Downand Related and Shoes Products	1416600	1255313	6169
木材加工和木、竹、藤、棕、草制品业	Timber Processing, Bamboo, Cane, Palm Fiber and Straw Products	239118	213340	1494
家具制造业	Furniture Manufacturing	1442265	1068292	10410

continued 1 (10000 yuan)

销售费用 Sales Expenses	管理费用 Management Expenses	财务费用 Financial Expenses	利息支出 Interest Expenditure	营业利润 Business Profits	利润总额 Total Profits	利税总额 Total Pre-tax Profits	本年应交增值税 Value Added Tax Payable
5331501	6616238	1082805	1352807	7481848	8286135	14710194	3663910
625989	1834550	532420	612784	2241472	2375679	3601704	828456
769933	1112498	134514	172867	860625	992648	1623836	546946
208022	521582	305393	322844	500120	584186	1027960	391949
121443	205814	38223	44116	260928	278335	432147	134446
89407	77449	17326	17799	181437	189594	275981	71063
182217	195096	36712	35847	243822	267484	427771	133734
278718	476233	65812	76772	401231	439060	710327	230838
7058	22321	6697	6534	19742	19460	37422	11512
2	142			186	185	433	92
	7	33	33	-41	-41	-41	
971	7532	1491	1518	2139	2164	6080	3325
6084	14640	5173	4982	17459	17153	30950	8095
5959039	7362087	1128977	1412534	7967500	8854610	15642831	3977987
49668	45561	16022	16151	58071	66866	102356	31074
291123	132236	7460	13058	77626	91185	193391	92491
414959	76169	10154	13153	149734	198729	334747	99883
86893	127175	1654	5324	255343	231085	2638719	404062
128648	377412	127490	157998	433300	446242	726054	239721
73275	202514	22328	29552	101713	119937	247646	111440
39024	56947	14655	23346	46891	49981	100489	44250
4051	11945	2820	3173	15268	16104	25224	7626
173338	77027	3461	13497	109769	125505	236499	100570

单位:万元　　4-11　续表2

项　目	Item	主营业务收入 Revenues in Main Business	主营业务成本 Costs in Main Business	主营业务税金及附加 Sales Taxes and Extra Charges in Main Business
造纸和纸制品业	Paper Making and Paper Products	3337068	2876514	23026
印刷和记录媒介复制业	Printing and Record Media	576399	482397	3085
文教、工美、体育和娱乐用品制造业	Cultural, Educational. Industrial Arts. Sports and Entertainment Goods	1692985	1533352	5774
石油加工、炼焦和核燃料加工业	Petroleum Processing, Coking and Nuclear Fuel Processing	74070	60263	670
化学原料和化学制品制造业	Raw Chemical Materials and Chemical Products	9486772	7524494	28513
医药制造业	Medical and Pharmaceutical Products	3997787	1759841	39858
化学纤维制造业	Chemical Fiber	4609419	4242237	9672
橡胶和塑料制品业	Rubber and Plastic Products	5824227	4996523	32927
非金属矿物制品业	Nonmetal Minerals Products	3831098	3280121	18850
黑色金属冶炼和压延加工业	Smelting and Processing of Ferrous Metals	1781796	1639717	5413
有色金属冶炼和压延加工业	Smelting and Processing of Nonferrous Metals	3417096	3183364	4522
金属制品业	Metals Products	4119529	3590924	17290
通用设备制造业	Ordinary Machinery	8548447	6821351	47823
专用设备制造业	For Special Purpose Equipment Manufacturing	1823632	1372232	12086
汽车制造业	Automobile Manufacturing	8421251	6608849	264882
铁路、船舶、航空航天和其他运输设备制造业	Railway. watercraft. Avigation spaceflight and other Equipment Manufacturing	466000	334476	5120
电气机械和器材制造业	Electric Equipment and Machinery	11529023	9290126	54367
计算机、通信和其他电子设备制造业	Computers. Telecommunications and Other Electronic Equipment Manufacturing	14659611	10862504	64085
仪器仪表制造业	Instruments and Meters Manufacturing	2335147	1598628	16750
其他制造业	Other Manufacturing	354636	313722	1535
废弃资源综合利用业	Multiple Utilization of Waste Resouces	728488	643791	2978
金属制品、机械和设备修理业	Metal Products, Machinery and Equipment Repair	3143	2373	9
电力、燃气及水的生产和供应业	Produotion and supply of electricity, gas & water	9068379	8335878	41939
电力、热力生产和供应业	Production and Supply of Electric Power and Hot Water	6710383	6159796	35545
燃气生产和供应业	Production and Supply of Gas	1943136	1831872	3912
水的生产和供应业	Production and Supply of Tap Water	414860	344210	2482

continued 2 (10000 yuan)

销售费用 Sales Expenses	管理费用 Management Expenses	财务费用 Financial Expenses	利息支出 Interest Expenditure	营业利润 Business Profits	利润总额 Total Profits	利税总额 Total Pre - tax Profits	本年应交增值税 Value Added Tax Payable
80474	165240	114330	116770	94933	144794	318162	150172
15607	46296	8603	8882	23056	25255	46888	18397
27457	57724	12945	15765	51706	53201	90776	31392
4325	3881	790	773	4645	5056	7773	2047
568241	691316	122734	132402	635519	717750	1036865	290426
1191852	355473	5973	23619	664232	707858	1091903	341914
25833	105665	91322	131927	221279	228482	300134	61972
212816	277838	91329	68378	215287	235316	410811	142408
154021	191249	74735	79505	179085	194977	335363	121292
21606	44330	24297	25094	56197	58752	93594	29406
20383	57534	50118	62265	113813	120182	211675	86965
83476	223922	52664	55838	150728	161748	272933	93473
303147	728355	65208	89367	678004	727341	1095208	318847
97431	236767	15314	21492	108457	127858	209571	69079
144096	540273	102385	78507	758831	784804	1176877	126828
18620	51871	1447	4627	13865	19042	38044	13852
631725	774871	100854	131441	750977	827940	1183110	300166
910241	1383958	-15913	67695	1646787	1950206	2517843	488000
175588	297768	-1582	15764	267515	328071	461253	116411
5474	11376	-571	1787	23093	23764	35797	10332
4981	8537	5857	5290	62579	67218	103669	33406
668	854	94	96	-801	-635	-540	85
37189	186421	105205	108274	582023	586537	876166	244492
1614	117466	64321	64696	521143	487940	727867	202228
18555	30514	13293	13552	64173	67659	97536	25577
17020	38441	27591	30026	-3293	30938	50763	16687

4－12 分行业规模以上工业

Main Economic Beneficial Indicators of Industrial

行 业	Sector
总 计	**Total**
煤炭开采和洗选业	Coal Mining and Dressing
黑色金属矿采选业	Ferrous Metals Mining and Dressing
有色金属矿采选业	Nonferrous Metals Mining and Dressing
非金属矿采选业	Nonmetal Minerals Mining and Dressing
农副食品加工业	Agricultural Products Processing
食品制造业	Food Manufacturing
酒、饮料和精制茶制造业	Wine, Beverage and Tea Manufacturing
烟草制品业	Tobacco Processing
纺织业	Textile Industry
纺织服装、服饰业	Textile Products and Costune Indnstry
皮革、毛皮、羽毛及其制品和制鞋业	Leather. Furs. Downand Related and Shoes Products
木材加工和木、竹、藤、棕、草制品业	Timber Processing, Bamboo, Cane, Palm Fiber and Straw Products
家具制造业	Furniture Manufacturing
造纸和纸制品业	Paper Making and Paper Products
印刷和记录媒介复制业	Printing and Record Media
文教、工美、体育和娱乐用品制造业	Cultural, Educational. Industrial Arts. Sports and Entertainment Goods
石油加工、炼焦和核燃料加工业	Petroleum Processing, Coking and Nuclear Fuel Processing
化学原料和化学制品制造业	Raw Chemical Materials and Chemical Products
医药制造业	Medical and Pharmaceutical Products

企业主要经济效益指标(2016 年)

Enterprises Above Designated Size by Sector(2016)

每百元固定资产原值实现利税(元) Pre tax Profits per 100 Yuan Original Value of Fixed Assets (yuan)	每百元主营业务收入实现利税(元) Pre tax Profits per 100 yuan Revenues in Main Business (yuan)	产品销售率(%) Rate of Production Sold (%)	出口交货值占工业销售(%) Export delivery Value of the proportion of total sales value (%)	新产品产值率(%) New Product ratio (%)
31.53	**13.39**	**99.43**	**13.66**	**37.37**
43.24	21.50	97.46		
	-1.86			
14.19	11.48	98.42		0.38
35.05	16.87	99.85		20.04
31.41	7.32	101.62	5.38	14.85
18.77	9.09	98.13	6.53	13.09
23.28	16.50	99.59	1.29	15.15
320.19	83.85	109.69	0.32	0.67
18.04	8.66	98.46	18.19	21.26
25.97	9.65	99.85	49.73	20.71
36.70	7.09	99.13	58.81	17.49
39.62	10.55	99.86	16.69	27.72
70.12	16.40	99.24	40.46	52.54
18.13	9.53	99.38	5.69	26.08
8.26	8.13	98.51	1.99	19.59
22.80	5.36	97.22	22.18	23.04
34.87	10.49	99.00	1.72	18.17
23.56	10.93	99.27	10.80	33.55
74.09	27.31	95.39	8.98	30.25

4－12 续表

行 业	Sector
化学纤维制造业	Chemical Fiber
橡胶和塑料制品业	Rubber and Plastic Products
非金属矿物制品业	Nonmetal Minerals Products
黑色金属冶炼和压延加工业	Smelting and Processing of Ferrous Metals
有色金属冶炼和压延加工业	Smelting and Processing of Nonferrous Metals
金属制品业	Metals Products
通用设备制造业	Ordinary Machinery
专用设备制造业	For Special Purpose Equipment Manufacturing
汽车制造业	Automobile Manufacturing
铁路、船舶、航空航天和其他运输设备制造业	Railway. watercraft. Avigation spaceflight and other Equipment Manufacturing
电气机械和器材制造业	Electric Equipment and Machinery
计算机、通信和其他电子设备制造业	Computers. Telecommunications and Other Electronic Equipment Manufacturing
仪器仪表制造业	Instruments and Meters Manufacturing
其他制造业	Other Manufacturing
废弃资源综合利用业	Multiple Utilization of Waste Resouces
金属制品、机械和设备修理业	Metal Products, Machinery and Equipment Repair
电力、热力生产和供应业	Production and Supply of Electric Power and Hot Water
燃气生产和供应业	Production and Supply of Gas
水的生产和供应业	Production and Supply of Tap Water

continued

每百元固定资产原值实现利税（元）Pre tax Profits per 100 Yuan Original Value of Fixed Assets (yuan)	每百元主营业务收入实现利税（元）Pre tax Profits per 100 yuan Revenues in Main Business (yuan)	产品销售率(%) Rate of Production Sold (%)	出口交货值占工业销售(%) Export delivery Value of the proportion of total sales value (%)	新产品产值率(%) New Product ratio (%)
15.78	6.51	97.17	6.24	25.14
14.74	7.05	100.41	13.82	31.62
16.04	8.75	99.18	4.26	22.83
15.86	5.25	99.07	1.55	17.52
35.79	6.19	99.71	6.69	19.27
21.21	6.63	98.48	14.45	37.13
35.50	12.81	98.18	15.76	50.44
21.93	11.49	98.35	24.52	38.89
37.39	13.98	99.55	5.53	76.58
17.06	8.16	96.21	30.75	27.75
36.41	10.26	99.54	17.33	51.30
102.10	17.18	100.42	24.21	73.36
77.52	19.75	100.27	16.21	51.23
61.52	10.09	105.08	8.08	49.63
87.96	14.23	97.07		33.91
-220.67	-17.19	104.88	0.29	16.36
8.75	10.85	100.02		2.02
8.83	5.02	100.08		
2.65	12.24	95.10		2.19

4－13 市区规模以上工业

Main Economic Indicators of Industrial Enterprises

单位:万元

项　目	Item	企业单位数（个）Number of Enterprises (unit)	亏损企业(个) Loss Making Enterprises (unit)	工业总产值（当年价格）Gross Industrial Output Value (current price)	新产品产值 Output of New Products
总　　计	**Total**	**4235**	**652**	**105688299**	**40304853**
按隶属关系分	**Grouped by Subordination**				
中　央　属	Central	27	5	5887797	664093
省　　属	Provincial	39	7	6664988	620365
市　　属	Municipal	69	11	5505040	1825551
按所有制分	**Grouped by Ownership**				
国有企业	State－owned Enterprises	11		5061048	7358
集体企业	Collective－owned Enterprises	2		6629	
股份合作企业	Cooperative Enterprises	7	1	46853	5310
联营企业	Joint Ownership Enterprises	1		4866	
有限责任公司	Limited Liability Corporations	722	113	33792529	16090300
股份有限公司	Share－holding Corporations Ltd.	169	23	9166962	4777235
私营企业	Private Enterprises	2492	343	26610626	7993424
外商及港澳台投资企业	Enterprises with Investment from Foreign、Hong Kong、Macao and Taiwan	831	172	30998787	11431228
其他企业	Other Enterprises				
按企业规模分	**Grouped by Size of Enterprises**				
大型企业	Large	115	15	33568227	19658142
中型企业	Medium－sized	556	67	30054055	11905612
小微企业	Small	3564	570	42066018	8741099
按轻重工业分	**Grouped by Light & Heavy Industry**				
轻工业	Light Industry	2025	313	39331082	10141488
重工业	Heavy Industry	2210	339	66357217	30163366

企业主要经济指标(2016 年)(一)

Above Designated Size in Urban District(2016)(Ⅰ)

(10000 yuan)

工业销售产值 Value of Industrial Products Sales	出口交货值 Export delivery value	实收资本 Total Capital Hold	国家资本 State Capital	个人资本 Personal Capital	港澳台资本 Hongkong, Macau and TaiWan Capital	外商资本 Foreign Capital	就业人员年平均人数(人) Annual Average Number of Staff and Workers (person)
105191682	**13573351**	**24832109**	**3120873**	**6024556**	**2305112**	**3397480**	**898117**
6297166	13506	745780	365705	7281	137500	14495	10769
6642318	156422	1149388	466818	125728	106204	94613	20030
5558414	869922	1463091	720994	100271	40488	205775	45342
5062465		203286	202727				5077
6653		508					55
44509	7	9269		9142			1036
4866		100					65
33791241	2827755	6466166	1722565	894034	185	2913	200995
9175002	980564	4159239	547331	1422421	43155	35413	82615
26252314	3331903	5289509	2690	3283366	60	4216	317063
30854631	6433122	8704034	645560	415593	2261711	3354938	291211
33377117	4755063	7457038	1611840	1231704	777113	878911	239042
29770618	4545756	6942284	838141	1298224	591497	1034733	276177
42043947	4272532	10432787	670892	3494628	936502	1483837	382898
39035484	5568374	8697310	695965	2135418	898413	1444153	421427
66156197	8004977	16134800	2424908	3889138	1406699	1953327	476690

单位:万元 4-13 续表1

项 目	Item	企业单位数(个) Number of Enterprises (unit)	亏损企业(个) Loss Making Enterprises (unit)	工业总产值(当年价格) Gross Industrial Output Value (current price)	新产品产值 Output of New Products
按国民经济行业分	**Grouped by Economic Sector**				
采掘业	Mining and Quarrying	12	3	97899	15773
黑色金属矿采选业	Ferrous Metals Mining and Dressing	1	1		
有色金属矿采选业	Nonferrous Minerals Mining and Dressing	2		19733	200
非金属矿采选业	Nonmetal Minerals Mining and Dressing	9	2	78167	15573
制造业	Manufacturing Industry	4166	640	97248815	40145314
农副食品加工业	Agricultural Products Processing	56	6	650116	135455
食品制造业	Food Manufacturing	81	14	1626572	197459
酒、饮料和精制茶制造业	Wine, Beverage and Tea Manufacturing	32	2	1334850	103134
烟草制品业	Tobacco Processing	2		3111240	20951
纺织业	Textile Industry	556	68	7039799	1573797
纺织服装、服饰业	Textile Products and Costume Industry	212	56	1809580	343763
皮革、毛皮、羽毛及其制品和制鞋业	Leather. Furs. Downand Related and Shoes Products	110	23	1166513	191741
木材加工和木、竹、藤、棕、草制品业	Timber Processing, Bamboo, Cane, Palm Fiber and Straw Products	16	2	124611	42043
家具制造业	Furniture Manufacturing	57	8	1293679	723305
造纸和纸制品业	Paper Making and Paper Products	200	27	2856510	716734
印刷和记录媒介复制业	Printing and Record Media	74	18	532287	109635
文教、工美、体育和娱乐用品制造业	Cultural, Educational. Industrial Arts. Sports and Entertainment Goods	83	12	1519837	315533
石油加工、炼焦和核燃料加工业	Petroleum Processing, Coking and Nuclear Fuel Processing	10	3	58350	5970
化学原料和化学制品制造业	Raw Chemical Materials and Chemical Products	234	38	7788725	2581139

continued 1 (10000 yuan)

工业销售产值 Value of Industrial Products Sales	出口交货值 Export delivery value	实收资本 Total Capital Hold	国家资本 State Capital	个人资本 Personal Capital	港澳台资本 Hongkong, Macau and TaiWan Capital	外商资本 Foreign Capital	就业人员年平均人数(人) Annual Average Number of Staff and Workers (person)
99068	–	42618	4080	17930	–	–	938
2201							5
18922		8980		8980			296
77945		33638	4080	8950			637
96764887	13573351	23152587	2156450	5983346	2235232	3335080	879981
673294	48589	157418		56829	28818	21334	6575
1595896	73270	591235	24907	95402	76307	191453	20919
1330726	18408	387760		14960	59297	164468	11792
3412769	10872	69040		3630	1400		3061
6918540	1207925	1464921	7951	605490	147951	172225	101391
1817901	816785	560777	3705	100413	277250	87003	51490
1153649	615970	218282	270	50505	29593	24440	19083
125096	22803	31444		14619			2187
1284597	446455	243406		48593	21060	61612	24010
2847621	77097	537711	26073	255803	8874	10010	27843
523877	6889	189870	23339	44089	31137	2739	8439
1475606	281973	238838	396	44977	25854	92544	15677
57452	804	10099		9715			362
7723335	685943	1792427	23597	236650	34389	198405	41537

单位:万元

4-13 续表2

项目	Item	企业单位数(个) Number of Enterprises (unit)	亏损企业(个) Loss Making Enterprises (unit)	工业总产值(当年价格) Gross Industrial Output Value (current price)	新产品产值 Output of New Products
医药制造业	Medical and Pharmaceutical Products	74	9	3818708	955658
化学纤维制造业	Chemical Fiber	107	12	4841242	1225419
橡胶和塑料制品业	Rubber and Plastic Products	219	28	4831002	1475526
非金属矿物制品业	Nonmetal Mineral Products	200	32	2807918	598397
黑色金属冶炼和压延加工业	Smelting and Processing of Ferrous Metals	74	16	1627309	279187
有色金属冶炼和压延加工业	Smelting and Processing of Nonferrous Metals	43	8	3281869	654255
金属制品业	Metal Products	241	42	3606398	1455470
通用设备制造业	Ordinary Machinery	388	51	6788688	3476633
专用设备制造业	For Special Purpose Equipment Manufacturing	195	34	1670455	652946
汽车制造业	Automobile Manufacturing	182	26	8461661	6542461
铁路、船舶、航空航天和其他运输设备制造业	Railway. watercraft. Avigation spaceflight and other Equipment Manufacturing	43	7	395678	106894
电气机械和器材制造业	Electric Equipment and Machinery	293	49	8800666	4611732
计算机、通信和其他电子设备制造业	Computers. Telecommunications and Other Electronic Equipment Manufacturing	231	32	12726734	9687410
仪器仪表制造业	Instruments and Meters Manufacturing	128	16	2333551	1212877
其他制造业	Other Manufacturing	20		249925	122598
废弃资源综合利用业	Multiple Utilization of Waste Resouces	4		91154	26673
金属制品、机械和设备修理业	Metal Products, Machinery and Equipment Repair	1	1	3189	522
电力、燃气及水的生产和供应业	Produotion and supply of electricity, gas & water	57	9	8341585	143767
电力、热力生产和供应业	Production and Supply of Electric Power and Hot Water	35	2	6064582	135454
燃气生产和供应业	Production and Supply of Gas	7	1	1916250	
水的生产和供应业	Production and Supply of Tap Water	15	6	360754	8313

continued 2 (10000 yuan)

工业销售产值 Value of Industrial Products Sales	出口交货值 Export delivery value	实收资本 Total Capital Hold	国家资本 State Capital	个人资本 Personal Capital	港澳台资本 Hongkong, Macau and TaiWan Capital	外商资本 Foreign Capital	就业人员年平均人数(人) Annual Average Number of Staff and Workers (person)
3630843	274215	862084	174992	48542	13079	224837	30387
4704711	296166	1256673		371809	84989	82398	23315
4865130	757702	867944	56304	250257	23962	216684	39599
2778272	149434	582900	8120	243848	26256	76607	25033
1612064	19811	254948	5571	90208	22912	7172	7874
3272919	223106	356320	6875	66769	3026	21671	6756
3555241	453392	764899	32680	349550	125191	40234	35654
6651462	1101676	1749994	58668	531951	136818	326954	79638
1645057	416926	665837	33806	197731	104730	146796	28883
8426726	469651	2684777	1155726	265211	351660	290765	47116
376988	136918	147467	30000	38027	1000	10572	6030
8799114	1330315	2487527	137156	362650	221114	354836	71900
12813991	3224877	3313115	343961	1271786	363370	437498	104808
2338746	385442	630180	2352	287839	15192	66486	33942
263403	19930	23147		15495		5037	3779
86520		10550		10000			800
3345	10	1000				300	101
8327727	–	1636905	960343	23280	69880	62401	17198
6067846		834082	321907	14055	38700	9819	10474
1917896		403836	308993	1225	28680	52582	2101
341984		398987	329443	8000	2500		4623

4-14 市区规模以上工业
Main Economic Indicators of Industrial

单位:万元

项 目	Item	资产合计 Total Assets	流动资产合计 Total Circulating Funds	应收账款 Receivables	存货 Stock
总 计	**Total**	**127108552**	**75255365**	**24322366**	**15485009**
按隶属关系分	**Grouped by Subordination**				
中 央 属	Central	6355619	3547283	785913	1877353
省 属	Provincial	5753113	1611827	520577	281774
市 属	Municipal	8136579	4151752	1063437	1198252
按所有制分	**Grouped by Ownership**				
国有企业	State - owned Enterprises	2557794	145549	16305	23128
集体企业	Collective - owned Enterprises	8806	8117	810	5
股份合作企业	Cooperative Enterprises	79138	64339	16357	5545
联营企业	Joint Ownership Enterprises	1044	980	364	527
有限责任公司	Limited Liability Corporations	40386043	22670647	8463165	5283654
股份有限公司	Share - holding Corporations Ltd.	21060403	10800365	3302195	2124604
私营企业	Private Enterprises	28027547	18338567	5569724	3878676
外商及港澳台投资企业	Enterprises with Investment from Foreign、Hong Kong、Macao and Taiwan	34987778	23226801	6953446	4168871
其他企业	Other Enterprises				
按企业规模分	**Grouped by Size of Enterprises**				
大型企业	Large	40659774	24383032	9984006	3783975
中型企业	Medium - sized	35338038	21015694	5650100	4230157
小微企业	Small	51110741	29856640	8688260	7470877
按轻重工业分	**Grouped by Light & Heavy Industry**				
轻工业	Light Industry	46522120	27819063	6154998	7095861
重工业	Heavy Industry	80586432	47436303	18167368	8389147

企业主要经济指标(2016 年)(二)

Enterprises Above Designated Size in Urban District(2016)(Ⅱ)

(10000 yuan)

产成品 Finished Products	固定资产合计 Fixed Assets	累计折旧 Accumulated Depreciation	本年折旧 Depreciation of the year	负债合计 Total Liabilities	流动负债合计 Total Current Liabilities	非流动负债合计 Total Non - current Liabilities	所有者权益合计 Creditors´Equity
6089969	**26192005**	**20953534**	**2897595**	**69712477**	**59582636**	**9400379**	**57114795**
271338	1889225	1312598	184254	3267461	2292022	742856	3158953
127975	2955660	3091336	333791	3293615	1484632	1806222	2459498
664752	2121056	1639746	210158	4612584	3528773	1069135	3523994
6705	2399508	2686708	290649	1919986	459147	1460323	637808
4	689	1183	111	5945	5945		2861
4242	6562	8445	863	44948	44889	60	34189
417	64	180	19	686	686		359
1682646	8352657	5746805	833138	25360344	20763316	4170107	14872198
891471	2564403	2027626	254248	7996669	6611188	1326390	13061866
1768246	5735332	4326660	693594	17117424	16276657	659364	10813320
1736238	7132792	6155928	824974	17266476	15420810	1784135	17692193
1508984	6685546	4926634	737907	21453097	18530663	2908208	19206676
1747711	8043372	6377259	895021	19089148	16243545	2488661	16041443
2833274	11463088	9649641	1264667	29170232	24808429	4003510	21866677
2665329	9934912	8304513	1059297	23850842	21327504	2173078	22410032
3424640	16257093	12649021	1838298	45861635	38255133	7227301	34704763

单位:万元　　　　4－14　续表1

项　目	Item	资产合计 Total Assets	流动资产合　计 Total Circulating Funds	应收账款 Receivables	存　货 Stock
按国民经济行业分	**Grouped by Economic Sector**				
采掘业	Mining and Quarrying	220343	141206	26967	6003
黑色金属矿采选业	Ferrous Metals Mining and Dressing	2516	2436	1797	326
有色金属矿采选业	Nonferrous Minerals Mining and Dressing	23424	12992	2819	1901
非金属矿采选业	Nonmetal Minerals Mining and Dressing	194403	125778	22351	3776
制造业	Manufacturing Industry	114431847	73235755	24073418	15417763
农副食品加工业	Agricultural Products Processing	584394	320925	93596	83565
食品制造业	Food Manufacturing	2470833	1477958	730562	193915
酒、饮料和精制茶制造业	Wine, Beverage and Tea Manufacturing	1247625	716247	188923	109555
烟草制品业	Tobacco Processing	3236095	2375615	390400	1711232
纺织业	Textile Industry	7822336	4644646	911719	1096850
纺织服装、服饰业	Textile Products and Costume Industry	2099519	1371553	285161	353127
皮革、毛皮、羽毛及其制品和制鞋业	Leather. Furs. Downand Related and Shoes Products	1163851	889010	238105	231307
木材加工和木、竹、藤、棕、草制品业	Timber Processing, Bamboo, Cane, Palm Fiber and Straw Products	135577	74292	16903	16763
家具制造业	Furniture Manufacturing	1244392	900010	195136	132176
造纸和纸制品业	Paper Making and Paper Products	3622620	2392244	625994	338817
印刷和记录媒介复制业	Printing and Record Media	733818	397418	158346	77931
文教、工美、体育和娱乐用品制造业	Cultural, Educational. Industrial Arts. Sports and Entertainment Goods	786950	501715	89080	211137
石油加工、炼焦和核燃料加工业	Petroleum Processing, Coking and Nuclear Fuel Processing	52955	40400	15366	8691
化学原料和化学制品制造业	Raw Chemical Materials and Chemical Products	8586873	4051494	761626	795099

continued 1 (10000 yuan)

产成品 Finished Products	固定资产合计 Fixed Assets	累计折旧 Accumulated Depreciation	本年折旧 Depreciation of the year	负债合计 Total Liabilities	流动负债合计 Total Current Liabilities	非流动负债合计 Total Non - current Liabilities	所有者权益合计 Creditors´Equity
3201	27648	22573	5894	140113	130077	10043	77714
					2971		
1560	3516	3311	421	12214	10249		11211
1641	24132	19261	5473	127900	116857	10043	66503
6077631	20568463	15934837	2349930	61755674	55599318	5437185	52406136
34765	144139	78158	14012	334050	307364	26648	250343
102101	600662	354547	59863	1069791	1033095	35945	1401041
35156	448630	556296	57986	628813	618496	10317	618812
172695	461297	363102	47780	874107	873693	414	2361988
555733	1905309	1933178	250816	4646330	4382257	153928	3095844
197694	474071	318665	38364	1027047	948803	53591	1073851
37431	156421	82875	13126	844662	821643	9644	319188
6222	25885	19055	2450	91475	90402	1073	44102
44429	204205	112386	17896	612506	610917	589	631885
147867	750548	706051	100191	2506359	2427160	53968	1116258
35394	269381	269636	31092	412304	360527	50703	321512
52348	200559	171092	19940	405894	389244	16034	381056
4322	7163	9086	1157	35373	34473	900	17582
376859	2294435	1456935	246098	4105623	3515003	578953	4481247

单位:万元

4－14 续表 2

项 目	Item	资产合计 Total Assets	流动资产合计 Total Circulating Funds	应收账款 Receivables	存货 Stock
医药制造业	Medical and Pharmaceutical Products	4462285	2563800	655496	657846
化学纤维制造业	Chemical Fiber	7166180	3509428	313702	660964
橡胶和塑料制品业	Rubber and Plastic Products	4685380	2765731	890126	619577
非金属矿物制品业	Nonmetal Mineral Products	3965768	2815766	1471284	333658
黑色金属冶炼和压延加工业	Smelting and Processing of Ferrous Metals	1433372	977638	145497	277679
有色金属冶炼和压延加工业	Smelting and Processing of Nonferrous Metals	2451262	1731643	209497	410439
金属制品业	Metal Products	3588601	2391247	780831	747603
通用设备制造业	Ordinary Machinery	9520520	6216110	2007952	1310836
专用设备制造业	For Special Purpose Equipment Manufacturing	2559458	1732360	608836	409305
汽车制造业	Automobile Manufacturing	9375797	5837190	3342165	703471
铁路、船舶、航空航天和其他运输设备制造业	Railway. watercraft. Avigation spaceflight and other Equipment Manufacturing	486567	299889	93726	68546
电气机械和器材制造业	Electric Equipment and Machinery	10534938	6870590	2569762	1396281
计算机、通信和其他电子设备制造业	Computers. Telecommunications and Other Electronic Equipment Manufacturing	16307945	12406022	5245232	1973865
仪器仪表制造业	Instruments and Meters Manufacturing	3790727	2722900	980653	443115
其他制造业	Other Manufacturing	211434	171764	16959	31961
废弃资源综合利用业	Multiple Utilization of Waste Resouces	101106	67843	40275	11480
金属制品、机械和设备修理业	Metal Products, Machinery and Equipment Repair	2671	2307	504	972
电力、燃气及水的生产和供应业	Produotion and supply of electricity, gas & water	12456362	1878404	221981	61242
电力、热力生产和供应业	Production and Supply of Electric Power and Hot Water	8574417	994659	155953	32733
燃气生产和供应业	Production and Supply of Gas	1320950	152541	35812	11958
水的生产和供应业	Production and Supply of Tap Water	2560995	731205	30217	16552

continued 2　　　　(10000 yuan)

产成品 Finished Products	固定资产合计 Fixed Assets	累计折旧 Accumulated Depreciation	本年折旧 Depreciation of the year	负债合计 Total Liabilities	流动负债合计 Total Current Liabilities	非流动负债合计 Total Non－current Liabilities	所有者权益合计 Creditors´Equity
239570	985392	444781	80755	2020438	1620354	398287	2441846
339152	958967	1038512	113020	3683868	3170863	371572	3310158
360636	1143828	1216114	169647	2557964	2389687	163174	2127413
171919	772447	682685	89725	2688994	2588678	84755	1276772
112448	270416	298634	40559	817544	748879	62670	615170
105436	407708	285128	44929	1797537	1659328	110308	649427
228797	658647	437361	70548	2128246	2059854	54997	1456470
515617	1450257	1050788	168353	4885556	4440357	416650	4626930
114793	518387	384551	52830	1280167	1128212	137909	1265919
363917	2019419	1102907	257768	6862639	6014534	847824	2513156
26790	136032	70158	12059	279354	263374	13350	205347
722294	1742818	1113869	141144	5574728	4501835	856690	4994819
809156	1200273	1044386	161933	7999240	7096282	847384	8308702
144140	322622	302745	41628	1433937	1352875	78907	2335214
13238	28405	24513	2745	92654	92654		118780
6566	10013	6529	1496	56129	56129		44976
148	129	116	24	2344	2344		327
9137	5595894	4996124	541772	7816689	3853242	3953152	4630945
5068	3855986	3758264	411125	5684390	2878322	2795772	2881301
4069	762131	317142	55553	799800	433654	366146	521149
	977777	920719	75094	1332500	541266	791234	1228495

4－15 市区规模以上工业

Main Economic Indicators of Industrial

单位:万元

项 目	Item	主营业务收入 Revenues in Main Business	主营业务成本 Costs in Main Business	主营业务税金及附加 Sales Taxes and Extra Charges in Main Business
总 计	**Total**	**105877597**	**83593183**	**2736082**
按隶属关系分	**Grouped by Subordination**			
中 央 属	Central	6125976	3473619	2034413
省 属	Provincial	6710401	6145228	20187
市 属	Municipal	5656046	4205150	36106
按所有制分	**Grouped by Ownership**			
国有企业	State－owned Enterprises	5070862	4879863	12085
集体企业	Collective－owned Enterprises	6653	5247	188
股份合作企业	Cooperative Enterprises	51169	43118	275
联营企业	Joint Ownership Enterprises	4866	4617	15
有限责任公司	Limited Liability Corporations	33693653	26094919	2330409
股份有限公司	Share－holding Corporations Ltd.	9811463	7241908	57151
私营企业	Private Enterprises	26329856	22639321	144815
外商及港澳台投资企业	Enterprises with Investment from Foreign、Hong Kong、Macao and Taiwan	30909076	22684190	191144
其他企业	Other Enterprises	－	－	－
按企业规模分	**Grouped by Size of Enterprises**			
大型企业	Large	33580429	25146808	384510
中型企业	Medium－sized	29915828	24379423	139501
小微企业	Small	42381341	34066952	2212071
按轻重工业分	**Grouped by Light & Heavy Industry**			
轻工业	Light Industry	38831641	28431964	2217985
重工业	Heavy Industry	67045957	55161219	518097

企业主要经济指标(2016 年)(三)

Enterprises Above Designated Size in Urban District(2016)(Ⅲ)

(10000 yuan)

销售费用 Sales Expenses	管理费用 Management Expenses	财务费用 Financial Expenses	利息支出 Interest Expenditure	营业利润 Business Profits	利润总额 Total Profits	利税总额 Total Pre－tax Profits	本年应交增值税 Value Added Tax Payable
5331501	**6616238**	**1082805**	**1352807**	**7481848**	**8286135**	**14710194**	**3663910**
137368	192456	71351	69575	143624	137372	2664081	491050
69902	166124	7562	19483	301259	283440	452842	148771
646877	457255	72352	65530	245379	321290	554533	196600
1720	8902	2971	3374	166197	124763	250536	112181
316	307	76	76	520	596	944	161
774	4557	1599	625	893	2151	4246	1820
77	141	–		16	16	121	89
1317086	1756811	344446	414874	2241792	2412512	5903247	1158492
732495	927006	79479	149734	930157	1107869	1534067	368710
657310	1480495	446129	480468	1136305	1251772	2168349	769996
2621723	2438020	208104	303656	3005968	3386456	4848683	1252461
–	–	–	–	–	–	–	–
2535514	2309865	210007	289180	3267878	3696923	5218187	1118887
1400922	1929631	309646	437392	2024694	2270286	3378747	966739
1395065	2376743	563151	626236	2189276	2318926	6113260	1578285
3049070	2347471	433099	589353	2649754	2927463	7030768	1880533
2282431	4268768	649706	763454	4832094	5358672	7679426	1783377

单位:万元

4－15 续表1

项　目	Item	主营业务收　入 Revenues in Main Business	主营业务成　本 Costs in Main Business	主营业务税金及附加 Sales Taxes and Extra Charges in Main Business
按国民经济行业分	**Grouped by Economic Sector**			
采掘业	Mining and Quarrying	97714	65147	3051
黑色金属矿采选业	Ferrous Metals Mining and Dressing	2201	2204	
有色金属矿采选业	Nonferrous Minerals Mining and Dressing	18922	14555	189
非金属矿采选业	Nonmetal Minerals Mining and Dressing	76591	48388	2862
制造业	Manufacturing Industry	97396558	75739691	2695129
农副食品加工业	Agricultural Products Processing	724183	622798	2222
食品制造业	Food Manufacturing	1884569	1408011	8594
酒、饮料和精制茶制造业	Wine, Beverage and Tea Manufacturing	1312506	897466	23820
烟草制品业	Tobacco Processing	3146976	710276	2003494
纺织业	Textile Industry	6839156	5954116	32850
纺织服装、服饰业	Textile Products and Costume Industry	1747847	1443229	11743
皮革、毛皮、羽毛及其制品和制鞋业	Leather. Furs. Downand Related and Shoes Products	1130633	1016201	5010
木材加工和木、竹、藤、棕、草制品业	Timber Processing, Bamboo, Cane, Palm Fiber and Straw Products	124246	112653	858
家具制造业	Furniture Manufacturing	1234989	892283	9488
造纸和纸制品业	Paper Making and Paper Products	2778853	2424730	19732
印刷和记录媒介复制业	Printing and Record Media	533302	444449	2909
文教、工美、体育和娱乐用品制造业	Cultural, Educational. Industrial Arts. Sports and Entertainment Goods	1479409	1358016	4692
石油加工、炼焦和核燃料加工业	Petroleum Processing, Coking and Nuclear Fuel Processing	58013	48906	345
化学原料和化学制品制造业	Raw Chemical Materials and Chemical Products	7950580	6209773	23234

continued 1 (10000 yuan)

销售费用 Sales Expenses	管理费用 Management Expenses	财务费用 Financial Expenses	利息支出 Interest Expenditure	营业利润 Business Profits	利润总额 Total Profits	利税总额 Total Pre - tax Profits	本年应交增值税 Value Added Tax Payable
4886	10574	4940	4780	8831	8879	15792	3861
	7	33	33	-41	-41	-41	
823	1917	797	797	641	623	2376	1564
4063	8650	4110	3950	8231	8297	13457	2298
5292989	6482926	981699	1249012	6951452	7750984	13928819	3460904
37299	32072	8841	9233	23732	30928	50621	17468
277110	120062	5033	10586	60731	72692	166567	85265
275828	58504	6668	8954	69227	108456	189428	57021
86893	127175	1654	5324	255343	231085	2638719	404062
109197	344156	113415	144157	335532	347261	582704	202141
64463	176317	14684	21625	54387	71354	170267	87055
28785	47474	12525	21853	23124	25292	65174	34782
2281	8234	2036	2368	7970	8477	13266	3931
165232	66666	3829	12463	97257	112569	216115	94044
53679	122680	108106	107335	65211	104494	254139	129770
14609	43799	8017	8217	22203	24281	44592	17252
20331	49354	11249	14187	36222	37393	67097	24717
3016	2252	585	577	3365	3551	5235	1339
512839	586398	108866	114798	565835	635518	917604	258683

单位:万元 4-15 续表2

项 目	Item	主营业务收入 Revenues in Main Business	主营业务成本 Costs in Main Business	主营业务税金及附加 Sales Taxes and Extra Charges in Main Business
医药制造业	Medical and Pharmaceutical Products	3559881	1555198	35862
化学纤维制造业	Chemical Fiber	4568369	4204628	9554
橡胶和塑料制品业	Rubber and Plastic Products	4698958	3982703	29172
非金属矿物制品业	Nonmetal Mineral Products	2813267	2438458	12477
黑色金属冶炼和压延加工业	Smelting and Processing of Ferrous Metals	1648514	1515878	4821
有色金属冶炼和压延加工业	Smelting and Processing of Nonferrous Metals	3259591	3043771	3739
金属制品业	Metal Products	3550977	3105764	13781
通用设备制造业	Ordinary Machinery	6856257	5389298	39714
专用设备制造业	For Special Purpose Equipment Manufacturing	1684836	1276752	11039
汽车制造业	Automobile Manufacturing	8237020	6457116	263802
铁路、船舶、航空航天和其他运输设备制造业	Railway. watercraft. Avigation spaceflight and other Equipment Manufacturing	390169	270425	4723
电气机械和器材制造业	Electric Equipment and Machinery	9001544	7196899	39515
计算机、通信和其他电子设备制造业	Computers. Telecommunications and Other Electronic Equipment Manufacturing	13446154	9826527	60091
仪器仪表制造业	Instruments and Meters Manufacturing	2296275	1564939	15924
其他制造业	Other Manufacturing	341125	302353	1461
废弃资源综合利用业	Multiple Utilization of Waste Resouces	95215	63705	456
金属制品、机械和设备修理业	Metal Products, Machinery and Equipment Repair	3143	2373	9
电力、燃气及水的生产和供应业	Produotion and supply of electricity, gas & water	8383325	7788345	37901
电力、热力生产和供应业	Production and Supply of Electric Power and Hot Water	6076865	5652813	31785
燃气生产和供应业	Production and Supply of Gas	1911916	1805362	3781
水的生产和供应业	Production and Supply of Tap Water	394545	330170	2335

continued 2 (10000 yuan)

销售费用 Sales Expenses	管理费用 Management Expenses	财务费用 Financial Expenses	利息支出 Interest Expenditure	营业利润 Business Profits	利润总额 Total Profits	利税总额 Total Pre - tax Profits	本年应交增值税 Value Added Tax Payable
1106550	315009	6411	21156	562409	604735	950635	307794
25198	104315	90578	131815	220685	227861	298517	61095
193131	236794	84465	61451	174145	191469	335493	114692
112109	138637	60673	68953	113646	123497	221580	85516
19974	40461	23643	24619	54297	56557	88829	27428
19371	54181	48903	61029	105021	111165	196928	82025
71584	191858	42475	46655	132401	141497	234378	78924
250611	592238	45815	68265	628856	672242	981517	268997
90567	220411	13543	19341	90679	108416	181665	61700
138520	528837	100887	77060	745701	771581	1156513	120865
17451	46103	853	4042	8461	12910	29390	11727
533767	606516	76955	101502	609871	671601	942887	231379
881217	1312037	- 18247	62746	1572385	1866239	2399341	457519
174913	296165	- 1765	15509	265275	325808	457643	115891
5028	10912	- 975	1384	22327	22997	34783	10159
772	2457	1883	1716	25955	29695	37731	7579
668	854	94	96	- 801	- 635	- 540	85
33626	122738	96165	99015	521565	526271	765583	199145
1475	58737	55282	55528	465153	432323	623557	157889
16469	28586	13321	13526	63597	67122	96142	24860
15682	35415	27563	29962	- 7185	26827	45884	16396

4－16 全市规模以上工业企业

Main Economic Indicators of Industrial Enterprises

单位：万元

项　目	Item	企业单位数（个）Number of Enterprises (unit)	亏损企业（个）Loss Making Enterprises (unit)	工业总产值（当年价格）Gross Industrial Output Value (current price)	新产品产值 Output of New Products
按登记注册类型分组	**Grouped by Status of Registration**	**5684**	**831**	**124209589**	**46423002**
内资企业	Domestic－funded Enterprises	4738	640	91381358	34402073
国有企业	State－owned Enterprises	15		5534102	7358
中央企业	Central Enterprises	3		1225476	
地方企业	Local Enterprises	12		4308625	7358
集体企业	Collective－owned Enterprises	4		12292	
股份合作企业	Cooperative Enterprises	7	1	46853	5310
联营企业	Joint Ownership Enterprises	1		4866	
集体联营企业	Collective Joint Ownership Enterprises	1		4866	
有限责任公司	Limited Liability Corporations	937	144	37802068	17735500
国有独资公司	State－funded Corporations	29	6	3826212	253730
其他有限责任公司	Other Limited Liability Corporations	908	138	33975857	17481771
股份有限公司	Share－holding Corporations Ltd.	219	30	11944766	6260042
私营企业	Private Enterprises	3554	465	36032209	10393864
私营独资企业	Private－funded Enterprises	136	12	736511	61885
私营合伙企业	Private Partnership Enterprises	16	1	88218	13992
私营有限责任公司	Private Limited Liability Corporations	3313	443	33338841	9336460
私营股份有限公司	Private Share－holding Corporations Ltd.	89	9	1868640	981527
港、澳、台商投资公司	Enterprises with Investment from Hong Kong, Macao and Taiwan	435	108	14056749	6295617
内地与港澳台合资经营企业	Joint－venture Enterprises with funds from Hong Kong, Macao and Taiwan	256	56	8994987	3278399
内地与港澳台合作经营企业	Cooperative Enterprises with funds from Hong Kong, Macao and Taiwan	3		57730	31950
港澳台商独资经营企业	Enterprises with Sole Investment from Hong Kong, Macao and Taiwan	168	48	3568720	1652995
港澳台商投资股份有限公司	Share－holding Corporations Ltd. with Investment from Hong Kong, Macao and Taiwan	5	1	1295198	1214921
其他港澳台商投资	Other Enterprises with Investment from Hong Kong, Macao and Taiwan	3	3	140115	117351
外商投资企业公司	Enterprises with Foreign Investment	511	83	18771481	5725312
中外合资经营企业	Joint－venture Enterprises	256	32	9546116	3609225
中外合作经营企业	Cooperation Enterprises	7	2	90077	25086
外商独资经营企业	Enterprises with Sole Foreign Investment	240	48	9025545	2046579
外商投资股份有限公司	Share－holding Corporations Ltd. with Foreign Investment	5	1	96770	44423

主要经济指标按登记注册类型分(2016 年)

Above Designated Size by Status of Registration(2016)

(10000 yuan)

工业销售产值 Value of Industrial Products Sales	出口交货值 Export delivery value	实收资本 Total Capital Hold	国家资本 State Capital	个人资本 Personal Capital	港澳台资本 Hongkong, Macau and TaiWan Capital	外商资本 Foreign Capital	就业人员年平均人数(人) Annual Average Number of Staff and Workers (person)
123496342	**16866200**	**28398613**	**3495114**	**7259031**	**2411081**	**3649697**	**1074178**
90837227	9630159	19173161	2845150	6813722	45863	68121	762373
5535519		341365	333436				6378
1225302		97902	97902				1524
4310216		243463	235534				4854
12280		739					111
44509	7	9269		9142			1036
4866		100					65
4866		100					65
37771125	3274708	7288517	1923798	1081126	185	28242	240826
4087760	20145	445238	344980				11480
33683365	3254563	6843279	1578818	1081126	185	28242	229346
11905744	1456695	5027132	580306	1822643	44059	35663	100875
35559082	4898749	6506021	7610	3900793	1619	4216	413046
721075	76649	45936		35470			8566
86043	5965	7755		7130			1465
32903368	4553485	5952310	7610	3686814	1619	4216	386305
1848596	262650	500020		171380			16710
14148236	2702181	4260771	452339	373497	2307670	152171	137418
8993961	1582547	2020887	193443	105671	805831	149246	72464
57770	22925	6510			580	1000	525
3659572	1030927	1452175		1084	1322477	300	51381
1297511	55318	700318	258896	266742	118901	1625	11831
139423	10464	80882			59882		1217
18510880	4533860	4964681	197625	71812	57548	3429405	174387
9357679	1817510	2181212	197625	69736	57527	993163	86265
88387	32937	35178		2076		27442	1825
8955064	2627754	2684761			21	2348446	84431
96941	48724	57083				53908	1459

4－17 分地区规上

Added Value of Industrial Enterprises Above

单位:亿元

年 份 Year	全 市 Whole City	市 区					
		上城区 Shangcheng	下城区 Xiacheng	江干区 Jianggan	拱墅区 Gongshu	西湖区 Xihu	高新(滨江)区 Hi－Tech (Binjiang)
2000	360.97						
2001	444.91						
2002	597.01						
2003	783.51						
2004	1019.47						
2005	1126.54						
2006	1363.17						
2007	1717.65						
2008	1743.20						
2009	1792.00						
2010	2153.83						
2011	2369.00	215.48	20.83	47.25	119.11	49.03	162.30
2012	2492.00	296.64	22.05	48.00	117.08	49.07	210.02
2013	2664.13	318.89	23.33	53.33	104.34	49.62	278.48
2014	2813.51	328.06	15.16	57.60	78.34	50.45	324.69
2015	2875.05	329.70	7.13	53.79	60.64	52.30	365.67
2016	2990.34	349.57	9.64	47.37	65.80	57.06	374.24

注:2000－2010 年为主营业务收入 500 万及以上;2011－2016 年为主营业务收入 2000 万及以上。

工业增加值(2000－2016 年)

Designated Size by Region (2000－2016)

(100 million yuan)

Urban District									
萧山区 Xiaoshan	大江东产业集聚区 Dajiangdong Industry Cluster District	余杭区 Yuhang	富阳区 Fuyang	经济技术开发区 Economic and Technological Development Zone	西湖风景名胜区 The West Lake Scenic Zone	桐庐县 Tonglu	淳安县 Chun'an	建德市 Jiande	临安市 Lin'an
77.95		31.54	22.05			9.29	2.24	10.13	11.83
106.28		38.50	31.69			11.98	2.99	8.86	14.71
145.26		40.29	38.87			14.08	3.40	13.05	18.55
199.34		69.17	52.52			18.98	5.46	16.82	25.09
245.57		86.96	63.65			29.73	6.59	27.62	32.25
311.61		129.16	80.22			31.60	9.29	28.54	37.84
385.34		150.85	103.73			42.10	12.70	37.88	47.54
401.88		195.17	136.42			57.06	17.35	50.54	62.53
482.29		212.97	160.31			68.41	20.56	61.38	74.51
538.91		225.60	167.30			62.17	23.48	60.03	80.02
606.90		297.10	182.30			76.63	29.18	76.13	98.91
721.27		243.41	162.41			71.74	32.66	68.09	98.20
727.65		250.64	165.25			80.02	38.69	76.19	106.67
704.46		275.99	198.03	380.51	0.06	81.63	43.44	81.74	115.18
712.21		301.62	200.53	405.16	0.12	94.92	47.53	85.18	123.24
706.49	189.07	334.30	200.89	457.66	0.76	102.26	52.06	83.67	127.85
742.23	215.14	349.74	201.89	541.62	－1.77	99.78	49.96	85.75	136.80

a) Data after 2011－2016 refer to all the industrial enterprises with annual Sales income of over 20 million yuan, data in 2000－2010 refer to all the industrial enterprises with annual sales income of over 5 million yuan.

4 - 18 分地区规上

Index of Added Value of Industrial

（上年 = 100）

年 份 Year	全 市 Whole City	上城区 Shangcheng	下城区 Xiacheng	江干区 Jianggan	拱墅区 Gongshu	西湖区 Xihu	高新(滨江)区 Hi - Tech (Binjiang)
2010	114.9	110.0	121.1	112.2	110.5	109.1	119.6
2011	112.7	112.1	104.0	109.4	112.3	111.8	118.2
2012	110.9	106.6	103.5	105.5	112.2	108.8	113.7
2013	108.0	106.3	107.7	109.4	104.5	109.6	115.1
2014	108.9	108.9	91.6	115.1	105.5	104.9	118.3
2015	105.4	106.0	90.1	100.5	95.2	101.0	117.8
2016	105.6	98.5	102.0	87.5	105.0	105.0	114.9

工业增加值发展指数(2010－2016年)

Enterprises Above Designated Size by Region(2010－2016)

(Preceding Year＝100)

萧山区 Xiaoshan	大江东产业集聚区 Dajiangdong Industry Cluster District	余杭区 Yuhang	富阳区 Fuyang	经济技术开发区 Economic and Technological Development Zone	西湖风景名胜区 The West Lake Scenic Zone	桐庐县 Tonglu	淳安县 Chun'an	建德市 Jiande	临安市 Lin'an
114.3		115.0	113.1	118.5	112.1	114.0	114.9	115.5	122.7
112.9		109.2	113.3	111.2	105.0	109.1	115.1	113.0	113.1
113.5		107.2	112.1	102.4	91.4	109.0	119.6	110.8	112.4
108.1		108.0	109.3	107.3	139.8	105.6	112.7	106.1	105.5
108.1		107.0	106.2	109.3	147.0	109.0	103.2	108.1	107.2
106.2	118.6	102.6	104.1	106.9	90.9	106.9	103.4	108.2	105.1
106.3	117.6	105.0	103.0	110.2	100.3	108.6	110.6	107.0	109.0

4-19 全市规上工业三大新兴产业发展情况(2013-2016年)

Development of the Three Recently Emerging Industries Above Designated Size(2013-2016)

指标 Item	高新技术产业 High-tech Industries		战略性新兴产业 Strategic Emerging Industries		装备制造业 Equipment Manufacturing Industries	
	增加值(亿元) Value-added (100 million yuan)	为上年(%) As Compared with the Preceding Year (%)	增加值(亿元) Value-added (100 million yuan)	为上年(%) As Compared with the Preceding Year (%)	增加值(亿元) Value-added (100 million yuan)	为上年(%) As Compared with the Preceding Year (%)
2013	785.4	108.9	636.6	107.1	900.5	108.6
2014	1096.6	110.5	813.1	113.0	921.4	109.3
2015	1212.6	109.8	877.3	109.4	1086.1	113.5
2016	1372.9	112.5	812.1	111.6	1249.6	114.6

4-20 主要工业产品生产量(2016年)
Output of Major Industrial Products(2016)

产品名称	Item	全市 Whole City 2016年	全市 Whole City 为上年(%) As Compared with the Preceding Year(%)	市区 Urban District
发电量 (亿千瓦时)	Generating Capacity (100 million kwh)	179.10	97.7	121.11
#水力发电 (亿千瓦时)	of which:Hydroelectric Generation (100 million kwh)	50.75	100.3	-
垃圾发电 (亿千瓦时)	Garbage Power (100 million kwh)	7.31	110.0	7.31
罐头 (万吨)	Canned Food (10000 tons)	5.96	91.7	1.81
乳制品 (吨)	Dairy Products (ton)	153346	104.4	124892
啤酒 (千升)	Beer (1000 litres)	932732.72	95.9	613841.00
软饮料 (万吨)	Soft Drinks (10000 tons)	735.48	112.7	404.74
精制茶 (吨)	Tea (ton)	29348	91.9	5285
卷烟 (亿支)	Cigarettes (100 million)	583.12	96.8	583.12
方便面 (吨)	Instant Noodle (ton)	283012	107.4	283012
化学纤维 (吨)	Chemical Fiber (ton)	6231482	99.4	6203981
#合成纤维 (吨)	Synthetic Fibre (ton)	6109894	99.8	6082393
纱 (万吨)	Yarn (10000 tons)	61.40	94.3	61.26
布 (万米)	Cloth (10000 m)	381004.07	97.0	295064.78
印染布 (万米)	Printed Fabric (10000 m)	628520.03	106.2	626957.53
蚕丝及交织机织物(含蚕丝≥50%) (万米)	Silk and Woven Fabrics (Containing Greater than or Equal 50% silk) (10000 m)	1913.42	85.1	1852.37
服装 (万件)	Garment (10000 units)	35363.68	94.8	26097.98
皮革鞋靴 (万双)	Leather Footwear (10000 units)	1256.76	85.1	1256.76
家具 (万件)	Furniture (10000 units)	3307.55	95.0	3077.71
塑料制品 (吨)	Plastic Membrane (ton)	1372698	101.9	1168402
机制纸及纸板 (万吨)	Machine Made Paper and Paperboard (10000 tons)	636.02	102.9	621.68

4－20 续表1 continued 1

产品名称	Item	全市 Whole City 2016年	为上年(%) As Compared with the Preceding Year(%)	市区 Urban District
盐酸(含量31%以上)(吨)	Mariatic Acid(above 31% percent) (ton)	134972	122.4	134972
氢氧化钠(烧碱)(折100%) (吨)	Caustic Soda (ton)	194072	103.9	194072
碳酸钠(纯碱) (吨)	Soda ash (ton)	307085	104.7	307085
初级形态的塑料(塑料树脂及共聚物)(吨)	Plastics in Primary Form(Plastic Resins and Copolymers) (ton)	340416	119.9	204558
合成氨 (吨)	Synthetic Ammonia (ton)	210097	102.8	190799
农用氮、磷、钾化学肥料总计(折纯)(吨)	Chemical Fertilizer (ton)	95728	104.1	88449
化学农药原药(折有效成分100%)(吨)	Chemical Pesticide (ton)	105454	100.9	12880
涂料(油漆) (吨)	Paint (ton)	162096	83.6	113213
合成洗涤剂 (吨)	Synthetic Detergent (ton)	134489	93.6	103828
化学药品原药(化学原料药) (吨)	Original Drug Chemicals (ton)	11122	101.7	10399
中成药 (吨)	Traditional Chinese Medicine (ton)	17775	107.9	16798
橡胶轮胎外胎(轮胎外胎) (万条)	Rubber Tires (10000 units)	5602.45	116.9	5591.55
水泥 (万吨)	Cement (10000 tons)	1609.45	89.5	851.42
铁合金 (万吨)	Iron Alloy (10000 tons)	4.70	92.8	-
钢材 (万吨)	Steel Products (10000 tons)	442.48	100.7	424.16
精炼铜(电解铜) (吨)	Refined Copper (ton)	253085	106.4	251739
工业锅炉 (蒸发量吨)	Industry Boiler (ton)	7970	102.1	7970
金属切削机床 (台)	Metal－cutting Machine Tools (unit)	37680	89.6	36206

4－20 续表2 continued 2

产品名称	Item	全市 Whole City 2016年	为上年(％) As Compared with the Preceding Year(％)	市区 Urban District
金属成形机床(锻压设备)(台)	Metal Forming Machine(Forge Equipment) (Tai)	5892	71.8	5892
泵(液体泵) (万台)	Pump (10000 sets)	89.87	111.6	89.02
滚动轴承(轴承) (万套)	Bearings (10000 units)	13028.58	102.4	13028.58
汽车 (辆)	Motor Vehicles (unit)	91127	64.6	91127
叉车 (台)	Forklift (unit)	71742	117.8	8100
两轮自行车(自行车) (万辆)	Bicycles (10000 units)	170.75	82.4	170.01
交流电动机 (万千瓦)	AC Motor (10000 kw)	119.30	123.5	110.75
钢绞线 (吨)	Strand (ton)	71765	136.7	71726
通信及电子网络用电缆 (万对千米)	Communication Cable (10000 km)	471.16	98.2	156.33
光缆(光纤通讯电缆)(万芯千米)	Electric Power Cable (10000 km)	3913.63	112.0	3817.45
家用电冰箱 (万台)	Household Refrigerators (10000 units)	111.20	106.5	111.20
家用洗衣机 (万台)	Household Washing Machines (10000 units)	298.49	95.8	298.49
吸排油烟机 (万台)	Smoke Absorbers (10000 units)	303.49	112.1	303.49
移动通信手持机(手机)(万部)	Mobile Telephone Sets (10000 units)	714.55	132.2	714.55
电工仪器仪表 (万台)	Electric Instrument and Apparatus (10000 units)	3126.38	111.8	3126.38
工业自动调节仪表与控制系统 (万台)	Industrial Automatic Adjustment Meter and Control System (10000 units)	165.68	106.0	165.64
电光源(灯泡) (亿只)	Light Bulbs (100 million units)	7.35	102.9	2.83
彩色电视机 (万部)	Color－Television Sets (10000 units)	0.55	8.8	0.55
微型计算机设备 (万台)	Micro－computer Equipment (10000 units)	132.44	99.4	132.44

4－21　分地区单位 GDP 能耗降低情况（2016 年）

Increase or Decrease of Energy Consumption Per Unit of GDP by Region（2016）

地　区	Region	单位 GDP 能耗（吨标准煤/万元）Energy Consumption Per Unit of GDP（tons of SCE/10000 yuan）		单位 GDP 电耗（千瓦时/万元）Electricity Consumption Per Unit of GDP（kwh/10000 yuan）		单位工业增加值能耗降低率 Decrease Rate of Energy Consumption Per Unit of Industriul Value－Added（±%）
		2016 年	降低率 Decrease Rate（±%）	2016 年	降低率 Decrease Rate（±%）	
杭州市	Hangzhou	0.37	6.9	617	4.1	6.3
#上城区	Shangcheng	－	－	223	2.8	－11.4
下城区	Xiacheng	－	－	263	－3.1	5.5
江干区	Jianggan	－	－	474	5.4	－5.1
拱墅区	Gongshu	－	－	593	30.6	19.2
西湖区	Xihu	－	－	417	－0.4	8.7
高新（滨江）区	Hi－Tech（Binjiang）	－	－	307	1.7	10.7
萧山区	Xiaoshan	0.59	5.2	1120	5.2	5.3
大江东产业集聚区	Dajiangdong Industry Cluster District	－	－	1747	12.5	11.0
余杭区	Yuhang	0.33	3.1	603	2.2	5.0
富阳区	Fuyang	0.8	0.6	1086	0.0	6.9
经济技术开发区	Economic and Technological Development Zone	－	－	685	－2.4	－2.5
桐庐县	Tonglu	0.41	0.5	585	－5.9	8.9
淳安县	Chun'an	0.28	－3.7	537	－4.1	6.4
建德市	Jiande	0.76	7.4	846	2.8	9.7
临安市	Lin'an	0.38	7.7	620	3.1	19.2

4－22　全市规模以上工业能源购进消费与库存(2016 年)

Purchasing,Consuming and Stocking of Energy in Industrial Enterprises Above Designated Size(2016)

能源名称		Item		购进量 Purchasing	消费量合计 Total Consumption	工业生产消费 Industry
原煤	(吨)	Raw Coal	(Ton)	11502300	11584071	11564094
洗精煤	(吨)	Washing Coal	(Ton)	－	－	－
煤制品	(吨)	Coal Puoducts	(Ton)	728295	720557	720557
焦炭	(吨)	Coke	(Ton)	25434	24471	24460
天然气(气态)	(万立方米)	Natural Gas(Gas)	(10000 cu. m)	178670	178808	178348
液化天然气(液态)	(吨)	Liquefied Natural Gas(Liquid)	(Ton)	33837	33842	33782
汽油	(吨)	Gasoline	(Ton)	46503	46599	16593
煤油	(吨)	Kerosene	(Ton)	4490	4468	4466
柴油	(吨)	Diesel Oil	(Ton)	135776	135963	115746
燃料油	(吨)	Fuel Oil	(Ton)	33233	32874	32856
液化石油气	(吨)	Liquefied Petroleum Gas	(Ton)	10999	11005	10866
润滑油	(吨)	Lubricating Oil	(Ton)	7131	6523	6519
溶剂油	(吨)	Solvent Oil	(Ton)	553	552	541
石油沥青	(吨)	Petroleum Asphalt	(Ton)	－	－	－
其他石油制品	(吨)	Other Petroleum Products	(Ton)	19884	19921	19921
热力	(百万千焦)	Heat	(Million kilo－joule)	78962776	92789501	92014560
电力	(万千瓦时)	Electricity	(10000 kwh)	3179405	3400666	3329559
煤矸石用于燃料	(吨)	Coal Gangue for Fuel	(Ton)	－	－	－
城市垃圾用于燃料	(吨)	Municipal Waste for Fuel	(Ton)	－	676806	676806
生物质废料用于燃料	(吨)	Biomass Waste for Fuel	(Ton)	166449	163580	163189
余热余压	(百万千焦)	Residual Heat and Pressure	(Million kilo－joule)	508841	9842649	9842648
其它工业废料用于燃料	(吨)	Other Industrial Waste for Fuel	(Ton)	101910	127590	127567
其它燃料	(吨标准煤)	Other Fuel	(Tons of SCE)	26693	42668	42668

4－23　工业企业主要能源

Energy Consumption of Industrial

行　业　Sector	原煤(吨) Raw Coal(Ton)	洗精煤(吨) Washing Coal(Ton)	焦炭(吨) Coke(Ton)	汽油(吨) Gasoline(Ton)	煤油(吨) Kerosene(Ton)
总　计 Total	**11584071**	**－**	**24471**	**46599**	**4468**
煤炭开采和洗选业 Coal Mining and Dressing	－	－	－	－	－
黑色金属矿采选业 Ferrous Metals Mining and Dressing	－	－	－	－	－
有色金属矿采选业 Nonferrous Minerals Mining and Dressing	－	－	－	30	－
非金属矿采选业 Nonmetal Minerals Mining and Dressing	27983	－	－	12	－
农副食品加工业 Agricultural Products Processing	4211	－	－	282	－
食品制造业 Food Manufacturing	8870	－	－	853	－
酒、饮料和精制茶制造业 Wine,Beverage and Tea Manufacturing	5318	－	－	68	－
烟草制品业 Tobacco Processing	－	－	－	23	－
纺织业 Textile Processing	631535	－	－	3569	3
纺织服装、服饰业 Textile Products and Costume Industry	2950	－	204	2032	2
皮革、毛皮、羽毛及其制品和制鞋业 Leather. Furs. Downand Related and Shoes Products	2901	－	－	1479	－
木材加工和木、竹、藤、棕、草制品业 Timber Processing,Bamboo,Cane,Plam Fiber and Straw Products	－	－	－	145	－
家具制造业 Furniture Manufacturing	8	－	34	576	8
造纸和纸制品业 Paper Making and Paper Products	67842	－	－	4164	3770
印刷和记录媒介复制业 Printing	－	－	－	671	－
文教、工美、体育和娱乐用品制造业 Cultural,Educational. Industrial Arts. Sports and Entertainment Goods	203	－	83	809	－
石油加工、炼焦和核燃料加工业 Petroleum Processing, Coking and Nuclear Fuel Processing	43	－	－	175	－

消费量按行业分(2016 年)
Enterprises by Sector(2016)

柴油(吨) Diesel oil(Ton)	燃料油(吨) Fuel Oil(Ton)	液化石油气(吨) Liquefied Petroleum Gas(Ton)	天然气(万立方米) Natural Gas (10000 cu. m)	其他石油制品(吨) Other Petroleum Products(Ton)	热力(百万千焦) Heat(Million kilo-joule)	电力(万千瓦时) Electricity (10000 kwh)
135963	**32874**	**11005**	**178808**	**19921**	**92789501**	**3400666**
–	–	–	–	–	–	172
–	–	–	–	–	–	9
3	–	–	–	–	–	2157
5210	–	–	–	–	–	10623
1109	94	46	887	–	266597	14053
1977	465	123	2251	–	1199808	28099
670	106	4	1364	–	1500552	54708
441	–	–	804	–	144135	8131
3914	3013	148	7173	9	26036783	465817
1432	–	5	403	–	621726	24511
580	–	1	603	–	127852	12887
233	–	–	18	–	1414	4768
941	77	–	782	–	78614	11866
2833	39	–	2135	–	29548526	263263
483	–	11	225	–	23458	14010
790	–	59	39	–	145826	16249
607	523	–	3	49	37490	419

4-23 续表

行业 Sector	原煤(吨) Raw Coal(Ton)	洗精煤(吨) Washing Coal(Ton)	焦炭(吨) Coke(Ton)	汽油(吨) Gasoline(Ton)	煤油(吨) Kerosene(Ton)
化学原料和化学制品制造业 Raw Chemical Materials and Chemical Products	1563172	–	–	2755	–
医药制造业 Medical and Pharmaceutical Products	55049	–	–	675	–
化学纤维制造业 Chemical Fiber	190995	–	–	568	–
橡胶和塑料制品业 Rubber and Plastic Products	233317	–	–	2283	13
非金属矿物制品业 Nonmetal Minerals Products	2421736	–	–	1681	7
黑色金属冶炼和压延加工业 Smelting and Processing of Ferrous Metals	4599	–	892	466	–
有色金属冶炼和压延加工业 Smelting and Processing of Nonferrous Metals	1116	–	22977	163	–
金属制品业 Metal Products	16465	–	73	2090	10
通用设备制造业 Ordinary Machinery	20985	–	206	5199	336
专用设备制造业 Special Purpose Equipment	196	–	–	1707	3
汽车制造业 Automobile Manufacturing	427	–	3	3467	300
铁路、船舶、航空航天和其他运输设备制造业 Railway. watercraft. Avigation spaceflight and other Equipment Manufacturing	156	–	–	1120	–
电气机械和器材制造业 Electric Equipment and Machinery	1052	–	–	3273	–
计算机、通信和其他电子设备制造业 Computers. Telecommunications and Other Electronic Equipment Manufacturing	688	–	–	2360	–
仪器仪表制造业 Instruments and Meters Manufacturing	188	–	–	1367	16
其他制造业 Other Manufacturing	259695	–	–	104	–
废弃资源综合利用业 Multiple Utilization of Waste Resouces	19162	–	–	57	–
金属制品、机械和设备修理业 Metal Products,Machinery and Equipment Repair	–	–	–	–	–
电力、热力生产和供应业 Production and Supply of Electric Power and Hot Water	6043209	–	–	1708	–
燃气生产和供应业 Production and Supply of Gas	–	–	–	301	–
水的生产和供应业 Production and Supply of Tap Water	–	–	–	368	–

continued

柴油(吨) Diesel oil(Ton)	燃料油(吨) Fuel Oil(Ton)	液化石油气(吨) Liquefied Petroleum Gas(Ton)	天然气(万立方米) Natural Gas (10000 cu. m)	其他石油制品(吨) Other Petroleum Products(Ton)	热力(百万千焦) Heat(Million kilo - joule)	电力(万千瓦时) Electricity (10000 kwh)
7899	14002	–	1577	16778	20023465	463008
1743	219	72	1962	–	812380	54328
707	–	–	866	–	4779231	350258
2876	6063	2576	735	–	4869277	210269
74076	3679	209	4590	2061	160845	207435
603	–	308	4015	108	322220	103105
1088	2174	119	2726	11	147891	75473
3714	2245	468	5223	4	328443	88792
7442	78	248	885	477	63163	115777
1256	5	417	280	–	200795	22478
3535	73	82	2119	400	161828	91436
258	17	241	228	–	–	6286
2598	–	5250	2060	3	339867	135324
3984	–	602	778	14	316656	115780
362	–	3	69	–	8299	17884
638	–	–	132	–	–	3753
55	–	–	–	5	58450	11306
–	–	–	–	–	–	43
1373	–	–	133835	2	463911	325536
347	–	–	41	–	–	626
184	–	14	1	–	–	70028

4－24 全市分行业电力消费量(2016 年)
Electricity Consumption by Sector(2016)

单位:万千瓦时 (10000 kwh)

项 目	Item	2016	2015	增长% Growth %
总 计	**Total**	**6782940**	**6463760**	**4.94**
#线路损失电量	#Losses in Transmission	221290	190625	16.09
农林牧渔业	Farming, Forestry, Animal Husbandry and Fishery Conservancy	47780	47248	1.13
工业	Industry	4015466	4070223	－1.35
#轻工业	Light Industry	2025716	1990274	1.78
重工业	Heavy Industry	1989750	2079949	－4.34
#采矿业	#Mining and Quarrying	26099	31828	－18.00
制造业	Manufacturing Industry	3566582	3664692	－2.68
电力、燃气及水的生产和供应业	Produotion and supply of electricity, gas & water	422785	373703	13.13
建筑业	Construction	131661	139136	－5.37
交通运输、仓储及邮政业	Transportation, Storage, Post & Telecommunications	141035	117160	20.38
信息传输、计算机服务和软件业	Information Transmission, Computer Services and Software	181098	146489	23.63
商业、住宿和餐饮业	Commerce, Catering and lodging	396025	355504	11.40
金融、房地产、商务及居民服务业	Finance, Real Estate Commerce and Service for the Residents	383163	314382	21.88
公共管理和社会组织	Public Management and Social Organizations	413742	371009	11.52
城乡居民生活用电	Residential Consumption	1072970	902609	18.87
#城市	Cities	676120	568580	18.91
乡村	#Rural Areas	396850	334030	18.81

4-25 水资源量和总用水量(2006-2016年)

Total Water Resources and Water Consumption(2006-2016)

单位:亿立方米 (100 million Cubic Meters)

		全市 Whole City	市区 Urban District	富阳区 Fuyang	桐庐县 Tonglu	淳安县 Chan'an	建德市 Jiangde	临安市 Lin'an
2006年	水资源量 Water Resources	109.80	15.14	10.36	11.70	38.42	13.41	20.75
	用水量 Water Consumption	48.73	31.39	7.13	2.39	1.42	2.68	3.72
2007年	水资源量 Water Resources	104.13	20.28	11.76	10.12	29.88	11.72	20.36
	用水量 Water Consumption	49.56	32.57	6.45	2.53	1.53	3.09	3.39
2008年	水资源量 Water Resources	154.38	24.58	14.20	14.95	49.22	18.52	32.92
	用水量 Water Consumption	56.70	39.57	6.49	2.90	1.32	2.69	3.70
2009年	水资源量 Water Resources	141.50	23.38	16.33	16.67	37.46	15.63	32.03
	用水量 Water Consumption	54.28	39.24	5.18	2.52	1.46	2.81	3.07
2010年	水资源量 Water Resources	190.40	29.58	17.92	19.03	63.61	30.36	29.91
	用水量 Water Consumption	54.95	39.00	4.80	2.79	1.61	2.88	3.87
2011年	水资源量 Water Resources	136.70	20.21	13.43	15.81	41.00	19.11	27.13
	用水量 Water Consumption	57.71	40.40	5.83	2.98	1.37	2.92	4.21
2012年	水资源量 Water Resources	221.26	36.20	23.57	24.89	66.73	31.08	38.83
	用水量 Water Consumption	56.45	39.69	5.75	2.67	1.40	2.84	4.10
2013年	水资源量 Water Resources	141.15	28.82	15.33	15.63	35.29	19.21	26.87
	用水量 Water Consumption	57.77	41.07	6.22	2.53	1.42	2.74	3.79
2014年	水资源量 Water Resources	163.00	34.87	14.39	18.37	58.11	24.30	27.36
	用水量 Water Consumption	37.14	27.04	4.27	2.57	1.40	2.76	3.37
2015年	水资源量 Water Resources	239.06	61.09	23.93	26.68	73.79	33.17	44.33
	用水量 Water Consumption	34.79	25.29	3.98	2.44	1.32	2.51	3.23
2016年	水资源量 Water Resources	213.10	36.14	20.44	22.86	63.56	26.85	43.25
	用水量 Water Consumption	34.24	21.21	3.93	2.28	1.31	2.35	3.16

4-26 规模以下工业主要指标(2016年)

Main Indicators of Industrial Enterprises Below Designated Size(2016)

指标名称		Item		2016
企业数	(万家)	Number of Enterprises	(10,000 Homes)	3.39
年末从业人数	(万人)	Total Number of Employed Persons at Year End	(10,000 persons)	36.38
资产总计	(亿元)	Total Assets	(100 million yuan)	1940.72
主营业务收入	(亿元)	Revenues in Main Business	(100 million yuan)	1142.00
主营业务成本	(亿元)	Costs in Main Business	(100 million yuan)	948.39
税金总额	(亿元)	Total taxes	(100 million yuan)	41.65
利润总额	(亿元)	Total Profits	(100 million yuan)	17.20
应付职工薪酬	(亿元)	Employee benefits Payable	(100 million yuan)	134.53

主要统计指标解释

工业总产值 是以货币表现的工业企业在报告期内生产的已出售或可供出售工业产品总量，它反映一定时间内工业生产的总规模和总水平，它包括：在本企业内不再进行加工，经检验、包装入库（规定不需包装的产品除外）的成品价值，对外加工费收入，自制半成品，在产品期末初差额价值。工业总产值采用“工厂法”计算，即以工业企业作为一个整体，按企业工业生产活动的最终成果来计算，企业内部不允许重复计算，不能把企业内部各个车间（分厂）生产的成果相加。

工业销售产值 是以货币表现的工业企业在一定时期内销售的本企业生产的工业产品总量。包括已销售的成品、半成品价值，对外提供的工业性作业和对本单位基本建设部门、生活福利部门等提供的产品和工业性作业及自制设备的价值。已销售的成品、半成品不论是本期生产的、还是上期生产的，只要是本期销售出去的均包括在内。对外提供的工业性作业是指企业按合同对外提供的工业性劳务。企业为本单位基本建设部门、生活福利部门等提供的产品和工业性作业及自制设备也应视同销售，这部分也作为销售统计。工业销售产值的计算范围、计算价格和计算方法与工业总产值一致，但两者计算的基础不同；工业销售产值计算的基础是产品销售总量，工业总产值计算的基础是工业产品生产总量。

工业增加值 是指工业行业在报告期内以货币表现的工业生产活动的最终成果。

固定资产原价 固定资产原值指企业在建造、购置、安装、改建、扩建、技术改造某项固定资产时所支出的全部货币总额。它一般包括买价、包装费、运杂费和安装费等。

固定资产净值 是指固定资产原价减去历年已提折旧额后的净额。

利税总额 指企业利润总额、产品销售税金及附加和应交增值税之和。

主营业务收入 指企业销售产品的销售收入和提供劳务等主要经营业务取得的收入总额。

主营业务成本 指企业销售产品和提供劳务等主要经营业务的实际成本。

主营业务税金及附加 指企业销售产品和提供工业性劳务等主要经营业务应负担的城市维护建设税、消费税、资源税和教育费附加。

主营业务利润 指企业销售产品和提供工业性劳务等主要经营业务收入和除其成本、费用、税金后的利润。

利润总额 指企业实现的利润。

应交增值税 指企业在报告期内应交纳的增值税额。

总资产 指企业拥有或控制的全部资产。包括流动资产、长期投资、固定资产、无形及递延资产、其他长期资产、递延税项等，即为企业资产负债表的资产总计项。

（1）流动资产指企业可以在一年内或者超过一年的一个生产周期内变现或耗用的资产合计。包括现金及各种存款、短期投资、应收及预付款项、存货等。

（2）固定资产指企业固定资产净值、固定资产清理、在建工程、待处理固定资产损失所占用的资金合计。

（3）无形资产指企业长期使用而没有实物形态的资产。包括专利权、非专利技术、商标权、著作权、土地使用权、商誉等。

总负债 指企业承担并需要偿还的全部债务。包括流动负债和长期负债、递延税项等，即为企业资产负债表的负债合计项。

（1）流动负债指企业在一年内或者超过一年的一个营业周期内需要偿还的债务合计，其中包括短期借款、应付及预收款项、应付工资、应交税金和应交利润等。

（2）长期负债指企业在一年以上或者超过一年的一个生产周期以上需要偿还的债务合计，其中包括长期借款、应付债务、长期应付款项等。

所有者权益 指企业投资人对企业净资产的所有权。企业净资产等于企业全部资产减去全部负债后的余额。其中包括投资者对企业的最初投入，以及资本公积金、盈余公积金和未分配利润，对股份制企业即为股东权益。

Explanatory Notes on Main Statistical Indicators

Gross Industrial Output Value is the total volume of industrial products sold or available for sale in value terms which reflects the total achievements and overall scale of industrial production during a given period. It includes the value of the finished products, which are not to be further processed in the enterprises and have been inspected, packed and put in storage, the value of industrial services rendered to other units, and the changes in the value of the semi – finished products and products in process between the beginning and closing of the period. The gross industrial output value is calculated with "factory method". No double calculations are to be made within the same enterprise. However, double counting does occur among different enterprises.

Industrial Sales Output Value is the total volume of industrial products sold in value term of an industrial enterprise during a given period. It includes the value of finished products, semi – finished products, industrial operations rendered to other units, products industrial operations & self – made equipment provided to the basic construction department, welfare department, etc. of the enterprise. For finished products & semi – finished products, whether produced in this calculation period or the previous one, if they are sold in this calculation period, they should be included. Industrial operations are industrial services rendered to other units according to contracts. Products, industrial operations & self – made equipment provided to basic construction department, welfare department, etc. of the enterprise should be regarded as act of sale, and included in sales statistics.

The scope , price and method of calculation of industrial sales output value are the same as those for gross industrial output value. But the calculation bases are different: the base for sales output value is the total volume of products sold; the base for gross industrial output value is total volume of production of industrial products.

Value – added of Industry refers to the final results of industrial production of the industrial trade in money terms during the reference period.

Original Value of Fixed Assets refers to the original value of all assets owned by industrial enterprises, calculated at the cost paid at the time of purchase, installation, reconstruction, expansion, and technical innovation and transformation of the said assets, which includes expenses on purchase, package, transportation, and installation, etc.

Net Value of Fixed Assets is obtained by deducting depreciation over years from the original value of fixed assets.

Total Pre – tax Profits refers to the sum of sales tax and extra charges adding total profits.

Sales Revenue of Industrial Products refers to the revenue from the sales of products by industrial enterprises and the revenue from services provided and etc.

Sales Cost of Industrial Products refers to the actual cost of products of industrial enterprises and industrial services provided, etc.

Tax and Extra Charges on Sales of Products refer to the tax on city maintenance and construction, consumption tax, resources tax and extra charges for education, which should be borne by the enterprises in selling products and providing industrial services.

Sales Profit of Products refers to the profit gained by the enterprises by deducting cost, charges and taxes from the business income of the enterprises obtained in selling products and providing industrial services.

Total Profits refer to the profits gained by the enterprises.

Value – added Tax Payable refers to the amount of the value added tax which should be paid by the enterprises in the reporting period.

Total Assets refer to all assets which are owned or controlled by enterprises, including circulating assets, long term investment, fixed assets, intangible assets and deferred assets, other long term assets, and deferred taxes, etc. The summation of above items is equal to total assets shown in the balance sheets of the enterprises.

(1) Circulating assets (working capital) refer to assets which can be cashed in or spent or consumed in an operating cycle of one year or over one year, including cash, all kinds of deposits, short term investment, receivables, advance payment, stock, etc.

(2) Fixed assets refer to the net value of fixed assets, clearance of fixed assets, project under construction, fixed assets losses in suspense. These are corporations' fund holdings.

(3) Intangible assets refer to assets without material form used by enterprises over a lone time, such as patents, non – patent technologies, trade marks, copyright, land use right, business reputation, etc.

Total Liabilities refer to the debts that enterprises are responsible for repayment, including liquid liabilities, long – term liabilities and deferred taxes, etc. Total liabilities correspond to the summation item of liabilities shown in the balance sheets of the enterprises.

(1) Liquid liabilities (also called quick liabilities or immediate liabilities) refer to enterprises' total debt payable within an operating cycle of one year or over one year, including short term loans, payables and advance payments, wages payable, taxes payable and profit payable, etc.

(2) Long term liabilities refers to total debt payable within an operating cycle of one year or over one year, including long – term loans, payable liabilities, long – term payables, etc.

Creditors' Equity refers to investors' ownership of net assets of the enterprise. It is equal to the total assets of the enterprise minus its total liabilities, including the primary input from investors, capital accumulation fund, surplus accumulation fund and undistributed profit. It is the shareholder's equity in share – holding companies.

五、建筑业

CONSTRUCTION

5 建筑业 Construction

主要统计指标 Major Statistical Indicators

建筑业总产值	Gross Output Value of Construction	4105.30	亿元	(100 million yuan)
为上年	As Compared with the Preceding Year	100.2	%	(%)
房屋建筑施工面积	Floor Space of Buildings Under Construction	27221	万平方米	(10, 000 sq.m)
为上年	As Compared with the Preceding Year	96.8	%	(%)
房屋建筑竣工面积	Floor Space of Buildings Completed	9754	万平方米	(10, 000 sq.m)
为上年	As Compared with the Preceding Year	96.2	%	(%)

5-01 全市分地区建筑业总产值(2016年)
Gross Output Value of Construction by Region(2016)

单位:万元 (10000 yuan)

地 区	Region	建筑企业单位数(个) Number of Construction Enterprises (unit)	建筑业总产值 Gross Output Value of Construction	建筑工程产值 Output Value of Construction Projects	安装工程产值 Output value of Installation Projects	其他产值 Other Output Values
全 市	**Total**	**1474**	**41052972**	**36106015**	**3978388**	**968569**
市 区	Urban District	1268	38833878	34178321	3761517	894038
#上城区	Shangcheng	83	2654282	1580291	1031844	42147
下城区	Xiacheng	69	1426086	1176907	233484	15695
江干区	Jianggan	100	2593612	2254847	311810	26956
拱墅区	Gongshu	159	3091018	2429755	612521	48741
西湖区	Xihu	154	8634016	8008012	424211	201792
高新(滨江)区	Hi-Tech (Binjiang)	58	4847115	4639270	82239	125606
萧山区	Xiaoshan	306	11746292	10593176	782821	370295
大江东产业集聚区	Dajiangdong Industry Cluster District	35	811284	776873	19916	14495
余杭区	Yuhang	188	2084594	1868338	208369	7887
富阳区	Fuyang	127	1296032	1204513	52135	39384
经济技术开发区	Economic and Technological Development Zone	20	210421	172853	22033	15535
西湖风景名胜区	The West Lake Scenic Zone	4	250410	250360	500	-
桐庐县	Tonglu	51	718940	642641	64422	11878
淳安县	Chun'an	62	310483	252659	35129	22695
建德市	Jiande	37	323842	275623	37752	10468
临安市	Lin'an	56	865829	756771	79568	29490

5-02 建筑总专包

Financial Indicators on Construction Enterprises of

单位:万元

指标名称	Item	二、年末资产 Asset and Liabilities 流动资产合计 Circulating Funds	固定资产合计 Fixed Assets	资产合计 Total Assets
总　计	**Total**	**25412440**	**2067226**	**31158063**
#特、一、二级企业	of Which: Special Grade, First Grade, Second Grade	23236002	1728297	28444021
#国有及国有控股企业	of Which: State-owned and State Holding Enterprises	6195957	422315	7512690
一、按登记注册类型分组	**Grouped by Registration Status**			
内资企业	Domestic Funded	25214060	2037234	30915769
国有企业	State-owned	286323	29899	332337
集体企业	Collective-owned	33186	4317	38705
股份合作企业	Share-holding Cooperative Enterprises			
联营企业	Joint Venture			
有限责任公司	Limited Liability Corporations	12503637	698163	14743419
股份有限公司	Share-holding Corporations Ltd.	3229696	357686	4617772
私营企业	Private Enterprises	9161218	947168	11183536
其他企业	Other Enterprises			
港、澳、台商投资企业	Funded from Hong Kong, Macao and Taiwan	173896	28042	214348
外商投资企业	Foreign Funded	24485	1950	27946
二、按国民经济行业分组	**Grouped by Sector**			
房屋建筑业	Housing Construction	13961200	824054	17145019
土木工程建筑业	Civil Engineering Construction	8461954	960045	10460561
建筑安装业	Installation of Lines, Pipelines and Equipment	1301149	132920	1580991
建筑装饰和其他建筑业	Fitting、Decoration of Building and Others Construction	1688137	150206	1971492

企业财务指标(2016 年)
General Contractors and Specialist Contractors(2016)

(10000 yuan)

负债 at Year - end				
流动负债合计 Liquid Liabilities	负债合计 Total Liabilities	所有者权益合计 Owners' Equity	实收资本 Paid - in Capitals	国家资本 State Capital
18752593	**20274680**	**10883382**	**5932301**	**384051**
17508185	18970589	9473432	4859403	373180
5571854	6115986	1396704	766003	378645
18588614	20088743	10827026	5901601	384051
212337	229990	102347	54973	54973
26369	26694	12010	5615	2550
9844306	10479118	4264301	2013574	250392
2770597	3159028	1458744	582253	76000
5735006	6193913	4989623	3245186	136
146300	168258	46090	25210	-
17679	17679	10267	5490	-
10352673	11308789	5836230	2959614	4579
6280654	6732044	3728517	2196707	334113
937742	998446	582545	303665	5170
1181524	1235402	736090	472316	40189

单位:万元 5-02 续表

指标名称	Item	三、损益 Expenditure, Income 工程结算收入 Revenue of Project Settlement Accounts	工程结算成本 Costs of Project Settlement Accounts
总　计	**Total**	**35753389**	**33038516**
#特、一、二级企业	of Which: Special Grade, First Grade, Second Grade	33065680	30681682
#国有及国有控股企业	of Which: State - owned and State Holding Enterprises	7733797	7246789
一、按登记注册类型分组	**Grouped by Registration Status**		
内资企业	Domestic Funded	35604941	32906554
国有企业	State - owned	408989	373998
集体企业	Collective - owned	35043	29914
股份合作企业	Share - holding Cooperative Enterprises		
联营企业	Joint Venture		
有限责任公司	Limited Liability Corporations	18366571	17186202
股份有限公司	Share - holding Corporations Ltd.	3912959	3499737
私营企业	Private Enterprises	12881379	11816703
其他企业	Other Enterprises		
港、澳、台商投资企业	Funded from Hong Kong, Macao and Taiwan	118709	104834
外商投资企业	Foreign Funded	29740	27129
二、按国民经济行业分组	**Grouped by Sector**		
房屋建筑业	Housing Construction	20929553	19641526
土木工程建筑业	Civil Engineering Construction	10406117	9411011
建筑安装业	Installation of Lines, Pipelines and Equipment	2007581	1785858
建筑装饰和其他建筑业	Fitting、Decoration of Building and Others Construction	2410139	2200120

continued (10000 yuan)

及分配 and Distribution					
工程结算 税金及附加 Taxes and Extra Charges Project Settlement Accounts	销售费用 Sales Expenses	管理费用 Management Expenditure	财务费用 Financial Expenditure	利润总额 Total Profits	应交所得税 Income Taxes Payable
533662	**85933**	**1042943**	**258903**	**950047**	**200153**
482404	65644	867497	241667	874123	179553
40859	7894	247824	36062	213046	39149
532125	84438	1035133	253064	949292	199836
4586	587	19016	768	12933	3027
638	606	2029	-110	1849	494
249853	26768	455680	106126	397276	89861
31975	16974	144561	42754	243475	35752
245073	39504	413848	103526	293759	70701
1178	1370	6452	5604	229	149
360	125	1358	235	525	169
320912	31296	401867	167050	483132	94893
150225	30839	433018	66287	354390	78084
27322	11365	113792	8891	58514	12365
35203	12433	94267	16675	54010	14812

5－03　建筑业企业生产情况(2012－2016年)

Statistics on Production of Construction Enterprises(2012－2016)

指标名称	Item	2012	2013	2014	2015	2016
一、建筑业合同情况	**Contract of Construction**					
签订的合同额（万元）	Total Value of Contracts (10000 yuan)	59279520	66234009	69933228	70729328	72311485
上年结转合同额（万元）	Value from Contracts Signed in 2015 (10000 yuan)	25205183	26548398	28874679	31220942	31413457
本年新签合同额（万元）	Value from New Contracts Signed in 2016 (10000 yuan)	34074337	39685611	41058549	39509226	40898029
二、承包工程完成情况	**Completion of Contracted Projects**					
直接从建设单位承揽工程完成的产值（万元）	Complete Output Value of Projects Contacted Directly from Investors (10000 yuan)	32845834	37176277	39364500	40695653	40898836
自行完成施工产值（万元）	Own－completed Output Value (10000 yuan)	31586124	35973925	38129851	39318980	39270784
分包出去工程的产值（万元）	Output Value of Out－sourced Projects (10000 yuan)	1259710	1202352	1234649	1377814	1628052
从建设单位以外承揽工程完成的产值（万元）	Completed Output Value of Projects Contacted from Non－investors (10000 yuan)	1489749	1580779	1584025	1657315	1782188
建筑业总产值（万元）	Gross Output Value (10000 yuan)	33075873	37554704	39713876	40975734	41052972
#装饰装修产值（万元）	of Which: Output Value of Fitting and Decoration of Buildings (10000 yuan)	2821922	3216682	3469325	3486860	3642482
#在外省完成的产值（万元）	of Which: Completed Output Value outside of Zhejiang Province (10000 yuan)	11179195	12048961	12425411	12018157	11675079
按构成分	by Structure					
建筑工程产值（万元）	Output Value of Construction Projects (10000 yuan)	28976550	33244948	34894095	36080625	36106015
安装工程产值（万元）	Output value of Installation Projects (10000 yuan)	3092140	3270944	3735431	3942809	3978388
其他产值（万元）	Other Output Values (10000 yuan)	1007183	1038812	1084350	951857	968569
竣工产值（万元）	Output Value of Buildings Completed (10000 yuan)	17563992	21021307	21665909	25994238	23746502
房屋建筑施工面积（万平方米）	Floor Space of Buildings Under Construction (10000 sq. m)	26363	29538	29581	28124	27221
#本年新开工面积（万平方米）	of Which: Beginning Projects in this Year (10000 sq. m)	10541	11964	11156	9596	8583
#实行投标承包面积（万平方米）	of Which: Floor Space of Biding System (10000 sq. m)	22684	24705	26927	23653	22615
房屋建筑竣工面积（万平方米）	Floor space of Buildings Completed (10000 sq. m)	8388	9613	9514	10137	9754
三、年末自有施工机械设备	**Machinery and Equipment Owned (year－end)**					
年末自有施工机械设备净值（万元）	Net Value of Machinery and Equipment Owned (10000 yuan)	799293	832466	796789	837565	782395
年末自有施工机械设备总台数（台）	Number of Machinery and Equipment Owned (set)	178639	185792	175738	173850	162491
年末自有施工机械设备总功率（千瓦）	Total Power of Machinery and Equipment Owned (1000 kw)	3355223	3460437	4076303	3279495	3301850
四、就业人员情况	**Number of Employed Persons**					
计算劳动生产率的平均人数（人）	Average Employed Persons Overall Labor Productivity (person)	1203387	1259282	1293740	1310577	1237441
年末就业人员数（人）	Employed Persons (year－end) (person)	1002886	1274082	-	1268020	1203999

5-04 全市具有资质等级建筑业企业主要生产经营指标(2010-2016年)

Major Economic Indicators of Construction Enterprises Having Class(2010-2016)

单位:万元 (10000 yuan)

指标名称 Item	2010	2011	2012	2013	2014	2015	2016
企业个数(个) Nomber of Enterprises (unit)	1331	1373	1430	1515	1476	1480	1474
亏损企业个数(个) Loss Making Enterprises (unit)	124	200	216	252	224	236	256
建筑业总产值 Gross Output Value of Construction	26638312	30324975	33073420	37554704	39713876	40975734	41052972
竣工产值 Output Value of Buildings Completed	16373795	16286512	17557004	21021307	21665909	25994238	23746502
房屋建筑施工面积(万平方米) Floor Space of Buildings Under Construction (10,000 sq. m)	22650	26104	26420	29538	29581	28124	27221
房屋建筑竣工面积(万平方米) Floor Space of Buildings Completed (10,000 sq. m)	8220	8556	8404	9613	9514	10137	9754
固定资产原价 Orginal Value of Fixed Assets	2511522	2846687	2967321	3293095	3393624	3488088	3239557
实收资本合计 Total Capital Hold	3472567	3888171	4394124	5019389	5493120	5799067	5932301
流动资产合计 Circulating Funds	13758468	16267419	17809148	19959672	22168981	23867659	25412440
其中:存货 Stock	3155492	3758947	4034742	4934518	5900549	6360774	6751318
在建工程 Projects wnder Construction	222328	198636	235510	320533	313490	211195	175075
固定资产合计 Fixed Assets	1896442	2199708	2233648	2371260	2826312	2829483	2067226
年末负债合计 Total Liabilities at Year-end	11760309	13868500	14970479	17591701	18186469	19365824	20274680
流动负债合计 Circulating Funds	11294749	13311213	17809148	16473990	16894050	17964478	18752593
所有者权益合计 Crediors´Equity	5689839	6634943	7381024	8559878	9656533	10453107	10883382
营业收入 Revenue of Business	24281416	27251719	29552959	33709184	34704862	35568492	36069232
营业成本 Operating Costs	21768815	24719576	27047034	30614028	31501139	32365477	33270805
营业税金及附加 Main Sales Tax and Extra Charges	757611	842437	880051	996370	1029405	1020437	541967
管理费用 Management Expenditure	651233	720238	853136	905194	918904	965161	1042943
财务费用 Financial Expenditure	178931	256538	295135	318198	330680	301313	258903
营业利润 Management Profits	683851	723488	759792	850362	888932	883320	917779
利润总额 Total Profits	676599	731358	791175	883887	913117	895484	950047

主要统计指标解释

建筑业总产值　建筑业总产值是以货币表现的建筑业企业在一定时期内生产的建筑业产品和服务的总和。建筑业总产值包括建筑工程产值、安装工程产值和其他产值三部分内容。

房屋建筑施工面积　指报告期内施过工的全部房屋建筑面积，它包括本期新开工的面积、上期跨入本期继续施工的房屋面积、上期停缓建在本期恢复施工的房屋面积、本期竣工的房屋面积以及本期施工后又停缓建的房屋面积。

房屋建筑竣工面积　指在报告期内房屋建筑按照设计要求已全部完工，达到了使用条件，经检查验收鉴定合格的房屋建筑面积。

工程结算收入（主营业务收入）　指本企业承包工程实现的工程价款结算收入以及向发包单位收取的除工程价款以外按规定列作营业收入的各种款项，如临时设施费、劳动保险费、施工机构调迁费等以及向发包单位收取的各种索赔款。

工程结算成本（主营业务成本）　指在报告期内与发包单位办理工程价款结算的已完工程实际成本。

Explanatory Notes on Main Statistical Indicators

Gross Output Value of Construction refers to total of construction products and services, expressed in money terms, produced or rendered by construction and installation enterprises during a given period of time. It includes: output value of construction projects, output value of installation projects and other output values.

Floor Space of Buildings Under Construction refers to floor space of buildings under construction during the reference period, including the floor space of buildings for which construction has newly started; buildings for which construction has started earlier and is continuing during the reference period; and buildings for which construction has been suspended earlier but has restarted during the reference period; buildings completed during the reference period; and buildings under construction but construction has subsequently been during the reference period.

Floor Space of Buildings Completed refers to the floor space of buildings that are completed in the reference period in accordance with the requirements of the design, up to the standard for being put into use, and having been checked and accepted by departments concerned as qualified ones.

Income from Settlement of Projects refers to the income received by the construction enterprise from the contracted project through settlement procedures, and other charges to the contractor as operational costs in addition to the value of the project, such as temporary facility fee, labor insurance premium, moving cost of construction equipment, as well as various types of claims to the contractor.

Project Settlement Costs refers to the contracting process works price of the actual settlement costs of projects have been completed during the reporting period.

六、交通运输邮电

TRANSPORTATION, POST AND TELECOMMUNICATIONS

6 交通运输、邮电
Transportation, Post and Telecommunications

主要统计指标
Major Statistical Indicators

客运量	Passenger Traffic	20541	万人次	(10, 000 person-times)
为上年	As Compared with the Preceding Year	85.8	%	(%)
货运量	Freight Traffic	30170	万吨	(10, 000 tons)
为上年	As Compared with the Preceding Year	102.7	%	(%)
邮电业务收入	Business Income of Post & Telecommunication Service	406.00	亿元	(100 million yuan)
为上年	As Compared with the Preceding Year	121.8	%	(%)
年末固定电话用户数	Number of Local Telephone Subscribers(year-end)	265.70	万户	(10, 000 subscribers)
为上年	As Compared with the Preceding Year	90.6	%	(%)
年末移动电话用户数	Number of Mobile Telephone Subscribers(year-end)	1734.41	万户	(10, 000 subscribers)
为上年	As Compared with the Preceding Year	100.4	%	(%)
年末宽带业务户数	Broadband Subscribers of Internet(year-end)	443.57	万户	(10, 000 subscribers)
为上年	As Compared with the Preceding Year	115.9	%	(%)

6-01 全市客运量(1978-2016年)
Total Passenger Traffic (1978-2016)

单位:万人次 (10,000 person-times)

年份 Year	合计 Total	铁路 Railways	公路 Highways	水路 Waterways	民航 Civil Aviation
1978	2878	485	-	-	3
1979	3122	560	1829	729	4
1980	3905	672	2358	870	5
1981	4484	769	2857	850	8
1982	5263	813	3377	1064	9
1983	5451	878	3530	1035	8
1984	6056	983	3912	1151	10
1985	6724	1004	4595	1111	14
1986	6765	1034	4768	941	22
1987	6905	1127	4852	896	30
1988	6593	1237	4445	877	34
1989	7493	1182	5488	801	22
1990	8119	1056	6350	691	22
1991	10701	1062	8876	710	53
1992	13358	1083	11538	670	67
1993	13070	1139	11403	454	74
1994	13373	1230	11669	390	84
1995	16620	1242	14921	339	118
1996	16714	1112	15184	273	145
1997	17034	1040	15623	260	111
1998	17395	1120	15925	235	115
1999	17882	1168	16369	235	110
2000	18607	1202	17102	179	124
2001	20342	1342	18707	148	145
2002	21089	1574	19213	108	194
2003	21348	1534	19510	89	215
2004	22833	1908	20372	237	316
2005	24124	2011	21431	304	378
2006	25810	2124	22961	267	458
2007	28026	2255	24836	306	629
2008	29084	2498	25630	277	679
2009	30116	2494	26454	372	796
2010	33772	2741	29671	456	904
2011	34778	2962	30305	595	916
2012	35819	3112	31126	592	989
2013	36409	3717	30994	547	1151
2014	24070	4689	17431	616	1334
2015	23942	5282	16591	597	1472
2016	20541	6053	12282	584	1622

注:1990年以前为交通系统数,1990年起为全社会数(后同)。2014年起运输量统计方法调整。

a) The data in the table only included transportation department before 1990, while extended to the whole society after 1990 (the same below). The statistical method has been adjusted since 2014.

6－02　全市货运量(1978－2016 年)

Total Freight Traffic (1978－2016)

单位:万吨　　　　(10000 tons)

年　份 Year	合　计 Total	铁　路 Railways	公　路 Highways	水　路 Waterways	民　航 Civil Aviation
1978	1706	418	633	655	
1979	1983	440	771	772	
1980	2070	444	762	864	
1981	1972	449	886	637	
1982	2261	485	795	981	
1983	2299	488	838	973	
1984	2385	510	888	987	
1985	2488	524	890	1074	
1986	2558	551	874	1133	
1987	2515	574	899	1041	1
1988	2416	555	823	1037	1
1989	7377	539	5095	1743	
1990	6522	449	4479	1594	
1991	7017	451	4891	1675	
1992	8434	534	6063	1836	1
1993	9082	580	6353	2148	1
1994	8962	491	6563	1907	1
1995	10347	482	7021	2842	2
1996	10962	445	7735	2780	2
1997	11015	406	7932	2676	1
1998	11329	418	8196	2713	2
1999	11684	403	8037	3241	3
2000	11459	417	7865	3173	4
2001	12443	452	8588	3398	5
2002	14347	446	10391	3504	6
2003	16815	438	12118	4253	6
2004	18895	480	13117	5289	9
2005	19909	525	13539	5833	12
2006	20924	569	14588	5754	13
2007	22569	573	16484	5500	12
2008	22550	483	16822	5232	13
2009	22372	427	16536	5396	13
2010	25915	379	19148	6371	17
2011	28831	331	21755	6727	18
2012	30089	322	23243	6503	20
2013	30734	284	23884	6545	22
2014	29335	312	23202	5797	24
2015	29384	307	23800	5251	25
2016	30170	274	25194	4673	29

6－03　客货运输量(2011－2016年)

Total Passenger and Freight Traffic(2011－2016)

项　目 Item	2011	2012	2013	2014	2015	2016
一、客运量合计(万人次) Passenger Traffic(10000 person－times)	**34778**	**35819**	**36409**	**24070**	**23942**	**20541**
铁路客运量 Passenger Railways	2962	3112	3717	4689	5282	6053
民航客运量 Passenger Civil Aviation	916	989	1151	1334	1472	1622
公路客运量 Passenger Highways	30305	31126	30994	17431	16591	12282
水路客运量 Passenger Waterways	595	592	547	616	597	584
二、旅客周转量合计(万人公里) Total Passenger－kilometers(10000 passenger－km)	**1529548**	**1598527**	**1573289**	**1151642**	**1085769**	**943874**
公路旅客周转量 Passenger－kilometers Highways	1522055	1590435	1566046	1143750	1078054	936574
水路旅客周转量 Passenger－kilometers Waterways	7493	8092	7243	7892	7715	7300
三、货运量合计(万吨) Total Freight Traffic(10000 tons)	**28831**	**30089**	**30734**	**29335**	**29384**	**30170**
铁路货运量 Freight Railways	331	322	284	312	307	274
民航货运量 Freight Civil Aviation	18	20	22	24	25	29
公路货运量 Freight Highways	21755	23243	23884	23202	23800	25194
水路货运量 Freight Waterways	6727	6503	6545	5797	5251	4673
四、货运周转量合计(万吨公里) Total Freight Ton－kilometers(10000 ton－km)	**4178684**	**4563560**	**4724588**	**4550550**	**4629814**	**4796677**
公路货物周转量 Freight Ton－kilometers Highways	2451057	2643428	2719204	2760873	3003728	3217983
水路货物周转量 Freight Ton－kilometers Waterways	1727627	1920132	2005384	1789677	1626086	1578694

6-04 分地区交通
Traffic and Transport

项　目		Item		全市 Whole City	市区 Urban District
铁路旅客运量	（万人）	Passenger Railways	(10,000 Persons)	6053	6053
铁路货物运量	（万吨）	Freight Railways	(10,000 tons)	274	150
公路客运量	（万人）	Passenger Highways	(10,000 Persons)	12282	9264
公路货运量	（万吨）	Freight Highway	(10,000 tons)	25194	22573
民用航空客运量	（万人）	Passenger Civil Aviation	(10,000 Persons)	1622	1622
民用航空货邮运量	（万吨）	Freight Civil Aviation	(10,000 tons)	29	29
水路客运量	（万人）	Passenger Waterways	(10,000 Persons)	584	294
水路货运量	（万吨）	Freight Waterways	(10,000 tons)	4673	4364
年末民用汽车拥有量	（辆）	Possession of Civil Vehicles(year-end)	(Unit)	2341536	2098672
#私人汽车拥有量	（辆）	in which:Possession of Private Vehicles	(Unit)	1922663	1715055

运输情况(2016 年)
Situation by Region(2016)

萧山区 Xiaoshan	余杭区 Yuhang	富阳区 Fuyang	桐庐县 Tonglu	淳安县 Chun'an	建德市 Jiande	临安市 Lin'an
–	88	–	–	–	–	–
40	89			70	54	
474	317	1038	812	694	973	539
3686	1073	733	991	332	778	520
1622	–	–	–	–	–	–
29	–	–	–	–	–	–
21	–	–	23	218	13	36
1552	1415	485	142	26	58	83
399518	309600	119157	63650	30956	49182	99076
335026	265970	102800	52733	26852	41523	86500

6-05 全市运输线路长度(2011-2016年)

Length of Transportation Routes(2011-2016)

单位:公里　　(km)

项　目 Item		2011	2012	2013	2014	2015	2016
公路通车里程 Length of Highways	(公里) (km)	15415	15747	15900	16024	16210	16306
#高速公路 Expressway	(公里) (km)	503	550	550	582	615	632
一级公路 First Class Highways	(公里) (km)	747	768	791	803	836	832
二级公路 Second Class Highways	(公里) (km)	1520	1542	1526	1570	1616	1615
内河通航里程 Length of Navigable Inland Waterways	(公里) (km)	2006	2006	2006	2006	2006	2006
民用航空航线 Number of Civil Aviation Routes	(条) (line)	159	144	185	222	235	240
国内航线 Domestic Routes	(条) (line)	123	117	156	186	196	195
国际航线 International Routes	(条) (line)	29	20	22	28	32	38
地区航线 Regional Routes	(条) (line)	7	7	7	8	7	7

6－06 民用机动车辆年末拥有量(2011－2016年末)

Total Number of Motor Vehicles End of the Year(End of 2011－2016)

单位:辆 (unit)

项 目	Item	2011	2012	2013	2014	2015	2016
全市合计	**Total**	**2078150**	**2267027**	**2542976**	**2696340**	**2733537**	**2633541**
一、汽车	Vehicles	1495503	1761001	2045618	2184000	2244767	2341536
1. 载客汽车	Passenger Vehicles	1313307	1570099	1860794	1992112	2056143	2127393
其中:大型	Large	15458	16118	17078	17485	18657	20017
中型	Medium	18620	18096	17849	14411	10797	10035
小型	Small	1244142	1499444	1794017	1936836	2002730	2076098
微型	Mini	35087	36441	31850	23380	23959	21243
其中:轿车	Car	–	–	1678453	1799442	1773864	1483128
2. 载货汽车	Trucks	171039	179399	173227	180475	177674	202775
其中:重型	Heavy	27989	31154	35917	39998	41999	49480
中型	Medium	27534	25242	17530	14444	8851	9422
轻型	Light	114592	122316	119205	125508	126321	143441
微型	Mini	924	687	575	525	503	432
3. 其他汽车	Vehicles	11157	11503	11597	11413	10950	11368
其中:三轮汽车	Vehicles	–	–	385	182	179	139
低速货车	Low Speed Trucks	–	–	384	416	549	806
二、摩托车	Motorcycles	576907	500080	490884	505360	481230	282477
1. 普通	Genera	515411	470779	466625	481027	463722	277238
2. 轻便	Light	61496	29301	24259	24333	17508	5239
三、挂车	Trailer	–	–	6433	6939	7464	9457
四、其他类型	Other	–	–	41	41	76	71

6-07 邮政、电信主要指标(2011-2016年)
Main Indicators of Post and Telecommunications(2011-2016)

项 目 Item	2011	2012	2013	2014	2015	2016
邮政业务总收入 (万元) Total Business Income of Postal Service (10,000 yuan)	1573563	533059	702664	1176704	1596884	2151732
#快递业务收入 (万元) Business Income of Express Mail Service (10,000 yuan)	-	427356	563459	1022279	1437542	1956944
电信业务收入 (万元) Total Business Income of Telecommunications Services (10,000 yuan)	-	1597344	1752286	1700825	1736600	1908315
函件 (万件) Number of Letters (10,000 pcs)	21144	21226	20133	17412	13256	9634
包裹 (万件) Number of Parcels (10,000 pcs)	84	129	133	113	81	49
快递 (万份) Pieces of Express Mail Service (10,000 copies)	-	25536	46852	84563	125707	180473
#国际及港澳台快递 (万份) Pieces of Express to overseas and HongKong,macao,Taiwan (10,000 copies)	-	525	738	1731	2046	2495
纪特邮票 (万枚) Stamps for Collettion (10,000 pcs)	2309	1744	1412	1151	1231	1295
年末固定电话用户数 (万户) Number of Local Telephone Subscribers(year-end) (10,000 subscribers)	353.76	346.22	334.87	311.14	293.44	265.70
年末移动电话用户数 (万户) Number of Subscribers of Mobile Telephone(year-end) (10,000 subscribers)	1218.11	1438.67	1546.83	1561.71	1726.76	1734.41
年末宽带业务户数 (万户) Number of Wide Band Subscribers (10,000 subscribers)	241.14	275.91	338.63	278.78	294.96	443.57

注:邮政业务总收入含规模以上快递企业。

a) The total business income of postal services included the express enterprises above designated sice.

主要统计指标解释

货(客)运量 指在一定时期内,各种运输工具实际运送的货物(旅客)数量。是反映运输业为国民经济和人民生活服务的数量指标,也是制定和检查运输生产计划、研究运输发展规模和速度的重要指标。货运按吨计算,客运按人计算。货物不论运输距离长短、货物类别,均按实际重量统计。旅客不论行程远近或票价多少,均按一人一次作为客运量统计;半价票、小孩票也按一人统计。

货物(旅客)周转量 指在一定时期内,由各种运输工具运送的货物(旅客)数量与其相应运输距离的乘积之总和。是反映运输业生产总成果的重要指标,也是编制和检查运输生产计划,计算运输效率、劳动生产率以及核算运输单位成本的主要基础资料。通常以吨公里和人公里为计算单位。计算货物周转量通常按发出站与到达站之间的最短距离,也就是计费距离计算。

移动电话用户 指在邮电部门登记,通过移动电话交换机进入移动电话网,占有移动电话号码的电话用户。用户数量以实际办理登记手续进入邮电部门移动电话网的户数进行计算,一部或一台移动电话统计为一户。

Explanatory Notes on Main Statistical Indicators

Freight(passenger) Traffic refers to the volume of freight (passenger) transported with various means. Freight transport is calculated in tons and passenger traffic is calculated in the number of persons. Despite the type of freight and traveling distance, the freight transport is calculated in the actual weight of the goods: and despite the traveling distance and ticket price, the passenger traffic is calculated by the principle that one person can be counted only once in one travel. The passenger who travel with a half – price ticket or a child ticket is also calculated as one person. The freight (passenger) traffic provides a quantitative measure to show how the transport industry serves the national economy and people, and is also an important indicator for plan the transport industry and for studying the development scale and speed of the transport industry.

Freight Ton – kilometers(Passenger – kilometers) refers to the sum of the products of the volume of transported cargo (passengers) multiplying by the transport distance, usually using ton – kilometer and passenger – kilometer as units for measurement . Normally, the shortest distance between the departure station and the terminal station (i. e. , the payable distance) is the basis to calculate the freight ton – kilometers. This is an important indicator to show the total results of the transport industry, to prepare and examine the transport plan and to measure the efficiency, the labour productivity and the unit cost of transport.

Mobile Telephone Subscribers refer to the persons who own mobile telephone number connected with the mobile telephone communication network and registered by post and telecommunications organization. The number of subscribers is calculated only when the subscribers who have gone through all the register formalities and entered into the mobile telephone network. One mobile telephone is treated as a subscriber.

七、固定资产投资

INVESTMENT IN FIXED ASSETS

7

固定资产投资
Investment in Fixed Assets

主要统计指标
Major Statistical Indicators

固定资产投资额	Investment in Fixed Assets	5842.42	亿元	(100 million yuan)
为上年	As Compared with the Preceding Year	105.1	%	(%)
第一产业	Primary Industry	39.36	亿元	(100 million yuan)
为上年	As Compared with the Preceding Year	125.1	%	(%)
第二产业	Secondary Industry	886.90	亿元	(100 million yuan)
为上年	As Compared with the Preceding Year	95.2	%	(%)
第三产业	Tertiary Industry	4916.16	亿元	(100 million yuan)
为上年	As Compared with the Preceding Year	107.0	%	(%)
房地产企业营业收入	Operating Revenue of Real Estate Enterprise	2650.47	亿元	(100 million yuan)
为上年	As Compared with the Preceding Year	136.3	%	(%)
房地产企业单位数	Number of Enterprises for Real Estate Developement	1639	个	(unit)
为上年	As Compared with the Preceding Year	103.3	%	(%)

7-01 全市固定资产投资总额(1978-2016年)

Investment in Fixed Assets (1978-2016)

单位:万元 (10000 yuan)

年份 Year	固定资产投资 Investment in Fixed Assets	房地产开发投资 Investment in Real Estate Development	项目投资 Projects Investment	基础设施投资 Investment in Infrastructure	工业投资 Industrial Investment	民间投资 Nongovernment Investment
1978	23941					
1979	34407					
1980	45752					
1981	51538					
1982	66123					
1983	68306					
1984	93244					
1985	141889					
1986	182398					
1987	200516					
1988	205967					
1989	202131					
1990	229214	20409				
1991	255696	25247				
1992	384136	41886				
1993	825382	218006				
1994	1059437	320532				
1995	1566280	527985				
1996	1819333	572749				
1997	2139012	572686				
1998	2681740	666244				
1999	3233609	848441				
2000	3766473	1015347				
2001	4634929	1409132				
2002	5623366	1982517				
2003	8952090	2588452	6363638	2907234	3194960	4192567
2004	11081993	3285409	7796584	3254648	4357950	5761350
2005	12777972	4105706	8672266	3715525	4438723	6723758
2006	13734482	4426534	9307948	3871462	4640261	7551249
2007	15837775	5187904	10649871	4056241	5271141	8215570
2008	18822936	6154060	12668876	5410313	5693385	9450542
2009	21951706	7046752	14904954	6018416	6091653	11127373
2010	26518839	9561970	16956869	6452236	6855587	13680327
2011	31000218	13027234	17972984	6437025	7474806	17507040
2012	37227544	15973611	21253933	7785196	8518653	20595909
2013	42638732	18532841	24105891	8524663	9104614	22536325
2014	49527010	23010823	26516187	10055306	9133973	28438054
2015	55563183	24720743	30842440	13551793	9300133	29768831
2016	58424194	26064090	32360104	16305335	8839451	30067802

注:2011年起固定资产投资口径由计划总投资500万元以上项目投资及房地产开发投资构成。
a) Since 2011, the date of investment in fixed Assets was composed by investment projects of which each is over 5 million yuan and investment in real estate.

7-02 市区固定资产投资总额(1990-2016年)
Investment in Fixed Assets of Urban District (1990-2016)

单位:万元 (10000 yuan)

年份 Year	固定资产投资 Investment in Fixed Assets	房地产开发投资 Investment in Real Estate Development	项目投资 Projects Investment	基础设施投资 Investment in Infrastructure	工业投资 Industrial Investment	民间投资 Nongovernment Investment
1990		12750				
1991		16509				
1992		29784				
1993		115116				
1994		189357				
1995		375816				
1996		439245				
1997		445316				
1998		538499				
1999		636705				
2000		737950				
2001		1255605				
2002		1724128				
2003	7409538	2176433	5233105	2535843	2424383	3316886
2004	8963515	3088508	6153009	2624214	3299235	5238005
2005	10358519	3485810	6872709	3071506	3247399	5802542
2006	10944075	3653393	7290682	3150192	3289532	5559199
2007	12630099	4298687	8331412	3396807	3617512	6218211
2008	15184281	5269947	9914334	4726734	3676567	7076219
2009	17797778	6261562	11536216	5070500	3821313	8632900
2010	21437496	8486495	12951001	5438685	4293707	10332997
2011	25202394	11409566	13792828	5451654	4801419	13302115
2012	30160782	13749412	16411370	6495070	5554286	15669790
2013	34029665	15978470	18051195	6728552	5787728	16735292
2014	42572154	21128840	21443314	8010162	7100359	24220917
2015	47507571	22981761	24525810	10960519	6835700	25114041
2016	49572744	24325359	25247385	13229143	6173050	24924679

7－03 全市固定资产投资总额发展指数(2011－2016年)

Indices of Investment in Fixed Assets(2011－2016)

(上年＝100) (Preceding Year＝100)

年 份 Year	固定资产投资 Investment in Fixed Assets	第一产业 Primary Industry	第二产业 Secondary Industry	第三产业 Primary Industry	民间投资 Nongovernment Investment	房地产开发投资 Investment in Real Estate Development	基础设施 Investment in Infrastructure	工业投资 Industrial Investment
2011	116.9	183.3	108.9	119.6	128.0	136.2	99.8	109.0
2012	120.1	55.5	114.0	122.3	117.6	122.6	120.9	114.0
2013	114.5	196.9	107.0	116.7	109.4	116.0	109.5	106.9
2014	116.2	227.0	100.3	120.2	126.2	124.2	118.0	100.3
2015	112.2	165.0	101.8	114.3	104.7	107.4	134.8	101.8
2016	105.1	125.1	95.2	107.0	101.0	105.4	120.3	95.0

7-04 分地区固定资产投资发展指数(2011-2016年)

Indices of Investment in Fixed Assets by Region(2011-2016)

(上年=100) (Preceding Year=100)

年份 Year	全市 Whole City	上城区 Shangcheng	下城区 Xiacheng	江干区 Jianggan	拱墅区 Gongshu	西湖区 Xihu	高新(滨江)区 Hi-Tech (Binjiang)	萧山区 Xiaoshan
2011	116.9	67.8	101.3	119.1	135.3	120.6	115.9	115.0
2012	120.1	109.4	116.6	129.8	120.7	121.5	118.9	118.9
2013	114.5	107.2	125.6	92.2	125.1	124.5	111.7	118.4
2014	116.2	121.6	66.5	118.7	124.6	118.4	118.9	116.4
2015	112.2	114.1	112.5	118.5	118.9	107.2	76.5	113.2
2016	105.1	123.1	129.3	101.3	97.8	80.1	126.5	112.0

(上年=100) 7-04 续表 continued (Preceding Year=100)

年份 Year	大江东产业集聚区 Dajiangdong Industry Cluster District	余杭区 Yuhang	富阳区 Fuyang	经济技术开发区 Economic and Technological Development Zone	西湖风景名胜区 The West Lake Scenic Zone	桐庐县 Tonglu	淳安县 Chun'an	建德市 Jiande	临安市 Lin'an
2011		118.8	106.5	116.5	46.7	115.7	118.9	120.9	118.6
2012		123.9	122.5	120.7	74.2	121.9	122.0	120.8	121.6
2013		123.3	122.4	118.7	712.7	122.2	123.1	122.3	119.2
2014		124.5	122.0	106.3	125.3	121.5	121.5	121.8	120.1
2015	115.6	117.0	115.3	68.2	136.9	117.9	104.3	122.7	117.1
2016	108.0	113.1	100.2	101.8	176.4	102.5	106.0	116.7	115.0

7-05 三次产业固定资产投资(1978-2016年)

Investment in Fixed Assets Grouped by Three Industries (1978-2016)

单位:万元 (10000 yuan)

年份 Year	绝对数(万元) Absolute Figure(10000 yuan)				比重(以投资总额为100) Proportion(%)		
	合计 Total	第一产业 Primary Industry	第二产业 Secondary Industry	第三产业 Tertiary Industry	第一产业 Primary Industry	第二产业 Secondary Industry	第三产业 Tertiary Industry
1978	23941	2174	14455	7312	9.1	60.4	30.5
1979	34407	2454	19927	12026	7.1	57.9	35.0
1980	45752	1608	26211	17933	3.5	57.3	39.2
1981	51538	850	29176	21512	1.6	56.6	41.8
1982	66123	1352	37648	27123	2.0	57.0	41.0
1983	68306	1297	37823	29186	1.9	55.4	42.7
1984	93244	2831	46619	43794	3.0	50.0	47.0
1985	141889	3207	71608	67074	2.3	50.5	47.2
1986	182398	2265	94394	85739	1.2	51.8	47.0
1987	200516	2994	106600	90922	1.5	53.2	45.3
1988	205967	4746	118736	82485	2.3	57.6	40.1
1989	202131	3038	117651	81442	1.5	58.2	40.3
1990	229214	2181	126263	100770	1.0	55.1	43.9
1991	255696	3204	132303	120189	1.3	51.7	47.0
1992	384136	4424	206659	173053	1.2	53.8	45.0
1993	825382	5650	346416	473316	0.7	42.0	57.3
1994	1059437	3905	354672	700860	0.4	33.5	66.1
1995	1566280	5821	534687	1025772	0.4	34.1	65.5
1996	1819333	3100	640273	1175960	0.2	35.2	64.6
1997	2139012	1712	595966	1541334	-	27.9	72.1
1998	2681740	4053	706948	1970739	0.2	26.4	73.4
1999	3233609	23546	764309	2445754	0.7	23.6	75.7
2000	3766473	774	844334	2921365	0.2	22.4	77.4
2001	4634929	595	953494	3680840	-	20.6	79.4
2002	5623366	6514	1104212	4512640	0.1	19.6	80.3
2003	8952090	10489	3208885	5732716	0.1	35.9	64.0
2004	11081993	15992	4369015	6696986	0.1	39.4	60.5
2005	12777972	13982	4451936	8312054	0.1	34.8	65.1
2006	13734482	17892	4651420	9065170	0.1	33.9	66.0
2007	15837775	23278	5286340	10528157	0.1	33.4	66.5
2008	18822936	30810	5705736	13086390	0.2	30.3	69.5
2009	21951706	31335	6115482	15804889	0.1	27.9	72.0
2010	26518839	41959	6875840	19601040	0.2	25.9	73.9
2011	31000218	76931	7486832	23436455	0.2	24.2	75.6
2012	37227544	42668	8531598	28653278	0.1	22.9	77.0
2013	42638732	84018	9125316	33429398	0.2	21.4	78.4
2014	49527010	190748	9152477	40183785	0.4	18.5	81.1
2015	55563183	314688	9317825	45930670	0.6	16.8	82.6
2016	58424194	393625	8869013	49161556	0.7	15.2	84.1

7－06　全市固定资产投资房屋建筑面积及造价(1978－2016年)
Floor Space of Buildings and Their Cost (1978－2016)

年　份 Year	施工面积(万平方米) Floor Space of Buildings Under Construction (10000sq. m)	住　宅 Residential Buildings	竣工面积(万平方米) Floor Space of Buildings Completed (10000 sq. m)	住　宅 Residential Buildings	竣工房屋价值(万元) Value of Buildings Completed (10000 yuan)	住　宅 Residential Buildings	每平方米造价(元) Cost Per Square (yuan)	住　宅 Residential Buildings
1978			101.95	39.58	8869	2810	87	71
1979			150.26	68.01	13223	4965	88	73
1980	456.54		202.58	104.44	19448	8564	96	82
1981	507.94		232.25	120.35	26709	12396	115	103
1982	554.89	258.09	281.63	148.66	34095	16470	121	111
1983	531.79	244.36	247.07	125.86	33938	15494	137	123
1984	620.71	293.21	267.85	138.71	42740	18398	160	133
1985	741.47	333.72	327.75	157.85	56561	22825	173	145
1986	674.58	278.19	338.19	160.19	50561	27338	238	170
1987	544.64	149.07	254.73	73.16	68801	14944	270	204
1988	526.70	156.92	230.21	75.44	68407	17820	297	236
1989	420.81	116.12	202.15	64.15	69750	18200	345	284
1990	472.59	209.50	236.44	112.77	93557	34266	396	304
1991	459.00	205.41	226.84	92.72	93158	28599	411	308
1992	604.85	301.21	262.11	114.97	116169	39834	452	350
1993	958.91	533.01	380.29	199.96	224251	105107	589	525
1994	1069.68	613.62	460.20	274.19	375211	212705	815	776
1995	1320.68	737.79	524.58	319.41	491705	274314	937	859
1996	1399.70	758.00	582.70	354.50	688569	370485	1182	1045
1997	1363.80	660.70	642.10	338.00	871361	449235	1357	1329
1998	1456.02	743.59	515.16	271.91	709730	390624	1378	1437
1999	1681.71	956.15	709.10	411.44	1119141	641717	1578	1560
2000	1721.58	949.32	744.42	419.80	1207767	709044	1622	1689
2001	2318.95	1251.92	830.05	402.46	1310380	679449	1579	1688
2002	2713.02	1586.28	890.05	492.95	1623662	956643	1820	1941
2003	4392.79	2083.58	1618.01	651.58	2732763	1353422	1689	2077
2004	5731.48	2909.03	1865.83	717.46	2791115	1313596	1496	1831
2005	6671.39	3628.34	1856.34	801.34	3265491	1865538	1759	2328
2006	7260.08	3747.60	1737.51	706.13	2900836	1580689	1670	2239
2007	7942.07	4040.54	1849.24	858.99	3750264	2329184	2028	2712
2008	9471.42	4160.27	2057.86	846.34	4113211	2171525	1999	2566
2009	10308.45	4441.84	2009.90	700.63	3626421	1684092	1804	2404
2010	12971.81	5534.10	2695.90	902.57	5274936	2285285	1957	2532
2011	15982.64	6442.52	3108.57	991.72	6209320	2498468	1997	2519
2012	17329.23	6938.29	2952.06	1048.95	6015778	2485123	2038	2369
2013	19226.78	7392.23	3666.67	1308.83	7744168	3530744	2112	2698
2014	20877.58	7757.60	4274.87	1350.19	9613177	3951202	2249	2926
2015	21686.34	8163.82	4877.76	1600.80	–	–	–	–
2016	17896.18	7370.57	3937.72	1443.96	12561050	5092235	3190	3527

注:2015年竣工房屋价值相关指标取消。

a) Since 2015, the indicators related to floor space of buildings completed have been cancelled.

7-07 市区固定资产投资房屋建筑面积及造价(1978-2016年)

Urban District Floor Space of Buildings and Their Cost (1978-2016)

年 份 Year	施工面积(万平方米) Floor Space of Buildings Under Construction (10000 sq. m)	住 宅 Residential Buildings	竣工面积(万平方米) Floor Space of Buildings Completed (10000sq. m)	住 宅 Residential Buildings	竣工房屋价值(万元) Value of Buildings Completed (10000 yuan)	住 宅 Residential Buildings	每平方米造价(元) Cost Per Square (yuan)	住 宅 Residential Buildings
1978			71.56	29.06	6941	2237	97	77
1979			109.23	53.37	10267	4056	94	76
1980			137.11	76.73	14396	6752	105	88
1981			163.36	90.12	20093	9643	123	107
1982	378.88	172.11	189.92	100.07	25200	11980	133	120
1983	376.32	169.17	157.14	81.68	24029	11045	153	135
1984	465.27	221.72	191.13	104.55	33863	14658	177	140
1985	532.66	258.19	219.79	114.26	40344	17489	184	153
1986	465.75	203.22	219.33	116.70	58619	21149	267	181
1987	336.85	86.05	150.59	41.72	46530	9513	309	228
1988	315.80	90.98	117.71	37.63	38501	10117	330	269
1989	253.41	56.39	99.86	28.89	38680	9087	387	315
1990	301.82	128.50	137.88	62.47	60551	20361	439	326
1991	265.61	118.99	114.19	42.31	53819	12892	471	305
1992	329.16	190.55	115.59	57.36	55758	19706	483	344
1993	500.08	266.80	175.22	104.83	101528	53540	579	511
1994	618.91	352.16	212.06	123.74	182730	102924	862	832
1995	821.03	463.98	244.94	152.10	250073	139666	1021	918
1996	969.10	538.50	350.10	229.00	437239	274244	1249	1196
1997	1017.30	485.20	442.00	232.70	675762	357624	1529	1537
1998	1055.24	541.41	321.17	184.18	516400	317402	1608	1723
1999	1204.30	656.07	489.23	294.85	908844	533675	1858	1810
2000	1176.29	617.80	497.64	269.94	916212	528385	1841	1957
2001	2053.02	1085.30	698.29	325.64	1193818	615802	1710	1891
2002	2330.97	1335.78	744.48	404.35	1483862	869969	1993	2152
2003	3637.82	1699.61	1325.48	516.33	2395039	1174735	1807	2275
2004	4740.42	2453.87	1389.30	528.26	2257386	1068708	1625	2023
2005	5533.58	3039.08	1478.07	661.56	2804402	1626514	1897	2459
2006	5898.15	3114.45	1327.37	580.22	2365342	1357671	1782	2340
2007	6496.01	3357.18	1355.43	674.97	3063585	1992874	2260	2953
2008	7812.71	3466.88	1537.69	668.13	3372465	1827426	2193	2735
2009	8558.17	3807.67	1398.49	537.39	2725150	1321357	1949	2459
2010	10738.49	4759.75	1983.33	732.55	4255543	1927150	2146	2631
2011	13259.13	5451.45	2091.12	797.96	4736356	2122126	2265	2659
2012	14385.57	5680.08	2169.11	889.73	4966296	2207085	2290	2481
2013	15693.30	5910.71	2637.83	986.35	6074353	2822878	2303	2862
2014	18219.47	6591.75	3516.92	1132.80	8406996	3536426	2390	3122
2015	18872.19	6972.04	3868.26	1269.66	-	-	-	-
2016	15655.38	6338.80	3192.00	1205.44	10907502	4524544	3417	3753

注:2015年竣工房屋价值相关指标取消。

a) Since 2015, the indicators related to floor space of buildings completed have been cancelled.

7-08 分地区

Investment in Fixed Assets

单位:万元

年 份 Year	全 市 Whole City	市区 Urban District	上城区 Shangcheng	下城区 Xiacheng	江干区 Jianggan	拱墅区 Gongshu	西湖区 Xihu	高新(滨江)区 Hi-Tech (Binjiang)
2003	8952090	7409538						
2004	11081993	8963515						
2005	12777972	10338519						
2006	13734482	10944075						
2007	15837775	12630099						
2008	18822936	15184281						
2009	21951706	17797778						
2010	26518839	21437496	802793	1030077	2901447	1508325	2188293	1609857
2011	31000218	25202394	544686	1043891	3456831	2041130	2638752	1866605
2012	37227544	30160782	595996	1217244	4486541	2463963	3205079	2220183
2013	42638732	34029665	638625	1528423	4138372	3081999	3991415	2480827
2014	49527010	42572154	776441	1017029	4914073	3838785	4723858	2948885
2015	55563183	47507571	885811	1144348	5823773	4565672	5064510	2254688
2016	58424194	49572744	1090808	1479399	5899757	4467059	4058658	2851746

固定资产投资(2003－2016年)
by Region(2003－2016)

(10000 yuan)

萧山区 Xiaoshan	大江东产业集聚区 Dajiangdong Industry Cluster Distr	余杭区 Yuhang	富阳区 Fuyang	经济技术开发区 Economic and Technological Development Zone	西湖风景名胜区 The West Lake Scenic Zone	桐庐县 Tonglu	淳安县 Chun'an	建德市 Jiande	临安市 Lin'an
1835889		1162453	563603			250100	135275	246594	346980
2246807		1478151	767880			352987	218730	299212	479669
2161067		1718028	896329			424962	275543	316779	525840
2424763		1758656	1017368			470450	324444	377875	600270
2745133		1929019	1155871			542615	403119	432576	673495
3184947		2317510	1334619			653234	475340	509484	665978
3769557		2823192	1534401			738391	542037	575374	763725
4515095		3480147	1796500	1732557	18393	1001737	668168	658530	956408
5190805		4134743	1913712	2018316	8594	1158682	794383	796301	1134746
6169275		5121242	2343812	2436859	6378	1412038	969471	961590	1379851
7307304		6312261	2868320	2891767	45458	1725986	1193796	1176467	1644498
8508518	2226738	7861506	3500717	3074966	56971	2096371	1450503	1432850	1975132
9631238	2574129	9200016	4037889	2098220	77986	2472662	1512184	1758713	2312053
10783163	2780042	10403247	4043949	2123585	137576	2534994	1603624	2053163	2659669

7－09 分地区分类型固定

Investment in Fixed Assets

单位:万元

指　　标	Item	全　市 Total	市　区 Urban District 合　计 Total
固定资产投资额	**Investment in Fixed Assets**	**58424194**	**49572744**
#民间投资	#Private Investment	30067802	24924679
#工业投资	Industrial Investment	8839451	6173050
#基础设施投资	Investment in Infrastructure	16305335	13229143
一、按投资、房地产分	**Grouped by Sector**		
投资项目完成额	Investment Projects	32360104	25247385
房地产开发完成额	Real Estate	26064090	24325359
二、按登记注册类型分	**Grouped by Status of Registration**		
内资	Domestic－funded	51785885	43273918
国有	State－owned	9834440	8399898
集体	Collective－owned	681056	477890
股份合作	Cooperative	86735	58167
国有联营	State Joint Ownership	5103	5103
国有与集体联营	Joint State－collective Ownership	15	15
其他联营	Other Joint	－	－
国有独资公司	State－owned Corporations	4992383	3790183
其他有限责任公司	Other Limited Liability Corporations	21931101	19880257
股份有限公司	Share－holding Corporations Ltd.	1137016	930717
私营	Private	12597000	9463295
其他	Other	521036	268393
港、澳、台商投资	Investment from Hong Kong, Macao and Taiwan	4883607	4678435
外商投资	Foreign Investment	1741858	1617377
个体经营	Individual	12844	3014

资产投资(2016 年)

by Region(2016)

(10000 yuan)

萧山区 Xiaoshan	余杭区 Yuhang	富阳区 Fuyang	桐庐县 Tonglu	淳安县 Chun'an	建德市 Jiande	临安市 Lin'an
10783163	**10403247**	**4043949**	**2534994**	**1603624**	**2053163**	**2659669**
5319851	6198873	2314860	1715249	946725	1034197	1446952
1975567	1001401	1763200	825086	326857	822231	692227
3361787	1904007	1144565	956316	445454	841735	832687
6864892	4534107	2970891	2194911	1207119	1807964	1902725
3918271	5869140	1073058	340083	396505	245199	756944
9487870	8801223	3634306	2485351	1522694	1928351	2575571
1370717	908465	263387	414701	225968	469809	324064
104695	111064	63352	123892	13370	63541	2363
1331	8453	33036	2081	16284	4756	5447
–	–	–	–	–	–	–
–	–	15	–	–	–	–
–	–	–	–	–	–	–
614520	1338922	767355	208344	201439	106620	685797
4302128	3603040	1143201	419538	440450	789087	401769
137293	213233	151724	20284	32189	51349	102477
2951920	2611104	1140007	1240293	552481	440687	900244
5266	6942	72229	56218	40513	2502	153410
728106	1273727	317835	32549	46558	51041	75024
565377	328297	90604	17094	33867	68608	4912
1810	–	1204	–	505	5163	4162

单位:万元　　　　7－09　续表

指　　标	Item	全　　市 Total	市　　区 Urban District 合　计 Total
三、按行业分	**Grouped by Sector**		
农林牧渔业	Agricultare, Forestry, Animal Husbandry and Fishery	393625	31866
采矿业	Mining	123354	5277
制造业	Manufacturing	7019382	4824721
电力、热力、燃气及水的生产和供应业	Production and Supply of Electric Power, Heat Power, Gas and Tap Water	1696715	1343052
建筑业	Construction	29562	19356
批发和零售业	Wholesale & Retail Trades	681871	540440
交通运输、仓储和邮政业	Transportation, Storage and Post	3887608	3327360
住宿和餐饮业	Hotels and Catering Services	617787	246618
信息传输、软件和信息技术服务业	Information Transmission, Softuare and Information Technology	1154495	1070993
金融业	Financial Intertnediation	231081	218423
房地产业	Real Estate	30902293	28636784
租赁和商务服务业	Leasing and Business Services	544823	520844
科学研究和技术服务业	Scientific Research and Technical Service	259019	187343
水利、环境和公共设施管理业	Management of Water Conservancy, Environment and Public Facilities	8101751	6303587
居民服务、修理和其他服务业	Residentid Service, Repairs and Other Service	16652	8192
教育	Education	1587853	1396061
卫生和社会工作	Health Care and Social Welfare	454956	337039
文化、体育和娱乐业	Culture, Sports and Entertainment	471044	368323
公共管理、社会保障和社会组织	Public Management, Social Security and Social Organizations	250323	186465

continued (10000 yuan)

萧山区 Xiaoshan	余杭区 Yuhang	富阳区 Fuyang	桐庐县 Tonglu	淳安县 Chun'an	建德市 Jiande	临安市 Lin'an
497	–	31369	84397	52018	57337	168007
–	–	5277	3001	20944	79300	14832
1733755	845324	1446379	745153	272159	608869	568480
241812	156077	311544	76932	33754	134062	108915
–	747	–	2845	2303	3370	1688
67743	55468	14816	59994	51567	16717	13153
1075633	234991	86615	137619	142988	117792	161849
57357	44835	2076	119314	217900	19316	14639
43686	539254	64647	–	72274	11228	–
7457	6763	–	2455	–	4756	5447
5336477	6823974	1256714	496666	431185	373451	964207
174797	46347	–	16907	–	7072	–
14332	90402	2871	3994	–	12572	55110
1878812	975692	548609	649465	176586	520336	451777
–	1880	1654	4529	629	3302	–
67026	433415	148374	46230	28667	22005	94890
37999	86669	33729	40934	27559	45831	3593
31937	35220	47144	16969	63177	9509	13066
13843	26189	42131	27590	9914	6338	20016

7－10 分地区分类型

Investment in Industrial

单位：万元

指标	Item	全市 Total	市区 Urban District 合计 Total
总计	**Total**	**8839451**	**6173050**
#技术改造投资	**Investment in Technique Innovation**	**6484218**	**4458305**
一、按登记注册类型分	**Grouped by Status of Registration**		
内资	Domestic－funded	7484194	4967865
国有	State－owned	745535	668276
集体	Collective－owned	11857	5491
股份合作	Cooperative	4959	3905
国有联营	State Joint Ownership	4825	4825
国有与集体联营	Joint State－collective Ownership	－	－
国有独资公司	State－funded Corporations	496368	386343
其他有限责任公司	Other Limited Liability Corporations	2075062	1526275
股份有限公司	Share－holding Corporations Ltd.	536410	353716
私营	Private	3602336	2019034
其他	Other	6842	－
港、澳、台商投资	Investment from Hong Kong, Macao and Taiwan	611087	562521
外商投资	Foreign Investment	736906	640250
个体经营	Individual	7264	2414
二、按行业分	**Grouped by Sector**		
采矿业	Mining	123354	5277
制造业	Manufacturing	7019382	4824721
#农副食品加工业	Processing of Food from Agricultural Products Processing	111032	50724
食品制造业	Food Manufacturing	196633	120341
酒、饮料和精制茶制造业	Wine, Beverage and Tea Manufacturing	154859	45577
烟草制品业	Tobacco Processing	35483	35483
纺织业	Textile Processing	368993	255258
纺织服装和服饰业	Textile Products and Costume Industry	193140	92813

工业投资(2016 年)
Sector by Region(2016)

(10000 yuan)

萧山区 Xiaoshan	余杭区 Yuhang	富阳区 Fuyang	桐庐县 Tonglu	淳安县 Chun'an	建德市 Jiande	临安市 Lin'an
1975567	**1001401**	**1763200**	**825086**	**326857**	**822231**	**692227**
1350783	**652970**	**1337567**	**632058**	**241088**	**619243**	**533524**
1537614	719121	1561684	786703	315332	743822	670472
92860	17548	7069	1943	12047	58577	4692
–	5491	–	995	–	4750	621
–	1495	2410	–	1054	–	–
–	–	–	–	–	–	–
–	–	–	–	–	–	–
50083	25738	168970	17889	19532	15104	57500
582601	189606	520716	109142	42545	306806	90294
120284	26993	148989	15681	32189	51349	83475
691786	452250	713530	641053	201315	307236	433698
–	–	–	–	6650	–	192
173816	147396	134180	23739	1105	7764	15958
262927	134884	66132	14644	10420	68608	2984
1210	–	1204	–	–	2037	2813
–	–	5277	3001	20944	79300	14832
1733755	845324	1446379	745153	272159	608869	568480
21341	22314	7069	9370	17114	6559	27265
81088	10378	4195	9524	16035	24189	26544
26839	6391	3501	29101	44716	35465	–
–	–	–	–	–	–	–
222275	28289	3449	39406	36555	18424	19350
10148	13492	52614	89660	2150	8517	–

单位:万元 7-10 续表

指标	Item	全市 Total	市区 Urban District 合计 Total
皮革、毛皮、羽毛(绒)及其制造业	Leather, Furs, Down and Related Products	35284	21536
木材加工及木、竹、藤、棕、草制品业	Timber Processing, Bamboo, Cane, Palm Fiber and Straw Products	39651	5116
家具制造业	Furniture Manufacturing	26326	16048
造纸及纸制品业	Paper Making and Paper Products	314000	208653
印刷业和记录媒介的复制业	Printing and Reproduction of Recording media	75704	42026
文教体育用品制造业	Cultural, Educational and Sports Goods	129292	67108
石油加工、炼焦及核燃料加工业	Petroleum and Nuclear Fuel Processing	660	-
化学原料及化学制品制造业	Raw Chemical Material and Chemical Products	419957	228795
医药制造业	Medical and Pharmaceutical Products	355133	330367
化学纤维制造业	Chemical Fiber	165807	164573
橡胶和塑料制造业	Rubber and Plastic Products	213969	111840
非金属矿制品业	Nonmetal Mineral Products	405186	180877
黑色金属冶炼和压延加工业	Smelting and Pressing of Ferrous Metals	83633	74506
有色金属冶炼和压延加工业	Smelting and Pressing of Nonferrous Metal	199809	180862
金属制品业	Metal Products	357885	241069
通用设备制造业	General Purpose Machinery	496666	303057
专业设备制造业	Special Purpose Machinery	207987	171671
汽车制造业	Automobile Manufacturing	703205	629760
铁路、船舶、航空航天等制造业	Railway, Watercraft, Avigation Spaceflight and other Equipment Manufacturing	54871	37602
电气机械及器材制造业	Electric Equipment and Machinery	646346	428672
计算机、通信和其他电子设备制造业	Computers, Telecommunications and other Electronic Equipment Manufacturing	699035	523017
仪器仪表制造业	Instruments and Meters Manufacturing	113331	91238
其他制造业	Other Manufacturing	107588	81789
废弃资源综合利用业	Multiple Utilization of Waste Resouces	97022	74226
金属制品、机械和设备修理业	Metal Products, Machinery and Equipment Repair	10895	10117
电力、热力、燃气及水的生产和供应业	Production and Supply of Electric Power, Heat Power, Gas and Tap Water	1696715	1343052

continued (10000 yuan)

萧山区 Xiaoshan	余杭区 Yuhang	富阳区 Fuyang	桐庐县 Tonglu	淳安县 Chun'an	建德市 Jiande	临安市 Lin'an
15835	669	3072	10704	–	1886	1158
424	4492	200	5222	8966	16869	3478
11667	2707	–	5108	–	1676	3494
8086	27522	164633	8978	–	8328	88041
19407	7440	4582	18233	3986	10603	856
27143	24185	10493	48983	5	10571	2625
–	–	–	–	–	660	–
178545	9569	36789	8460	5202	147110	30390
46604	29520	164535	11439	–	5256	8071
132826	800	28444	–	–	1234	–
26607	23327	41677	27765	1192	52870	20302
56762	27974	85495	63827	22216	110257	28009
8130	4401	61975	5129	–	3998	–
12064	36391	132407	–	–	16787	2160
91262	31808	95251	41249	4624	45090	25853
89506	128827	39517	92832	4682	24319	71776
53611	41225	23651	30390	41	1879	4006
408571	143257	53370	10139	28887	3132	31287
30998	4752	1852	–	1844	7402	8023
115331	105004	147120	35965	45053	22888	113768
29885	71866	120304	120850	9406	5950	39812
8800	25426	7350	2465	14611	–	5017
–	3425	78364	11986	4767	4196	4850
–	2533	71693	8368	107	11976	2345
–	7340	2777	–	–	778	–
241812	156077	311544	76932	33754	134062	108915

7-11 分地区房地产
Investment in Real Estate

指　标	Item	全　市 Total	市　区 Urban District 合　计 Total
房地产开发投资额　（万元）	**Investment in Real Estate Development (10000 yuan)**	**26064090**	**24325359**
住宅　（万元）	Residential Buildings (10000 yuan)	15599790	14389769
办公楼　（万元）	Office Buildings (10000 yuan)	2528303	2477181
商业营业用房　（万元）	Buildings for Business Use (10000 yuan)	3042491	2833754
其他　（万元）	Others (10000 yuan)	4893506	4624655
房屋建筑面积	**Floor space of Buildings**		
施工面积　（万平方米）	Under Construction (10000 sq. m)	11562.96	10253.68
#住宅　（万平方米）	#Residential Buildings (10000 sq. m)	6000.56	5109.23
新开工面积　（万平方米）	Started This Year (10000 sq. m)	2135.90	1913.32
#住宅　（万平方米）	#Residential Buildings (10000 sq. m)	1224.33	1088.13
竣工面积　（万平方米）	Construction Completed (10000 sq. m)	1922.99	1735.25
#住宅　（万平方米）	#Residential Buildings (10000 sq. m)	1113.35	969.77
商品房销售情况	**Selling of Commercialized Buildings**		
销售金额　（万元）	Total Sales of Buildings (10000 yuan)	36654771	34431256
#住宅　（万元）	#Residential Buildings (10000 yuan)	30596076	28525948
现房销售额　（万元）	Sales of Completed Buildings (10000 yuan)	7381840	6683832
#住宅　（万元）	#Residential Buildings (10000 yuan)	5944791	5318448
期房销售金额　（万元）	Sales of Future Buildings (10000 yuan)	29272931	27747424
#住宅　（万元）	#Residential Buildings (10000 yuan)	24651285	23207500
销售面积　（万平方米）	Floor Space of Buildings Sold (10000 sq. m)	2326.69	2058.66
#住宅　（万平方米）	#Residential Buildings (10000 sq. m)	1887.11	1636.13
现房销售面积　（万平方米）	Floor Space of Completed Buildings Sold (10000 sq. m)	555.85	467.28
#住宅　（万平方米）	#Residential Buildings (10000 sq. m)	434.44	354.82
期房销售面积　（万平方米）	Floor Space of Futures Buildings Sold (10000 sq. m)	1770.84	1591.38
#住宅　（万平方米）	#Residential Buildings (10000 sq. m)	1452.67	1281.31

开发投资(2016年)
Development by Region(2016)

萧山区 Xiaoshan	余杭区 Yuhang	富阳区 Fuyang	桐庐县 Tonglu	淳安县 Chun'an	建德市 Jiande	临安市 Lin'an
3918271	**5869140**	**1073058**	**340083**	**396505**	**245199**	**756944**
2599419	3862956	600224	231962	249901	148524	579634
292805	360514	50767	24493	2423	13146	11060
248074	585156	242512	58713	76070	18107	55847
777973	1060514	179555	24915	68111	65422	110403
1880.53	3340.81	448.93	333.82	303.60	224.42	447.44
979.27	2012.49	274.62	224.47	189.57	163.61	313.67
323.31	657.47	129.41	43.63	44.29	26.96	107.70
207.32	386.55	64.90	23.20	24.65	23.13	65.23
266.09	534.10	75.50	42.09	19.48	79.53	46.63
142.35	382.46	47.38	37.09	12.53	65.36	28.60
5840845	8050284	1284345	483778	365878	310244	1063615
4933615	7235746	1210926	442115	354790	252273	1020950
884159	1729584	246985	213402	142150	30638	311818
693090	1600156	221520	192617	132744	23361	277621
4956686	6320700	1037360	270376	223728	279606	751797
4240525	5635590	989406	249498	222046	228912	743329
393.01	679.87	110.62	63.85	43.14	33.89	127.14
313.44	590.16	104.81	59.50	42.11	29.97	119.40
64.84	164.79	18.08	27.72	15.02	4.34	41.49
46.79	146.71	16.08	25.97	14.20	3.57	35.88
328.18	515.08	92.54	36.13	28.12	29.55	85.66
266.65	443.45	88.73	33.54	27.91	26.40	83.52

7－12 房屋建筑面积及造价(2016年)

Floor Space of Buildings and Their Cost(2016)

指　　标	Item	施工面积(万平方米) Floor Space of Buildings Under Construction (10000 sq. m)	竣工面积(万平方米) Floor Space of Buildings Completed (10000 sq. m)	竣工房屋的价值(万元) Value of Buildings Completed (10000 yuan)	每平方米造价(元) Cost Per Square Meter (yuan)
全　市	**Total**				
房屋建筑面积合计	**Floor Space of Buildings**	**17896.18**	**3937.72**	**12561050**	**3190**
#住宅	#Residential Buildings	7370.57	1443.96	5092235	3527
房地产开发	Real Estate Development	11562.96	1922.99	7405055	3851
#住宅	#Residential Buildings	6000.56	1113.35	4387923	3941
市　区	**Urban District**				
房屋建筑面积合计	**Floor Space of Buildings**	**15655.38**	**3192.00**	**10907502**	**3417**
#住宅	#Residential Buildings	6338.80	1205.44	4524544	3753
房地产开发	Real Estate Development	10253.68	1735.25	6847623	3946
#住宅	#Residential Buildings	5109.23	969.77	3982469	4107
#萧山区	**Xiaoshan**				
房屋建筑面积合计	**Total Floor Space of Buildings**	**2903.81**	**784.48**	**2127538**	**2712**
#住宅	#Residential Buildings	1238.16	248.26	812019	3271
房地产开发	Real Estate Development	1880.53	266.09	923918	3472
#住宅	#Residential Buildings	979.27	142.35	574426	4035
余杭区	**Yuhang**				
房屋建筑面积合计	**Total Floor Space of Buildings**	**4620.86**	**771.75**	**2121724**	**2749**
#住宅	#Residential Buildings	2183.43	407.98	1265520	3102
房地产开发	Real Estate Development	3340.81	534.10	1608673	3012
#住宅	#Residential Buildings	2012.49	382.46	1213833	3174

7－12 续表 continued

指　　标	Item	施工面积（万平方米）Floor Space of Buildings Under Construction (10000 sq. m)	竣工面积（万平方米）Floor Space of Buildings Completed (10000 sq. m)	竣工房屋的价值（万元）Value of Buildings Completed (10000 yuan)	每平方米造价（元）Cost Per Square Meter (yuan)
富 阳 区	**Fuyang**				
房屋建筑面积合计	**Total Floor Space of Buildings**	**931.05**	**330.03**	**978197**	**2964**
#住宅	#Residential Buildings	327.11	65.07	225770	3470
房地产开发	Real Estate Development	448.93	75.50	271669	3598
#住宅	#Residential Buildings	274.62	47.38	182697	3856
桐 庐 县	**Tonglu**				
房屋建筑面积合计	**Total Floor Space of Buildings**	**547.75**	**152.06**	**381619**	**2510**
#住宅	#Residential Buildings	243.57	49.63	143852	2899
房地产开发	Real Estate Development	333.82	42.09	98627	2343
#住宅	#Residential Buildings	224.47	37.09	88848	2395
淳 安 县	**Chun'an**				
房屋建筑面积合计	**Total Floor Space of Buildings**	**422.12**	**92.39**	**214783**	**2325**
#住宅	#Residential Buildings	193.47	13.04	32375	2483
房地产开发	Real Estate Development	303.60	19.48	46742	2400
#住宅	#Residential Buildings	189.57	12.53	30445	2430
建 德 市	**Jiande**				
房屋建筑面积合计	**Total Floor Space of Buildings**	**485.85**	**244.30**	**470681**	**1927**
#住宅	#Residential Buildings	220.30	95.49	211414	2214
房地产开发	Real Estate Development	224.42	79.53	186397	2344
#住宅	#Residential Buildings	163.61	65.36	154287	2360
临 安 市	**Lin'an**				
房屋建筑面积合计	**Total Floor Space of Buildings**	**785.09**	**256.98**	**586465**	**2282**
#住宅	#Residential Buildings	374.43	80.36	180050	2240
房地产开发	Real Estate Development	447.44	46.63	225666	4839
#住宅	#Residential Buildings	313.67	28.60	131874	4611

7－13 分注册类型和资质等级

Financial Statistics of Enterprises for Real Estate Development

单位:万元

项目	Item	法人企业数(个) Number of Enterprises (unit)	年末 Asset and		
			流动资产合计 Circulating Funds	应收账款 Account Receivable	固定资产合计 Fixed Assets
总计	**Total**	**1639**	**134597562**	**2156716**	**2225258**
一、按登记注册类型分组	**Grouped by Registration Status**				
内资企业	Domestic Funded	1500	110710291	1245452	1540659
国有企业	State－owned	7	960989	7278	4273
集体企业	Collective－owned	－	－	－	－
股份合作企业	Share－holding Cooperative Enterprises	－	－	－	－
联营企业	Joint Venture	2	55639	12572	598
有限责任公司	Limited Liability Corporations	931	80114449	894442	1025581
股份有限公司	Share－holding Corporations Ltd.	24	3371220	15032	152784
私营企业	Private Enterprises	536	26207994	316128	357422
其他企业	Other Enterprises	－	－	－	－
港澳台商投资企业	Funded from Hong Kong，Macao and Taiwan	106	16284586	762641	500101
外商投资企业	Foreign Funded	33	7602685	148623	184498
二、按企业资质等级分	**Grouped by Quali Fication Grade**				
一级	Grade Ⅰ	48	12905426	67592	176567
二级	Grade Ⅱ	120	8282194	109117	218883
三级	Grade Ⅲ	197	9283197	260026	471126
四级	Grade Ⅳ	58	1940021	54294	15861
暂定	Tentatine	804	68630895	1263723	754248
其他	Others	412	33555830	401965	588573

房地产开发企业财务状况(2016 年)

Grouped by Registration Status and Qualification Grade(2016)

(10000 yuan)

资产负债 Liabilities at Year - end						所有者权益合计 Creditors′ Equity	
固定资产原价 Orginal Value of Fixed Assets	累计折旧 Accumulated Depreciation	#本年折旧 Depreciation This Year	在建工程 Projects wnder Construction	资产合计 Total Assets	负债合计 Total Liabilities		实收资本 Capital Hold
2573779	**608630**	**89543**	**2291202**	**159053761**	**120397375**	**38656386**	**29147533**
1916103	548708	71755	1768962	130696630	103838879	26857751	19835839
5677	2406	163	2487	989231	807279	181952	34000
–	–	–	–	–	–	–	–
–	–	–	–	–	–	–	–
1954	1356	121	–	151859	93278	58580	2800
1237615	343974	45887	1718696	95719550	76804997	18914554	14583689
191427	46152	7439	3191	5267899	2466349	2801549	1037156
479431	154821	18145	44588	28568091	23666976	4901116	4178194
–	–	–	–	–	–	–	–
537378	37652	14326	436778	18494316	9582795	8911520	7907222
120298	22270	3462	85462	9862815	6975701	2887114	1404473
289162	117410	11845	–	20782009	14447635	6334374	1982410
307420	108433	11296	13318	11404031	8093090	3310942	1657622
567376	146104	17368	1129891	12525945	8911875	3614070	1604189
33788	18235	1836	388600	2503270	2167254	336016	178979
762219	137912	29314	482608	75918280	59176482	16741798	15993837
613814	80535	17884	276786	35920226	27601040	8319186	7730498

单位:万元　　7－13　续表

项　　目	Item	营业收入 Revenue of Business	#主营业务收入 Main Revenue of Business	营业成本 Operating Costs	#主营业务成本 Main Cost of Business
总计	**Total**	**26504734**	**26384000**	**21807672**	**21722844**
一、按登记注册类型分组	**Grouped by Registration Status**				
内资企业	Domestic Funded	22165937	22068043	18605561	18528393
国有企业	State－owned	7500	7500	4785	4785
集体企业	Collective－owned	–	–	–	–
股份合作企业	Share－holding Cooperative Enterprises	–	–	–	–
联营企业	Joint Venture	23425	23301	14822	14822
有限责任公司	Limited Liability Corporations	16781795	16692572	14062217	13996713
股份有限公司	Share－holding Corporations Ltd.	189917	188925	91157	90236
私营企业	Private Enterprises	5163301	5155745	4432581	4421838
其他企业	Other Enterprises	–	–	–	–
港澳台商投资企业	Funded from Hong Kong，Macao and Taiwan	3394959	3393798	2595368	2587947
外商投资企业	Foreign Funded	943838	922159	606743	606505
二、按企业资质等级分	**Grouped by Quali Fication Grade**				
一级	Grade Ⅰ	1331166	1291545	922298	914405
二级	Grade Ⅱ	1176264	1169884	851710	844988
三级	Grade Ⅲ	2301041	2290906	1515453	1514592
四级	Grade Ⅳ	203522	203351	174300	172792
暂定	Tentatine	18781298	18722942	16110716	16043606
其他	Others	2711443	2705373	2233196	2232461

continued (10000 yuan)

营业税金及附加 Main Sales Tax and Extra Charges	销售费用 Cost of Sales	管理费用 Administration Cost	财务费用 Financil Cost	#利息支出 Interest Expenditure	营业利润 Management Profits	利润总额 Total Profits	应交所得税 Income Tax
1804450	**917826**	**793044**	**546179**	**521281**	**1838541**	**1879297**	**562571**
1490334	750719	648116	538773	420950	1230402	1279380	416046
299	480	2707	-283	-	2259	2488	420
-	-	-	-	-	-	-	-
-	-	-	-	-	-	-	-
904	86	3949	-572	15	4236	4224	1300
1123855	547103	462928	462580	347039	944703	984976	322331
46960	11089	24713	-8383	12628	185345	186120	17458
318317	191961	153820	85431	61268	93860	101573	74536
-	-	-	-	-	-	-	-
217033	111591	86594	12466	24485	380181	375832	105225
97082	55517	58334	-5059	75846	227957	224085	41300
151425	34147	123638	85169	202365	614431	626168	48414
78713	49882	77060	66702	50955	219909	237252	36162
221468	59779	115439	136145	63787	356145	375881	82384
9362	6346	8965	1030	1961	5327	7063	1792
1179828	605831	341705	203402	163090	603539	575946	339824
163655	161843	126237	53731	39124	39190	56987	53995

7-14 全市分行业基础设施投资(2010-2016年)
Investment in Infrastructure by Sector(2010-2016)

单位:亿元 (100 million yuan)

年份 Year	基础设施投资 Investment in Infrastructure	水利、环境和公共设施 Water, Environment and Public Facilities	电力、燃气及水的生产供应业 Produotion and supply of Electricity, Gas & Water	交通运输、仓储和邮政业 Transportation, Storage and Post	电信和其他信息传输服务业 Telecommunications and Other Information Transmission Services	教育设施 Education Facilities	卫生设施 Sanitary Facilities
2010	6452236	2593603	682482	2415265	162166	339381	165668
2011	6437025	2529677	809813	2193350	142099	382672	167024
2012	7785196	2725934	1275603	2572604	162947	572350	201913
2013	8524663	3486809	1167072	2375342	199444	643681	261722
2014	10055306	3940406	1131323	3129697	180788	959814	241614
2015	13551793	5899889	1616380	3892605	201924	1234331	231015
2016	16305335	8101751	1696715	3887608	231813	1587853	358314

主要统计指标解释

固定资产投资额　固定资产投资完成额是以货币表现的建造和购置固定资产的工作量以及与此有关的费用的总称。它是反映固定资产投资规模、速度、比例关系和使用方向的综合性指标。

房地产开发投资　包括各种经济类型的房地产开发公司、商品房建设公司及其他房地产开发单位统一开发的包括统代建、拆迁还建的住宅、厂房、仓库、饭店、宾馆、度假村、写字楼、办公楼等房屋建筑物和配套的服务设施、土地开发工程,如道路、给水、排水、供电、供热、通讯、平整场地等基础设施工程的投资。不包括单纯的土地交易活动。

施工和竣工房屋建筑面积　房屋建筑面积是从房屋外墙线算起的各层平面面积的总和,包括房屋结构(如柱、墙)占用的面积和地下室面积。多层建筑按各自然层面积总和计算,包括房屋内的楼隔层,突出墙面的眺望间、门斗、有柱雨罩的面积。不包括突出墙面结构的构件、艺术装饰等所占的面积,如台阶等。凹阳台、挑阳台按其水平投影面积一半计算建筑面积。

房屋新开工面积　指在报告期内新开工建设的房屋面积。不包括上期跨入报告期继续施工的房屋面积和上期停缓建而在本期恢复施工的房屋面积。房屋的开工应以房屋正式开始破土刨槽(地基处理或打永久桩)的日期为准。

商品房销售面积　指报告期内出售商品房屋的合同总面积(即双方签署的正式买卖合同中所确定的建筑面积)。由现房销售建筑面积和期房销售建筑面积两部分组成。

(1)现房销售面积:是指在报告期内正式签订买卖合同、已经竣工达到入住条件的商品房屋建筑面积。包括以一次性付款方式和分期付款方式销售的现房建筑面积。

(2)期房销售面积:是指在报告期内正式签订买卖合同、正在建设尚未竣工交付使用的商品房屋建筑面积。包括以一次性付款方式和分期付款方式销售的商品房屋建筑面积。期房销售建筑面积竣工后不再转为现房销售建筑面积。

新增固定资产　指通过投资活动所形成的新的固定资产价值。包括已经建成投入生产或交付使用的工程价值和达到固定资产标准的设备、工具、器具的价值及有关应摊入的费用。它是以价值形式表示的固定资产投资成果的综合性指标,可以综合反映不同时期、不同部门、不同地区的固定资产投资成果。

Explanatory Notes on Main Statistical Indicators

Total Investment in Fixed Assets refer to the volume of activities in construction and purchases of fixed assets in monetary terms and other relative expenses. It is a comprehensive indicator which shows the size, pace, proportional relations and use orientation of investment in fixed assets.

Investment in Real Estate Development include the investment by the real estate development companies, commercial buildings construction companies and other real estate development units of various types of ownership in the construction of house buildings, such as residential buildings, factory buildings, warehouses, hotels, guesthouses, holiday supply, water drainage, power supply, heating, telecommunications, land leveling and other projects of infrastructure, it excludes the activities in simple land transaction.

Floor space of Building Under Construction and Completed refer to total floor space in each story of buildings calculate from the outside line of building walls, including the space occupied by construction like pillars or walls and basements. The floor space of multi - story building includes the total floor space of each story, including area occupied by separating walls, watching rooms, door - ways, and pillars, but excluding protruding wall structures, artistic decoration, etc. (for example, flight of steps). The space of balcony is counted by half of the projection area.

Beginning to Construction Floor Space of Building refer to the area space which constructed in report period, not including the floor whose construction lasted to report period and which stopped in the last period to continue construction in the report period. And the beginning of construction of floor space should base on the date of breaking the earth(disposal the basement or piling).

Selling of the Commercial Building refer to the total area that sold by contract(which reflected in the contract), which include completed and future buildings.

(1) Floor Space of Completed Building: refer to the area which formal contract has been signed and which has been completed and reached the condition of living, including payment in one time and installment payment.

(2) Floor Space of Future Building: refer to the area which signed by formal contract and under constructing, including payment in one time and installment payment. Which can not be turned into completed building's sale when they completed.

Newly Increased Fixed Assets refer to the newly increased value of fixed assets through investment, including the value of projects completed and put into production, the value of equipment, tools, and vessels considered as fixed assets, as well as the relevant expenses as investment in fixed assets. This is a comprehensive indicator of investment in fixed assets, reflecting the achievements of investment in fixed assets in different periods, different sectors, and different regions.

八、国内贸易

DOMESTIC TRADE

8

国内贸易
Domestic Trade

主要统计指标
Major Statistical Indicators

社会消费品零售总额	Total Retail Sales of Consumer Goods	5176.20	亿元	(100 million yuan)
为上年	As Compared with the Preceding Year	110.5	%	(%)
批发和零售贸易业	Wholesale and Retail Trades	4635.71	亿元	(100 million yuan)
为上年	As Compared with the Preceding Year	110.7	%	(%)
住宿和餐饮业	Hotels and Catering Services	540.49	亿元	(100 million yuan)
为上年	As Compared with the Preceding Year	108.6	%	(%)

8－01 社会消费品零售总额(1978－2016 年)

Total Retail Sale of Consumer Goods(1978－2016)

单位:万元 (10,000 yuan)

年　份 Year	全　市 Total	市　区 Urban District	县(市)合计 All Counties
1978	119509	73653	45856
1979	150462	93342	57120
1980	205381	128440	76941
1981	236188	148152	88036
1982	251068	154582	96486
1983	273664	169508	104156
1984	343722	215901	127821
1985	478117	308901	169216
1986	557963	360479	197484
1987	657838	426745	231093
1988	866373	557374	308999
1989	927019	600816	326203
1990	981713	650278	331435
1991	1155476	777559	377917
1992	1408525	928586	479939
1993	1901509	1300037	601472
1994	2616477	1733572	882905
1995	2993250	1930140	1063110
1996	3478156	2310619	1167537
1997	3815537	2537537	1278000
1998	4178013	2794171	1383842
1999	4574924	3053983	1520941
2000	5146789	3436536	1710253
2001	5790138	4993078	797060
2002	6606548	5701707	904841
2003	7425760	6401970	1023790
2004	8554476	7385662	1168814
2005	9784275	8440559	1343716
2006	11191900	9630210	1561690
2007	13082930	11247539	1835391
2008	15775872	13542665	2233207
2009	18378198	15793645	2584553
2010	22250034	19141417	3108616
2011	26902226	23152666	3749561
2012	31651929	27196536	4455393
2013	38648394	33483819	5164575
2014	42014577	37855211	4159366
2015	46864334	42192730	4671604
2016	51762033	46581230	5180803

注:1)根据国家统一规定,2013 年经济普查后对 2009－2013 年度数据作了相应调整。
2)从 2013 年开始,零售总额口径从“在地口径”调整为“法人口径”。
a)According to the standards by NBS, the data of 2009－2013 are adjusted by the resuct of economic census.
b)The donotation of retail sale has been adjusted to "legal" from" regional".

8－02 分地区社会消费品

Total Retail Sale of Consumer Goods

单位:万元

年份 Year	全市 Whole City		市区 Urban District					
	合计 Total	为上年(%) As Compared with the Preceding Year(%)	合计 Total	上城区 Shangcheng	下城区 Xiacheng	江干区 Jianggan	拱墅区 Gongshu	西湖区 Xihu
2001	5790138	113.6	4993078					
2002	6606548	114.1	5701707					
2003	7425760	112.4	6401970					
2004	8554476	115.2	7385662					
2005	9784275	114.4	8440559	875997	2211413	921149	1214351	973276
2006	11191900	114.4	9630210	1009624	2525806	1037537	1276948	1123397
2007	13082930	116.9	11247539	1187213	2974715	1182818	1462099	1301510
2008	15775872	120.6	13542665	1453850	3481959	1383411	1701815	1566397
2009	18378198	116.5	15793645	1658259	4038155	1613453	2001549	1827286
2010	22250034	121.1	19141417	1835792	4674657	1974898	2457354	2461164
2011	26902226	120.9	23152666	2185077	5626892	2400276	2981552	2984970
2012	31651929	117.7	27196536	2535185	6570798	2830689	3480268	3521955
2013	38648394	115.1	33483819	2846236	7457146	3195632	3982649	4197443
2014	42014577	108.7	37855211	3064010	8184312	3484859	4159942	4606757
2015	46864334	111.8	42192730	3418056	9162747	3887534	4617536	5139067
2016	51762033	110.5	46581230	3794726	10092262	4315163	5080110	5676221

零售总额(2001 －2016 年)
by Region(2001 －2016)

(10000 yuan)

高新(滨江)区 Hi－Tech(Binjiang)	萧山区 Xiaoshan	大江东产业集聚区 Dajiangdong Industry Cluster Distr	余杭区 Yuhang	富阳区 Fuyang	经济技术开发区 Economic and Technological Development Zone	西湖风景名胜区 The West Lake Scenic Zone	桐庐县 Tonglu	淳安县 Chun'an	建德市 Jiande	临安市 Lin'an
	690721		446812	223782			166892	90133	128754	187499
	795711		508919	254887			188087	101581	144849	215437
	929390		584748	289297			209153	114990	163244	247106
	1069728		674799	331534			237598	130974	185772	282936
61378	1234568		778848	382960	99577	70006	272394	149456	212138	326768
71889	1462157		906960	450365	130145	75745	317484	173272	247425	373144
86073	1721511		1064956	526750	168722	97921	371057	201769	288873	446942
220282	2059811		1302135	643169	256127	116877	451356	244069	350854	543759
263639	2425882		1534222	745144	288218	142982	522835	282629	406299	627647
432557	2955860		1849231	895185	336766	163138	624511	338317	499388	751216
537647	3578930		2248637	1081323	415098	193588	752559	409590	602059	904030
656956	4270442		2616486	1285095	502576	211180	896018	488301	714702	1071278
889240	4871438		3077344	1504100	610530	225115	1030908	563508	823344	1242715
928820	5156481		3494348	1707917	715540	238287	1173697	640460	934093	1411117
1066796	5739163	400901	3912097	1980415	833283	264499	1323402	721510	1044830	1581862
1180895	6350442	461386	4331598	2224502	883476	291033	1478405	808981	1152578	1740840

8－03 社会消费品
Total Retail Sale of

单位：万元

地 区	Region	合 计 Total
全 市	**Total**	**51762033**
市 区	Urban District	46581230
#上城区	Shangcheng	3794726
下城区	Xiacheng	10092262
江干区	Jianggan	4315163
拱墅区	Gongshu	5080110
西湖区	Xihu	5676221
高新(滨江)区	Hi－Tech(Binjiang)	1180895
萧山区	Xiaoshan	6350442
余杭区	Yuhang	4331598
富阳区	Fuyang	2224502
桐庐县	Tonglu	1478405
淳安县	Chun'an	808981
建德市	Jiande	1152578
临安市	Lin'an	1740840

零售总额(2016 年)
Consumer Goods(2016)

(10000 yuan)

按经营地分 By Location		按行业分 By Sector	
城镇 Urban Areas	乡村 Rural Areas	批发和零售贸易业 Wholesale and Retail Trades	住宿和餐饮业 Hotels and Catering Services
49046087	**2715946**	**46357120**	**5404913**
45867104	714126	42010466	4570763
3794726	–	3328359	466367
10092262	–	9388316	703946
4315163	–	3926306	388857
5080110	–	4812292	267818
5676221	–	5164685	511536
1180895	–	1080245	100650
6350442	–	5569516	780926
4331598	–	3951633	379964
1510376	714126	2020881	203621
912019	566386	1265803	212602
484488	324493	638845	170136
790970	361608	935865	216713
991507	749333	1506140	234700

8-04 按登记注册类型分限额以上批发零售贸易企业商品销售总额(2016年)

Sales of Wholesale and Retail Trades Above Designated Size by Status of Registration(2016)

单位:万元 (10000 yuan)

项目	Item	法人企业(个) Number of Enterprises (unit)	销售总额 Total Sales	批发额 Wholesale	零售额 Retail
总计	**Total**	**4134**	**153805814**	**124765707**	**29040107**
1.内资企业	**Domestic-funded Enterprises**	**3993**	**145726390**	**121172480**	**24553910**
国有企业	State-owned Enterprises	17	1990958	1928869	62089
集体企业	Collective-owned Enterprises	7	49929	5482	44447
股份合作企业	Cooperative Enterprises	2	1887	-	1887
联营企业	Joint Ownership Enterprises	5	40617	471	40146
国有联营企业	State Joint Ownership Enterprises	-	-	-	-
集体联营企业	Collective Joint Ownership Enterprises	-	-	-	-
国有与集体联营企业	Joint State-collective Enterprises	5	40617	471	40146
其他联营企业	Other Joint Ownership Enterprises	-	-	-	-
有限责任公司	Limited Liability Corporations	1144	80590375	66741798	13848577
国有独资公司	State-funded Corporations	50	7548521	7289967	258554
其他有限责任公司	Other Limited Liability Corporations	1094	73041854	59451831	13590023
股份有限公司	Share-holding Corporations Ltd.	115	18015088	13829685	4185403
私营企业	Private Enterprises	2648	44919821	38588767	6331055
私营独资企业	Private-funded Enterprises	17	41708	14144	27564
私营合伙企业	Private Partnership Enterprises	1	1251	-	1251
私营有限责任公司	Private Limited Liability Corporations	2592	43731497	37536446	6195051
私营股份有限公司	Private Share-holding Corporations Ltd.	38	1145366	1038177	107189
其他企业	Other Enterprises	55	117714	77409	40305
2.港、澳、台商投资企业	**Enterprises With Investment from Hong Kong, Macao and Taiwan**	**70**	**4863966**	**2808517**	**2055448**
合资经营企业(港或澳、台资)	Joint-venture Enterprises (With Funds from Hong Kong, Macao and Taiwan)	21	1745686	843148	902538
合作经营企业(港或澳、台资)	Coorperative Enterprises (With Funds from Hong Kong, Macao and Taiwan)	1	32706	-	32706
港、澳、台商独资经营企业	Enterprises With Sole Investment from Hong Kong, Macao and Taiwan	45	3066881	1950870	1116011
港、澳、台商投资股份有限公司	Share-holding Corporations Ltd. With Investment from Hong Kong, Macao and Taiwan	1	4193	-	4193
其他港澳台投资企业	Other Enterprises With Investment from Hong Kong, Macao and Taiwan	2	14499	14499	-
3.外商投资企业	**Enterprises With Foreign Investment**	**71**	**3215458**	**784710**	**2430749**
中外合资经营企业	Joint-venture Enterprises	16	1283756	450740	833016
中外合作经营企业	Cooperation Enterprises	1	7837	-	7837
外资企业	Enterprises With Sole Foreign Investment	53	1875240	285344	1589896
外商投资股份有限公司	Share-holding Corporations Ltd. With Foreign Investment	-	-	-	-
其他外商投资企业	Other Enterprises With Foreign Investment	1	48626	48626	-

8-05 按国民经济行业分限额以上批发零售贸易企业商品销售总额(2016年)
Sales of Wholesale and Retail Trades Above Designated Size by Sector(2016)

单位:万元 (10000 yuan)

项目	Item	法人企业(个) Number of Enterprises (unit)	销售总额 Total Sales	批发额 Wholesale	零售额 Retail
总计	**Total**	**4134**	**153805814**	**124765707**	**29040107**
一、批发业	**Wholesale**	**2825**	**126292786**	**121737510**	**4555276**
农、林、牧产品批发	Wholesale of Farm, Forestry and Animal Husbandry Products	43	835979	827607	8372
食品、饮料及烟草制品批发	Wholesale of Food, Beverages and Tobaccos	205	10670636	10439631	231005
纺织、服装及家庭用品批发	Wholesale of Textile Products, Garments and Household Articles	692	15419898	14963591	456307
文化、体育用品及器材批发	Wholesale of Cultural and Sports Goods	116	3889530	3710279	179251
医药及医疗器材批发	Wholesale of Medicines and Medical Appliances	162	8437245	5534375	2902869
矿产品、建材及化工产品批发	Wholesale of Mineral Products, Building and Chemical Materials	1104	69845486	69388946	456540
机械设备、五金产品及电子产品批发	Wholesale of Machinery, Hardware and Electronic Products	462	16630880	16314287	316592
#汽车、摩托车及零配件批发	Wholesale of Automobiles, Motorcycle and Parts	95	8067668	7906665	161003
贸易经纪与代理	Trade Agenly	5	34336	34186	149
其他批发业	Other	36	528797	524606	4191
二、零售业	**Retail Trade**	**1309**	**27513028**	**3028197**	**24484830**
综合零售	Comprehensive Retail Trade	130	6150136	604331	5545805
食品、饮料及烟草制品专门零售	Specialism Retail of Food, Beverages and Tobaccos	130	411340	52879	358461
纺织、服装及日用品专门零售	Specialism Retail of Textile Products, Garments, Shoes and Caps	96	1071805	128564	943241
文化、体育用品及器材专门零售	Specialism Retail of Cultural and Sports Goods	55	529179	137966	391213
医药及医疗器材专门零售	Specialism Retail of Medicines and Medical Appliances	91	1088160	145221	942939
汽车、摩托车、燃料及零配件专门零售	Specialism Retail of Automobiles, Motorcycle, Fuels and Parts	476	12395277	1041059	11354218
#汽车零售	Specialism Retail of Automobiles	303	9270513	770751	8499762
家用电器及电子产品专门零售	Specialism Retail of Household Electric Applianes, and Electronic Products	115	1836504	363952	1472552
五金、家具及室内装饰材料专门零售	Specialism Retail of Hardware and Upholstery Materials	51	250184	16269	233915
货摊、无店铺及其他零售业	Stall, Non-shop and Other Retails	165	3780445	537957	3242488

8-06 按登记注册类型分限额以上

Main Financial Indicators of Enterprises Above Designated Size in

单位:万元

项目	Item	法人企业数(个) Number of Enterprises (unit)	年末资产负债 Assets and Liabilities 流动资产合计 Circulating Funds	存货 Inventory	固定资产原价 Orginal Value of Fixed Assets
批发零售贸易业企业合计	**Total**	**4134**	**58347294**	**8595127**	**4788429**
1. 内资企业	**Domestic - funded Enterprises**	**3993**	**54697952**	**8225603**	**4117676**
国有企业	State - owned Enterprises	17	829238	110210	130996
集体企业	Collective - owned Enterprises	7	7928	1736	2359
股份合作企业	Cooperative Enterprises	2	2820	140	2395
联营企业	Joint Ownership Enterprises	5	6083	234	1531
国有联营企业	State Joint Ownership Enterprises	-	-	-	-
集体联营企业	Collective Joint Enterprises	-	-	-	-
国有与集体联营企业	Joint State - collective Enterprises	5	6083	234	1531
其他联营企业	Other Joint Ownership Enterprises	-	-	-	-
有限责任公司	Limited Liability Corporations	1144	27500850	4674943	1809756
国有独资公司	State - funded Corporations	50	2692894	860839	193186
其他有限责任公司	Other Limited Liability Corporations	1094	24807957	3814104	1616570
股份有限公司	Share - holding Corporations Ltd.	115	6727872	979185	840753
私营企业	Private Enterprises	2648	19599807	2455777	1321064
私营独资企业	Private - funded Enterprises	17	14647	2541	2066
私营合伙企业	Private Partnership Enterprises	1	591	201	23
私营有限责任公司	Private Limited Liability Corporations	2592	19134631	2399619	1279039
私营股份有限公司	Private Share - holding Corporations Ltd.	38	449938	53416	39937
其他企业	Other Enterprises	55	23355	3378	8822
2. 港、澳、台商投资企业	**Enterprises With Investment from Hong Kong, Macao and Taiwan**	**70**	**1975169**	**157416**	**260043**
合资经营企业(港或澳、台资)	Joint - venture Enterprises (With Funds from Hong Kong, Macao and Taiwan)	21	653434	51440	154000
合作经营企业(港或澳、台资)	Coorperative Enterprises (With Funds from Hong Kong, Macao and Taiwan)	1	16902	567	13004
港、澳、台商独资经营企业	Enterprises With Sole Investment from Hong Kong, Macao and Taiwan	45	1291402	104902	91036
港、澳、台商投资股份有限公司	Share - holding Corporations Ltd. With Investment from Hong Kong, Macao and Taiwan	1	636	405	1679
其他港澳台投资企业	Other Enterprises With Investment from Hong Kong, Macao and Taiwan	2	12795	103	324
3. 外商投资企业	**Enterprises With Foreign Investment**	**71**	**1674173**	**212109**	**410710**
中外合资经营企业	Joint - venture Enterprises	16	203366	57564	162507
中外合作经营企业	Cooperation Enterprises	1	5681	872	3771
外资企业	Enterprises With Sole Foreign Investment	53	1462654	152073	244431
外商投资股份有限公司	Share - holding Corporations Ltd. With Foreign Investment	-	-	-	-
其他外商投资企业	Other Enterprises With Foreign Investment	1	2472	1600	2

批发零售贸易企业财务状况(2016 年)

Wholesale and Retail Trades by Status of Registration(2016)

(10000 yuan)

累计折旧 Accumulated Depreciation	本年折旧 Depreciation	资产总计 Total Assets	负债合计 Total Liabilities	所有者权益合计 Creditors´ Equity
1876186	**273294**	**77925817**	**57690434**	**20235383**
1621150	**233086**	**72784634**	**54195378**	**18589256**
70461	7856	939397	222363	717034
1226	97	9061	3577	5484
631	41	8077	7626	451
727	76	6887	2696	4191
–	–	–	–	–
–	–	–	–	–
727	76	6887	2696	4191
–	–	–	–	–
672053	90877	36200928	28266182	7934746
62418	4502	4155028	2478981	1676047
609636	86375	32045900	25787201	6258699
321764	44455	10563654	6003457	4560197
552572	89237	25022677	19673831	5348845
676	96	16912	12892	4019
6	1	697	644	54
534763	86853	24139820	19094802	5045018
17128	2287	865248	565494	299755
1715	448	33954	15646	18308
112881	**17579**	**2918487**	**1905445**	**1013042**
70004	10335	990123	660335	329788
8914	–134	28315	2176	26139
32751	7228	1885716	1237302	648414
1071	110	1249	1840	–592
142	40	13084	3791	9292
142155	**22629**	**2222697**	**1589611**	**633085**
46811	6603	369777	325134	44643
2466	337	11391	2108	9283
92877	15690	1839056	1261274	577783
–	–	–	–	–
1	–	2472	1096	1376

项　目	Item	营业收入 Revenue of Business	主营业务收入 Main Revenue of Business	主营业务成本 Main Cost of Business	主营业务税金及附加 Main Sales Tax and Extra Charges
批发零售贸易业企业合计	**Total**	**137348654**	**136031511**	**127802840**	**380849**
1. 内资企业	**Domestic - funded Enterprises**	**130322902**	**129139823**	**121688334**	**356898**
国有企业	State - owned Enterprises	1724852	1719229	1228056	205577
集体企业	Collective - owned Enterprises	43684	43671	37124	126
股份合作企业	Cooperative Enterprises	2256	1616	1507	1
联营企业	Joint Ownership Enterprises	34716	34714	27431	155
国有联营企业	State Joint Ownership Enterprises	-	-	-	-
集体联营企业	Collective Joint Enterprises	-	-	-	-
国有与集体联营企业	Joint State - collective Enterprises	34716	34714	27431	155
其他联营企业	Other Joint Ownership Enterprises	-	-	-	-
有限责任公司	Limited Liability Corporations	71285714	70667424	67267648	70802
国有独资公司	State - funded Corporations	6605882	6583948	6404375	2915
其他有限责任公司	Other Limited Liability Corporations	64679832	64083476	60863273	67887
股份有限公司	Share - holding Corporations Ltd.	17084979	16692152	15590375	19290
私营企业	Private Enterprises	40033910	39868232	37430071	60784
私营独资企业	Private - funded Enterprises	34136	34105	30853	70
私营合伙企业	Private Partnership Enterprises	1069	1069	914	2
私营有限责任公司	Private Limited Liability Corpora tions	38960268	38804188	36475101	59651
私营股份有限公司	Private Share - holding Corporations Ltd.	1038437	1028869	923204	1060
其他企业	Other Enterprises	112791	112785	106123	163
2. 港、澳、台商投资企业	**Enterprises With Investment from Hong Kong, Macao and Taiwan**	**4168930**	**4128925**	**3705805**	**13539**
合资经营企业(港或澳、台资)	Joint - venture Enterprises (With Funds from Hong Kong, Macao and Taiwan)	1394950	1372646	1213818	4917
合作经营企业(港或澳、台资)	Coorperative Enterprises (With Funds from Hong Kong, Macao and Taiwan)	34937	34937	28355	140
港、澳、台商独资经营企业	Enterprises With Sole Investment from Hong Kong, Macao and Taiwan	2720617	2702916	2448087	8422
港、澳、台商投资股份有限公司	Share - holding Corporations Ltd. With Investment from Hong Kong, Macao and Taiwan	4193	4193	2826	19
其他港澳台投资企业	Other Enterprises With Investment from Hong Kong, Macao and Taiwan	14232	14232	12718	42
3. 外商投资企业	**Enterprises With Foreign Investment**	**2856822**	**2762764**	**2408701**	**10412**
中外合资经营企业	Joint - venture Enterprises	1121068	1077829	1002202	1983
中外合作经营企业	Cooperation Enterprises	8011	8011	5906	151
外资企业	Enterprises With Sole Foreign Investment	1686183	1635363	1360139	8273
外商投资股份有限公司	Share - holding Corporations Ltd. With Foreign Investment	-	-	-	-
其他外商投资企业	Other Enterprises With Foreign Investment	41561	41561	40453	5

continued (10000 yuan)

销售费用 Cost of Sales	管理费用 Administration Cost	财务费用 Financil Cost	营业利润 Management Profits	利润总额 Total Profits	应交所得税 Income Tax	从业人员平均人数(人) Average Number of Employees (person)
4365456	**2075605**	**701527**	**2227541**	**2391725**	**511869**	**253732**
3842243	**1853009**	**682521**	**2103131**	**2235942**	**460625**	**229457**
28491	46289	-28391	243812	244278	60707	1647
1392	500	9	4534	1381	1087	135
99	452	-1	7	12	2	41
1189	191	-33	5781	5847	1470	98
-	-	-	-	-	-	-
-	-	-	-	-	-	-
1189	191	-33	5781	5847	1470	98
-	-	-	-	-	-	-
1872148	743094	381211	875545	981141	210007	101041
66493	61820	13643	135558	171993	12568	3714
1805655	681275	367569	739988	809148	197438	97327
682415	266238	64020	708641	700748	82073	31588
1255344	794487	265543	261489	298987	105204	94074
1034	711	167	1269	1198	93	339
-	63	46	44	44	2	8
1219234	770175	246410	225006	252999	98289	91652
35076	23538	18920	35171	44745	6820	2075
1164	1759	163	3320	3549	75	833
299429	**97697**	**12345**	**52392**	**78192**	**27962**	**10694**
121415	42906	-245	12366	15040	14605	4132
1543	3484	78	1336	1435	359	311
176200	49404	12561	38043	61528	12700	6168
60	1687	14	-413	-1008	-	54
210	216	-63	1060	1197	299	29
223784	**124900**	**6661**	**72018**	**77592**	**23281**	**13581**
76420	25575	7357	6879	9669	4805	4624
1725	18	32	346	346	74	57
145635	99261	-727	63690	66449	18307	8899
-	-	-	-	-	-	-
4	46	-1	1104	1128	96	1

8－07 按国民经济行业分限额以上

Main Financial Indicators of Enterprises Above Designated

单位:万元

项　　目	Item	法人企业数(个) Number of Enterprises (unit)	年末资产负债 Assets and Liabilities 流动资产合计 Circulating Funds	存　货 Inventory	固定资产原价 Orginal Value of Fixed Assets
总　　计	**Total**	**4134**	**58347294**	**8595127**	**4788429**
一、批发业	**Wholesale**	**2825**	**48780938**	**6496757**	**2586063**
农、林、牧产品批发	Wholesale of Farm, Forestry and Animal Husbandry Products	43	376893	64674	42026
食品、饮料及烟草制品批发	Wholesale of Food, Beverages and Tobaccos	205	4897526	780457	443674
纺织、服装及家庭用品批发	Wholesale of Textile Products, Garments and Household Articles	692	7182877	924142	465870
文化、体育用品及器材批发	Wholesale of Cultural and Sports Goods	116	1487190	489931	98628
医药及医疗器材批发	Wholesale of Medicines and Medical Appliances	162	3316982	722726	189533
矿产品、建材及化工产品批发	Wholesale of Mineral Products, Building and Chemical Materials	1104	25224103	2652065	1063541
机械设备、五金产品及电子产品批发	Wholesale of Machinery, Hardware and Electronic Products	462	6048330	833792	273344
#汽车、摩托车及零配件批发	Wholesale of Automobiles, Motorcycle and Parts	95	2206763	144666	65704
其他批发业	Other	36	234384	24050	9135
二、零售业	**Retail Trade**	**1309**	**9566356**	**2098371**	**2202366**
综合零售	Comprehensive Retail Trade	130	2875164	278390	777595
食品、饮料及烟草制品专门零售	Specialism Retail of Food, Beverages and Tobaccos	130	176314	38299	43534
纺织、服装及日用品专门零售	Specialism Retail of Textile Products, Garments, Shoes and Caps	96	559719	214269	276768
文化、体育用品及器材专门零售	Specialism Retail of Cultural and Sports Goods	55	336269	137982	83761
医药及医疗器材专门零售	Specialism Retail of Medicines and Medical Appliances	91	423041	101536	63856
汽车、摩托车、燃料及零配件专门零售	Specialism Retail of Automobiles, Motorcycle, Fuels and Parts	476	3175398	693169	645407
#汽车零售	Specialism Retail of Automobiles	303	2771025	623717	436361
家用电器及电子产品专门零售	Specialism Retail of Household Electric Applianes, and Electronic Products	115	675892	164296	63215
五金、家具及室内装饰材料专门零售	Specialism Retail of Hardware and Upholstery Materials	51	117594	25046	109991
货摊、无店铺及其他零售业	Stall, Non－shop and Other Retails	165	1226966	445383	138240

批发零售贸易企业财务状况（2016年）

Size in Wholesale and Retail Trades by Sector(2016)

(10000 yuan)

累计折旧 Accumulated Depreciation	本年折旧 Depreciation	资产总计 Total Assets	负债合计 Total Liabilities	所有者权益合计 Creditors′ Equity
1876186	**273294**	**77925817**	**57690434**	**20235383**
1063437	**148791**	**64166423**	**47556985**	**16609438**
15211	2078	689413	500436	188976
175881	28111	6374974	3976577	2398397
212240	29829	8794759	6906310	1888450
42785	2861	1928591	1339375	589215
81883	15031	4138254	2612083	1526170
408260	50851	34641800	26420810	8220990
123467	19828	7287854	5580524	1707330
29525	7322	2428146	2243426	184720
3513	177	297999	210936	87063
812750	**124503**	**13759394**	**10133449**	**3625945**
354826	40835	4262421	2822245	1440176
14699	3337	337621	250028	87593
53960	9055	944606	843593	101013
30821	3702	423201	281635	141567
20704	4164	848724	548059	300665
256897	44990	4313484	3345713	967771
165215	33384	3562942	2923160	639782
25037	3424	855484	617098	238386
19764	5448	261725	190429	71296
36042	9549	1512128	1234649	277479

项　目	Item	营业收入 Revenue of Business	主营业务收入 Main Revenue of Business	主营业务成本 Main Cost of Business	主营业务税金及附加 Main Sales Tax and Extra Charges
总　计	**Total**	**137348654**	**136031511**	**127802840**	**380849**
一、批发业	**Wholesale**	**113377070**	**112566132**	**107109946**	**307269**
农、林、牧产品批发业	Wholesale of Farm , Forestry and Animal Husbandry Products	819672	781684	740246	1182
食品、饮料、烟草制品批发	Wholesale of Food, Beverages and Tobaccos	9647321	9437368	8074501	219998
纺织、服装及家庭用品批发	Wholesale of Textile Products, Garments and Household Articles	14121009	14052304	12993375	14075
文化、体育用品及器材批发	Wholesale of Cultural and Sports Goods	3535656	3514777	3317913	4777
医药及医疗器材批发	Wholesale of Medicines and Medical Appliances	7400094	7359454	6790403	11565
矿产品、建材及化工产品批发	Wholesale of Mineral Products, Building and Chemical Materials	62563074	62188930	60740945	42065
机械设备、五金产品及电子产品批发	Wholesale of Machinery, Hardware and Electronic Products	14773587	14715187	13962106	12675
#汽车、摩托车及零配件批发	Wholesale of Automobiles, Motorcycle and Parts	6934586	6926485	6696882	3506
其他批发业	Other	485801	485575	463381	916
二、零售业	**Retail Trade**	**23971584**	**23465379**	**20692894**	**73580**
综合零售	Comprehensive Retail Trade	5225062	4949377	4196047	28010
食品、饮料及烟草制品专门零售	Specialism Retail of Food, Beverages and Tobaccos	389472	374469	297349	2467
纺织、服装及日用品专门零售	Specialism Retail of Textile Products, Garments, Shoes and Caps	894841	862418	602093	7212
文化、体育用品及器材专门零售	Specialism Retail of Cultural and Sports Goods	468240	463776	392969	3731
医药及医疗器材专门零售	Specialism Retail of Medicines and Medical Appliances	961520	954256	813231	2788
汽车、摩托车、燃料及零配件专门零售	Specialism Retail of Automobiles, Motorcycle, Fuels and Parts	10774014	10642985	9974541	17852
#汽车零售	Specialism Retail of Automobiles	8141109	8045671	7579447	13961
家用电器及电子产品专门零售	Specialism Retail of Household Electric Applianes, and Electronic Products	1652198	1637267	1489894	3200
五金、家具及室内装饰材料专门零售	Specialism Retail of Hardware and Upholstery Materials	222067	220047	163174	1423
货摊、无店铺及其他零售业	Stall, Non－shop and Other Retails	3384171	3360785	2763597	6895

continued (10000 yuan)

销售费用 Cost of Sales	管理费用 Administration Cost	财务费用 Financil Cost	营业利润 Management Profits	利润总额 Total Profits	应交所得税 Income Tax	从业人员平均人数(人) Average Number of Employees (person)
4365456	**2075605**	**701527**	**2227541**	**2391725**	**511869**	**253732**
2532319	**1336125**	**579879**	**1790079**	**1891830**	**391004**	**130536**
15785	18283	15242	6896	11473	2635	1385
612283	201218	3045	593178	625331	113114	30294
534525	295774	99937	189425	216919	53155	36377
83162	53509	11683	62697	64323	6925	4781
255483	141707	42975	228323	228736	38558	13068
582034	418191	376222	550859	581443	136239	25001
444791	201040	22816	142449	152690	39417	18912
256467	43013	1315	-67731	-61444	2913	4536
2555	5438	7925	15190	9859	689	573
1833137	**739480**	**121648**	**437462**	**499896**	**120865**	**123196**
588168	200517	-7356	201856	207168	41871	38918
51267	22208	7362	-1760	469	1189	5743
184526	77401	24751	2043	7837	6736	11386
40011	19993	3013	8442	8774	705	3987
76360	46389	6487	25553	26720	5893	8721
325016	202466	54717	177011	187620	40936	28520
230616	173144	52356	80592	94250	23343	22791
94293	43667	8624	22391	25147	4722	9935
24882	17054	4335	5939	5623	1140	1945
448615	109785	19715	-4012	30538	17673	14041

8－08 分地区限额以上

The Situation of Wholesale

单位:万元

地 区	Region	企业法人数(个) Number of Enterprises (unit)	商品销售总额 Total Sales of Commodities	主营业务收入 Main Revenue of Business	主营业务成本 Main Cost of Business	主营业务税金及附加 Main Sales Tax and Extra Charges
全 市	**Total**	**4134**	**153805814**	**136031511**	**127802840**	**380849**
市 区	Urban District	3665	150586096	133110792	125148330	371010
#上城区	Shangcheng	353	18378760	17156297	15785868	227044
下城区	Xiacheng	495	31881443	27992175	26739327	32195
江干区	Jianggan	392	19565793	17203699	16192870	15132
拱墅区	Gongshu	364	16016149	14030799	13415961	14617
西湖区	Xihu	298	11961582	10464731	9444871	17839
高新(滨江)区	Hi－Tech(Binjiang)	222	17031006	14950271	14270224	12308
萧山区	Xiaoshan	739	18632155	16309442	15482763	25477
大江东产业集聚区	Dajiangdong Industry Cluster District	73	1849765	1644165	1519367	1593
余杭区	Yuhang	529	9502329	8317866	7690613	13110
富阳区	Fuyang	200	4501979	3965125	3760411	6406
经济技术开发区	Economic and Technological Development Zone	63	3089889	2697739	2348868	6702
西湖风景名胜区	The West Lake Scenic Zone	10	25011	22650	16555	179
桐庐县	Tonglu	140	962428	868153	793586	1476
淳安县	Chun'an	87	672091	550027	456762	1498
建德市	Jiande	70	373233	369585	328353	1139
临安市	Lin'an	172	1211966	1132955	1075808	5726

批发零售业主要指标(2016 年)
and Retail Trades by Region(2016)

(10000 yuan)

销售费用 Cost of Sales	管理费用 Administration Cost	财务费用 Financil Cost	利润总额 Total Profits	本年应交增值税 Value Added Tax Payable	从业人员平均人数(人) Average Number of Employees (person)
4365456	**2075605**	**701527**	**2391725**	**1889066**	**253732**
4237318	2005420	681456	2302929	1854848	239963
438108	291968	83604	467879	216112	25390
664545	371286	105682	507325	1014409	35065
501169	253224	70183	356153	95088	29693
312860	174136	123094	70080	69362	24241
742726	243913	36714	337779	142218	37873
413743	156028	79990	145231	74574	16421
485372	198886	70796	177053	92977	28105
125501	23687	2944	-10126	12989	2320
308431	187169	83614	101687	55591	24088
132992	68714	22825	14336	36724	9139
235218	57538	4893	123792	56811	9526
2154	2560	63	1615	983	422
22644	22898	6132	23275	8722	3308
61823	15274	1590	20392	11605	4712
19562	9295	2624	13519	6906	1945
24109	22719	9725	31609	6985	3804

8－09 按注册类型、行业分限额以上

Main Financial Indicators of Hotels and Catering Services

单位:万元

项　　目	Item	法人企业数(个) Number of Enterprises (unit)	年末资产负债 Assets and Liabilities 流动资产合计 Circulating Funds	存　货 Inventory	固定资产原价 Orginal Value of Fixed Assets
总　计	**Total**	**894**	**1820730**	**127304**	**2998167**
(一)按登记注册类型分组	**Grouped By Registered Type**				
1. 内资企业	**Domestic－funded Enterprises**	**859**	**1461490**	**104883**	**2404257**
国有企业	State－owned Enterprises	42	135038	3269	220547
集体企业	Collective－owned Enterprises	11	12118	1052	59631
股份合作企业	Cooperative Enterprises	2	1181	151	1546
联营企业	Joint Ownership Enterprises	1	5028	62	4808
有限责任公司	Limited Liability Corporations	245	718814	74493	1425928
股份有限公司	Share－holding Corporations Ltd.	8	61823	1878	67053
私营企业	Private Enterprises	547	525659	23843	621760
其他企业	Other Enterprises	3	1829	135	2985
2. 港、澳、台商投资企业	**Enterprises With Investment from Hong Kong, Macao and Taiwan**	**21**	**214572**	**17067**	**341690**
3. 外商投资企业	**Enterprises With Foreign Investment**	**14**	**144668**	**5355**	**252220**
(二)按国民经济行业分组	**Grouped By Sector**				
1. 住宿业	**Lodging**	**417**	**1326932**	**98095**	**2333070**
旅游饭店	Restaurants for Junketing	253	1207522	93656	2094793
一般旅馆	General Hotel	164	119410	4439	238277
2. 餐饮	**Catering Services**	**477**	**493798**	**29209**	**665097**
正餐服务	Dinner Services	433	411067	22943	546760
快餐服务	Short Order Services	21	61015	5306	108041
饮料及冷饮服务	Beverages and Services	14	4633	481	1792
其他餐饮业	Others Catering Services	9	17083	480	8505

住宿业和餐饮业财务状况(2016 年)

Enterprises Above Designated Size by Status of Registration and Sector(2016)

(10000 yuan)

累计折旧 Accumulated Depreciation	本年折旧 Depreciation	资产总计 Total Assets	负债合计 Total Liabilities	所有者权益合计 Creditors′ Equity
1252065	**155452**	**4473068**	**3203448**	**1269620**
979740	**108827**	**3631913**	**2511417**	**1120496**
119671	8477	282792	94948	187844
35220	1733	45852	34182	11670
1196	61	1532	903	629
3577	156	6262	895	5366
537503	65863	2009682	1395642	614040
28664	2441	169193	67709	101484
253839	30069	1111828	916589	195239
71	29	4773	549	4225
159781	**13924**	**425138**	**318279**	**106859**
112544	**32700**	**416017**	**373753**	**42265**
1001823	**99906**	**3311715**	**2312415**	**999300**
922377	86730	2944124	2073679	870445
79446	13176	367591	238736	128855
250242	**55546**	**1161353**	**891033**	**270320**
186784	35006	944174	726851	217323
57246	19653	188686	155020	33667
1342	167	5476	3046	2430
4870	720	23017	6117	16901

单位:万元 8－09 续表

项目	Item	营业收入 Revenue of Business	主营业务收入 Main Revenue of Business	主营业务税金及附加 Business Tax and Extra Charges
总计	**Total**	**2446519**	**2411500**	**53886**
(一)按登记注册类型分组	**Grouped By Registered Type**			
1. 内资企业	**Domestic－funded Enterprises**	**1702072**	**1680978**	**37643**
国有企业	State－owned Enterprises	125855	119140	2775
集体企业	Collective－owned Enterprises	18743	18631	461
股份合作企业	Cooperative Enterprises	3249	3249	69
联营企业	Joint Ownership Enterprises	4792	4792	94
有限责任公司	Limited Liability Corporations	656312	647023	14179
股份有限公司	Share－holding Corporations Ltd.	87764	87520	1508
私营企业	Private Enterprises	803685	798950	18437
其他企业	Other Enterprises	1673	1673	119
2. 港、澳、台商投资企业	**Enterprises With Investment from Hong Kong, Macao and Taiwan**	**172463**	**166733**	**4690**
3. 外商投资企业	**Enterprises With Foreign Investment**	**571984**	**563789**	**11553**
(二)按国民经济行业分组	**Grouped By Sector**			
1. 住宿业	**Lodging**	**1035964**	**1016988**	**24435**
旅游饭店	Restaurants for Junketing	847506	830677	19880
一般旅馆	General Hotel	188458	186311	4555
2. 餐饮	**Catering Services**	**1410555**	**1394513**	**29450**
正餐服务	Dinner Services	801562	791163	17629
快餐服务	Short Order Services	552780	549235	10855
饮料及冷饮服务	Beverages and Services	11088	10833	236
其他餐饮业	Others Catering Services	45126	43282	731

continued (10000 yuan)

销售费用 Cost of Sales	管理费用 Administration Cost	财务费用 Financil Cost	营业利润 Management Profits	利润总额 Total Profits	应交所得税 Income Taxes Payable	从业人员平均人数(人) Average Number of Employees (person)
817018	**548241**	**71111**	**51915**	**69476**	**30505**	**96622**
570474	**440774**	**57106**	**-17161**	**-1249**	**12051**	**68906**
43706	45089	-537	-3111	-1222	1723	5086
7474	6039	65	-286	-292	106	809
949	575	7	225	246	61	66
1753	1508	-67	548	560	140	137
227497	214521	35430	-38109	-31135	3426	27427
35009	12361	696	24995	26879	759	3633
253661	159770	21510	-420	3628	5837	31564
425	912	-	-1002	89	-	184
61918	**37881**	**10750**	**12257**	**13388**	**1846**	**6053**
184626	**69587**	**3255**	**56819**	**57337**	**16607**	**21663**
368214	**370475**	**55169**	**-46232**	**-35936**	**6201**	**40910**
307616	310495	49247	-41931	-33637	5074	33633
60599	59981	5922	-4301	-2300	1127	7277
448803	**177766**	**15942**	**98147**	**105412**	**24304**	**55712**
259861	119917	13498	32884	39879	7094	32002
175021	49281	2356	61611	61839	16383	21133
1328	4477	10	291	322	83	375
12594	4091	78	3362	3372	743	2202

8-10 按登记注册类型和国民经济行业分限额以上住宿业和餐饮业经营情况(2016年)

Management Conditions of Hotels and Catering Services Enterprises Above Designated Size by Status of Registration and Sector(2016)

单位:万元 (10000 yuan)

项目	Item	法人企业(个) Number of Enterprises (unit)	营业额 Revenue of Business	客房收入 Revenue of Guest Rooms	餐饮收入 Revenue of Catering Services	商品销售收入 Revenue of Goods Sales
一、按登记注册类型分	**Grouped By Registered Type**					
总计	**Total**	**894**	**2501235**	**608882**	**1737175**	**13411**
1. 内资企业	**Domestic - funded Enterprises**	**859**	**1739390**	**536164**	**1065977**	**12539**
国有企业	State - owned Enterprises	42	124151	55326	54291	680
集体企业	Collective - owned Enterprises	11	19110	12060	4045	129
股份合作企业	Cooperative Enterprises	2	3376	1511	1757	15
联营企业	Joint Ownership Enterprises	1	4996	2612	1868	69
国有联营企业	State Joint Ownership Enterprises	-	-	-	-	-
集体联营企业	Collective Joint Enterprises	-	-	-	-	-
国有与集体联营企业	Joint State - collective Enterprises	1	4996	2612	1868	69
其他联营企业	Other Joint Ownership Enterprises	-	-	-	-	-
有限责任公司	Limited Liability Corporations	245	667269	261043	326962	2941
国有独资公司	State - funded Corporations	15	64809	17905	26326	266
其他有限责任公司	Other Limited Liability Corporations	230	602460	243138	300636	2675
股份有限公司	Share - holding Corporations Ltd.	8	94483	11817	79525	585
私营企业	Private Enterprises	547	824330	191539	596161	8119
私营独资企业	Private - funded Enterprises	20	14183	1459	12449	171
私营合伙企业	Private Partnership Enterprises	4	2121	-	2094	17
私营有限责任公司	Private Limited Liability Corporations	514	798781	187066	576036	7917
私营股份有限公司	Private Share - holding Corporations Ltd.	9	9245	3014	5582	14
其他企业	Other Enterprises	3	1675	257	1369	-

单位:万元　　8－10　续表　continued　　(10000 yuan)

项　目	Item	法人企业(个) Number of Enterprises (unit)	营业额 Revenue of Business	客房收入 Revenue of Guest Rooms	餐饮收入 Revenue of Catering Services	商品销售收入 Revenue of Goods Sales
2. 港、澳、台商投资企业	**Enterprises With Investment from Hong Kong, Macao and Taiwan**	**21**	**170748**	**50960**	**109251**	**740**
合资经营企业(港或澳、台资)	Joint－venture Enterprises(With Funds from Hong Kong, Macao and Taiwan)	10	100314	36672	55405	31
合作经营企业(港或澳、台资)	Coorperative Enterprises (With Funds from Hong Kong, Macao and Taiwan)	1	521	493	7	1
港、澳、台商独资经营企业	Enterprises With Sole Investment from Hong Kong, Macao and Taiwan	8	42306	5164	36345	63
港、澳、台商投资股份有限公司	Share－holding Corporations Ltd. With Investment from Hong Kong, Macao and Taiwan	2	27608	8630	17494	645
3. 外商投资企业	**Enterprises With Foreign Investment**	**14**	**591097**	**21759**	**561947**	**132**
中外合资经营企业	Joint－venture Enterprises	2	450101	8288	440846	－
中外合作经营企业	Cooperation Enterprises	1	4039	2435	1260	124
外资企业	Enterprises With Sole Foreign Investment	9	135411	10157	119176	7
外商投资股份有限公司	Share－holding Corporations Ltd. With Foreign Investment	2	1546	879	665	1
二、按国民经济行业分	**Grouped By Sector**					
总　计	**Total**	**894**	**2501235**	**608882**	**1737175**	**13411**
1. 住宿业	**Lodging**	**417**	**1048094**	**558785**	**375800**	**4320**
旅游饭店	Restaurants for Junketing	253	855750	431527	327074	3989
一般旅馆	General Hotel	164	192344	127258	48727	331
2. 餐饮业	**Catering Services**	**477**	**1453141**	**50097**	**1361375**	**9091**
正餐服务	Dinner Services	433	820984	50097	742559	8822
快餐服务	Short Order Services	21	573150	－	562467	－
饮料及冷饮服务	Beverages and Services	14	11208	－	10665	269
其他餐饮业	Others Catering Services	9	47799	－	45684	－

8－11 分地区限额以上

The Situation of Lodging

单位:万元

地 区 Region		企业法人数(个) Number of Enterprises (unit)	营业额 Revenue of Business	客房收入 Revenue of Guest Rooms	餐饮收入 Revenue of Catering Services	主营业务收入 Main Revenue of Business
全 市	**Total**	**894**	**2501235**	**608882**	**1737175**	**2411500**
市 区	Urban District	768	2320838	531186	1644441	2238397
#上城区	Shangcheng	137	406855	116119	271751	394873
下城区	Xiacheng	97	300315	74355	209094	284907
江干区	Jianggan	81	168670	55435	93219	166898
拱墅区	Gongshu	66	127980	34200	83237	122300
西湖区	Xihu	126	717090	85477	585121	693822
高新(滨江)区	Hi－Tech(Binjiang)	36	58576	19965	37404	56747
萧山区	Xiaoshan	62	236930	49530	178203	226511
大江东产业集聚区	Dajiangdong Industry Cluster District	2	5753	911	4437	5538
余杭区	Yuhang	54	62021	20855	35009	59634
富阳区	Fuyang	29	26922	7141	17561	26190
经济技术开发区	Economic and Technological Development Zone	23	32048	7289	21132	28320
西湖风景名胜区	The West Lake Scenic Zone	57	183433	60819	112710	178195
桐庐县	Tonglu	25	35175	14802	18105	31553
淳安县	Chun'an	51	96972	47359	45155	93656
建德市	Jiande	15	10988	2226	8272	11071
临安市	Lin'an	35	37261	13309	21203	36822

住宿餐饮业主要指标(2016 年)

and Catering by Region(2016)

(10000 yuan)

主营业务税金及附加 Business Tax and Extra Charges	销售费用 Cost of Sales	管理费用 Administration Cost	财务费用 Financil Cost	利润总额 Total Profits	从业人员平均人数(人) Average Number of Employees (person)
54313	**817018**	**548241**	**71111**	**69476**	**96622**
50085	763008	492425	62269	79537	88230
8899	142324	88954	17758	31325	13731
6219	129409	55948	14844	-3587	12390
3474	51274	47118	1552	3067	5177
2628	45142	30138	1412	-1714	4874
14905	191956	111988	5216	63695	27336
1308	16070	13340	535	2248	2329
5613	97151	32365	16508	1081	10052
87	334	982	13	222	172
1624	13150	23475	1391	-5381	3465
630	6935	10970	1914	-1686	1834
519	9843	9183	535	-3787	1097
4266	59753	68947	606	-5724	5945
903	9339	9694	4515	-4848	1696
2229	34196	32703	2375	-4891	4131
292	2553	3107	337	-249	767
804	7923	10312	1614	-73	1798

8-12 个体工商业登记注册情况(2016年末)
Statistics of Individual Owned Business(End of 2016)

项目	Item	全市 Whole City		市区 Urban District	
		合计 Total	#城镇 Urban	合计 Total	#城镇 Urban
户数(户)	**Number of Households (household)**	**426028**	**309743**	**330867**	**256843**
农、林、牧、渔业	Farming, Forestry, Animal Husbandry and Fishery	6924	2422	4706	1797
农、林、牧、渔服务业	Service for Farming, Forestry, Animal Husbandry and Fishery	364	157	245	125
采矿业	Mining and Quarrying	50	11	20	2
开采辅助活动	Support Activity for Mining and Quarrying				
制造业	Manufacturing	19535	6944	11907	4156
金属制品、机械和设备修理业	Metal Products, Machinery and Equipment Repair	115	53	71	35
电力、热力、燃气及水的生产和供应业	Production and Supply of Electricity, Gas and Water	47	23	16	6
建筑业	Construction	1374	725	998	505
批发和零售业	Wholesale and Retail Trade & Catering Services	276601	205960	220096	174444
交通运输、仓储和邮政业	Transportation, Storage and Post	6423	3690	4710	2850
住宿和餐饮业	Lodging and Catering	58074	46554	44089	37808
信息传输、软件和信息技术服务业	Information Transmission, Computer Services and Software	779	613	551	472
金融业	Banking and Insurance	7	6	4	3
房地产业	Real Estate	128	117	90	86
租赁和商务服务业	Renting and Business Service	6447	4738	4882	3704
科学研究和技术服务业	Scientific Research and Technical Service	1228	983	946	784
水利、环境和公共设施管理业	Water Conservancy, Environment and Public Utility	61	39	48	29
居民服务、修理和其他服务业	Service for the Residents and Other Service Sector	45565	34672	35743	28428
教育	Education	412	330	334	276
卫生和社会工作	Health Care, Sports & Social Welfare	532	379	286	213
文化、体育和娱乐业	Culture, Sports and Entertainment	1833	1530	1434	1273
其他	Others	8	7	7	7

8－12 续表1 continued 1

项 目	Item	全市 Whole City		市区 Urban District	
		合计 Total	#城镇 Urban	合计 Total	#城镇 Urban
从业人员(人)	**Employed Persons(person)**	**844532**	**604722**	**628898**	**483445**
农、林、牧、渔业	Farming, Forestry, Animal Husbandry and Fishery	18592	5793	11058	3609
农、林、牧、渔服务业	Service for Farming, Forestry, Animal Husbandry and Fishery	935	393	549	278
采矿业	Mining and Quarrying	252	48	99	9
开采辅助活动	Support Activity for Mining and Quarrying				
制造业	Manufacturing	71835	22213	33787	9851
金属制品、机械和设备修理业	Metal Products, Machinery and Equipment Repair	265	114	158	69
电力、热力、燃气及水的生产和供应业	Production and Supply of Electricity, Gas and Water	98	55	21	9
建筑业	Construction	5002	1971	3363	1088
批发和零售业	Wholesale and Retail Trade & Catering Services	452291	340251	356398	283559
交通运输、仓储和邮政业	Transportation, Storage and Post	10499	5936	7270	4366
住宿和餐饮业	Lodging and Catering	147460	121690	111658	97198
信息传输、软件和信息技术服务业	Information Transmission, Computer Services and Software	1642	1327	1077	941
金融业	Banking and Insurance	38	37	4	3
房地产业	Real Estate	205	188	148	142
租赁和商务服务业	Renting and Business Service	13611	10153	9703	7509
科学研究和技术服务业	Scientific Research and Technical Service	2713	2267	1892	1644
水利、环境和公共设施管理业	Water Conservancy, Environment and Public Utility	202	94	152	50
居民服务、修理和其他服务业	Service for the Residents and Other Service Sector	111915	86268	86500	68592
教育	Education	1259	991	961	833
卫生和社会工作	Health Care, Sports & Social Welfare	1323	960	788	602
文化、体育和娱乐业	Culture, Sports and Entertainment	5567	4453	3992	3413
其他	Others	28	27	27	27

8－12 续表2 continued 2

项目	Item	全市 Whole City 合计 Total	全市 Whole City #城镇 Urban	市区 Urban District 合计 Total	市区 Urban District #城镇 Urban
注册资金(万元)	**Capital Registered(10000 yuan)**	**3743654**	**2613835**	**2570541**	**1960525**
农、林、牧、渔业	Farming, Forestry, Animal Husbandry and Fishery	226495	78232	123112	46477
农、林、牧、渔服务业	Service for Farming, Forestry, Animal Husbandry and Fishery	9156	4272	6411	3786
采矿业	Mining and Quarrying	2735	806	537	101
开采辅助活动	Support Activity for Mining and Quarrying				
制造业	Manufacturing	226396	82157	103393	36773
金属制品、机械和设备修理业	Metal Products, Machinery and Equipment Repair	1123	633	589	338
电力、热力、燃气及水的生产和供应业	Production and Supply of Electricity, Gas and Water	234	74	89	16
建筑业	Construction	30582	11457	21912	6635
批发和零售业	Wholesale and Retail Trade & Catering Services	1913208	1456242	1412830	1146591
交通运输、仓储和邮政业	Transportation, Storage and Post	73947	41785	51739	31883
住宿和餐饮业	Lodging and Catering	714224	538927	453001	391238
信息传输、软件和信息技术服务业	Information Transmission, Computer Services and Software	4764	3624	3263	2651
金融业	Banking and Insurance	39	36	28	25
房地产业	Real Estate	442	336	274	188
租赁和商务服务业	Renting and Business Service	89921	55676	57984	39414
科学研究和技术服务业	Scientific Research and Technical Service	8814	7712	6042	5350
水利、环境和公共设施管理业	Water Conservancy, Environment and Public Utility	1192	478	679	267
居民服务、修理和其他服务业	Service for the Residents and Other Service Sector	405214	298682	303573	225023
教育	Education	4130	2717	2640	2210
卫生和社会工作	Health Care, Sports & Social Welfare	8405	6520	4804	3926
文化、体育和娱乐业	Culture, Sports and Entertainment	32851	28314	24581	21697
其他	Others	61	60	60	60

8－13 私营企业登记注册情况(2016 年末)

Statistics of Private Owned Business(End of 2016)

项目	Item	全市 Whole City		市区 Urban District	
		合计 Total	#城镇 Urban	合计 Total	#城镇 Urban
户数(户)	**Number of Households (household)**	**400586**	**316695**	**362135**	**296750**
农、林、牧、渔业	Farming, Forestry, Animal Husbandry and Fishery	6298	2561	3843	1748
农、林、牧、渔服务业	Service for Farming, Forestry, Animal Husbandry and Fishery	908	481	729	427
采矿业	Mining and Quarrying	163	37	70	17
开采辅助活动	Support Activity for Mining and Quarrying	4	2	3	2
制造业	Manufacturing	49044	18219	37926	14832
金属制品、机械和设备修理业	Metal Products, Machinery and Equipment Repair	268	190	250	179
电力、热力、燃气及水的生产和供应业	Production and Supply of Electricity, Gas and Water	523	190	201	114
建筑业	Construction	18985	14605	17293	13525
批发和零售业	Wholesale and Retail Trade & Catering Services	137335	114417	125856	107786
交通运输、仓储和邮政业	Transportation, Storage and Post	5648	4021	4702	3417
住宿和餐饮业	Lodging and Catering	6762	5359	5943	4843
信息传输、软件和信息技术服务业	Information Transmission, Computer Services and Software	33690	31117	31938	29728
金融业	Banking and Insurance	5024	4384	4545	4038
房地产业	Real Estate	8731	7054	7835	6445
租赁和商务服务业	Renting and Business Service	61442	55813	58849	53931
科学研究和技术服务业	Scientific Research and Technical Service	36839	33860	35636	33042
水利、环境和公共设施管理业	Water Conservancy, Environment and Public Utility	1325	932	947	696
居民服务、修理和其他服务业	Service for the Residents and Other Service Sector	17249	13816	16008	13010
教育	Education	1840	1667	1741	1591
卫生和社会工作	Health Care, Sports & Social Welfare	1188	786	1038	685
文化、体育和娱乐业	Culture, Sports and Entertainment	8445	7811	7731	7273
其他	Others	55	46	33	29

8－13 续表1 continued 1

项 目	Item	全市 Whole City 合计 Total	全市 Whole City #城镇 Urban	市区 Urban District 合计 Total	市区 Urban District #城镇 Urban
从业人员(人)	**Employed Persons(person)**	**2817035**	**1908807**	**2499749**	**1767081**
农、林、牧、渔业	Farming, Forestry, Animal Husbandry and Fishery	36588	14364	20817	9066
农、林、牧、渔服务业	Service for Farming, Forestry, Animal Husbandry and Fishery	5102	2726	3968	2323
采矿业	Mining and Quarrying	2472	539	1147	131
开采辅助活动	Support Activity for Mining and Quarrying	29	22	26	22
制造业	Manufacturing	456167	132566	310124	99861
金属制品、机械和设备修理业	Metal Products, Machinery and Equipment Repair	1585	1043	1479	987
电力、热力、燃气及水的生产和供应业	Production and Supply of Electricity, Gas and Water	3676	1280	1522	705
建筑业	Construction	135982	93830	121959	84657
批发和零售业	Wholesale and Retail Trade & Catering Services	902566	634315	845789	598490
交通运输、仓储和邮政业	Transportation, Storage and Post	36699	23635	28382	17608
住宿和餐饮业	Lodging and Catering	45683	36021	39317	31463
信息传输、软件和信息技术服务业	Information Transmission, Computer Services and Software	219546	186497	208901	177859
金融业	Banking and Insurance	40344	33456	35635	30057
房地产业	Real Estate	52104	39783	45732	34939
租赁和商务服务业	Renting and Business Service	452939	371527	435377	358332
科学研究和技术服务业	Scientific Research and Technical Service	249326	201352	239216	195893
水利、环境和公共设施管理业	Water Conservancy, Environment and Public Utility	7672	5084	5499	3675
居民服务、修理和其他服务业	Service for the Residents and Other Service Sector	103786	74515	95852	69574
教育	Education	10632	8769	9953	8208
卫生和社会工作	Health Care, Sports & Social Welfare	6888	4818	5832	4064
文化、体育和娱乐业	Culture, Sports and Entertainment	53594	46152	48496	42344
其他	Others	371	304	199	155

8－13 续表2 continued 2

项 目	Item	全 市 Whole City		市 区 Urban District	
		合 计 Total	#城 镇 Urban	合 计 Total	#城 镇 Urban
注册资金(万元)	**Capital Registered(10000 yuan)**	**266020927**	**228544176**	**246341296**	**215473975**
农、林、牧、渔业	Farming, Forestry, Animal Husbandry and Fishery	1935965	875432	1022561	531915
农、林、牧、渔服务业	Service for Farming, Forestry, Animal Husbandry and Fishery	359824	183527	281551	165358
采矿业	Mining and Quarrying	151529	61861	90809	36174
开采辅助活动	Support Activity for Mining and Quarrying	21500	21000	21000	21000
制造业	Manufacturing	20257090	8447257	16705331	7019288
金属制品、机械和设备修理业	Metal Products, Machinery and Equipment Repair	79166	57375	68620	55265
电力、热力、燃气及水的生产和供应业	Production and Supply of Electricity, Gas and Water	438013	282675	287541	211081
建筑业	Construction	13257991	10880582	11827801	9758673
批发和零售业	Wholesale and Retail Trade & Catering Services	36479583	32106273	34010114	30386084
交通运输、仓储和邮政业	Transportation, Storage and Post	2087819	1570283	1673206	1247761
住宿和餐饮业	Lodging and Catering	1419394	1138393	1129045	986836
信息传输、软件和信息技术服务业	Information Transmission, Computer Services and Software	16795419	15403224	15863531	14626830
金融业	Banking and Insurance	15343678	14315702	12422188	11598577
房地产业	Real Estate	13577296	11316998	12357499	10377439
租赁和商务服务业	Renting and Business Service	115376492	106045232	111990400	104014947
科学研究和技术服务业	Scientific Research and Technical Service	18712247	16980278	17796354	16355170
水利、环境和公共设施管理业	Water Conservancy, Environment and Public Utility	896468	726266	673802	567361
居民服务、修理和其他服务业	Service for the Residents and Other Service Sector	5308830	4668690	4948432	4382008
教育	Education	396741	362758	365384	354850
卫生和社会工作	Health Care, Sports & Social Welfare	534834	502876	365964	360309
文化、体育和娱乐业	Culture, Sports and Entertainment	3033538	2843859	2799994	2648387
其他	Others	18000	15537	11340	10285

8－14 分行业、类型规模以上
Main Indicators of Service

单位:亿元

项　目	Item	单位数(个) Number of Enterprise (Unit)	资产总计 Total Assets	固定资产原价 Orginal Value of Fixed Assets
总　计	**Total**	**3486**	**18951**	**3129**
按登记注册类型分	**Grouped By Registered Type**			
国有企业	State－owned Enterprises	96	814	82
集体企业	Collective－owned Enterprises	64	270	85
股份合作企业	Cooperative Enterprises	12	63	52
联营企业	Joint Ownership Enterprises	3	1	－
有限责任公司	Limited Liability Corporations	1299	10353	1867
股份有限公司	Share－holding Corporations Ltd.	170	1497	262
私营企业	Private Enterprises	1631	2017	293
其他企业	Other Enterprises	28	26	5
港澳台商投资企业	Enterprises With Investment from Hong Kong, Macao and Taiwan	96	3352	371
外商投资企业	Enterprises With Foreign Investment	87	557	112
按国民经济行业分	**Grouped by Sector**			
交通运输、仓储和邮政业	Transportation,Storage and Post	637	2161	952
信息传输、软件和信息技术服务业	Information Transmission,Softuare and Information Technology	708	5894	683
房地产业(除房地产开发经营)	Real Estate	239	391	91
租赁和商务服务业	Leasing and Business Services	831	8256	1015
科学研究和技术服务业	Scientific Research and Technical Service	546	1063	151
水利、环境和公共设施管理业	Water Conservancy,Environment and Public Utility	125	546	140
居民服务、修理和其他服务业	Service for the Residents and Other Service Sector	88	25	8
教育	Education	67	18	7
卫生和社会工作	Health Care and Social Welfare	103	42	15
文化、体育和娱乐业	Culture,Sports and Entertainment	142	554	68

服务业企业主要经济指标(2016 年)
Enterprises by Sector and Type(2016)

(100 million yuan)

本年折旧 Depreciation	负债合计 Total Liabilities	所有者权益合计 Total Owners' Equities	营业收入 Revenue of Business	主营业务收入 Main Revenue of Business	营业成本 Operating Costs	主营业务成本 Main Cost of Business	营业税金及附加 Sales Taxes and Extra Charges in Main Business
207	**9134**	**9816**	**6639**	**6512**	**4111**	**4039**	**47**
5	272	542	252	249	176	175	2
3	118	152	35	33	15	14	2
1	19	43	6	6	1	1	1
–	1	–	2	2	2	2	–
101	5315	5039	2010	1963	1451	1414	16
19	930	567	457	451	290	288	3
25	1007	1010	1344	1321	992	977	8
–	14	12	29	29	19	19	–
46	1122	2230	1660	1617	365	353	13
7	336	221	844	840	800	797	2
44	1132	1029	734	711	631	606	4
78	2450	3445	3582	3526	1854	1833	18
4	213	178	156	150	105	102	4
57	4224	4033	1059	1029	722	705	14
11	648	415	671	667	521	519	3
6	269	277	155	149	118	114	2
1	13	12	27	26	17	17	–
1	12	7	22	22	12	12	–
1	27	15	56	56	34	34	–
4	148	406	177	174	97	96	2

项　目	Item	主营业务税金及附加 Main Sales Tax and Extra Charges	销售费用 Cost of Sales	管理费用 Administration Cost
总　计	**Total**	**46**	**341**	**932**
按登记注册类型分	**Grouped By Registered Type**			
国有企业	State－owned Enterprises	2	7	26
集体企业	Collective－owned Enterprises	2	2	10
股份合作企业	Cooperative Enterprises	1	－	2
联营企业	Joint Ownership Enterprises	－	－	－
有限责任公司	Limited Liability Corporations	15	92	227
股份有限公司	Share－holding Corporations Ltd.	3	31	71
私营企业	Private Enterprises	8	80	191
其他企业	Other Enterprises	－	2	5
港澳台商投资企业	Enterprises With Investment from Hong Kong, Macao and Taiwan	12	108	379
外商投资企业	Enterprises With Foreign Investment	2	17	19
按国民经济行业分	**Grouped by Sector**			
交通运输、仓储和邮政业	Transportation,Storage and Post	4	16	49
信息传输、软件和信息技术服务业	Information Transmission,Softuare and Information Technology	17	221	609
房地产业（除房地产开发经营）	Real Estate	4	11	22
租赁和商务服务业	Leasing and Business Services	14	49	113
科学研究和技术服务业	Scientific Research and Technical Service	3	19	84
水利、环境和公共设施管理业	Water Conservancy,Environment and Public Utility	2	4	14
居民服务、修理和其他服务业	Service for the Residents and Other Service Sector	－	3	4
教育	Education	－	3	4
卫生和社会工作	Health Care and Social Welfare	－	7	12
文化、体育和娱乐业	Culture,Sports and Entertainment	2	9	19

continued (100 million yuan)

其中:税金 Tax	财务费用 Financil Cost	营业利润 Management Profits	利润总额 Total Profits	应交所得税 Income Tax	应付职工薪酬 Payroll Payable	应交增值税 Value Added Tax Payable	从事服务业活动的从业人员平均人数（万人） Average Number of Employed Persons (10000 Persons)
8	**43**	**1352**	**1443**	**174**	**904**	**153**	**68.92**
–	–8	55	57	3	44	7	3.84
–	–	12	13	2	6	1	0.46
–	–	2	1	–	–	–	0.06
–	–	–	–	–	–	–	0.02
3	90	255	300	35	326	38	28.81
1	2	65	73	12	97	14	9.37
2	12	85	100	16	148	26	18.69
–	–	3	3	–	8	1	0.51
1	–54	869	882	102	246	62	5.21
1	1	7	15	5	28	4	1.94
1	21	2	48	17	131	12	11.53
2	–59	977	1002	114	405	99	15.69
1	4	13	14	3	51	3	9.32
2	75	231	239	23	111	14	12.58
1	1	49	53	10	131	16	11.43
–	3	19	19	3	23	2	2.82
–	–	1	2	–	10	1	1.87
–	–	2	2	–	7	–	0.81
–	1	4	4	1	13	–	1.33
–	–3	55	59	2	23	7	1.55

8－15　规模以上服务业企业主要经济指标(2011－2016年)

Main Indicators of Service Enterprises Above Designated Size(2011－2016)

单位:亿元　　(100 million yuan)

		2011	2012	2013	2014	2015	2016
单位数(个)	Number of Enterprises(Unit)	5533	4571	4770	4393	3238	3486
资产总计	Total Assets	7816	10826	13208	14340	15412	18951
固定资产原价	Orginal Value of Fixed Assets	2006	2195	2399	2716	2847	3129
本年折旧	Depreciation	109	120	138	156	177	207
负债合计	Total Liabilities	3999	5657	6789	7181	7463	9134
所有者权益合计	Total Owners´Equities	3999	5169	6418	7160	7949	9816
营业收入	Revenue of Business	2494	3014	3719	4353	5236	6639
主营业务收入	Main Revenue of Business	2439	2909	3609	4247	5111	6512
营业成本	Main Cost of Business	1630	1918	2335	2650	3215	4111
主营业务成本	Main Cost of Business	1612	1863	2288	2609	3170	4039
营业税金及附加	Sales Taxes and Extra Charges in Main Business	70	82	59	58	59	47
主营业务税金及附加	Main Sales Tax and Extra Charges	68	79	56	54	57	46
销售费用	Cost of Sales	199	196	221	257	314	341
管理费用	Administration Cost	291	379	468	621	765	932
其中:税金	Taxes	6	7	8	9	10	8
财务费用	Financil Cost	53	70	70	62	65	43
营业利润	Management Profits	346	484	725	858	1020	1352
利润总额	Total Profits	411	560	795	934	1110	1443
应交所得税	Income Tax	47	65	76	123	110	174
应付职工薪酬	Employee benefits Payable	326	377	486	588	718	904
应交增值税	Value Added Tax Payable	14	19	61	107	106	153
从事服务业活动的从业人员平均人数(万人)	Average Number of Employed Persons(10000 persons)	44.67	48.70	57.74	60.29	63.22	68.92

注:1.规上服务业企业不包括批发零售业、住宿餐饮业、房地产开发业和金融业企业。

2.规模以上服务业企业统计标准有调整,2011年执行杭州标准,2012年－2014年执行浙江省标准,2015年起执行国家标准。

a)The enterprises of service enterprises above designated size excluded wholesale retail,residential catering,real estate development and financial industry enterprises.

b)The service enterprises above designated size were counted according to Hangzhou municipal statistical standard in 2011, Zhejiang provincial statistical standard in 2012－2014, and national statistical standard in 2015－2016.

8－16　规模以上服务业非企业单位主要经济指标(2011－2016年)

Main Indicators of Service Non－Enterprise Units Above Designated Size(2011－2016)

单位:亿元　　(100 million yuan)

年　份 Year	单位数 (个) Number of Enterprise (Unit)	从业人员平均人数 (万人) Average Number of Employees(10000 person)	年末资产 Total Assets at the End of Year	固定资产原价 Orginal Value of Fixed Assets
2011	4141	36.72	3414	1306
2012	2321	32.39	5531	1211
2013	2356	34.10	6058	1346
2014	2367	35.14	6401	1499
2015	2382	35.69	6497	1628
2016	2376	36.26	7263	1708

单位:亿元　　8－16　续表　continued　　(100 million yuan)

年　份 Year	收入合计 Total Revenue	支出合计 Total Expenditure	工资福利支出 Wages and Welfare Expenses	商品和服务支出 Goods and Services Spending	对个人和家庭的补助 For Individual and Family Allowance
2011	1557	1481	316	604	133
2012	1497	1439	314	577	140
2013	1610	1527	352	594	138
2014	1672	1601	391	638	156
2015	1814	1787	469	699	172
2016	2027	1975	572	768	165

8－17　分行业规模以上服务业非企业

Main Indicators of Service Non－Enterprise Units

单位:亿元

项　目	Item	单位数(个) Number of Enterprise (Unit)	从业人员平均人数(万人) Average Number of Employees(10000 person)	年末资产 Total Assets at the End of Year
总　计	**Total**	**2376**	**36.26**	**7263**
按国民经济行业分	**Grouped by Sector**			
交通运输、仓储和邮政业	Transportation, Storage and Post	16	0.24	23
信息传输、软件和信息技术服务业	Information Transmission, Softuare and Information Technology	20	0.14	12
房地产业(除房地产开发经营)	Real Estate	10	0.05	8
租赁和商务服务业	Leasing and Business Services	61	0.23	161
科学研究和技术服务业	Scientific Research and Technical Service	140	1.36	684
水利、环境和公共设施管理业	Water Conservancy, Environment and Public Utility	88	1.06	106
居民服务、修理和其他服务业	Service for the Residents and Other Service Sector	19	0.08	8
教育	Education	723	12.75	1340
卫生和社会工作	Health Care and Social Welfare	320	9.36	579
文化、体育和娱乐业	Culture, Sports and Entertainment	123	0.70	90
公共管理、社会保障和社会组织	Public Management, Social Security and Social Organizations	851	10.16	1148

单位主要经济指标(2016 年)

Above Designated Size by Sector(2016)

(100 million yuan)

固定资产原价 Orginal Value of Fixed Assets	收入合计 Total Revenue	支出合计 Total Expenditure	工资福利支出 Wages and Welfare Expenses	商品和服务支出 Goods and Services Spending	对个人和家庭的补助 For Individual and Family Allowance
1708	**2027**	**1975**	**572**	**768**	**165**
13	20	19	3	1	1
7	7	7	1	3	–
1	1	1	1	–	–
28	15	13	3	4	1
80	132	107	19	28	5
38	37	36	9	14	2
3	3	3	1	2	–
717	469	440	190	132	64
327	573	561	171	340	24
59	33	31	9	10	3
424	734	715	163	230	64

主要统计指标解释

社会消费品零售额　指各种经济类型的批发零售贸易业、住宿餐饮业对城乡居民和社会集团的消费品零售额总和。这个指标反映通过各种商品流通渠道向居民和社会集团供应的生活消费品来满足他们生活需要，是研究人民生活、社会消费品购买力、货币流通等问题的重要指标。社会消费品零售额包括：(1)售给城乡居民作为生活用的商品和修建房屋用的建筑材料；(2)售给机关、团体、学校、部队、企业、事业单位的职工食堂各种食品、燃料；(3)售给部队干部、战士生活用的粮食、副食品、衣着品、日用品、燃料；(4)售给来华的外国人、华侨、港澳台同胞的消费品；(5)售给社会集团的办公用品、纸张、帐册、文印用品、计算工具、书刊杂志和奖品；公共用品和纺织品、针织品；学校用的教学用具；文体用品；非专用的劳动保护用品，如工作服、套袖、围裙、手套、毛巾、肥皂等；日用百货和杂品，包括职工食堂用的餐具、炊具、设备和清洁卫生工具等；家具、设备、日用电器、电讯设备、电影器材和照相器材等；取暖用的设备和燃料、防暑、降温的饮料；非生产经营用的交通工具，如小轿车、面包车、工具车、卡车和油料；零星修理的各种零配件、材料、工具、建筑材料等；举办各种招待会、茶话会、宴会用的烟酒茶和各种食品及馈赠的礼品；从公费医疗经费中开支的中、西药品、中药材和医疗器材以及其他非生产性设备和用品。

限额以上批发零售业　指批发业年主营业务收入在2000万元及以上，零售业年主营业务收入在500万元及以上的各种经济类型商贸企业。

商品销售总额　指对本企业(单位)以外的单位和个人出售(包括对国(境)外直接出口)的商品金额。这个指标反映批发零售贸易业在国内市场上销售商品以及出口商品的总量。商品销售总额包括：(1)售给城乡居民和社会集团消费用的商品；(2)售给工业、农业、建筑业、运输邮电业、批发零售贸易业、餐饮业、服务业等作为生产、经营使用的商品；(3)售给批发零售贸易业作为转卖或加工后转卖的商品；(4)对国(境)外直接出口的商品，不包括：出售本企业(单位)自用的废旧包装用品，未通过买卖行为付出的商品，经本单位介绍，由买卖双方直接结算，本单位只收取手续费的业务，购货退出的商品以及商品损耗和损失等。

Explanatory Notes on Main Statistical Indicators

Total Retail Sales of Consumer Goods referring to the sum of retail sales of consumer goods sold by wholesale and retail, catering and lodging to urban and rural residents and social groups. This indicator is used to show the supply of consumer goods through various channels to households and institutions, and is very important for the study on people' s livelihood, on the purchasing power of consumer goods and on the circulation of money. The retail sales of consumer goods include: (1) commodities sold to urban and rural residents for their daily use and building materials sold to them for the construction or repair of houses; (2) food and fuels sold to canteens of institutions, enterprises, schools and military units; (3) grains and non – staple food, clothing, daily articles and fuels sold to military personnel; (4) consumer goods sold to foreigners, overseas Chinese, and Chinese compatriots form Taiwan, Hong Kong and Macao during their stay in the mainland of China; (5) commodities sold to social groups. included under this heading are : office appliances, paper, account books, printing articles, calculaters, newspapers, magazines and prizes; public articles, textiles and knitgoods; realias for schools; cultural and sports articles; working articles for unspecial use i. e. working clothes, raglan sleeves, gloves, towels and soaps; commidities and miscellaneous goods for daily use i. e. dishwares, cookers and cleaning articles for canteens of institutions, enterprises, schools; furnishings, appliances, communications facilities , film and photograph equipments and materials; heating facilities, fuels and beverages; vehicles (exclude for business use) such as cars, microbuses, trucks and oils; parts , fittings, instruments and building materials, tobaccoes, alcohols, teas, foods for all kinds of reception meetings and banquets and prizes for presenting; Chinese and Western medicines, herbs and medical facilities expenditured by medical insurance fund and other non – production goods and equipments.

Wholesale And Retail Trade Above Designated Size wholesale trade, with year main business revenue over 20 million yuan of different status of registration; retail sale trade, with year main business revenue over 5 million yuan of different status of registration.

Total Sales of Commodities refer to selling of commodities by the establishments to other establishments and individuals (including direct export). This indictor is used to show the total value of sales of commodities at domestic markets and export. The total sales include: (1) commodities sold to urban and rural residents and social groups for their consumption; (2) commodities sold to establishments in industry, agriculture, construction, transportation, post and telecommunications, wholesale and retail trades, catering trade and public utility for their production and operation; (3) commodities sold to wholesale and retail establishment for re – selling, with or without further processing; and (4) commodities for direct export to other countries. Excluded are selling of waste packaging materials used by the establishments(units) themselves, commodities transferred without buying or selling procedures, commission income from brokerage in transactions whose settlement is directly handled by buyers and sellers, rejected commodities in the purchase, loss in commodities, etc.

九、对外经济旅游

FOREIGN ECONOMIC COOPERATION AND TOURISM

9

对外经济、旅游
Foreign Economic Cooperation and Tourism

主要统计指标
Major Statistical Indicators

实际利用外资金额	Foreign Investments Actually Utilized	72.09	亿美元	(USD 100 million)
为上年	As Compared with the Preceding Year	101.4	%	(%)
进出口总额	Total Imports and Exports	679.92	亿美元	(USD 100 million)
为上年	As Compared with the Preceding Year	102.2	%	(%)
# 出口总额	Total Exports	502.59	亿美元	(USD 100 million)
为上年	As Compared with the Preceding Year	100.5	%	(%)
接待境外旅游者人数	Number of Oversea Visitor Arrivals	363.23	万人次	(10000 person-times)
为上年	As Compared with the Preceding Year	106.3	%	(%)
旅游外汇收入	Total Foreign Exchange Earnings from International Tourism	31.49	亿美元	(USD 100 million)
为上年	As Compared with the Preceding Year	107.5	%	(%)

9－01 外商直接投资情况（1978－2016年）
Foreign Direct Investment（1978－2016）

单位:万美元 （USD 10000）

年 份 Year	项目个数（个） Number of Projects (unit)	协议总投资额 Total Investments of Agreements	协议利用外资金额 Contracted Foreign Investment	实际利用外资金额 Foreign Investments Actually Utilized
1978				
1979				
1980	3	153	128	
1981				
1982				
1983	2	356	100	
1984	9	6932	2697	
1985	21	6638	1731	907
1986	9	5722	2017	683
1987	10	2685	1256	1470
1988	23	6781	2734	696
1989	34	3897	1569	1860
1990	68	7817	3951	751
1991	121	11107	5551	2129
1992	583	125224	60915	9678
1993	1078	222325	121947	35713
1994	624	174406	110541	41098
1995	427	136662	90207	42659
1996	221	108150	70982	53651
1997	174	51682	27888	41187
1998	216	98219	51400	38425
1999	212	83416	56742	42025
2000	315	89781	64548	43093
2001	483	154447	103023	50324
2002	587	247888	96720	52186
2003	869	432660	200104	100850
2004	802	629727	307746	140982
2005	756	770941	400503	171274
2006	747	1080602	537986	225536
2007	574	854907	558059	280181
2008	483	862523	622788	331154
2009	554	948323	696486	401370
2010	545	1188055	770911	435627
2011	500	1291015	817108	472230
2012	510	1342616	826516	496061
2013	415	1419926	913144	527633
2014	408	1329217	723838	633460
2015	475	1649709	1038042	711253
2016	462	1503411	847841	720915

9－02 分行业外商直接投资情况（2016年）
Foreign Direct Investment by Sector（2016）

单位：万美元 （USD 10,000）

行　业 Sector	项目数（个） Projects（unit）	占总数 % Proportion（%）	实际利用外资金额 Foreign Investments Actually Utilized	占总数（%） Proportion（%）
合　计 Total	**462**	**100**	**720915**	**100**
第一产业 Primary Industry	**5**	**1.08**	**2255**	**0.31**
农　业 Agriculture	5	1.08	2255	0.31
第二产业 Secondary Industry	**43**	**9.31**	**153200**	**21.26**
采矿业 Mining	–	–	269	0.04
制造业 Manufacturing	39	8.44	145089	20.13
电力、燃气及水的生产和供应业 Production & Supply of Electricity, Gas & Water	–	–	4624	0.64
建筑业 Construction	4	0.87	3218	0.45
第三产业 Tertiary Industry	**414**	**89.61**	**565460**	**78.43**
交通运输、仓储、邮政业 Transportation, Storage and Post	5	1.08	33575	4.66
信息传输、计算机服务和软件业 Information Transmission, Computer Service and Software	61	13.20	99590	13.81
批发和零售贸易、餐饮业 Whole sale and Retail Tvade. Catering Services	125	27.06	75180	10.43
金融业 Banking and Insurance	12	2.60	104335	14.47
商住用房开发经营 Commercial and Residential Housing Development and Management	5	1.08	52355	7.26
纯住宅开发经营 Pure Residential Development and Management	1	0.22	68276	9.47
物业管理 Estate Management	1	0.22	669	0.09
租赁及商务服务业 Renting and Business Service	97	21.00	60583	8.40
科学研究和综合技术服务业 Scientific research and Integrated Technical Service	102	22.08	68157	9.45
其他行业 Others	5	1.08	2740	0.38

9-03 分国别(地区)外商直接投资情况(2016年)

Foreign Direct Investment by Region or Territory(2016)

单位:万美元 (USD 10000)

国别(地区)	Country (territory)	历年累计 Accumulated 项目(个) Projects (unit)	总投资额 Total Investments	协议外资金额 Total Contracted Foreign Investments	2016年 In Year 2016 项目(个) Projects (unit)	总投资额 Total Investments	协议外资金额 Total Contracted Foreign Investments	实际利用外资 Foreign Investments Actually Utilized
合 计	**Total**	**13351**	**16854432**	**10140984**	**462**	**1503411**	**847841**	**720915**
#香港	#Hong Kong	5832	11151914	6718038	221	1279362	704469	578630
澳门	Macao	73	76469	45569	2	5348	5116	-
台湾	Taiwan	1531	423595	232527	39	33737	24230	15113
日本	Japan	768	531286	232220	4	8069	-5792	1720
泰国	Thailand	42	12878	3502	1	89	29	8
马来西亚	Malaysia	82	41574	22818	1	1	1	-
新加坡	Singapore	330	484783	299119	11	-14903	-1807	27645
印度	India	24	5855	5275	8	374	324	-
韩国	Republic of Korea	352	110604	70766	29	6218	6736	401
德国	Germany	215	110458	66381	10	3684	1546	267
法国	France	127	73058	40611	1	79	-53	177
意大利	Italy	225	152577	71015	6	893	3513	2842
荷兰	Netherlands	89	101730	22615	-	-	-	30
英国	Britain	203	190824	130610	4	259	2353	234
西班牙	Spain	72	67760	26497	2	175	113	-
奥地利	Austria	24	29697	21344	-	897	897	665
俄罗斯联邦	The Russion Federation	19	3310	1572	2	172	97	-
英属维尔京群岛	The British Virgin Islands	579	1439031	688818	13	78631	17225	28922
加拿大	Canada	230	108998	72271	9	1031	2757	2147
美国	U. S. A	1686	1165129	588206	46	8803	16919	17804
澳大利亚	Australia	198	101559	78810	14	2006	919	253
新西兰	New Zealand	41	12587	8674	1	151	15	-

9－04 分地区外商直接投资情况(2016年)

Foreign Direct Investment by Region(2016)

单位:万美元 (USD 10000)

区域 Region		批准项目个数(个) Number of Projects(unit)		实际利用外资金额 Foreign Investments Actually Utilized	
		2016年 In Year 2016	历年累计 Accumulated Until the End of 2016	2016年 In Year 2016	历年累计 Accumulated Until the End of 2016
全 市	**Total**	**462**	**13351**	**720915**	**6107322**
市 区	Urban District	413	11909	665929	5615115
#上城区	Shangcheng	24	719	23610	252380
下城区	Xiacheng	25	767	40959	66672
江干区	Jianggan	42	737	34321	277190
拱墅区	Gongshu	23	971	38142	375903
西湖区	Xihu	51	1089	58872	468142
高新(滨江)区	Hi－Tech(Binjiang)	48	1106	80648	730898
萧山区	Xiaoshan	109	1758	155159	898006
余杭区	Yuhang	46	1567	9545	623174
富阳区	Fuyang	12	730	29142	262650
桐庐县	Tonglu	20	557	18250	148590
淳安县	Chun'an	5	198	1264	94210
建德市	Jiande	5	254	14759	84460
临安市	Lin'an	19	433	20713	164947

9-05　分地区国内招商引资情况(2015-2016年)
Domestic Investment by Region(2015-2016)

单位:亿元　　(100 million yuan)

区　域　Region		批准项目个数(个) Number of Projects(unit)		实际利用资金 Investments Actually Utilized	
		2016 In Year 2016	2015 In Year 2015	2016年 In Year 2016	2015年 In Year 2015
全　市	**Total**	**2733**	**2376**	**1397.07**	**1249.27**
市　区	Urban District	2149	1898	1231.03	1100.37
#上城区	Shangcheng	125	88	94.81	86.46
下城区	Xiacheng	206	322	165.14	146.18
江干区	Jianggan	240	207	161.03	144.39
拱墅区	Gongshu	595	527	172.27	153.43
西湖区	Xihu	304	186	186.27	165.36
高新(滨江)区	Hi-Tech(Binjiang)	86	65	85.26	77.91
萧山区	Xiaoshan	330	249	167.10	148.35
余杭区	Yuhang	108	121	111.21	101.00
富阳区	Fuyang	77	73	52.69	46.69
桐庐县	Tonglu	110	115	45.29	40.51
淳安县	Chun'an	147	66	28.17	25.34
建德市	Jiande	201	161	43.96	40.22
临安市	Lin'an	126	136	48.62	42.83

9－06 国家级开发区

The Construction of National－

项 目	Item	合计 Total	杭州经济技术开发区 Hangzhou Economic and Technological Development Zone
规划面积 （平方公里）	Area of planning (sq. km)	812.13	64.25
已开发面积 （平方公里）	Area of Development (sq. km)	226.82	49.42
历年累计基础设施投资额 （亿元）	Accumulative Total Investments in Infrastructure (100 million yuan)	2099.82	514.21
历年累计批准进区企业 （个）	Accumulative Number of Enterprises Approved (unit)	79162	17083
#三资企业 （个）	Foreign Investments Enter－prises (unit)	3120	837
历年累计协议利用外资 （亿美元）	Accumulative Total Foreign Investments of Agreements (USD 100 million)	275.70	131.81
历年累计实际利用外资 （亿美元）	Accumulative Total Foreign Investments Actually Used (USD 100 million)	263.20	79.67
年末实有投产企业个数 （个）	Number of Enterprises in Production or Operation at the Year－end (unit)	56565	11627
#三资企业 （个）	Foreign Investments Enter－prises (unit)	1892	588
当年规模以上工业总产值 （亿元）	Gross Industrial Output Value of the Year (100 million yuan)	7239.07	1972.75
当年规模以上企业主营业务收入 （亿元）	Fulfilled Profits and Tax of the Year (100 million yuan)	9404.60	2407.17
当年规模以上企业实现利润 （亿元）	Fulfilled Profits of the Enterprises above the Designated Size of the Year (100 million yuan)	659.58	195.35
当年出口创汇 （亿美元）	Foreign Exchange Earmings of Export of the Year (USD 100 million)	168.60	57.23
当年财政总收入 （亿元）	Total Financial Revenue of the Year (100 million yuan)	657.38	173.70
#税收收入 （亿元）	Tax Revenue (unit)	580.74	168.08

建设发展情况(2016 年)

Class Development Zones(2016)

杭州高新技术开发区 Hangzhou High - tech Development Zone	萧山经济技术开发区 Xiaoshan Economic and Technological Development Zone	富阳经济技术开发区 Fuyang Economic and Technological Development Zone	余杭经济技术开发区 Yuhang Economic and Technological Development Zone	临江国家高新区 Linjiang National High - Tech Zone
12.64	105.20	126.10	76.94	427.00
12.64	35.13	24.42	35.21	70.00
336.75	210.34	516.52	330.00	192.00
29719	8033	10920	8194	5213
541	652	508	432	150
-	82.86	29.80	31.23	-
74.40	43.93	21.30	17.69	26.21
24241	7126	5595	2978	4998
541	338	150	193	82
1355.60	1174.10	1065.19	524.81	1146.62
1456.50	2021.63	1664.35	510.56	1344.39
196.40	86.48	59.57	43.59	78.19
54.40	27.90	12.86	4.64	11.57
235.40	76.01	72.70	21.00	78.57
228.50	76.01	58.53	21.00	28.62

9－07　省级产业集聚区建设发展情况(2015－2016 年末)

Development Statistics on Provincial－level Industry Cluster Districts(End of 2015－2016)

项　　目	Item	大江东产业集聚区 Dajiangdong Industry Cluster District		城西科创产业集聚区 Chengxi Technological and Creative Industry Cluster District	
		2016 年末 End of 2016	2015 年末 End of 2015	2016 年末 End of 2016	2015 年末 End of 2015
入区企业数(个)	Proposed Enterprises (unit)	1034	812	13297	5413
投产企业数(个)	Operating Enterprises (unit)	261	250	667	482
已开发建设面积(平方千米)	Land Space under Construction (sq. km)	23.88	23.88	36.70	36.12
已建成投产面积(平方千米)	Land Space Completed (sq. km)	22.69	22.69	34.20	24.73
当年产业增加值(亿元)	Current year's Value－added (100 million yuan)	202.16	142.33	1013.70	578.61
#工业增加值(亿元)	Value－added of Industry (100 million yuan)	195.00	116.00	147.00	92.00
#服务业增加值(亿元)	Value－added of the Tertiary Industry (100 million yuan)	7.16	3.22	835.70	486.60
当年实际引进内资(亿元)	Current Year's Amount of Domestic Investment (100 million yuan)	66.89	57.45	63.60	73.94
当年实际利用外资(亿美元)	Current Year's Amount of Foreign Investment Actually Utilized (100 million USD)	6.58	5.94	3.20	4.16
当年科技活动经费支出(亿元)	Current Year's S & T Expenditure (100 million yuan)	15.27	10.54	166.00	17.86
科技活动人员数(人)	S & T Personnel (person)	4174	3044	17156	6919
当年财政预算总收入(亿元)	Current Year's Total Financial Revenue (100 million yuan)	69.15	51.23	169.10	127.56
当年固定资产投资完成额(亿元)	Current Year's Investment in Fixed Assets (100 million yuan)	228.40	210.73	366.90	296.26
当年工业总产值(亿元)	Current Year's Gross Industrial Output Value (100 million yuan)	1013.40	629.63	518.90	475.21
当年服务业营业收入(亿元)	Current Year's Operating Revenue of the Tertiary Industry (100 million yuan)	170.96	154.32	2494.70	1483.50
当年出口交货值(亿元)	Current Year's Export Delivery Value (100 million yuan)	49.00	39.77	87.30	68.23
当年利税总额(亿元)	Current Year's Total Taxes and Profits (100 million yuan)	107.00	56.11	822.60	481.47
#利润总额(亿元)	Total Profits (100 million yuan)	64.80	31.94	725.50	457.19

9-08 特色小镇发展情况(2016年)
Development of Characteristic Towns(2016)

	企业数（家）Number of Enterprises (unit)	本年新入驻企业数（家）Number of new Enterprises to enter this year (unit)	"新四军"人数（个）Number of XinSiJun (unit)	固定资产投资（不包括商业住宅和商业综合体项目）（亿元）Investment in Fixed Assets (Excluding commercial housing and commercial complex projects) (100 million yuan)
合 计 Total	**26647**	**8691**	**6582**	**506.56**
省级特色小镇创建对象 Provincial Characteristic Towns to Create Objects	12753	5596	4819	301.84
省级特色小镇培育对象 Provincial Characteristic Towns to Cultivate Objects	12155	2313	1226	121.00
市级特色小镇 Municipal Characteristic Towns	1739	782	537	83.72

注:"新四军"创业人员数:包括大学生创业者、大企业高管及其他连续创业者、科技人员创业者、留学归国人员创业者等创业人员数。包括个体工商户和企业中有技术、资本入股的人员。

a)"New Fourth Army" Entrepreneurs: including college student entrepreneurs, big business executives and other serial entrepreneurs, tech entrepreneurs, overseas returnees entrepreneurs and so on. Also including people with technical capital and equity of individual industrial and commercial businesses or enterprises.

9-08 续表 continued

	特色产业投资（亿元）Characteristic Industry Investment (100 million yuan)	工业企业主营业务收入（亿元）Industrial Enterprise Revenues in Main Business (100 million yuan)	服务业营业收入（亿元）Service Revenues (100 million yuan)	税收收入（亿元）Tax Revenues (100 million yuan)
合 计 Total	**303.59**	**1437.16**	**1371.26**	**172.78**
省级特色小镇创建对象 Provincial Characteristic Towns to Create Objects	183.74	691.46	632.42	70.63
省级特色小镇培育对象 Provincial Characteristic Towns to Cultivate Objects	74.22	576.35	703.80	93.07
市级特色小镇 Municipal Characteristic Towns	45.62	169.34	35.04	9.08

9－09 进出口情况(1989－2016年)
Imports and Exports (1989－2016)

单位:亿美元 (USD 100 million)

年份 Year	进出口 Exports And Imports		出口 Exports		进口 Imports	
	总值 Total Value	为上年% As Compared with the Preceding Year(%)	总值 Total Value	为上年% As Compared with the Preceding Year(%)	总值 Total Value	为上年% As Compared with the Preceding Year(%)
1989	0.84		0.50		0.34	
1990	1.45	172.6	0.99	198.0	0.46	135.3
1991	2.18	150.3	1.48	149.5	0.70	152.2
1992	3.42	156.9	2.16	146.0	1.26	180.0
1993	8.73	255.3	4.92	227.8	3.81	302.4
1994	34.96	400.5	26.11	530.7	8.85	232.3
1995	45.18	129.2	33.18	127.1	12.00	135.6
1996	43.52	96.3	31.11	93.8	12.41	103.4
1997	48.83	112.2	37.43	120.3	11.40	91.8
1998	59.73	122.3	44.16	118.0	15.57	136.6
1999	73.40	122.9	50.79	115.0	22.61	145.3
2000	104.76	142.7	69.65	137.1	35.11	155.3
2001	112.98	107.9	72.84	104.6	40.14	114.3
2002	131.07	116.0	84.81	116.4	46.26	115.3
2003	182.38	139.2	109.55	129.2	72.83	157.4
2004	244.96	134.3	151.75	138.6	93.21	128.0
2005	298.70	121.9	198.04	130.5	100.66	108.0
2006	389.09	130.3	262.28	132.4	126.81	126.0
2007	434.26	111.7	299.66	114.3	134.60	106.2
2008	480.65	110.7	336.14	112.2	144.51	107.4
2009	404.20	84.1	271.80	80.9	132.40	91.6
2010	523.55	129.5	353.37	130.0	170.18	128.6
2011	639.72	122.2	415.21	117.5	224.50	131.9
2012	616.83	96.4	412.62	99.4	204.22	91.0
2013	650.71	105.5	447.66	108.5	203.05	99.5
2014	679.98	104.5	491.66	109.8	188.32	92.8
2015	665.66	97.9	500.67	101.8	165.00	87.7
2016	679.92	102.2	502.59	100.5	177.34	107.6

9－10 分经济类型进出口情况(2015－2016年)

Statistics on Imports and Exports of Econimic Types(2015－2016)

单位:亿美元 (USD 100 million)

项目	Item	2016年 In Year 2016	2015年 In Year 2015	为上年(%) As Compared with year 2015 (%)
全市进出口总值(海关口径)	Total Exports And Imports	679.92	665.66	102.2
一、出口总额	Exports	502.59	500.67	100.5
1.国有企业	State－owned Enterprises	64.30	76.23	84.3
2.三资企业	Foreign Investment Enterprises	108.27	124.78	86.8
(1)中外合作企业	Cooperation Enterprises	0.63	0.61	103.3
(2)中外合资企业	Joint－Venture Enterprises	51.25	59.77	85.7
(3)外商独资企业	Enterprises With Sole Foreign Investment	56.39	64.40	87.6
3.集体企业	Collective－owned Enterprises	16.53	18.49	89.4
4.私营企业	Private Enterprises	312.17	280.75	111.2
二、进口总额	Imports	177.34	165.00	107.6

9－11 分地区外贸进出口情况(2016年)

Imports and Exports by Region(2016)

单位:万美元 (USD 10000)

区　域	Region	进出口总值 Total Imports and Exports	为上年(%) As Compared with the Preceding Year(%)	出口总值 Exports of This Year	为上年(%) As Compared with the Preceding Year(%)	进口总值 Imports of This Year	为上年(%) As Compared with the Preceding Year(%)
全市合计	**Total**	**6799241**	**102.2**	**5025852**	**100.5**	**1773389**	**107.6**
#不含省属	#Non－provincial	6229000	105.1	4578531	103.1	1650469	111.1
#上城区	Shangcheng	219033	109.0	129579	109.7	89454	108.0
下城区	Xiacheng	289824	91.6	205820	91.7	84004	91.3
江干区	Jianggan	206699	100.0	190630	100.3	16069	96.3
拱墅区	Gongshu	211965	105.5	176050	105.7	35915	104.9
西湖区	Xihu	337540	109.0	240556	103.2	96984	126.6
高新(滨江)区	Hi－Tech(Binjiang)	670780	102.8	526642	102.7	144138	102.9
萧山区	Xiaoshan	1120689	94.3	897135	97.9	223554	82.0
余杭区	Yuhang	520195	96.7	477435	95.5	42760	112.8
富阳区	Fuyang	273306	96.2	140370	92.8	132936	100.1
桐庐县	Tonglu	139150	94.4	132399	94.2	6752	98.7
淳安县	Chun'an	18377	87.8	16514	91.3	1863	65.5
建德市	Jiande	105623	104.6	99710	105.3	5913	94.6
临安市	Lin'an	223014	106.1	185321	105.5	37694	108.9

9－12 分地区外贸进出口总值(2004－2016 年)
Imports and Exports by Region(2004－2016)

单位:万美元 (USD 10000)

年份 Year	全市 Whole City	市区 Urban District				桐庐县 Tonglu	淳安县 Chun'an	建德市 Jiande	临安市 Lin'an
		合计 Total	#萧山区 Xiaoshan	#余杭区 Yuhang	#富阳区 Fuyang				
2004	2449671	2364434	414374	88538	52399	32333	4461	19525	28918
2005	2986993	2892191	510950	128999	72357	30489	5211	25841	33262
2006	3890853	3769910	610201	183930	81616	38522	6797	34132	41492
2007	4342666	4181699	795487	255534	105765	48811	8319	48295	55542
2008	4806503	4545719	953377	324421	126829	71753	12478	101692	74862
2009	4041991	3821965	829827	285496	116158	60064	12039	77470	70454
2010	5235549	4946409	1135326	385736	166652	73919	17183	96651	101387
2011	6397180	6044765	1432742	484903	216575	93464	20459	105763	132729
2012	6168325	5814547	1367290	512531	224446	103153	21604	86681	142340
2013	6507102	6115754	1408929	555640	265788	119539	19692	87023	165094
2014	6799775	6355378	1384823	601220	284980	133392	23802	94202	193001
2015	6656636	6178381	1189039	537405	285540	147326	20814	100965	209150
2016	6799241	6313076	1120689	520195	273306	139150	18377	105623	223014

9－13　出口企业前20位排名(2016年)
The List of Top Twenty Export Enterprises(2016)

单位:万美元　　　　(USD 10000)

企业名称	Name of Enterprises	位次 Ranks	出口额 Export Value
浙江一达通企业服务有限公司	Zhejiang One Touch Business Service Co. ,Ltd.	1	541193
杭州海康威视科技有限公司	Hangzhou Hikvision Digital Technology Co. ,Ltd.	2	123973
中策橡胶集团有限公司	Zhongce Rubber Group Co. ,Ltd.	3	79155
东芝信息机器(杭州)有限公司	Toshiba Information Equipment (Hangzhou) Co. , Ltd.	4	73894
浙江大华科技有限公司	Zhejiang Dahua Technology Co. ,Ltd.	5	59145
杭州华三通信技术有限公司	Hangzhou H3C Tech Co. ,Ltd.	6	52611
杭州巨星科技股份有限公司	Hangzhou Greatstar Industrial Co. ,Ltd.	7	48935
杭州融易通进出口有限公司	Hangzhou Ueasy Business Service Co. ,Ltd.	8	31885
杭州市轻工工艺纺织品进出口有限公司	Hangzhou Hardicrafts and Textiles Import and Export Corporation	9	29852
浙江物产国际贸易有限公司	Zhejiang Materials Industry International Co. ,Ltd.	10	27869
杭州热联国贸股份有限公司	Hangzhou CIEC International Co. ,Ltd.	11	26372
博世电动工具(中国)有限公司	Bosch Power Tools(China) Co. ,Ltd.	12	24814
奥的斯机电电梯有限公司	XiZi Otis Elevator Co. ,Ltd.	13	24632
顾家家居股份有限公司	Jason Furniture(Hangzhou)Co. ,Ltd.	14	26151
浙江恒逸石化有限公司	Zhejiang Hengyi Petrochemical Co. ,Ltd.	15	22710
杭州杭丝时装进出口有限公司	Hangzhou Hangsi Fashionable Dress Export & Import Co. ,Ltd.	16	21344
汇孚集团有限公司	Wellfull Group Co. ,Ltd.	17	19986
杭州鼎胜进出口有限公司	Hangzhou Dingsheng Import & Export Co. ,Ltd.	18	19928
杭州大和热磁电子有限公司	Hangzhou Dahe Thermo－Maretics Co. ,Ltd.	19	19800
浙江中大技术进出口集团有限公司	Zhejiang Zhongda Technology Import and Export Group Co. ,Ltd.	20	19227

9-14 外贸出口分国别(地区)情况(2015-2016年)

Export of Foreign Trade by Main Countries or Regions(2015-2016)

单位:万美元 (USD 10000)

国别(地区)	Country (territory)	2016年 In Year 2016	2015年 In Year 2015	为上年(%) As Compared with the Preceding Year(%)
合 计	**Total**	**5025852**	**5001751**	**100.5**
#香港	Hong Kong	91265	97551	93.6
台湾	Taiwan	56240	54037	104.1
美国	U. S. A	1015565	1009827	100.6
日本	Japan	317434	315349	100.7
德国	Germany	205134	208032	98.6
英国	Britain	201912	199272	101.3
印度	India	196021	207662	94.4
越南	Vietnam	150220	123320	121.8
韩国	Republic of Korea	140446	123017	114.2
荷兰	Netherlands	140270	151331	92.7
意大利	Italy	110896	109001	101.7
法国	France	108550	105449	102.9
俄罗斯	Russia	104824	94766	110.6
澳大利亚	Australia	102960	109202	94.3
印度尼西亚	Indonesia	97796	85859	113.9
西班牙	Spain	89138	84850	105.1
加拿大	Canada	88312	91180	96.9
巴西	Brazil	85670	92437	92.7
墨西哥	Mexico	80960	86014	94.1
泰国	Thailand	80829	86002	94.0
"一带一路"国家	One Belt and One Road Countries	1546011	1502506	102.9

9－15 旅游发展情况(1995－2016 年)
Development of Tourism(1995－2016)

年份 Year	旅游总收入 (亿元) Total Tourism Revenue (100 million yuan)	国内旅游收入 (亿元) Domestic Earnings (100 million yuan)	旅游外汇收入 (亿美元) Foreign Exchange Earnings from International Tourism (USD 100 million)	旅游总人数 (万人次) Total Tourists (10000 person－times)	国内游客人数 (万人次) Domestic Tourists (10000 person－times)
1995	106.0	94.3	1.45	2148	2104
1996	136.5	122.6	1.67	2055	2009
1997	158.8	142.1	2.01	2150	2100
1998	163.4	146.0	2.10	2172	2121
1999	186.0	166.7	2.37	2266	2207
2000	214.3	190.0	2.92	2376	2305
2001	249.7	218.9	3.37	2592	2510
2002	294.4	254.8	4.77	2758	2652
2003	325.9	290.9	4.22	2862	2776
2004	410.1	361.2	5.97	3139	3016
2005	465.1	403.6	7.58	3417	3266
2006	543.7	471.2	9.09	3864	3682
2007	630.1	548.6	11.19	4320	4112
2008	707.2	617.2	12.96	4773	4552
2009	803.1	708.9	13.80	5324	5094
2010	1025.7	910.9	16.90	6581	6305
2011	1191.0	1063.8	19.60	7487	7181
2012	1392.3	1253.2	22.02	8568	8237
2013	1603.7	1469.9	21.60	9725	9409
2014	1886.3	1743.9	23.18	10933	10606
2015	2200.7	2019.7	29.31	12382	12040
2016	2571.8	2362.6	31.49	14059	13696

9－16　境外旅游者人数(1978－2016年)
Number of International Tourists (1978－2016)

单位:人次　　　　(person－times)

年　份 Year	合　计 Total	外国人 Foreigners	港澳台同胞 Compatriots from Hong Kong, Macao and Taiwan	平均逗留天数 Average days of Staying
1978	53475	728	26648	
1979	84914	44714	39131	2.59
1980	124960	61710	61382	2.70
1981	154745	87727	65014	2.71
1982	152897	89100	61314	2.49
1983	160564	97803	59625	2.18
1984	179200	105771	70915	2.12
1985	238385	156311	75063	2.18
1986	266370	170960	87092	2.38
1987	300603	183477	100078	2.38
1988	349246	149512	159745	2.08
1989	248502	66094	163589	2.08
1990	388345	86621	268131	2.09
1991	390197	136809	229690	2.00
1992	489578	183781	267256	2.03
1993	459620	199796	234640	2.06
1994	337362	201692	124346	2.10
1995	441262	249418	177236	2.06
1996	462313	273477	178845	2.07
1997	504276	288949	205267	2.20
1998	507243	261353	231609	2.20
1999	591853	324625	257978	2.09
2000	707148	400906	306242	2.15
2001	819438	447689	371749	2.41
2002	1056266	631576	424690	2.50
2003	861163	482073	379090	2.72
2004	1234063	791616	442447	2.59
2005	1513585	1020840	492745	2.63
2006	1820171	1236792	583379	2.57
2007	2085997	1453650	632347	2.67
2008	2213329	1543665	669654	2.73
2009	2304045	1572838	731207	2.87
2010	2757147	1878528	878619	2.94
2011	3063140	2108263	954877	2.96
2012	3311225	2298763	1012462	2.95
2013	3160058	2198187	961871	2.93
2014	3261337	2254866	1006471	2.93
2015	3415619	2378461	1037158	2.99
2016	3632252	2556247	1076005	3.14

注:从1995年起为全市数。

a) Data in this table has included the tourists of whole municipality since 1995.

9-17 接待境外游客及居民出境旅游情况(2015-2016年)

Number of International Tourists and Outbound Tourists(2015-2016)

项　目	Item	2016年 In Year 2016	2015年 In Year 2015	为上年(%) As Compared with the preceding year(%)
一、接待境外游客	**International Tourists**			
全年接待人数(人次)	**Number of Foreign Tourists(person-times)**	**3632252**	**3415619**	**106.3**
#外国人	#Foreigners	2556247	2378461	107.5
港澳台同胞	Compatriots From Hong Kong, Macao and Taiwan	1076005	1037158	103.7
全年接待人天数(人天)	**Total Person-days (person-days)**	**11414114**	**10236003**	**111.5**
#外国人	#Foreigners	8409339	7428277	113.2
港澳台同胞	Compatriots From Hong Kong, Macao and Taiwan	3004775	2807726	107.0
平均逗留天数(天)	**Average Days of Staying (days)**	**3.14**	**2.99**	**105.0**
#外国人	#Foreigners	3.29	3.12	105.4
港澳台同胞	Compatriots From Hong Kong, Macao and Taiwan	2.79	2.71	103.0
旅游外汇总收入(万美元)	**Total Foreign Exchange Earnings From International Tourism (USD 10000)**	**314944**	**293065**	**107.5**
二、居民出境旅游	**Outbound Tourism**			
居民出境旅游人数(人次)	**Outbound Tourists(Person-time)**	**1598969**	**1507250**	**106.1**

注:2015年旅游外汇总收入统计口径调整,同比增速按可比口径计算。

a) Since 2015, the date of the total foreign exchange earnings from international tourism were adjusted, the growth rate were calculated at comparable prices.

9-18 接待境外游客分国别(地区)情况(2015-2016年)

Number of International Tourists by Country or Territory(2015-2016)

单位:人次 (person-times)

国别(地区)	Country (territory)	2016年 In Year 2016	2015年 In Year 2015	为上年(%) As Compared with the Preceding Year(%)
合计	**Total**	**3632252**	**3415619**	**106.3**
#香港	#Hong Kong	409723	390266	105.0
澳门	Macao	60785	58740	103.5
台湾	Taiwan	605479	588152	103.0
日本	Japan	206004	210743	97.8
美国	U.S.A	243223	224628	108.3
新加坡	Singapore	103915	98497	105.5
澳大利亚	Australia	49705	45001	110.5
泰国	Thailand	96103	89702	107.1
意大利	Italy	31834	29284	108.7
荷兰	Netherlands	26047	24213	107.6
西班牙	Spain	21274	20748	102.5
马来西亚	Malaysia	106738	100186	106.5
韩国	Republic of Korea	649096	626821	103.6
法国	France	63951	57114	112.0
德国	Germany	80463	74287	108.3
加拿大	Canada	49906	44039	113.3
英国	Britain	69216	62545	110.7
印度尼西亚	Indonesia	24665	26888	91.7
印度	India	31786	29247	108.7
菲律宾	Filipine	16138	17145	94.1

主要统计指标解释

利用外资 指我市政府部门,企业和其他经济组织通过对外借款,吸收外商直接投资以及用其他方式筹措的境外现汇、设备、技术等。

外商直接投资 是指外国企业和经济组织或个人(包括华侨、港澳台胞以及我国在境外注册的企业)按我国有关政策、法规,用现汇、实物、技术等在我市境内开办外商独资企业、与我市境内的企业或经济组织共同举办中外合资经营企业、合作经营企业或者合作开发资源的投资(包括外商投资收益的再投资)以及经政府有关部门批准的项目投资总额内,企业从境外借入的资金。

进出口总额 海关进出口总额指实际进出我国国境的货物总金额。包括对外贸易实际进出口货物,来料加工装配进出口货物,国家间、联合国及国际组织无偿援助物资和赠送品,华侨、港澳台同胞和外籍华人捐赠品,租赁期满归承租人所有的租赁货物,进料加工进出口货物,边境地方贸易及边境地区小额贸易进出口货物(边民互市贸易除外),中外合资经营企业、中外合作经营企业、外商独资经营企业进出口货物和公用物品,到、离岸价格在规定限额以上的进出口货样和广告品(无商业价值、无使用价值和免费提供出口的除外),从保税仓库提取在中国境内销售的进口货物,以及其他进出口货物。进出口总额以观察一个国家在对外贸易方面的总规模。我国规定出口货物按离岸价格统计,进口货物按到岸价格统计。

境外旅游者人数 指来我市参观、访问、旅行、探亲、访友、休养、考察、参加会议和从事经济、科技、文化、教育、体育、宗教等活动的外国人、华侨、港澳和台湾同胞的人数。不包括外国在我市的常驻机构,如使领馆、通讯社、企业办事处的工作人员;来我市常住的外国专家、留学生以及在岸逗留不过夜人员。

境外旅游(外汇)收入 指入境旅游的外国人、华侨、港澳台同胞在杭州旅游过程中发生的一切旅游支出,对我市来说就是境外旅游(外汇)收入。

Explanatory Notes on Main Statistical Indicators

Utilization of Foreign Capital refers to remittance, equipment and technology financed from abroad, by loans, foreign direct investment and other forms undertaken by the government units of Hangzhou, by various departments, enterprises and other economic units.

Direct Investment by Foreign Entrepreneurs refers to the investments inside China by foreign enterprises and economic organizations or individuals (including overseas Chinese, compatriots from Hong Kong, Macao and Taiwan, and Chinese enterprises registered abroad), following the relevant policies and laws of China, for the establishment of ventures exclusively with foreign own investment, Sino – foreign joint ventures and cooperative enterprises or for co – operative exploration of resources with enterprises or economic organizations in Hangzhou. It includes the re – investment of the foreign entrepreneurs with the profits gained from the investment and the funds that enterprises borrow from abroad in the total investment of projects which are approved by the relevant department of the government.

Total Imports and Exports at Customs refer to the value of commodities imported into and exported from the boundary of China. They include the actual imports and exports through foreign trade, imported and exported goods under the processing and assembling trades and materials, supplies and gifts as aid given gratis between governments and by the United Nations and other international organizations, and contributions donated by overseas Chinese, compatriots in Hong Kong, Macao and Chinese foreign citizenship, leasing commodities owned by tenant at the expiration of leasing period, the imported and exported commodities processed with imported materials, commodities trading in border areas (excluding mutual exchange goods), the imported and exported commodities and articles for public use of the Sino – foreign joint ventures, cooperative enterprises and ventures exclusively with foreign own investment. Also included are import or export of samples and advertising goods for whose CIF or FOB value are beyond the permitted ceiling (excluding goods of no trading or use value and free commodities for export), imported goods sold in China from bonded warehouses and other imported or exported goods. The indicator of the total imports and exports at customs can be used to observe the total size of external trade in a country. In accordance with the stipulation of Chinese government, imports are calculated at CIF, while exports are calculated at FOB.

Number of International Tourists refer to foreigners, overseas Chinese compatriots from Hong Kong, Macao and Taiwan coming to Hangzhou for sightseeing, visits, tours, family reunions, vacations, study tours, conferences and other activities of a business, scientific and technological, cultural, educational and religious nature. It does not include representatives and employees of resident institutions of foreign countries in China such as embassies, consulates, news agencies and offices of foreign companies and organizations, nor does it include long – term foreign experts or students residing in Hangzhou, or persons in transition without spending a night in China.

Foreign Exchange Earnings from International Tourism refer to the total expenditures of foreigners, overseas Chinese, Chinese compatriots from Hong Kong, Macao and Taiwan during their stay in the mainland of China, which are earnings of foreign exchange form international tourism from the point of vies from China.

十、财政、金融保险

FINANCE,BANKING AND INSURANCE

10 财政、金融、保险
Finance, Banking and Insurance

主要统计指标
Major Statistical Indicators

财政总收入	Total Financial Revenue	2558.41	亿元	(100 million yuan)
为上年	As Compared with the Preceding Year	114.0	%	(%)
一般公共预算收入	General Public Budget Revenue	1402.38	亿元	(100 million yuan)
为上年	As Compared with the Preceding Year	113.2	%	(%)
一般公共预算支出	General Public Financial Budgetary Expenditure	1404.31	亿元	(100 million yuan)
为上年	As Compared with the Preceding Year	116.4	%	(%)
年末金融机构各项存款余额	Balance of Deposits of Financial Institutions at Year-end	33386.04	亿元	(100 million yuan)
为上年	As Compared with the Preceding Year	111.8	%	(%)
# 住户存款余额	The Increased Amount of Household Deposits	8493.27	亿元	(100 million yuan)
为上年	As Compared with the Preceding Year	111.5	%	(%)
年末金融机构各项贷款余额	Balance of Loans of Financial Institutions at Year-end	26169.00	亿元	(100 million yuan)
为上年	As Compared with the Preceding Year	112.2	%	(%)

10－01 财政收入及支出(1978－2016年)

Financial Revenue and Expenditure (1978－2016)

单位:万元 (10000 yuan)

年份 Year	财政总收入 Financial Revenue		一般公共预算收入 General Public Budget Revenue		一般公共预算支出 General Public Budget Expenditure	
	全市 Total	市区 Urban District	全市 Total	市区 Urban District	全市 Total	市区 Urban District
1978	94102	73396	–	–	16170	7779
1979	103259	81885	–	–	20334	11289
1980	118529	94015	–	–	21726	11867
1981	128564	100645	–	–	23964	13891
1982	140510	107298	–	–	24945	13687
1983	153941	116559	–	–	32765	17822
1984	172996	130757	–	–	46937	28710
1985	186472	131923	–	–	57710	35435
1986	205952	141943	–	–	73213	43959
1987	226262	152268	–	–	70717	41011
1988	246961	161208	–	–	95655	53031
1989	255003	156649	–	–	113571	61534
1990	252503	149904	–	–	118167	62587
1991	267597	158130	–	–	123134	62403
1992	286394	168341	–	–	132814	65984
1993	394946	233670	–	–	185168	90545
1994	484597	300014	197292	116733	215415	102430
1995	551262	339828	230431	135041	249050	120084
1996	635334	414557	268438	169987	302390	151016
1997	740725	485650	312797	196885	363834	197054
1998	869824	585615	368484	236269	424478	237221
1999	1026577	689394	449593	288002	563524	335243
2000	1428519	970937	691891	599910	734328	445698
2001	1884608	1612225	1042789	884738	1049330	849479
2002	2571408	2235021	1183153	1022964	1410199	1166298
2003	3297091	2861459	1503888	1290778	1635948	1340463
2004	3957516	3488744	1974523	1712813	1956282	1602303
2005	5207930	4584112	2504565	2172575	2383344	1957619
2006	6244906	5484645	3013888	2616084	2754809	2254347
2007	7884237	6929667	3916195	3421403	3357153	2747060
2008	9105489	7991043	4553531	3972842	4196674	3454599
2009	10194264	8965758	5207899	4535191	4903983	4000324
2010	12454323	10988265	6713413	5894414	6165836	4988197
2011	14889206	13009046	7851524	6822765	7475004	5971740
2012	16278879	14244888	8599875	7475989	7862800	6222930
2013	17349750	15157584	9452020	8207264	8557370	6662314
2014	19201076	17750305	10273169	9426504	9611771	8077961
2015	22387456	20738698	12338820	11360166	12054777	10235061
2016	25584128	23844189	14023826	12988095	14043065	12019355

10－02 分地区财政
Local Financial

单位:万元

指 标	Item	全 市 Total	市 区 Urban District	上城区 Shangcheng
财政总收入合计	**Total**	**25584128**	**23844189**	**1283388**
一、一般公共预算收入	General Public Budget Revenue	14023826	12988095	723906
(一)税收收入	Tax Revenue	12892210	11971781	689715
1. 国内增值税	Domestic Value－added Tax	2097640	1872504	68105
2. 改征增值税	Newly Changed Value－added Tax	1705813	1614476	92507
3. 营业税	Business Tax	1988053	1856681	142744
4. 企业所得税	Corporate Income Tax	2215439	2084202	137337
5. 个人所得税	Individual Income Tax	1155176	1097107	109385
6. 城市维护建设税	City Construction and Maintenance Tax	890160	832986	36840
7. 房产税	Real Estate Tax	443407	409180	43456
8. 城镇土地使用税	Urban Land Use Tax	147437	112205	3505
9. 土地增值税	Land Appreciation Tax	851760	791672	44588
10. 耕地占用税	Tax on the Use of Arable Land	40610	29747	－
11. 契税	Contract Tax	1056441	1001049	－
12. 其他税收	Others Tax	300274	269972	11248
(二)非税收入	Non－tax Revenue	1131616	1016314	34191
1. 专项收入	Special Revenue	1102959	1027919	31478
#教育费附加	Revenue from Extra－Charges for Education	334644	308411	13357
地方教育附加收入	Local Education Additional Revenue	223646	206209	8899
水利建设专项收入	Special Revenue of Water Coservancy Construction	145059	131935	3932
残疾人就业保障金收入	Employment Security for The Disabled Revenue	91585	86130	5290
教育资金收入	Educational Fund Revenue	169120	164761	－
农田水利建设资金收入	Fund in The Farmland Irrigation Construction Revenue	108237	105447	－
2. 行政事业性收费收入	Income from Administrative Fees	10968	5810	－
3. 罚没收入	Penalty and Confiscatory Income	160147	135852	2306
4. 国有企业计划亏损补贴	Subsides to Loss－making of state－owned Enterprises	－250873	－237900	－
5. 国有资源(资产)有偿使用收入	Compensation for the Use of Seate－owned Assets Income	58175	46077	407
6. 政府住房基金收入	Government Housing Fund Income	47146	38370	－
7. 其他收入	Others Revenue	1119	93	－
二、上划中央“六税”小计	Subtotal Revenue of Central Government	11560302	10856094	559482
1. 消费税	Consumption Tax	1971548	1961383	1932
2. 国内增值税	Domestic Value－added Tax	2977758	2666325	93627
3. 企业所得税	Corporate Income Tax	3323162	3126305	206006
4. 个人所得税	Individual Income Tax	1732766	1645663	164078
5. 改征增值税	Newly Changed Value－added Tax	1185950	1109644	72025
6. 营业税	Business Tax	369118	346774	21814

总收入(2016年)
Revenue by Region(2016)

(10000 yuan)

下城区 Xiacheng	江干区 Jianggan	拱墅区 Gongshu	西湖区 Xihu	高新(滨江)区 Hi－Tech (Binjiang)	萧山区 Xiaoshan
1358497	**1427113**	**1309836**	**2213922**	**2353665**	**3459863**
794139	874915	796566	1231126	1253661	1951629
751604	841792	750262	1166148	1184935	1735907
96955	93986	107492	121638	181489	417027
110918	106701	104857	202670	210781	137960
126679	201084	195916	206237	115859	301203
129231	134736	120010	187730	264048	268974
79352	50225	39887	239938	206932	91725
42124	51192	49672	64293	86329	141191
43704	44303	32599	52453	37784	44777
3246	4765	3782	5609	4179	36282
40595	140902	84666	69044	59590	119856
–	–	–	–	–	13431
–	–	–	–	–	112697
78800	13898	11381	16536	17944	50784
42535	33123	46304	64978	68726	215722
39175	43286	42524	56560	66738	182572
15254	18411	16765	23254	31540	53919
10166	12271	11804	15523	21032	35943
5556	6045	6566	6827	5740	25682
8199	6559	7389	10889	8426	10366
–	–	–	–	–	33512
–	–	–	–	–	21447
15		87	2249		67
3167	4585	3108	5226	1698	24526
–	－15000	–	–	–	－8500
178	252	585	943	290	8665
–	–	–	–	–	8208
–	–	–	–	–	91
564358	552198	513270	982796	1100004	1508234
3827	1332	1691	602	108	203186
146261	145358	161143	171233	260100	587634
193847	202104	180015	281595	396072	403461
119028	75338	59831	359907	310398	137588
84537	88590	81828	140463	119796	115751
16858	39476	28762	28996	13530	60614

指标	Item	大江东产业集聚区 Dajiangdong Industry Cluster District	余杭区 Yuhang	富阳区 Fuyang
财政总收入合计	**Total**	**785737**	**4000319**	**971747**
一、一般公共预算收入	General Public Budget Revenue	314590	2442888	576102
(一)税收收入	Tax Revenue	286232	2267761	493234
1. 国内增值税	Domestic Value－added Tax	127157	240888	141155
2. 改征增值税	Newly Changed Value－added Tax	18848	477666	41993
3. 营业税	Business Tax	19515	290296	55486
4. 企业所得税	Corporate Income Tax	51286	413698	64880
5. 个人所得税	Individual Income Tax	9328	191473	36478
6. 城市维护建设税	City Construction and Maintenance Tax	40233	125538	35120
7. 房产税	Real Estate Tax	－2729	56618	17062
8. 城镇土地使用税	Urban Land Use Tax	7643	29429	15566
9. 土地增值税	Land Appreciation Tax	6590	189598	24404
10. 耕地占用税	Tax on the Use of Arable Land	－	100	5415
11. 契税	Contract Tax	－	218282	37059
12. 其他税收	Others Tax	8361	34175	18616
(二)非税收入	Non－tax Revenue	28358	175127	82868
1. 专项收入	Special Revenue	27913	156761	50014
#教育费附加	Revenue from Extra－Charges for Education	15322	47598	15272
地方教育附加收入	Local Education Additional Revenue	10213	31732	10140
水利建设专项收入	Special Revenue of Water Coservancy Construction	1338	21038	10625
残疾人就业保障金收入	Employment Security for The Disabled Revenue	1040	8592	3633
教育资金收入	Educational Fund Revenue	－	26000	3537
农田水利建设资金收入	Fund in The Farmland Irrigation Construction Revenue	－	16640	2264
2. 行政事业性收费收入	Income from Administrative Fees	－	1101	1599
3. 罚没收入	Penalty and Confiscatory Income	4	18733	13359
4. 国有企业计划亏损补贴	Subsides to Loss－making of state－owned Enterprises	－	－7000	－3000
5. 国有资源(资产)有偿使用收入	Compensation for the Use of Seate－owned Assets Income	441	5498	8033
6. 政府住房基金收入	Government Housing Fund Income	－	34	12863
7. 其他收入	Others Revenue	－	－	－
二、上划中央"六税"小计	Subtotal Revenue of Central Government	471147	1557431	395645
1. 消费税	Consumption Tax	191800	7824	1019
2. 国内增值税	Domestic Value－added Tax	169175	338435	196095
3. 企业所得税	Corporate Income Tax	76929	620547	97320
4. 个人所得税	Individual Income Tax	13992	287210	54717
5. 改征增值税	Newly Changed Value－added Tax	5058	46411	10180
6. 营业税	Business Tax	14193	257004	36314

continued (10000 yuan)

经济技术开发区 Economic and Technological Development Zone	西湖风景名胜区 The West Lake Scenic Zone	桐庐县 Tonglu	淳安县 Chun'an	建德市 Jiande	临安市 Lin'an
1272893	**92745**	**430440**	**272873**	**388730**	**647896**
635098	52204	261681	173613	227059	373378
593712	49740	226029	155553	204833	334014
264782	2889	58599	21678	64499	80360
41925	8721	27931	19382	20019	24005
31102	10810	25663	37919	20380	47410
128496	14001	26463	22622	25753	56399
31162	4884	16317	7541	10554	23657
53532	2180	11382	7194	13187	25411
26201	5238	9265	5942	8399	10621
4914	644	10159	2604	8249	14220
3719	–	13747	12346	10620	23375
–	–	4461	2011	3636	755
–	–	15801	13139	9071	17381
7879	373	6241	3175	10466	10420
41386	2464	35652	18060	22226	39364
39066	2156	17840	12808	17448	26944
19441	784	6173	4022	6000	10038
12967	523	4108	2650	4008	6671
2164	231	3796	2049	3074	4205
4494	618	1127	956	1180	2192
–	–	951	1543	1080	785
–	–	609	988	691	502
169	32	1418	280	401	3059
792	256	6784	4087	5151	8273
–	–	–	–	-4700	-8273
1357	20	8420	393	294	2991
–	–	1190	454	3632	3500
2	–	–	38	–	988
637795	40541	168759	99260	161671	274518
12058	–	49	3815	2747	3554
351896	4077	77017	28462	85287	120667
192744	21002	39695	33933	38630	84599
46743	7326	24475	11311	15831	35486
5624	1272	4040	6260	3373	8671
28730	6864	23483	15479	15803	21541

10－03 分地区公共

General Public

单位:万元

指标	Item	全市 Total	市区 Urban District	上城区 Shangcheng
一般公共预算支出	**General Public Budget Expenditure**	**14043065**	**12019355**	**329788**
一、一般公共服务	Expenditure for General Public Services	1125425	954778	34250
二、国防	Expenditure for National Defense	9702	7814	21
三、公共安全	Expenditure for Public Security	926471	825028	31199
四、教育	Expenditure for Education	2530114	2126150	73675
#教育费附加支出	Expenditure on Extra－Charges for Educations	261254	239328	13500
五、科学技术	Expenditure for Science and Technology	749190	674862	13824
六、文化体育与传媒	Expenditure for Culture,Sports and Media	283936	243583	4149
七、社会保障和就业	Expenditure for Social Safety Net and Employment Effort	1492895	1250880	63953
八、医疗卫生与计划生育	Expenditure for Medical and Health Care and Birth Control	970504	790805	19936
九、节能环保	Expenditure for Energy Conservation Environmental Protection	408576	341035	56
#排污费支出	Sewage Expenses	7835	7658	
十、城乡社区	Expenditure for Urban and Rural Community	2338331	2210800	53661
十一、农林水	Expenditure for Agriculture,Forestry and Water Conservancy	914373	631235	29
十二、交通运输	Expenditure for Trarssportation	518178	349852	10
十三、资源勘探信息等	Resources Exploration Information,etc	504023	476779	12087
十四、商业服务业等	Expenditure for Commercial Service Industry	294333	274004	5332
十五、金融支出	Expenditure for Financial Supervision	15105	14682	7502
十六、援助其他地区	Expenditure for Aiding Other Territories	57282	54015	1404
十七、国土海洋气象等	Expenditure for Land, Ocean and Meteorological Services	56504	41756	697
十八、住房保障	Expenditure on Housing Support	219590	170061	
十九、粮油物资储备	Expenditure for Grain and Oil Reservation and other Materials Services	22562	17056	
二十、债务付息支出	Expenditure for Interest Payment of Government debt	197106	160090	2565
二十一、其他	Other Expenditure	408865	404090	5438

预算支出(2016 年)
Expenditure by Region(2016)

(10000 yuan)

下城区 Xiacheng	江干区 Jianggan	拱墅区 Gongshu	西湖区 Xihu	高新(滨江)区 Hi-Tech (Binjiang)	萧山区 Xiaoshan
325327	**535048**	**385544**	**695927**	**1074539**	**2045491**
32639	46729	44266	63355	29026	157925
311	50	29	798	29	1788
38796	42143	40304	59818	30035	110845
65830	97642	92756	145960	130012	433599
10705	14342	15364	18432	33217	49271
11596	38494	13115	32406	117067	73444
7418	5251	4774	10014	25311	19389
55500	63129	43213	88871	99270	172186
21197	25801	21007	42078	27563	205229
–	7572	4115	405	6007	111818
–	–	–	–	–	1678
61782	94366	101810	155417	437021	219966
2192	19589	1360	21999	20530	155363
–	15	–	30	10	128661
4970	2806	3320	49103	110573	122112
12595	2075	11159	9134	14221	21691
25	324	420	260	750	505
–	–	1241	3823	7128	8719
653	722	1001	3480	1583	6042
7033	–	–	3728	10905	37689
–	–	–	–	–	14861
2785	8705	489	4647	4999	30563
5	79635	1165	601	2499	13096

单位:万元

10－03 续表

指标	Item	大江东产业集聚区 Dajiangdong Industry Cluster District	余杭区 Yuhang	富阳区 Fuyang
一般公共预算支出	**General Public Budget Expenditure**	**457974**	**2214988**	**661607**
一、一般公共服务	Expenditure for General Public Services	34420	171198	71022
二、国防	Expenditure for National Defense	－	2774	54
三、公共安全	Expenditure for Public Security	17879	94875	37811
四、教育	Expenditure for Education	112620	373331	176693
#教育费附加支出	Expenditure on Extra－Charges for Educations	521	33933	8404
五、科学技术	Expenditure for Science and Technology	4509	118293	34916
六、文化体育与传媒	Expenditure for Culture,Sports and Media	1209	28731	14879
七、社会保障和就业	Expenditure for Social Safety Net and Employment Effort	13343	181712	43102
八、医疗卫生与计划生育	Expenditure for Medical and Health Care and Birth Control	32506	155623	47856
九、节能环保	Expenditure for Energy Conservation Environmental Protection	44084	100686	24323
#排污费支出	Sewage Expenses	－	－	1980
十、城乡社区	Expenditure for Urban and Rural Community	81132	395588	24101
十一、农林水	Expenditure for Agriculture,Forestry and Water Conservancy	29767	118118	93671
十二、交通运输	Expenditure for Trarssportation	1654	61530	22126
十三、资源勘探信息等	Resources Exploration Information,etc	58154	110976	6860
十四、商业服务业等	Expenditure for Commercial Service Industry	1698	163011	4621
十五、金融支出	Expenditure for Financial Supervision	85	786	97
十六、援助其他地区	Expenditure for Aiding Other Territories	－	11054	2618
十七、国土海洋气象等	Expenditure for Land,Ocean and Meteorological Services	939	7577	4041
十八、住房保障	Expenditure on Housing Support	13408	83491	20456
十九、粮油物资储备	Expenditure for Grain and Oil Reservation and other Materials Services	－	145	481
二十、债务付息	Expenditure for Interest Payment of Government debt	3842	22545	31879
二十一、其他	Other Expenditure	6725	12944	－

continued (10000 yuan)

经济技术开发区 Economic and Technological Development Zone	西湖风景名胜区 The West Lake Scenic Zone	桐庐县 Tonglu	淳安县 Chun'an	建德市 Jiande	临安市 Lin'an
477640	**139282**	**409353**	**600733**	**411925**	**601699**
43091	4974	25949	56171	37077	51450
58	–	461	252	496	679
26244	16350	21690	28544	21419	29790
59587	2979	98204	88862	86857	130041
20000	–	6238	2900	2452	10336
44493	294	16804	10670	15129	31725
968	12094	10374	10885	8776	10318
5666	2509	58395	71663	53501	58456
4449	1844	42142	52189	38315	47053
1769	2	9493	31025	14145	12878
–	–	–	144	33	–
225724	94937	12246	60801	13389	41095
13497	1378	65014	88418	70126	59580
–	–	18798	50435	19591	79502
30534	162	1448	10731	2563	12502
7851	485	3103	8681	3092	5453
483	–	227	–	13	183
5855	170	1131	–	910	1226
1058	240	5355	2520	2928	3945
2571	–	11438	12541	11945	13605
–	–	3008	2056	39	403
3742	–	3992	14289	7670	11065
–	864	81	–	3944	750

10-04 全市分税种、支出科目财政收支情况(2011-2016年)

Local Public Financial Budgetary Expenditure by Tax and Expenditure Account(2011-2016)

单位:万元 (10000 yuan)

指标 Item	2011	2012	2013	2014	2015	2016
财政总收入合计 Total	**14889206**	**16278879**	**17349750**	**19201076**	**22387456**	**25584128**
一、一般公共预算收入 General Public Budget Revenue	7851524	8599875	9452020	10273169	12338820	14023826
(一)税收收入 Tax Revenue	7582715	8302478	9106690	9952111	11259532	12892210
1. 国内增值税 Domestic Value-added Tax	1018017	1094696	1122297	1224336	1301043	2097640
2. 改征增值税 Newly Changed Value-added Tax			593744	837724	1000427	1705813
3. 营业税 Business Tax	2409436	2970123	2670660	2650471	3094627	1988053
4. 企业所得税 Corporate Income Tax	1308761	11448553	1518112	1723639	1928567	2215439
5. 个人所得税 Individual Income Tax	510554	498726	573227	681449	920917	1155176
6. 城市维护建设税 City Construction and Maintenance Tax	549604	604523	658593	693932	792815	890160
7. 房产税 Real Estate Tax	245337	317711	323897	378171	398528	443407
8. 城镇土地使用税 Urban Land Use Tax					155914	147437
9. 土地增值税 Land Appreciation Tax					551468	851760
10. 耕地占用税 Tax on the Use of Arable Land	103448	102820	91622	72117	64426	40610
11. 契税 Contract Tax	722185	465946	674188	805656	761861	1056441
12. 其他税收 Others Tax	715373	799380	880350	884616	288939	300274
(二)非税收入 Non-tax Revenue	268809	297397	345330	321058	1079288	1131616
1. 专项收入 Special Revenue	231881	245863	267287	278423	1073893	1102959

指标 Item	2011	2012	2013	2014	2015	2016
2. 行政事业性收费收入 Income from Administrative Fees	16844	19137	19738	13988	12213	10968
3. 罚没收入 Penalty and Confiscatory Income	115948	128549	148738	148190	149897	160147
4. 国有企业计划亏损补贴 Subsides to Loss－making of state－owned Enterprises	－113682	－105032	－105699	－147887	－197823	－250873
5. 国有资源(资产)有偿使用收入 Compensation for the Use of Seate－owned Assets Income	17666	8870	14314	27927	38904	58175
6. 政府住房基金收入 Government Housing Fund Income	－	－	－	－	－	47.46
7. 其他收入 Others Revenue	152	10	952	417	2204	47146
二、一般公共预算支出 General Public Budget Expenditure	7475004	7862800	8557370	9611771	12054777	14043065
1. 一般公共服务 Expenditure for General Public Services	857578	893776	915881	892027	1011605	1125425
2. 教育 Expenditure for Education	1320537	1469266	1624445	1826924	2234425	2530114
3. 科学技术 Expenditure for Science and Technology	350657	401878	462600	524082	701490	749190
4. 文化体育与传媒 Expenditure for Culture, Sports and Media	185042	207869	223604	242375	449192	283936
5. 社会保障和就业 Expenditure for Social Safety Net and Employment Effort	775422	871431	946033	1082564	1309862	1492895
6. 医疗卫生与计划生育 Expenditure for Medical and Health Care and Birth Control	513455	559225	621518	716754	766328	970504
7. 节能环保 Expenditure for Energy Conservation Environmental Protection	141227	161518	197392	300159	445749	408576
8. 城乡社区 Expenditure for Urban and Rural Community	1231576	1042885	1064358	1143602	1586419	2338331
9. 农林水 Expenditure for Agriculture, Forestry and Water Conservancy	392344	448764	506246	562286	880440	914373
10. 交通运输 Expenditure for Trarssportation	212663	253757	305919	306032	389625	518178
11. 住房保障 Expenditure on Housing Support	60192	65066	77290	93521	122825	219590

10－05　全市金融机构存、贷款余额（1978－2016年）

Balance of Deposits and Loans of Financial Institutions（1978－2016）

单位：万元　　　　(10000 yuan)

年份 Year ＼ 项目 Item	各项存款 Deposits	住户存款 Household Deposits	城镇住户存款 Urban Household Deposits	各项贷款 Loans
1978	86824	20714	17056	136759
1979	108998	28937	22640	135713
1980	180707	40447	30896	174153
1981	226949	51440	38889	236678
1982	262156	67192	50113	216040
1983	303130	86635	64736	236203
1984	388305	115766	85439	329195
1985	484999	159596	115592	580180
1986	635514	222110	153572	769841
1987	776105	302762	207505	967477
1988	839680	351943	241839	1145989
1989	1017087	501592	346318	1338984
1990	1646165	697515	479031	1803266
1991	2036334	904490	616308	2136903
1992	2652966	1144737	763309	2651983
1993	3469954	1563328	1048413	3415527
1994	5061345	2394370	1642498	4450932
1995	7079650	3423379	2448787	5672105
1996	9619291	4638458	3459439	7434243
1997	12251840	5583306	4229591	9388500
1998	14948225	6701158	5155548	11620537
1999	17886717	7425967	5760527	14937506
2000	20884723	7885579	6151084	16866431
2001	26215100	9418400	7396800	20877000
2002	33731500	11834000	9492300	27523800
2003	46527300	15899600	13079600	38187000
2004	57072000	18351700	15016100	48000400
2005	67487200	21916600	17960100	55453000
2006	78555500	25552400	20789600	66038600
2007	93109600	26348300	21154300	84306800
2008	113333500	34765900	27584600	100690500
2009	142842104	42869189	34027871	131133023
2010	170843548	49909744	39352353	150787269
2011	183965719	55474824	43464332	165737441
2012	201487672	60899841	46965391	180908011
2013	221747107	64085856	47733077	193504605
2014	244505093	67672009	49107745	213168315
2015	298638294	76177515	55659016	233279520
2016	333860429	84932733	62521938	261689982

注：1. 1989年以前数据均为银行机构存贷款，1990年及以后年份数据为调整后金融机构存贷款。2003年起金融机构存贷款为本外币合并数据。
2. 2015年起，各项存款和各项贷款分类调整。

a) Data before 1989 belonged to banking system, data after 1990 adjusted for deposits and loans of financial institutions, data of 2003 included both RMB and foreign currency.

b) Since 2015, the classification in deposits and Loans has been adjusted.

10－06　市区金融机构存、贷款余额(1978－2016 年)

Balance of Deposits and Loans of Financial Institutions of Urban District(1978－2016)

单位:万元　　　　(10000 yuan)

年份 Year \ 项目 Item	各项存款 Deposits	住户存款 Household Deposits	城镇住户存款 Urban Household Deposits	各项贷款 Loans
1978	58372	13774	13246	101144
1979	73720	18055	17241	98792
1980	134275	24702	23282	121231
1981	172721	31358	29345	170539
1982	198350	39756	37047	142091
1983	226160	50439	46833	155297
1984	293145	66108	61934	194977
1985	359825	89114	82868	418214
1986	458142	115818	106703	557763
1987	565429	156704	142642	714313
1988	610601	180341	163466	846998
1989	737388	256238	229518	1000731
1990	1062574	354316	297390	1271779
1991	1309462	451756	397322	1469671
1992	1695011	572660	479248	1774158
1993	2263969	762234	662234	2298124
1994	3383877	1242379	1085363	3033010
1995	4851774	1853512	1639875	3907199
1996	6828786	2734904	2371657	5350499
1997	8831147	3287475	2873638	6772221
1998	10785066	3905602	3440607	8615412
1999	13051806	4336058	3835542	11462505
2000	15436286	4620235	4101716	13105849
2001	23765400	7976400	6460200	19237800
2002	30638400	10139800	8370100	25476700
2003	42522000	13834200	11693000	30297500
2004	52542100	16014700	13479900	44517600
2005	62249500	19231800	16208400	51455900
2006	72269600	22391800	18737800	61190700
2007	86197300	23124600	19132300	78456200
2008	104930100	30665200	24996500	93838100
2009	131800234	37837816	30801878	121473548
2010	156776515	43676938	35370599	138671334
2011	168052916	48263525	38996516	151756838
2012	183719227	52347969	41789531	156426086
2013	201596137	54488059	42142666	175670366
2014	222558892	57202595	43243610	191888081
2015	284321331	68516344	51360093	222078475
2016	317723682	76306727	57718389	249684325

10－07 全市金融机构本外币

Balance of Deposits and

单位:万元

指 标	Item	全 市 Total 绝对值 Absolute Value	全 市 Total 为上年(%) As Compared with the Preceding Year(%)	市 区 Urban District 小计 Subtotal
一、各项存款	**Deposits**	**333860429**	**111.79**	**317723682**
(一)境内存款	Domestic Deposits	332544482	111.66	316425746
1.住户存款	Household Deposits	84932733	111.49	76306727
(1)活期存款	Current Deposits	37034570	120.79	33438529
(2)定期及其他存款	Term and Other Deposits	47898163	105.23	42868198
2.非金融企业存款	Non－financial Enterprise Deposits	144762855	110.33	140072010
(1)活期存款	Current Deposits	50053129	120.71	47465055
(2)定期及其他存款	Term and Other Deposits	94709726	105.54	92606955
3.广义政府存款	General Government Deposits	57904505	123.40	55165862
(1)财政性存款	Treasury Deposits	5171743	85.64	5051350
(2)机关团体存款	Organization Deposits	52732762	128.97	50114513
4.非银行业金融机构存款	Non－banking Financial Institutions Deposits	44944388	103.29	44881146
(二)境外存款	Overseas Deposits	1315947	161.73	1297936
二、各项贷款	**Loans**	**261689982**	**112.18**	**249684325**
(一)境内贷款	Domestic Loans	259440758	112.25	247435277
1.住户贷款	Household Loans	78007685	133.13	72289068
(1)短期贷款	Short－term Loans	19993614	106.63	17985236
(2)中长期贷款	Medium and Long term Loans	58014071	145.60	54303831
2.非金融企业及机关团体贷款	Non－financial Enterprise and Organization Loans	181249670	105.12	174962807
(1)短期贷款	Short－term Loans	73976328	100.84	70755162
(2)中长期贷款	Medium and Long term Loans	82192307	104.24	79285213
(3)票据融资	Note Financing	16789851	128.04	16638382
(4)融资租赁	Finance lease	7833919	118.06	7833919
(5)各项垫款	Advance Money	457266	99.48	450132
3.非银行业金融机构贷款	Non－banking Financial Institutions Loans	183403	147.49	183403
(二)境外贷款	Overseas Loans	2249224	105.00	2249047

存、贷款余额(2016 年末)

of Financial Institutions(End of 2016)

(10000 yuan)

萧山区 Xiaoshan	余杭区 Yuhang	富阳区 Fuyang	桐庐县 Tonglu	淳安县 Chun'an	建德市 Jiande	临安市 Lin'an
35345696	**23110968**	**9335808**	**4076868**	**2863553**	**3512762**	**5683565**
35276763	23092559	9332266	4063959	2862680	3511139	5680957
14507660	9953559	4119760	2239347	1506490	2208966	2671203
5159856	3486606	1732573	869816	646654	818079	1261492
9347804	6466953	2387187	1369531	859837	1390887	1409711
14561297	7719586	3940425	1213195	702150	751129	2024371
5576394	3491664	1495313	642292	443753	417047	1084983
8984903	4227922	2445112	570903	258397	334083	939388
5761806	5380837	1194537	602687	650041	525959	959955
458838	985623	81285	17392	32170	42888	27943
5302968	4395214	1113252	585295	617871	483071	932012
446000	38577	77543	8731	3999	25084	25427
68933	18409	3542	12909	873	1623	2607
30131901	**15490552**	**10656871**	**3322338**	**1866763**	**2447146**	**4369410**
30128246	15489020	10656871	3322338	1866763	2447131	4369248
7481841	5689438	3295446	1580210	1115959	1054868	1967581
2349333	1527805	1163771	414661	424971	352394	816352
5132508	4161633	2131675	1165549	690988	702473	1151229
22646405	9799582	7361426	1742129	750804	1392264	2401667
14968239	4494878	4927614	1025317	303659	722458	1169731
6596748	4385447	2078956	692932	418715	631762	1163685
1000222	896046	316418	22718	28429	34183	66139
81197	23211	38437	1162		3860	2112
3655	1531				15	161

10－08 全市金融机构人民币

Balance of RMB Deposits, RMB Loans

单位:万元

指 标	Item	全市 Total 绝对值 Absolute Value	全市 Total 为上年(%) As Compared with the Preceding Year(%)	市区 Urban District 小计 Subtotal
一、各项存款	**Deposits**	**325146405**	**112.11**	**309316484**
(一)境内存款	Domestic Deposits	324409739	112.07	308596379
1. 住户存款	Household Deposits	83131325	110.74	74566987
(1)活期存款	Current Deposits	35963567	119.75	32396708
(2)定期及其他存款	Term and Other Deposits	47167758	104.73	42170279
2. 非金融企业存款	Non－financial Enterprise Deposits	138536592	111.39	134087622
(1)活期存款	Current Deposits	47157145	120.01	44787433
(2)定期及其他存款	Term and Other Deposits	91379447	107.41	89300190
3. 广义政府存款	General Government Deposits	57889065	123.83	55152168
(1)财政性存款	Treasury Deposits	5171743	85.64	5051350
(2)机关团体存款	Organization Deposits	52717322	129.49	50100818
4. 非银行业金融机构存款	Non－banking Financial Institutions Deposits	44852757	103.66	44789602
(二)境外存款	Overseas Deposits	736666	129.06	720105
二、各项贷款	**Loans**	**254648309**	**113.71**	**242670360**
(一)境内贷款	Domestic Loans	254312515	113.67	242334743
1. 住户贷款	Household Loans	77996857	133.14	72278413
(1)短期贷款	Short－term Loans	19983079	106.63	17974876
(2)中长期贷款	Medium and Long term Loans	58013777	145.60	54303537
2. 非金融企业及机关团体贷款	Non－financial Enterprise and Organization Loans	176132256	106.73	169872927
(1)短期贷款	Short－term Loans	70825112	102.00	67631481
(2)中长期贷款	Medium and Long term Loans	80232257	106.42	77325163
(3)票据融资	Note Financing	16789851	128.04	16638382
(4)融资租赁	Finance lease	7833919	118.06	7833919
(5)各项垫款	Advance Money	451118	102.27	443984
3. 非银行业金融机构贷款	Non－banking Financial Institutions Loans	183403	147.49	183403
(二)境外贷款	Overseas Loans	335793	150.85	335617

存、贷款余额(2016 年末)
of Financial Institutions(End of 2016)

(10000 yuan)

萧山区 Xiaoshan	余杭区 Yuhang	富阳区 Fuyang	桐庐县 Tonglu	淳安县 Chun′an	建德市 Jiande	临安市 Lin′an
34132756	**22720167**	**9125825**	**3979881**	**2848578**	**3438079**	**5563384**
34088102	22702217	9122472	3967901	2847718	3436691	5561051
14398952	9904414	4096444	2205960	1501391	2197981	2659006
5097377	3452404	1717533	858167	643067	812199	1253426
9301575	6452010	2378911	1347793	858324	1385782	1405581
13481843	7378843	3756766	1150523	692287	689461	1916699
5143317	3305298	1435362	587563	435576	356630	989944
8338526	4073545	2321404	562960	256712	332831	926755
5761697	5380358	1191720	602687	650041	524251	959919
458838	985623	81285	17392	32170	42888	27943
5302859	4394735	1110435	585295	617871	481363	931975
445610	38601	77543	8730	3999	24998	25427
44654	17951	3353	11980	861	1388	2333
29663453	**15381601**	**10638218**	**3320846**	**1865963**	**2428792**	**4362346**
29659797	15380069	10638218	3320846	1865963	2428778	4362185
7481440	5689274	3295266	1580162	1115945	1054826	1967510
2348933	1527641	1163643	414613	424957	352352	816281
5132508	4161633	2131623	1165549	690988	702473	1151229
22178357	9690795	7342952	1740684	750018	1373952	2394674
14508410	4386688	4909534	1023872	302874	704147	1162738
6592834	4384851	2078956	692932	418715	631762	1163685
1000222	896046	316418	22718	28429	34183	66139
76891	23211	38044	1162		3860	2112
3655	1531				15	161

10－09　住户(本外币)存款余额(2016 年末)

Balance of Savings Deposits of Rural and Urban Residents(End of 2016)

单位:万元　　　　(10000 yuan)

地区 Region	总计 Total		城镇住户 Urban Residents		农村住户 Rural Residents	
	2016 年末 At the End of Year 2016	为上年(%) As Compared with the Preceding Year(%)	2016 年末 At the End of Year 2016	为上年(%) As Compared with the Preceding Year(%)	2016 年末 At the End of Year 2016	为上年(%) As Compared with the Preceding Year(%)
全　市　Total	**84932733**	**111.49**	**62521938**	**112.33**	**22410796**	**109.22**
市　区　Urban District	76306727	111.37	57718389	112.38	18588338	108.35
#萧山区　Xiaoshan	14507660	109.83	8058675	111.11	6448985	108.26
余杭区　Yuhang	9953559	111.18	5258018	112.74	4695541	109.48
富阳区　Fuyang	4119760	108.19	2287331	109.98	1832429	106.04
桐庐县　Tonglu	2239347	112.56	1206082	111.24	1033264	114.14
淳安县　Chun'an	1506490	111.42	811657	111.40	694833	111.44
建德市　Jiande	2208966	112.29	1344808	111.63	864159	113.32
临安市　Lin'an	2671203	113.55	1441001	112.45	1230202	114.87

10－10　金融机构人民币信贷收支表(资金来源,2011－2016年)

Credit Funds Balance Sheet of Financial Institution (RMB,Sources of Funds,2011－2016)

单位:亿元　　(100 million yuan)

项　目	Item	2011	2012	2013	2014	2015	2016
资金来源合计	**All Sources**	**18618.72**	**19629.31**	**22028.95**	**25403.81**	**30190.21**	**36881.85**
一、各项存款	Deposits	18322.33	19857.46	22386.39	25721.84	29003.07	32514.64
(一)境内存款	Domestic Deposits	18286.35	19795.13	22322.27	25642.26	28945.99	32440.97
1.住户存款	Household Deposits	5670.76	6198.63	6831.58	7223.78	7507.09	8313.13
2.非金融企业存款	Non－financial Enterprise Deposits	9531.38	9842.96	10733.60	11508.67	12437.24	13853.66
3.广义政府存款	General Government Deposits	2266.98	2784.09	3476.44	4218.53	4674.92	5788.91
4.非银行业金融机构存款	Non－banking Financial Institutions Deposits	817.24	969.45	1280.64	2691.28	4326.75	4485.28
(二)境外存款	Overseas Deposits	35.98	62.33	64.12	79.58	57.08	73.67
二、金融债券	Bonds	57.80	137.57	130.65	168.43	239.84	342.64
三、卖出回购资产	Sell Repurchase Assets	2.80	7.18	27.11			
四、借款及非银行业金融机构拆入	Borrowing and Non Banking Financial Institutions Borrowing	115.08	178.71	216.25	258.90	0.30	15.35
五、联行往来(净)	Interbank Transactions (net)						
六、应付及暂收款	Accounts Payable and Temporary Collection of Money	503.35	549.14	699.24	907.61	935.16	1008.12
七、各项准备	All Reserves	360.19	456.58	399.37	480.22	600.05	733.19
八、所有者权益	Creditor' s Equity	684.84	660.01	828.71	929.92	967.10	1104.44
其中:实收资本	Paid－in Capital	135.20	152.95	180.29	201.14	283.48	315.27
九、其他	Others	－1427.67	－2217.33	－2658.76	－3063.11	－1555.31	1163.46

10-11 金融机构人民币信贷收支表(资金运用,2011-2016年)

Credit Funds Balance Sheet of Financial Institution (RMB, Use of Funds, 2011-2016)

单位:亿元 (100 million yuan)

项 目	Item	2011	2012	2013	2014	2015	2016
资金运用合计		**18618.72**	**19629.31**	**22028.95**	**25403.81**	**30190.21**	**36881.85**
一、各项存款	**Deposits**	**15787.41**	**17106.54**	**18426.94**	**20388.37**	**22395.29**	**25464.83**
(一)境内贷款	**Domestic Loans**	**15779.75**	**17099.47**	**18420.12**	**20382.37**	**22373.03**	**25431.25**
1. 住户贷款	**Household Loans**	**3541.85**	**3778.53**	**4372.82**	**4918.01**	**5858.42**	**7799.69**
(1)短期贷款	Short-term Loans	1156.29	1290.02	1481.46	1770.03	1874.03	1998.31
(2)中长期贷款	Medium and Long term Loans	2385.56	2488.51	2891.37	3147.99	3984.39	5801.38
2. 非金融企业及机关团体贷款	**Non-financial Enterprise and Organization Loans**	**12215.57**	**13266.48**	**14019.88**	**15432.16**	**16502.18**	**17613.23**
(1)短期贷款	Short-term Loans	6363.93	6884.25	7074.96	6909.51	6943.84	7082.51
(2)中长期贷款	Medium and Long term Loans	5275.70	5477.42	5958.28	7145.36	7539.38	8023.23
(3)票据融资	Note Financing	232.58	421.60	441.08	731.55	1311.28	1678.99
(4)融资租赁	Finance lease	333.59	416.64	484.62	589.24	663.57	783.39
(5)各项垫款	Advance Money	9.78	66.57	60.95	56.49	44.11	45.11
3. 非银行业金融机构贷款	**Non-banking Financial Institutions Deposits**	**22.32**	**54.46**	**27.41**	**32.20**	**12.44**	**18.34**
(二)境外贷款	**Overseas Loans**	**7.66**	**7.06**	**6.82**	**6.00**	**22.26**	**33.58**
二、债券投资	**Bond Investment**	**652.04**	**802.06**	**1021.41**	**1667.86**	**2005.65**	**2032.81**
三、股权及其他投资	**Equity and other Investment**	**70.00**	**224.96**	**814.64**	**1076.84**	**1738.10**	**2642.37**
四、买入返售资产	**Bug Assets Repurchased**	**3.47**	**79.28**	**589.67**	**336.63**	**62.63**	**48.35**
五、存放非银行业金融机构款项	**Deposit of non Banking Financial Institutions**	**0.31**	**0.34**	**0.11**	**0.27**	**0.97**	**1.11**
六、联行往来(净)	**Interbank Transactions (net)**	**1607.01**	**927.52**	**410.23**	**1315.59**	**3374.29**	**5960.97**
七、金银占款	**Funds Outstanding for Gold and Silver**						
八、外汇买卖	**Foreign Exchange Trading**	**-5.37**	**11.33**	**68.01**	**-33.91**	**-7.34**	
九、应收及预付款	**Collectable Account and Advance Payment**	**308.31**	**262.68**	**475.07**	**420.79**	**391.61**	**488.74**
十、投资性房地产	**Investment Property**	**1.71**	**1.10**	**2.77**	**2.75**	**2.63**	**5.74**
十一、固定资产	**Fitness Assets**	**193.83**	**213.50**	**220.11**	**228.62**	**226.38**	**236.93**

10－12 保险业务情况(2014－2016年)

Development of Insurance Business(2014－2016)

单位:万元 (10000 yuan)

指 标	Item	保险费收入 Premium			赔付金额 Indemnity Expenditure		
		2014	2015	2016	2014	2015	2016
全市总计	**Total**	**3204138**	**3743769**	**5183992**	**1190338**	**1396924**	**1588847**
为上年%	As Compared with the Preceding Year(%)	114.8	116.8	138.5	116.3	117.4	113.7
一、财产保险	Property Insurance	1410891	1569067	1724886	832313	937229	1000353
企业财产险	Enterprise Property Insurance	93834	90317	93299	58793	42398	40793
家庭财产险	Family Property Insurance	4516	10012	9084	817	4641	6606
机动车辆险	Transportation Equipment Insurance	1075684	1153742	1212797	642940	702258	734273
工程险	Project Insurance	9945	19167	20089	3965	7798	6579
责任险	Responsibilihty Insurance	31039	42734	62457	12101	15975	29742
信用险	Export Credit Insurance	111468	130809	148168	73037	101830	95939
保证险	Guarantee Insurance	24767	39963	66594	8160	13759	17314
船舶险	Shipping Insurance	5458	4326	4538	4723	4078	3795
货运险	Cargo Insurance	19005	21933	39567	10457	10172	23571
特殊风险保险	Special Pisks Insurance	6154	5455	7014	528	320	174
农业保险	Agriculture Insurance	13722	17775	18038	5939	9312	12479
其他险	Other	15301	32834	43242	10853	24688	29088
二、人身险	Personal Insurance	1793247	2174702	3459106	358025	459695	588494
寿险	Life Insurance	1470213	1612350	2300127	272796	392062	503930
意外伤害险	Accidental Insurance	86671	125954	178268	16820	23802	32600
健康险	Health Insurance	236363	436398	980711	68409	43831	51964

主要统计指标解释

财政收入　包括:(1)各项税收。主要有增值税、营业税、土地增值税、城市维护建设税、资源税、城市土地使用税、印花税、个人所得税、企业所得税、关税和耕地占用税等。

(2)专项收入包括征收排污费、征收城市水资源费收入,教育费附加收入等。

存款　企业、机关、团体或居民根据可以收回的原则,把货币资金存入银行或其他信用机构保管并取得一定利息的一种信用活动形式。根据存款对象的不同可划分为企业存款、财政存款、机关团体存款、基本建设存款、城镇储蓄存款、农村存款等科目。它是银行信贷资金的主要来源。

贷款　银行或其他信用机构根据必须归还的原则,按一定利率,为企业、个人等提供资金的一种信用活动形式。我国银行贷款分为流动资金贷款、固定资产贷款、城乡个体工商户贷款、城乡个体工商户贷款以及农业贷款等科目。

Explanatory Notes on Main Statistical Indicators

Financial Revenue It includes the following main items: (1) various tax revenues, including value added tax, business tax, land value added tax, tax on city maintenance and construction, resources tax, tax on use of urban land, stamp tax, personal income tax, enterprise income tax and tax on occupancy of cultivated land, etc. (2) Special revenues, including revenue collected from imposing fee on sewage treatment, revenue collected from imposing fee on urban water resources, and extra – charges for education, etc.

Deposit is a form of credit by which enterprises, institutions, organizations or households can put money into banks and other credit institutions for safekeeping and interest earning under the principle of free withdrawal. According to different depositors, deposits are divided into enterprise deposits, treasury deposits, deposits of government agencies and organizations, capital construction deposits, urban savings deposits, rural deposits and other deposits. Deposits are major sources of the credit funds of banks.

Loan is a form of credit by which banks and other credit institutions provide funds at certain interest rate to enterprises and individuals in the light of the principle of unconditional repayment. Loans from Chinese banks include circulating capital loans, fixed assets loans, loans to urban and rural individuals engaged in industrial and commercial business and agricultural loans.

十一、城市建设环境保护

URBAN CONSTRUCTION AND ENVIRONMENTAL PROTECTION

11 城市建设、环境保护
Urban Construction and Environmental Protection

主要统计指标
Major Statistical Indicators

市区建成区面积	Developed Area in Urban District	541.38	平方千米	(sq.km)
市区实有道路面积	Area of Roads in Urban District at Year-end	6932	万平方米	(10, 000 sq.m)
市区用电量	Electricity Consumption of Urban District	583.96	亿千瓦时	(100 million kw/h)
# 工业用电	Industrial Electricity Consumption	337.04	亿千瓦时	(100 million kw/h)
生活用电	Electricity Consumption for Residential Use	93.03	亿千瓦时	(100 million kw/h)
市区供水能力	Water-supply Capacity of Urban District	384	万吨/日	(10, 000 tons/day)
市区供水总量	Annual Volume of Tap Water Supplied in Urban District	65087	万吨	(10, 000 tons)
市区气化率	Percentage of Population with Access to Gas in Urban District	100	%	(%)
市区公园绿地面积	Park Green Area in Urban District	8118	公顷	(hectare)
市区空气质量达标(AQI < 100)天数	The Number of Days of Air Quality Reaching(AQI<100) the Standards	260	天	(day)

11-01 市区公共交通情况(主要年份)
Urban Public Transportation in Urban Districts(Main Years)

指 标	Item	2000	2005	2010	2012	2013	2014	2015	2016
一、轨道交通	**Rail Transit**								
年末运营线路总长度(千米)	Length of Operating Routes (year-end) (km)	-	-	-	47.97	47.97	66.30	81.5	81.5
客运总量 (万人次)	Passenger Traffic (10,000 person-times)	-	-	-	561	9237	14521	22348	26877
二、公共汽车	**Bus**								
年末运营线路条数(条)	Number of Operating Routes (year-end) (unit)	163	368	548	620	645	703	756	758
年末运营线路总长度(千米)	Length of Operating Routes (year-end) (km)	2016	4902	8594	11351	11445	12032	12791	13866
#BRT线路长度(千米)	BRT line length (km)					122	113	128	151
年末运营公共汽车(辆)	Number of Public Transportation Vehicles(year-end) (unit)	1781	3997	7209	7450	8249	8656	8555	8770
#无轨电车 (辆)	Number of Operating Trolleys (unit)	223	189	65	51	101	115	150	150
客运总量 (万人次)	Passenger Traffic (10,000 person-times)	57986	70653	127967	131901	132221	140928	142312	141441
三、出租汽车	**Tax**								
年末实有出租汽车数(辆)	Number of Taxis(year-end) (unit)	6300	8320	9362	10344	10904	11913	11963	12209

11－02 市区城市供电、供水情况(主要年份)

Urban Electricity and Water Supply in Urban Districts(Main Years)

指 标	Item	2000	2005	2010	2012	2013	2014	2015	2016
一、城市供电	**Urban Electricity Supply**								
全年用电总量（亿千瓦时）	Total Electricity Consumption (100 million kwh)	60.19	244.78	392.64	444.95	484.05	552.71	559.54	583.96
#工业（亿千瓦时）	Industrial Electricity Consumption (100 million kwh)	33.52	172.56	258.35	278.93	296.08	355.06	345.23	337.04
生活（亿千瓦时）	Electricity Consumption for Residential Use (100 million kwh)	9.86	27.98	50.74	63.62	71.52	72.56	78.27	93.03
二、城市供水（自来水）	**Urban Water Supply**								
总售水量（万吨）	Total Annual Volume of Tap Water Saled (10,000 tons)	27510	58332	45666	49549	51709	56401	56478	55566
平均日供水（万吨）	Per Capita Daily Consumption of Tap Water (10,000 tons)	92	201	147	159	166	181	183	178
供水能力（万吨/日）	Capacity of Water Supply (10,000 tons/day)	146	253	320	320	350	380	380	384
供水总量（万吨）	Total Annual Volume of Tap Water Supplied (10,000 tons)	33725	73331	53565	58183	60747	66172	66760	65087
#生产用水（万吨）	For Productive Use (10,000 tons)	8100	27327	11479	12478	13005	14792	14902	14161
生活用水（万吨）	For Residential Use (10,000 tons)	19410	35220	30978	22861	23733	26894	26162	25078
用水普及率（%）	Percentage of Population with Access to Tap Water (%)	100	100	100	100	100	100	100	100

11－03 市区市政建设情况(主要年份)

Public Utilities in Urban Districts(Main Years)

指 标	Item	2000	2005	2010	2012	2013	2014	2015	2016
一、市政建设	**Urban Infrastructure**								
建成区面积(平方公里)	Constructed Area (sq. m)	–	314.45	412.59	452.62	462.48	495.22	506.09	541.38
年末实有道路面积(万平方米)	Area of Roads (year－end) (10,000 sq. m)	1183	3175	4754	5284	5426	6145	6540	6932
年末实有道路长度(公里)	Length of Roads(year－end) (km)	1050	1782	2194	2458	2479	2748	2991	3075
年末实有桥梁数(座)	Number of Bridges(year－end) (unit)	291	991	1021	1129	1165	1235	1337	1353
排水管道长度(公里)	Length of Drainage Pipelines (km)	1431	2945	3904	4280	4455	5012	5370	5944
城市污水排放量(万立方米)	Volume of Sewage Drained (10,000 cu. m)	27010	55141	43746	47330	48432	53111	56974	57916
城市污水处理总量(万立方米)	the Total Volume of Urban Sewage Treatment (10,000 cu. m)	–	43352	41733	45197	46251	50318	54137	55061
二、城市液化气	**Urban Liquefied Petroleum Gas**								
供气总量 (万吨)	Total Volume of Liquefied Petroleum Gas Supply (10,000 tons)	7.47	15.28	11.44	11.17	11.92	9.87	12.38	13.14
#家庭用气(万吨)	Supply for Residential Use (10,000 tons)	5.08	9.51	5.77	5.90	4.70	5.08	6.08	5.90
三、人工煤气及天然气	**Coal Gas and Natural Gas**								
家庭用气总量(万立方米)	Total Volume of Coal Gas Consumed (10,000 cu. m)	4367	3225	10053	13397	13869	18019	20659	21878
家庭用气户数(万户)	Residential Households with Access to Gas (10,000 households)	14.46	25.48	62.85	81.72	91.08	111.30	128.94	139.03
四、全社会气化率 %	**Percentage of Population with Access to Gas** (%)	**95.7**	**99.17**	**100**	**100**	**100**	**100**	**100**	**100**

11-04 市区园林绿化情况(主要年份)

Urban Forestation(Main Years)

指 标	Item	2000	2005	2010	2012	2013	2014	2015	2016
建城区绿化覆盖面积(公顷)	The Green Areas Coveraged in Constructed Areas (hectare)	6083	11734	16483	18135	18606	20031	20464	22035
园林绿地面积(公顷)	Total Area of Parks, Gardens and Green Areas (hectare)	6035	10774	15118	16647	17071	18386	18949	20118
#公园绿地(公顷)	Public Green Area (hectare)	976	2564	5017	5635	5820	6304	7640	8118
建城区绿化覆盖率(%)	Rate of the Green Areas Coveraged in Constructed Areas (%)	34.33	37.31	39.95	40.07	40.23	40.57	40.43	40.70
公园景点个数(个)	Number of Parks and Scenic Resorts (unit)	70	184	176	185	190	207	217	222
公园景点面积(公顷)	Area of Parks and Scenic Resorts (hectare)	489	997	1906	2065	2094	2298	2488	2754

11－05 环境保护情况(2016 年)

Environmental Protection Situation (2016)

指标名称		Item		全市 Whole City	市区 Urban District
工业废水排放量	(万吨)	Industrial Wastewater Emissions	(10,000 tons)	28382	25237
工业废水中 COD 排放量	(吨)	COD Emissions in Industrial Wastewater	(tons)	17571	15649
工业废水中氨氮排放量	(吨)	Ammonia emissions in Industrial wastewater	(tons)	765	667
工业二氧化硫产生量	(吨)	Industrial Sulfur Dioxide Produced	(tons)	114894	99282
工业二氧化硫排放量	(吨)	Industrial Emissions of Sulfur Dioxide	(tons)	39499	28697
工业氮氧化物排放量	(吨)	Industrial Nitrogen Oxide Emissions	(tons)	42311	27509
工业烟(粉)产生量	(吨)	Industrial Smoke (Powder) Production	(tons)	3987001	1740396
工业烟(粉)尘排放量	(吨)	Industrial Smoke, Powder and Dust Emissions	(tons)	20414	11818
一般工业固体废物综合利用率	(%)	Comprehensive Utilization Rate of General Industrial Solid Waste	(%)	85.1	86.1
城市污水集中处理率	(%)	Centralized Treatment Rate of Urban Sewage	(%)	94.5	95.1
城市生活垃圾无害化处理率	(%)	Harmless Treatment Rate of City's Living Garbage	(%)	100	100
空气质量优良天数	(天)	Air Quality Days	(days)	-	260
集中式饮用水源地水质达标率	(%)	Compliance Rate of Centralized Sources of Drinking Water	(%)	100	-

注:1. 以上数据为环统数据,未经国家环保部最终核定;

2. 2016 年起环境统计方法有调整。

a) The above data is environmental statistics and is not approved by the ministry of environmental Protection.

b) The environmental statistical method has been adjusted since 2016.

主要统计指标解释

自来水生产能力　指年底城建部门管理的自来水厂实际生产能力。

生活用水量　指居民日常生活与公共福利设施的用水量。包括居民、饮食店、旅馆、医院、理发店、浴池、洗衣店、游泳池、商店、学校、机关、部队等单位的用水量。

供气总量　指全年售给各类用户的全部煤气量。包括工业用量、家庭用量和其他用量。

年末实有道路长度　指除土路外，路面经过铺装宽度在3.5米以上的道路，包括高级、次高级道路和普通道路。

城市桥梁　指城市范围内，修建在河道上的桥梁和道路与道路立交、道路跨越铁路的立交桥，以及人行天桥。包括永久性桥和半永久性桥，不包括临时性桥、铁路桥、涵洞。

营运线路长度　指设置的固定营运线路的长度，包括郊区营运线路长度。不包括临时行驶的线路长度。

用水普及率　指城市用水的非农业人口数（不包括临时人口和流动人口）与城市非农业人口总数之比。计算公式为：

$$用水普及率=\frac{城市用水非农业人口数}{城市非农业人口数}\times 100\%$$

城市园林绿地面积　指城市公共绿地、专用绿地、生产绿地、防护绿地、郊区风景名胜区的全部面积。

公园绿地面积　指供游览休息的各种公园、动物园、植物园、陵园以及花园、游园和供游览休息用的林荫道绿地、广场绿地。不包括一般栽植的行道树及林荫道的面积。

Explanatory Notes on Main Statistical Indicators

Production Capacity of Tap Water refers to the actual comprehensive production capacity of the waterworks administered by the urban construction department.

Consumption of water for Residential Use refers to the water consumption of households for daily life and the water consumption of public welfare facilities, including the consumption of restaurants, hotels, hospitals, barber shops, public bathhouses, laundries, swimming pools, shops, schools, institutions, army units and other units.

Volume of Gas Supply refers to the total volume of gas Sold to users in a year, including the volume for industrial use, residential use and other uses.

Length of Roads at the Year – end refers to the length of roads with a paved surface, and with a width of more than 3 – 5 meters, including high quality, medium quality and ordinary roads.

Urban Bridges refers to bridges over river courses, great separated junctions and overpasses in urban areas. Permanent bridges and semi – permanent bridges are included. Temporary bridges, railway bridges and culverts are excluded.

Length in Operation refers to the length of the roads in fixed operation, including the suburb one, but excluding the tomporary ones.

Percentage of Urban Population with Access to Tap Water refers to the ratio of the urban non – agricultural population (excluding temporary and mobile population) with access to tap water to the tolal urban non – agricultural population. The formula is:

$$\text{Percentage of Poputalion with Access to Tap Water} = \frac{\text{Urban Non – agricultural Population with Access to Tap Water}}{\text{Urban Non – agricultural Population}} \times 100\%$$

Area of Urban Gardens and Green Areas refers to the total area of urban public green land, special green land, production green land, protection green land and suburban scenic spots.

Park Green Area refers to green area of various parks, zoos, botanical gardens, cemeteries, amusement parks, tree – flanked boulevards Greenland squares for tourism and relaxing. Areas with trees planted along – side the streets and boulevards are excluded.

十二、科技、教育文化、卫生、体育

SCIENCE AND TECHNOLOGY,EDUCATION,
CULTURE,PUBLIC HEALTH AND SPORTS

12 科技、教育、文化、卫生、体育
Science and Technology, Education, Culture, Public Health and Sports

主要统计指标
Major Statistical Indicators

高等学校数	Number of Regular Institution of Higher Education	39	个	(unit)
高等学校在校学生数	Number of Students in Regular Institution of Higher Education	48.10	万人	(10, 000 person)
高中在校学生数	Number of Students in Senior High Schools	11.04	万人	(10, 000 person)
初中在校学生数	Number of Students in Junior High Schools	21.58	万人	(10, 000 person)
小学在校学生数	Number of Students in Primary Schools	54.30	万人	(10, 000 person)
医疗病床数	Number of Beds in Health Institutions	6.95	万张	(10, 000 bed)
# 医院	Number of Beds in Hospitals	6.40	万张	(10, 000 bed)
卫生技术人员数	Number of Medical Technical Personnel	10.12	万人	(10, 000 person)
# 执业(助理)医师	Number of Registered (Assistant) Doctors	3.82	万人	(10, 000 person)
公共图书馆	Public Library	15	个	(unit)

12－01 全市科技活动情况(2012－2016年)

The Situation of the City's Scientific and Technological Activities(2012－2016)

指 标 Item	2012	2013	2014	2015	2016
一、全社会科技活动 **The Scientific and Technological Activities in whole Society**					
研究与试验发展活动折合全时人员 (人年) Full－time Equivalent of R&D Personnel	78275	81617	90193	94323	94696
研究与试验发展经费支出 (亿元) R&D Financial Expenditure (0.1 billion yuan)	228.00	248.73	274.00	302.19	346.36
研究与试验发展经费支出与GDP之比 (%) The Proportion of R&D Financial Expenditure in GDP (%)	2.92	2.96	2.98	3.01	3.06
二、规模以上工业科技活动 **The Scientific and Technological Activities of Industrial Enterprises Above designated Size**					
有研究与试验发展活动企业数 (个) The Number of Scientific and Technological Activities Enterprises (Unit)	1229	1453	1518	1671	1753
研究与试验发展项目数 (个) Projeet on R&D (Unit)	5854	7342	7383	8265	8943
企业有科技机构 (个) Scientific and Technological Institutions of Enterprises (Unit)	1197	1273	1346	1354	1410
科技机构仪器和设备原价 (亿元) Original Value of Machines of Scientlfic and Technological (0.1 billion yuan)	92.75	87.06	99.61	100.73	126.23
研究与试验发展人员 (万人) R&D Personnel (10,000)	6.12	6.88	7.41	8.01	7.92
每万名从业人员中研究与试验发展活动人员数 (人) The Number of R&D Activities Personnel per 10,000 Employees (Person)	501	578	644	725	743
研究与试验发展经费支出 (亿元) R&D Financial Expenditure (0.1 billion yuan)	143.47	160.21	177.39	198.06	215.03
研究与试验发展经费支出占主营业务收入的比例 (%) The Proportion of R&D Financial Expenditure in Main Business Income (%)	1.15	1.33	1.42	1.66	1.79

12－02　全社会 R&D 经费投入情况(2011－2016 年)
Basic Statistics on R&D Activities Funds(2011－2016)

单位:亿元　　(100 million yuan)

年　份 Year	总计 Total	按执行部门分 By Sector			
		研究机构 Research and Development Institutions	高等院校 Colleges and Universties	工业企业 Enterprises	其他部门 Others
2011	202.35	10.23	34.62	119.87	37.64
2012	228.00	14.96	38.12	143.47	31.44
2013	248.73	15.91	39.78	160.21	32.83
2014	274.00	17.34	42.06	177.39	37.21
2015	302.19	20.88	46.04	198.06	37.21
2016	346.36	16.55	40.79	215.03	73.99

12－03　规模以上工业企业 R&D 经费投入情况(2011－2016 年)
Basic Statistics on R&D Activities of Industrial Enterprises above Designated Size(2011－2016)

单位:亿元　　(100 million yuan)

年　份 Year	总计 Total	按经费来源分 By Source			
		政府资金 Government Appropriation Funds	企业资金 Self－raised Funds by Enterprise	境外资金 Overseas Capital	其他资金 Other
2011	119.87	3.26	115.57	0.33	0.70
2012	143.47	4.63	137.73	0.41	0.70
2013	160.21	4.35	154.42	0.26	1.19
2014	177.39	5.24	171.18	0.10	0.89
2015	198.06	5.35	191.03	0.24	1.43
2016	215.03	3.88	209.98	0.08	1.09

12－04 分地区、行业非私营及规上私营单位年末人才资源(2016 年)

Trained Personnel Resource Including Private Units above Designated Size by Region(2016)

单位:人 (person)

项 目	Item	合计 Total	非私营单位 Non－Private	#专业技术人员 Technical Personnel	非私营单位 Non－Private	#技术工人 Technical Workers	非私营单位 Non－Private
全市	**Whole City**	**2926290**	**1929775**	**948535**	**693564**	**1404115**	**821352**
市区	Urban District	2645123	1780119	858501	636387	1276943	770961
#上城区	Shangcheng	163427	125838	63288	53686	62842	41983
下城区	Xiacheng	178067	158092	79325	70685	51630	47050
江干区	Jianggan	249020	120272	68176	40891	132099	45345
拱墅区	Gongshu	212728	104767	49413	29807	129194	50996
西湖区	Xihu	403337	334022	123550	100002	204517	171742
高新(滨江)区	Hi－Tech(Binjiang)	227073	173941	129750	110376	56039	32762
萧山区	Xiaoshan	581978	364253	151176	99470	338338	205854
大江东产业集聚区	Dajiangdong Industry Cluster District	79771	53262	24657	18673	43914	28040
余杭区	Yuhang	309317	175115	99356	61527	142730	69164
富阳区	Fuyang	181804	100469	54042	33504	94191	48089
经济技术开发区	Economic and Technological Development Zone	125783	111598	35770	32145	60981	53799
西湖风景名胜区	The West Lake Scenic Zone	12589	11752	4655	4294	4382	4177
桐庐县	Tonglu	79790	33946	23413	12350	40909	12227
淳安县	Chun'an	40130	23901	15516	11007	13340	4294
建德市	Jiande	56911	32688	18895	11820	24758	12412
临安市	Lin'an	104336	59121	32210	22000	48165	21458

单位:人 12－04 续表 continued (person)

项 目	Item	合计 Total	非私营单位 Non－Private	#专业技术人员 Technical Personnel	非私营单位 Non－Private	#技术工人 Technical Workers	非私营单位 Non－Private
按国民经济行业分组	**Total**						
农、林、牧、渔业	Farming, Forestry, Animal Husbandry and Fishery	659	655	98	97	335	334
采矿业	Mining	1444	604	274	71	857	416
制造业	Manufacturing	712239	446082	172741	118948	411906	252129
电力、热力、燃气及水生产和供应业	Production & Supply of Electricity, Heat, Gas & Water	16894	15819	3375	3113	10119	9547
建筑业	Construction	1100822	546100	227204	101148	795867	407333
批发和零售业	Wholesale & Retail Trades	114171	72542	32085	20685	26387	20390
交通运输、仓储和邮政业	Transportation, Storage and Posts	98510	79288	13234	8284	68940	60342
住宿和餐饮业	Hotels and Catering Services	29628	19388	5596	3170	10282	7002
信息传输、软件和信息技术服务业	Information Transmission, Software and Information Technology	126373	100613	91553	75355	6181	4497
金融业	Financial Intermediation	68646	68444	43187	43097	3887	3873
房地产业	Real Estate	70793	58997	18956	14923	20144	18585
租赁和商务服务业	Leasing and Business Services	70598	46211	24640	12794	13823	8698
科学研究、技术服务业	Scientific Research, Technical Services	94066	73297	71131	55913	6007	4765
水利、环境和公共设施管理业	Management of Water Conservancy, Environment and Public Facilities	18904	12756	6091	3663	6963	4767
居民服务、修理和其他服务业	Service to Honseholds, Repair and Other Services	10473	5655	1868	1013	5221	2738
教育	Education	150406	147122	122161	120413	7658	6708
卫生和社会工作	Health Care and Social Work	103774	99464	90114	86915	4734	4652
文化、体育和娱乐业	Culture, Sports and Entertainment	19468	18316	13820	13555	1164	936
公共管理、社会保障和社会组织	Public Management, Social Security and Social Organizations	118422	118422	10407	10407	3640	3640

12-05 专利申请与授权情况(2007-2016年)

Patent Application and Authorization(2007-2016)

单位:件 (item)

年份 Year	专利申请合计 Patent Applications	发明 Inventions	实用新型 Utility Models	外观设计 Designs	专利授权合计 Patent Applications Granted	发明 Inventions	实用新型 Utility Models	外观设计 Designs
2007	13295	4592	4332	4371	7563	1320	3638	2605
2008	18549	5130	5796	7623	9831	1923	4637	3271
2009	26077	6703	9806	9568	15507	2535	5806	7166
2010	29732	7766	13108	8858	26483	3238	11888	11357
2011	40890	9717	18783	12390	29249	4511	14556	10182
2012	53785	11960	25313	16512	40651	5526	20400	14725
2013	58280	14031	25523	18726	41518	4903	23159	13456
2014	48569	14779	21711	12079	33548	5552	18147	9849
2015	60839	17777	29048	14014	46245	8296	24764	13185
2016	73546	24951	32187	16408	41052	8647	21763	10642

12－06　全市分地区专利申请与授权情况（2016 年）

Patent Application and Authorization by Region（2016）

单位：件　　　　　　　　　　　　　　　　　　　　　　　　　　　　　　（item）

地　区	Region	专利申请合计 Patent Applications	发明 Inventions	实用新型 Utility Models	外观设计 Designs	专利授权合计 Patent Applications Granted	发明 Inventions	实用新型 Utility Models	外观设计 Designs
全市	**Whole City**	**73546**	**24951**	**32187**	**16408**	**41052**	**8647**	**21763**	**10642**
市区	Urban District	66797	23836	29674	13287	37156	8326	20136	8694
#上城区	Shangcheng	1871	534	826	511	1288	182	586	520
下城区	Xiacheng	5104	2133	1905	1066	2634	808	1271	555
江干区	Jianggan	10949	4184	4952	1813	6212	1729	3250	1233
拱墅区	Gongshu	3020	645	1505	870	1783	237	1102	444
西湖区	Xihu	10752	5842	3761	1149	5808	2365	2589	854
高新（滨江）区	Hi－Tech（Binjiang）	14247	5902	5374	2971	6700	1466	3271	1963
萧山区	Xiaoshan	5678	1240	3629	809	4085	677	2725	683
余杭区	Yuhang	12027	2537	5796	3694	6687	607	3976	2104
富阳区	Fuyang	3149	819	1926	404	1959	255	1366	338
桐庐县	Tonglu	2595	233	716	1646	1799	49	506	1244
淳安县	Chun'an	538	152	270	116	291	19	226	46
建德市	Jiande	1365	95	475	795	692	56	253	383
临安市	Lin'an	2251	635	1052	564	1114	197	642	275

12－07 全市文化事业单位数(2000－2016 年)

Number of Institutions for Culture(2000－2016)

单位:个　　(unit)

年　份 Year	电影院数 Cinemas	剧场 Theaters	剧团 Opera Troupes	文化馆 Cultural Centers	文化站 Cultural Stations	图书馆 Libraries	博物馆 Museums	展览馆 Exhibition Buildings
2000	16	9	18	13	268	10	9	1
2001	16	15	18	13	226	10	11	1
2002	18	13	18	13	221	10	11	1
2003	20	11	18	13	220	10	11	1
2004	18	16	18	13	165	10	12	1
2005	22	12	19	13	204	12	12	1
2006	22	12	19	13	197	13	12	1
2007	22	12	19	13	195	14	12	1
2008	23	12	19	13	195	14	13	1
2009	22	12	20	13	198	16	35	1
2010	31	12	21	13	199	16	65	1
2011	30	11	21	15	190	15	65	1
2012	40	11	21	15	192	15	65	1
2013	48	11	21	15	189	15	65	1
2014	66	12	21	15	189	15	65	1
2015	90	11	20	15	189	15	67	1
2016	90	11	20	15	189	15	68	1

12－08　全市分地区文化部门机构数(2016 年末)

Number of Institutions for Culture by Region(End of 2016)

单位:个　　　　(unit)

指　标	Item	剧场 Theaters	剧团 Opera Troupes	文化馆 Cultural Centers	文化站 Cultural Stations	图书馆 Libraries	博物馆 Museums	展览馆 Exhibition Buildings
全市	**Total**	**11**	**20**	**15**	**189**	**15**	**68**	**1**
市区	Urban District	11	18	11	118	11	60	1
#萧山区	Xiaoshan	–	1	1	27	1	9	–
余杭区	Yuhang	2	1	1	19	1	5	–
富阳区	Fuyang	–	1	1	24	1	3	–
桐庐县	Tonglu	–	1	1	14	1	2	–
淳安县	Chun'an	–	–	1	23	1	1	–
建德市	Jiande	–	1	1	16	1	4	–
临安市	Lin'an	–	–	1	18	1	1	–

12-09 市区文化事业单位数(1978-2016年)
Cultural Institutions of Urban District (1978-2016)

单位:个 (unit)

年份 Year	电影院数 Cinemas	剧团 Opera Troupes	剧场 Theaters	文化馆 Cultural Centers	文化站 Cultural Stations	图书馆 Libraries	博物馆 Museums
1978	7	13	6	5	-	2	1
1979	8	14	7	5	27	2	1
1980	8	15	7	5	37	2	1
1981	8	17	7	6	40	2	1
1982	9	17	7	6	45	3	1
1983	9	15	3	6	46	3	1
1984	9	15	4	6	49	3	1
1985	8	16	9	6	47	3	2
1986	8	15	8	6	48	3	2
1987	8	15	9	6	38	3	2
1988	7	14	9	6	50	3	2
1989	7	14	9	6	48	2	2
1990	9	14	9	5	48	3	2
1991	10	14	8	5	48	3	2
1992	11	14	8	5	48	3	6
1993	10	14	9	5	42	3	6
1994	11	13	9	5	48	3	6
1995	11	13	9	5	67	3	6
1996	10	13	8	5	55	3	6
1997	10	13	8	5	52	3	6
1998	9	13	8	6	55	3	7
1999	9	13	6	6	52	3	8
2000	8	12	6	6	52	3	9
2001	49	14	11	8	89	5	11
2002	-	14	10	8	90	4	11
2003	19	14	11	13	92	4	11
2004	18	14	14	8	93	5	12
2005	16	15	10	8	94	7	12
2006	16	15	10	8	94	8	12
2007	16	15	10	8	92	9	12
2008	18	15	11	8	92	9	13
2009	15	16	11	8	95	11	34
2010	25	17	11	8	96	11	54
2011	23	17	10	10	94	10	54
2012	31	17	10	10	96	10	54
2013	31	17	11	10	94	10	54
2014	55	18	11	11	118	11	57
2015	78	18	11	11	118	11	59
2016	78	18	11	11	118	11	60

12－10 分地区艺术表演团体演出情况（2016 年）

Basic Statistics on Performance of Art Troupes by Region（2016）

指 标	Item	艺术表演场所演出场次（场）Number of Performances in Artistic Performance Place（scene）	艺术表演场所演出收入（万元）Income of Performances in Artistic Performance Place（10000 yuan）	剧团演出场次（场）Number of Performances of Opera Troupes（scene）	农 村（场）Rural Areas（scene）	剧团演出观众人数（万人次）Number of Spectators of Opera Troupes（10000 person－times）	剧团演出收入（万元）Income of Performances of Opera Troupes（10000 yuan）
全市	**Total**	**1560**	**2331**	**5618**	**2017**	**515.22**	**8815**
为上年（%）	As Compared with the Preceding Year （%）	90.5	221.6	91.6	71.2	87	128.8
市区	Urban District	1560	2331	5030	1587	424.3	8642.3
#萧山区	Xiaoshan	－	－	66	47	8.95	
余杭区	Yuhang	19	－	153	140	29.8	29
富阳区	Fuyang	－	－	120	100	24	177.8
桐庐县	Tonglu	－	－	280	150	30	57.7
淳安县	Chun'an	－	－	－	－	－	－
建德市	Jiande	－	－	308	280	60.92	115
临安市	Lin'an	－	－	－	－	－	－

12－11 图书出版数量(2015－2016 年)
Number of Books Published(2015－2016)

项 目 Item	本版图书种数(种) Number of Publications (kind)		租型图书种数(种) Number of Publications for Lease (kind)		总印数(万册、万份) Total Printed Copies (1000 copies)		总印张(千印张) Total Printed Sheets (1000 sheets)	
	2015	2016	2015	2016	2015	2016	2015	2016
图书总计 Total	**13035**	**13412**	**394**	**485**	**36228.1**	**39309.53**	**2571790**	**2868085.6**
使用《中国标准书号》部分合计 Publication wirh "China Standard Book Number"	12959	13331	394	485	35971.31	39241.25	2555543.55	2865370.71
#哲学 Philosophy	128	118	–	–	63.48	96.23	8609.52	13064.65
社会科学总论 General Social Science	211	229	–	–	114.75	100.22	17727.02	14094.11
文化、科学、教育、体育 Culture, Science, Education and Sports	7128	6895	393	445	27785.07	30259.1	1827265.11	2054432.06
文学 Literature	1557	1891	–	–	4484.64	5167.45	385364.67	440667.42
艺术 Arts	1378	1535	–	36	558.88	735.51	56798.51	68303.78
自然科学总论 General Natural Science	29	44	–	–	22.92	30.27	3142.47	4017.93
不使用《中国标准书号》部分合计 Publications without "China Standard Book Number"	76	81	–	–	256.79	68.28	16246.5	2714.91

12－12 幼儿园基本情况(1978－2016年)

Basic Statistics on Kindergartens(1978－2016)

单位:人　　　　　　　　　　　　　　　　　　　　　　(person)

年份 Year	园数(个) Kindergartens(unit)	在园幼儿数 Number of Children	教职员工数 Teachers and Staff	教师 Number of Full－time Teachers
1978	266	37597	2570	1439
1979	216	59245	3731	2201
1980	518	82182	4763	3398
1981	676	82808	5275	3691
1982	853	95733	6357	4269
1983	1034	95676	6271	4135
1984	1749	112095	7238	4900
1985	1743	115766	7360	5278
1986	1607	118792	7898	5659
1987	1678	133773	8622	6335
1988	1541	139883	9221	6608
1989	1397	132947	9595	6849
1990	1526	136277	9808	7167
1991	1422	150982	10472	7388
1992	1431	133773	9240	6487
1993	1328	171005	10779	7886
1994	1470	165860	10718	7891
1995	1493	149497	10102	7943
1996	1437	150587	10203	7625
1997	1504	146530	10480	7743
1998	1695	153035	10691	7956
1999	1787	156372	10719	8107
2000	2037	168414	11740	8770
2001	1249	174204	11447	7880
2002	1268	175891	11988	8086
2003	1285	176862	13702	9076
2004	1098	186472	14991	9544
2005	1188	188991	16161	10288
2006	1188	195552	17550	11053
2007	1071	212754	19330	12168
2008	1037	235867	21193	12917
2009	972	246336	22970	14211
2010	969	267352	25525	15203
2011	970	271128	27458	16023
2012	914	283421	29843	17811
2013	860	285406	32037	18945
2014	881	295036	35212	20088
2015	910	313385	38238	21404
2016	930	325495	40833	22955

12－13　小学基本情况(1978－2016年)

Basic Statistics on Primary Schools(1978－2016)

单位:人　　　　(person)

年　份 Year	学校数(个) Number of Schools (unit)	在校学生数 Enrolment	毕业生数 Graduates	教职员工数 Number of Teachers and Staff	专职教师数 Number of Full－time Teachers
1978	4959	605137	－	24103	22291
1979	4850	577811	－	25089	23220
1980	4781	560244	－	25388	22902
1981	4668	525503	－	22468	20832
1982	4528	479264	－	22213	20289
1983	4417	444301	－	20842	18945
1984	4345	427763	－	20496	18500
1985	4286	414839	－	20945	18415
1986	4250	413507	－	20796	18464
1987	4205	405856	－	21067	18751
1988	4137	426842	－	21658	19236
1989	4106	459162	－	22660	20177
1990	4077	460514	－	20542	18099
1991	3972	453055	－	20781	18369
1992	3654	450496	－	21452	19067
1993	3473	477026	－	22141	19775
1994	3352	504867	－	22751	20462
1995	3172	513988	－	23743	21380
1996	3006	525674	－	24553	22197
1997	2762	538390	－	25269	23022
1998	2395	532845	－	25718	23499
1999	1996	512874	－	26350	24120
2000	1659	485679	100405	25938	23876
2001	1354	467982	93365	25535	23179
2002	1197	456535	89752	25425	23138
2003	1044	448969	84051	25304	22955
2004	897	447971	74872	25396	23066
2005	791	458942	75337	25793	23541
2006	605	459529	79070	26040	23848
2007	437	456152	81767	26455	24251
2008	418	452143	82620	26894	24743
2009	417	445132	80441	27445	25424
2010	408	453897	76126	27881	25709
2011	409	465289	73465	27862	26395
2012	415	472613	74547	25620	27777
2013	419	483489	73682	30373	28949
2014	421	502688	73244	31490	30139
2015	443	524513	71398	32815	31280
2016	447	543038	77726	33873	32549

12－14　初中基本情况(1978－2016 年)
Basic Statistics on Junior Middle Schools(1978－2016)

单位:人　　　　(person)

年　份 Year	学校数(个) Number of Schools (unit)	在校学生数 Enrolment	毕业生数 Graduates	专职教师数 Number of Full－time Teachers
1978	254	247209	－	11978
1979	363	208484	－	11020
1980	369	204073	－	10695
1981	359	194024	－	10015
1982	367	193135	－	10107
1983	370	190221	－	9948
1984	368	192971	－	9679
1985	361	196889	－	9799
1986	376	199638	－	9821
1987	385	195426	－	10264
1988	380	170079	－	10055
1989	376	151223	－	9825
1990	382	160111	－	9564
1991	387	185590	－	10020
1992	367	212022	－	10603
1993	365	203896	－	10876
1994	371	205388	－	11495
1995	373	216300	－	12058
1996	374	229466	－	12810
1997	368	227809	－	13370
1998	359	222191	－	13493
1999	339	239174	－	13723
2000	330	269484	68347	14529
2001	314	285203	75722	15685
2002	315	282951	91056	15758
2003	316	268824	98412	15836
2004	303	252291	93042	16042
2005	289	241374	90094	16205
2006	263	235527	85436	16374
2007	262	238252	76194	16591
2008	260	244464	74827	16965
2009	252	241899	77268	17317
2010	245	236014	78379	17795
2011	246	223545	78431	17652
2012	244	215701	75489	17992
2013	241	213452	71006	18260
2014	241	213936	67988	18671
2015	243	211323	69200	18909
2016	249	215756	69674	19469

12-15 高中基本情况(1978-2016年)

Basic Statistics on Senior High Schools(1978-2016)

单位:人 (person)

年份 Year	学校数(个) Number of Schools (unit)	在校学生数 Enrolment	毕业生数 Graduates	专职教师数 Number of Full-time Teachers
1978	352	102815	-	5235
1979	182	58866	-	3471
1980	151	43661	-	3173
1981	118	34606	-	2825
1982	113	35136	-	2740
1983	111	38580	-	2740
1984	105	43167	-	2781
1985	104	47510	-	3016
1986	95	46379	-	2972
1987	92	44697	-	3006
1988	89	42196	-	2947
1989	88	39994	-	2898
1990	86	39829	-	2922
1991	82	37809	-	2896
1992	74	34620	-	2791
1993	72	32483	-	2641
1994	75	35720	-	2673
1995	72	40771	-	2880
1996	70	43692	-	3135
1997	69	47975	-	3388
1998	75	55688	-	3693
1999	82	64459	-	4172
2000	85	73049	17484	4745
2001	88	79632	22012	5262
2002	81	91635	22630	6126
2003	77	108116	25429	6879
2004	81	115303	30630	7510
2005	80	120883	34486	8041
2006	82	124177	39484	8421
2007	80	122939	39805	8542
2008	76	120294	40551	8646
2009	75	118057	41408	8751
2010	72	116983	39319	8871
2011	71	117089	38579	9061
2012	70	115652	38623	9069
2013	70	113894	37810	9125
2014	72	110478	38489	9378
2015	75	109983	37303	9630
2016	77	110431	36022	10016

12－16 中等专业学校基本情况(1978－2016年)

Basic Statistics on Specialized Secondary Schools(1978－2016)

单位:人 (person)

年 份 Year	学校数(个) Number of Schools (unit)	在校学生数 Enrolment	毕业生数 Graduates	教职员工数 Teachers and Staff	专职教师数 Number of Full－time Teachers
1978	26	8711	–	3044	1080
1979	27	11093	–	2601	1124
1980	26	9453	–	2450	1101
1981	35	7309	–	3122	1276
1982	37	8284	–	3694	1529
1983	37	10516	–	3716	1604
1984	42	13419	–	4194	1758
1985	46	16527	–	5095	1959
1986	50	19114	–	5641	2336
1987	52	20929	–	6081	2623
1988	51	22117	–	6144	2741
1989	54	23302	–	6602	2888
1990	55	23564	–	6679	2948
1991	55	23331	–	6584	2770
1992	55	26373	–	6786	2825
1993	56	30336	–	6732	2780
1994	57	36079	–	6881	2840
1995	57	42784	–	6851	2888
1996	58	49593	–	6789	2904
1997	57	51752	–	6731	2896
1998	56	55796	–	6554	2746
1999	50	52272	–	5023	2272
2000	28	45238	15674	2950	1421
2001	26	32763	15202	2053	1051
2002	14	26255	13355	1251	566
2003	13	21735	11866	1058	457
2004	11	21262	6399	869	416
2005	10	20344	6661	893	443
2006	8	12540	5830	410	184
2007	8	8927	4849	414	194
2008	8	5514	4130	345	152
2009	8	4016	2025	233	65
2010	6	3999	1092	348	151
2011	5	4071	934	369	154
2012	5	3909	1252	376	150
2013	5	3656	1215	390	158
2014	7	3974	1077	469	226
2015	7	3968	1134	494	244
2016	7	4402	982	504	262

12 – 17 高等学校基本情况(1978 – 2016 年)

Basic Statistics on Regular Institutions of Higher Education(1978 – 2016)

单位:人 (person)

年份 Year	学校数(个) Number of Schools (unit)	招生数 Entrants	在校学生数 Enrolment	毕业生数 Graduates	教职员工数 Teachers and Staff	专职教师数 Number of Full – time Teachers
1978	9	–	13319	–	8966	3946
1979	12	–	17518	–	10182	4458
1980	13	–	23545	–	12400	5278
1981	13	–	28936	–	13090	5359
1982	13	–	25821	–	14363	6067
1983	14	–	27443	–	15267	6172
1984	16	–	31384	–	15889	6387
1985	20	–	36996	–	17507	7247
1986	22	–	40051	–	18968	7845
1987	21	–	39922	–	18965	7876
1988	21	–	40787	–	19582	8133
1989	21	–	40330	–	19680	8107
1990	21	–	39866	–	19495	8075
1991	21	–	42192	–	19489	7737
1992	19	–	43787	–	19841	7561
1993	19	–	51063	–	19787	7561
1994	19	–	59109	–	19903	7703
1995	20	–	63124	–	19883	7799
1996	20	–	66023	–	19693	7824
1997	20	–	69391	–	19540	7793
1998	17	–	76546	–	19320	7723
1999	18	–	89109	–	20136	8135
2000	32	46070	122386	17004	23791	10477
2001	33	63001	174894	22756	25805	11866
2002	34	74656	224048	27213	27307	13605
2003	35	85865	269798	41192	34508	18141
2004	36	96810	313599	53288	33325	18445
2005	36	101374	351918	63989	34816	19583
2006	36	103885	373563	80069	36929	21375
2007	36	110371	392770	90944	38843	23197
2008	36	114714	409559	97778	39762	24017
2009	36	114568	429774	96101	40420	24765
2010	37	113529	434811	101681	41582	25003
2011	38	117892	446721	104486	42222	25735
2012	38	121331	459181	107484	43216	26689
2013	38	123046	471820	108688	43992	27544
2014	38	122099	474652	110512	44710	28265
2015	39	139002	475558	125013	44825	28868
2016	39	138819	480953	128434	45512	29222

注:在校学生数包括各高校研究生。

a) Number of students include graduate students in all colleges and universities.

12－18　小学、幼儿园及特殊

Basic Statistics on Primary Schools,

单位：人

指　标	Item	全　市 Total	市　区 Urban District	萧山区 Xiaoshan
小　　学	**Primary Schools**			
学校数(所)	Number of Schools(unit)	447	317	73
班数(班)	Number of Classes(unit)	14405	11762	2399
在校学生数	Number of Students	543038	453180	94166
本年招生数	Number of New Students Enrollment	99783	85040	16952
本年毕业生数	Number of Graduates	77726	62884	15143
专职教师数	Full－time Teachers	32549	26503	5528
2017 年预计毕业生数	Number of Students Will Graduate in 2017	84273	69057	15552
幼儿园	**Kindergartens**			
园数(个)	Number of Kindergartens(unit)	930	729	174
班数(班)	Number of Classes(unit)	11116	9279	1752
在园幼儿数	Number of Children	325495	274650	50776
教师数	Full－time Teachers	22955	19607	3403
盲聋哑学校	**Schools for the Blind,Deaf and Deaf－mute**			
学校数(个)	Number of Schools(unit)	2	2	－
在校学生数	Number of Students	457	457	－
本年招生数	Number of New Students Enrollment	71	71	－
本年毕业生数	Number of Graduates	84	84	－
专职教师数	Number of Full－time Teachers	152	152	－
弱智学校	**Schools for Weaken in Intelligence**			
学校数(个)	Number of Schools(unit)	12	8	1
在校学生数	Number of Students	1138	936	256
本年招生数	Number of New Students Enrollment	181	158	68
本年毕业生数	Number of Graduates	175	157	67
专职教师数	Number of Full－time Teachers	342	295	65
工读学校	**Reformatory Schools**			
学校数(个)	Number of Schools(unit)	1	1	－
在校学生数	Number of Students	288	288	－
本年招生数	Number of New Students Enrollment	113	113	－
本年毕业生数	Number of Graduates	159	159	－
专任教师数	Number of Full－time Teachers	63	63	－

教育基本情况(2016 年)

Kindergartens and Special Education(2016)

(person)

余杭区 Yuhang	富阳区 Fuyang	桐庐县 Tonglu	淳安县 Chun'an	建德市 Jiande	临安市 Lin'an
48	45	27	37	28	38
2302	1228	643	605	583	812
91679	44365	23736	15699	20739	29684
17474	7128	3997	2399	3383	4964
12944	7460	3651	3058	3380	4753
5088	2596	1430	1568	1261	1787
13974	7667	3971	2906	3467	4872
114	82	49	36	40	76
1791	831	432	309	454	642
55411	23987	13077	7753	12312	17703
3889	1728	794	480	803	1271
–	–	–	–	–	–
–	–	–	–	–	–
–	–	–	–	–	–
–	–	–	–	–	–
–	–	–	–	–	–
1	1	1	1	1	1
91	70	48	33	31	90
8	8	3	10	6	4
7	–	–	13	5	–
26	20	11	7	9	20
–	–	–	–	–	–
–	–	–	–	–	–
–	–	–	–	–	–
–	–	–	–	–	–
–	–	–	–	–	–

12－19 普通中学、职业中学
Basic Statistics on Senior, Junior High

单位：人

指　标	Item	全　市 Total	市　区 Urban District	萧山区 Xiaoshan
高　　中	**Senior High Schools**			
学校数(所)	Number of Schools(unit)	77	57	10
在校学生数	Number of Students	110431	83923	18961
本年招生数	Number of New Students Enrollment	37506	29138	6425
本年毕业生数	Number of Graduates	36022	26456	6309
专职教师数	Full－time Teachers	10016	7599	1699
2017 年预计毕业生数	Number of Students Will Graduate in 2017	35378	26304	6213
初　　中	**Junior High Schools**			
学校数(所)	Number of Schools(unit)	249	184	38
在校学生数	Number of Students	215756	173540	39062
本年招生数	Number of New Students Enrollment	76129	61746	14008
本年毕业生数	Number of Graduates	69674	54737	12349
专职教师数	Full－time Teachers	19469	15242	3230
2017 年预计毕业生数	Number of Students Will Graduate in 2017	69553	55363	12308
职业中学	**Vocational Schools**			
学校数(所)	Number of Schools(unit)	30	23	4
在校学生数	Number of Students	60261	48622	11046
本年招生数	Number of New Students Enrollment	20362	16522	3579
本年毕业生数	Number of Graduates	21153	17054	4676
专职教师数	Full－time Teachers	4452	3517	772
2017 年预计毕业生数	Number of Students Will Graduate in 2017	19907	16050	3942
技工学校	**Technical Schools**			
学校数(所)	Number of schools(unit)	19	16	1
在校学生数	Number of Students	27272	25222	2184
专职教师数	Full－time Teachers	1902	1720	230

和技工学校基本情况(2016 年)

Schools and Vacational, Technical Schools(2016)

(person)

余杭区 Yuhang	富阳区 Fuyang	桐庐县 Tonglu	淳安县 Chun'an	建德市 Jiande	临安市 Lin'an
11	7	4	5	6	5
13431	12186	5090	6031	8177	7210
4576	4003	1672	1861	2572	2263
4338	4361	1751	2173	2933	2709
1206	1071	509	553	716	639
4313	4054	1723	2046	2798	2507
34	17	13	17	17	18
34110	20035	9952	9071	10104	13089
12657	7190	3413	3078	3386	4506
9901	6516	3334	3439	3955	4209
2828	1596	953	1042	1161	1071
10409	6350	3278	3136	3483	4293
5	2	2	2	1	2
10454	7121	2879	3403	1737	3620
3665	2414	957	1166	424	1293
3452	2664	824	1213	860	1202
736	551	211	246	136	342
3318	2470	859	1115	766	1117
1	1	-	1	1	1
144	411	-	-	1277	773
-	42	-	25	102	55

12－20　高等学校

Basic Statistics on Regular

单位:人

单位名称	Item	在校学生数 Enrolment 2016	为上年(%) As Compared with the Preceding Year(%)
全　　市	**Total**	**427978**	**100.6**
#市　　区	**Urban District**	**406031**	**100.6**
浙江大学	Zhejiang University	24133	101
杭州电子科技大学	Hangzhou Dianzi University	16172	98.66
浙江工业大学	Zhejiang Univesity of Technology	20091	97.78
浙江理工大学	Zhejiang Sci－Tech University	17657	100
浙江农林大学	Zhejiang Forestry University	14419	0.3
浙江中医药大学	Zhejiang University of Traditional Chinese Medicine	7210	107.5
杭州师范大学	Hangzhou Normal University	17679	105.6
浙江工商大学	Zhejiang Gongshang University	15283	99.48
中国美术学院	China Academy of Art	7382	95.63
中国计量大学	China JiLiang University	15116	102.5
浙江科技学院	Hangzhou Application Engineering and Technology College	16631	104.1
浙江广播电视大学	Zhejiang Radio & TV University	10055	85.6
浙江水利水电专科学校	Zhejiang Water Conservancy and Hydroelectricity College	9108	110.6
浙江财经大学	Zhejiang University of Finance and Economics	13262	99.64
浙江警察学院	Zhejiang Police College	4091	100.1
浙江传媒学院	Zhejiang Institute of Media and Communications	13683	105.7
浙江树人大学	Zhejiang Shuren University	15419	101.9
浙江大学城市学院	Zhejiang University City College	13154	100.3

注:本表不含在校研究生。

基本情况(2016 年)
Institutions of Higher Education(2016)

(person)

本年招生数 Entrants	本年毕业生数 Graduates	教职员工数 Number of Teachers and Staff	
		合　计 Total	其中:专职教师 Full - time Teachers
121614	**114737**	**45512**	**29222**
115997	**109262**	**43445**	**27762**
5972	5517	8305	3497
3955	4026	1878	1512
4531	4746	3131	2086
4422	4363	1950	1461
3721	3577	1601	1056
2008	1433	1045	722
4205	4008	2240	1532
4068	3797	1810	1390
1630	2208	986	631
3846	3471	1530	1018
4204	3588	1314	975
3092	3430	266	73
2722	2404	668	510
3555	3656	1443	985
1031	858	481	239
3438	3294	1269	749
4114	3898	829	605
3343	3136	1009	693

a) Data in this table does not contain post - graduate students.

12－21 各级成人教育

Basic Statistics on

单位:人

指　标	Item	成人高等学历教育 Higher Education for Adults	成人高校 Adult Institutions of Higher Education	普通高校成人高等学历教育 Adult Higher Education in Ordinary Universities
全　　市	**Total**			
学校数(所)	Number of Schools(unit)	3	3	
在校学生数	Number of Students	107585	13243	94342
本年招生数	Number of New Students Enrollment	45662	4378	41284
本年毕业生数	Number of Graduates	55047	5351	49696
教职员工数	Number of Teachers and Staff	440	440	–
#专职教师	#Full－time Teachers	167	167	–
市　　区	**Urban District**			
学校数(所)	Number of Schools(unit)	3	3	–
在校学生数	Number of Students	101409	13243	88166
本年招生数	Number of New Students Enrollment	42674	4378	38296
本年毕业生数	Number of Graduates	52360	5351	47009
教职员工数	Number of Teachers and Staff	440	440	–
#专职教师	#Full－time Teachers	167	167	–

基本情况(2016 年)
Various Adult Education(2016)

(person)

成人中等学历教育 Adult Secondary Education	成人中等专业 Adult Secondary Specialized	成人中学 Secondary Schools for Adults
140	6	134
242160	15800	226360
7474	7474	–
232973	6644	226329
2039	704	1335
1226	347	879
75	6	69
109439	15800	93639
7474	7474	–
101720	6644	95076
1744	704	1040
976	347	629

12－22 医疗卫生机构数(1978－2016年)

Number of Health Institutions(1978－2016)

单位:个 (unit)

年 份 Year	全市合计 Total	医 院 Hospitals	市区合计 Urban District	医 院 Hospitals
1978	1361	421	689	45
1979	1390	426	696	50
1980	1381	425	675	51
1981	1476	424	749	51
1982	1540	432	798	56
1983	1540	435	800	58
1984	1574	437	807	54
1985	1582	404	787	47
1986	1636	407	826	53
1987	1693	420	865	55
1988	1710	438	878	55
1989	1721	443	882	57
1990	1738	440	890	58
1991	1789	441	889	58
1992	1767	436	885	58
1993	1730	403	882	68
1994	1717	416	882	72
1995	1712	414	883	72
1996	1712	416	893	83
1997	1711	411	891	81
1998	1491	419	757	89
1999	1530	400	789	85
2000	1599	396	853	85
2001	1496	391	1072	191
2002	1817	116	1277	88
2003	1901	99	1323	73
2004	1985	114	1396	87
2005	2196	127	1604	97
2006	2570	134	1886	107
2007	2607	138	1872	104
2008	2544	141	1813	108
2009	2687	144	1887	111
2010	2819	151	1906	113
2011	2958	167	1992	122
2012	3017	198	2004	146
2013	4139	208	2233	156
2014	4198	218	2763	173
2015	4428	244	2982	198
2016	4691	277	3214	226

12－23 医疗病床数(1978－2016年)

Number of Beds in Health Institutions(1978－2016)

单位:张 (bed)

年 份 Year	全 市 Total	医 院 Hospitals	市 区 Urban District	医 院 Hospitals
1978	14042	11704	6588	5789
1979	15124	12682	7335	6282
1980	16317	13478	8244	6940
1981	17408	13576	9646	7185
1982	17179	14350	9194	7580
1983	17338	14584	9411	7833
1984	17694	14691	9536	7867
1985	19637	15010	11095	7933
1986	20555	16035	11657	8448
1987	21465	16770	12203	8863
1988	23394	17954	13204	9651
1989	24111	18363	13581	9773
1990	24121	18879	13219	10041
1991	24966	19444	13968	10437
1992	25606	20243	14206	10821
1993	25653	20884	14058	10982
1994	25984	20870	14231	11045
1995	26684	21360	14731	11336
1996	28141	22217	15427	12132
1997	26616	22341	15076	12190
1998	27327	23110	15530	12766
1999	26713	22952	14988	12691
2000	27166	23303	15496	13068
2001	27063	23520	20523	17770
2002	27609	22797	21200	18667
2003	29144	22036	22641	18205
2004	31738	24444	25008	20338
2005	33251	25907	26732	21931
2006	33972	27186	27172	23184
2007	36928	29987	29884	25664
2008	38114	31416	30663	26882
2009	40226	33094	32412	28031
2010	42828	36148	34693	30639
2011	45291	39363	36633	33291
2012	49471	44019	40534	37383
2013	52056	46636	42506	39489
2014	55779	50805	48406	44639
2015	63632	58400	55540	51672
2016	69452	63994	60666	56522

12-24 全市

Number of

单位:个

指标	Item	全市 Total	市区 Urban District
总计	**Total**	**4691**	**3214**
一、医院	**Number of Hospitals**	**277**	**226**
1. 综合医院	General Hospitals	131	112
2. 中医医院	Hospitals of Chinese Medicine	35	21
3. 中西医结合医院	Chinese Therapeutics with Western	6	5
4. 专科医院	Specialized Hospitals	93	76
#口腔医院	Hospitals for Mouth	13	12
眼科医院	Hospitals for Eye	6	5
耳鼻喉科医院	ENT Hospitals	–	–
肿瘤医院	Tumor Hospitals	3	3
心血管病医院	Cardiovascular Hospitals	2	2
胸科医院	Chest Hospitals	–	–
血液病医院	Blood Diseases Hospitals	–	–
妇产(科)医院	Hospitals for Pregnant Woman	12	11
儿童医院	Children Hospitals	3	3
精神病医院	Mental Hospitals	7	3
传染病医院	Hospitals for Infectious Diseases	1	1
皮肤病医院	Dermatology Hospital	3	3
结核病医院	Tuberculosis Hospitals	–	–
麻疯病医院	Leprosy Hospitals	–	–
职业病医院	Occupational Disease Hospitals	–	–
骨科医院	Orthopaedics Hospitals	8	4
康复医院	Healing Hospitals	14	12
整型外科医院	Plastic Hospitals	1	1
美容医院	Beauty Hospitals	10	9
其他专科医院	Other Special Hospitals	10	7
5. 护理院	Nursing Centers	12	12
二、基层医疗卫生机构	**Community Medical Institutions**	**4313**	**2911**
1. 社区卫生服务中心(站)	Health Service Centers for Community	1275	1021
#社区卫生服务中心	Health Service Centers	134	122
社区卫生服务站	Health Service Stations	1141	899
2. 卫生院	Health Service Centers	88	9
#街道卫生院	Rural Township Hospitals in Subdistrict	–	–
乡镇卫生院	Rural Township Hospitals in Country	88	9
3. 村卫生室	Health Offices in Village	917	240
4. 门诊部	Clinics	518	467
5. 诊所、卫生所、医务室、护理站	Other Health Care Institutions	1515	1174
三、专业公共卫生机构	**Professional Public Health Institutions**	**60**	**39**
疾病预防控制中心	Centers for Disease Prevention and Control	15	11
专科疾病防治所(所、站)	Specialized Centers for Disease Prevention and Control(stations)	2	–
健康教育所(站、中心)	Education Center for Health(stations)	–	–
妇幼保健院(所、站)	Maternity and Child Care Centers(stations)	9	5
急救中心(站)	First - aid Centers(stations)	10	5
采供血机构	Blood Supplying Agencies	3	2
卫生监督所	Institutions of Public Health Inspection	16	12
计划生育服务机构	Family Planning Service Institutions	5	4
四、其他卫生机构	**Other Health Care Institutions**	**41**	**38**
疗养院	Sanatoriums	8	8
医学科学研究机构	Research Institutions of Medical Science	1	1
医学在职培训机构	Medical Training Organization for Incumbent	6	3
临床检验中心(所、站)	Clinical Laboratory Center	7	7
统计信息中心	Statistical Information Centers	2	2
其他	Other	17	17

医疗卫生机构数(2016 年末)

Health Institutions(End of 2016)

(unit)

萧山区 Xiaoshan	余杭区 Yuhang	富阳区 Fuyang	桐庐县 Tonglu	淳安县 Chun'an	建德市 Jiande	临安市 Lin'an
718	**492**	**460**	**320**	**315**	**392**	**450**
51	**20**	**14**	**11**	**7**	**8**	**25**
42	9	6	5	3	2	9
4	1	3	2	2	1	9
–	–	–	–	–	1	–
5	6	5	4	2	4	7
1	2	1	–	–	–	1
–	–	1	–	–	1	–
–	–	–	–	–	–	–
–	–	1	–	–	–	–
–	–	–	–	–	–	–
–	–	–	–	–	–	–
–	–	–	–	–	–	–
–	1	–	–	–	–	1
–	–	–	–	–	–	–
–	1	1	1	1	1	1
–	–	–	–	–	–	–
1	–	–	–	–	–	–
–	–	–	–	–	–	–
–	–	–	–	–	–	–
–	–	–	–	–	–	–
–	2	–	1	–	1	2
1	–	–	–	1	1	–
–	–	–	–	–	–	–
–	–	–	–	–	–	1
2	–	1	2	–	–	1
–	4	–	–	–	–	–
659	**463**	**438**	**306**	**299**	**377**	**420**
318	180	172	106	50	21	77
29	20	25	3	2	2	5
289	160	147	103	48	19	72
–	–	9	10	21	22	26
–	–	–	–	–	–	–
–	–	9	10	21	22	26
122	–	118	122	174	232	149
50	84	26	17	3	17	14
169	199	113	51	51	85	154
6	**5**	**4**	**3**	**8**	**6**	**4**
1	1	1	1	1	1	1
–	–	–	–	1	1	–
–	–	–	–	–	–	–
–	1	1	1	1	1	1
2	1	1	–	3	1	1
1	–	–	–	–	1	–
1	1	1	1	1	1	1
1	1	–	–	1	–	–
2	**4**	**4**	**–**	**1**	**1**	**1**
1	1	4	–	–	–	–
–	–	–	–	–	–	–
–	1	–	–	1	1	1
1	2	–	–	–	–	–
–	–	–	–	–	–	–
–	–	–	–	–	–	–

12－25 全市

Total Number of

单位：张

指 标	Item	全 市 Total	市区 Urban District
总 计	**Total**	**69452**	**60666**
一、医院	**Number of Hospitals**	**63994**	**56522**
1.综合医院	General Hospitals	35676	31324
2.中医医院	Hospitals of Chinese Medicine	8209	6601
3.中西医结合医院	Chinese Therapeutics with Western	4153	3956
4.专科医院	Specialized Hospitals	14618	13303
#口腔医院	Hospitals for Mouth	223	198
眼科医院	Hospitals for Eye	240	220
耳鼻喉科医院	ENT Hospitals	–	–
肿瘤医院	Tumor Hospitals	2631	2631
心血管病医院	Cardiovascular Hospitals	868	868
胸科医院	Chest Hospitals	–	–
血液病医院	Blood Diseases Hospitals	–	–
妇产(科)医院	Hospitals for Pregnant Woman	1880	1860
儿童医院	Children Hospitals	1610	1610
精神病医院	Mental Hospitals	2184	1629
传染病医院	Hospitals for Infectious Diseases	600	600
皮肤病医院	Dermatology Hospital	110	110
结核病医院	Tuberculosis Hospitals	–	–
麻疯病医院	Leprosy Hospitals	–	–
职业病医院	Occupational Disease Hospitals	–	–
骨科医院	Orthopaedics Hospitals	833	388
康复医院	Healing Hospitals	2147	1992
整型外科医院	Plastic Hospitals	120	120
美容医院	Beauty Hospitals	203	183
其他专科医院	Other Special Hospitals	969	894
5.护理院	Nursing Centers	1338	1338
二、基层医疗卫生机构	**Community Medical Institutions**	**3304**	**2649**
1.社区卫生服务中心(站)	Health Service Centers for Community	2731	2611
#社区卫生服务中心	Health Service Centers	2709	2611
社区卫生服务站	Health Service Stations	22	–
2.卫生院	Health Service Centers	563	38
#街道卫生院	Rural Township Hospitals in Subdistrict	–	–
乡镇卫生院	Rural Township Hospitals in Country	563	38
3.村卫生室	Health Offices in Village	–	–
4.门诊部	Clinics	10	–
5.诊所、卫生所、医务室、护理站	Other Health Care Institutions	–	–
三、专业公共卫生机构	**Professional Public Health Institutions**	**1247**	**588**
疾病预防控制中心	Centers for Disease Prevention and Control	–	–
专科疾病防治所(所、站)	Specialized Centers for Disease Prevention and Control(stations)	300	–
健康教育所(站、中心)	Education Center for Health(stations)	–	–
妇幼保健院(所、站)	Maternity and Child Care Centers(stations)	928	588
急救中心(站)	First – aid Centers(stations)	19	–
采供血机构	Blood Supplying Agencies	–	–
卫生监督所(中心)	Institutions of Public Health Inspection	–	–
计划生育服务机构	Family Planning Service Institutions	–	–
四、其他卫生机构	**Other Health Care Institutions**	**907**	**907**
#疗养院	Sanatoriums	907	907
医学科学研究机构	Research Institutions of Medical Science	–	–
医学在职培训机构	Medical Training Organization for Incumbent	–	–
临床检验中心(所、站)	Clinical Laboratory Center	–	–
统计信息中心	Statistical Information Centers	–	–
其他	Other	–	–

医疗病床数(2016 年末)

Beds in Health Institutions(End of 2016)

(bed)

萧山区 Xiaoshan	余杭区 Yuhang	富阳区 Fuyang	桐庐县 Tonglu	淳安县 Chun'an	建德市 Jiande	临安市 Lin'an
9173	**4965**	**3423**	**1857**	**1721**	**2551**	**2657**
8688	**3915**	**2301**	**1599**	**1491**	**1847**	**2535**
6783	2275	1391	1116	862	890	1484
1264	400	625	390	489	250	479
–	–	–	–	–	197	–
641	870	285	93	140	510	572
15	15	15	–	–	–	25
–	–	20	–	–	20	–
–	–	–	–	–	–	–
–	–	20	–	–	–	–
–	–	–	–	–	–	–
–	–	–	–	–	–	–
–	–	–	–	–	–	–
–	35	–	–	–	–	20
–	–	–	–	–	–	–
–	520	150	–	90	315	150
–	–	–	–	–	–	–
40	–	–	–	–	–	–
–	–	–	–	–	–	–
–	–	–	–	–	–	–
–	–	–	–	–	–	–
–	300	–	38	–	70	337
152	–	–	–	50	105	–
–	–	–	–	–	–	–
–	–	–	–	–	–	20
434	–	80	55	–	–	20
–	370	–	–	–	–	–
425	**680**	**250**	**178**	**80**	**304**	**93**
425	680	212	24	–	54	42
425	680	212	22	–	34	42
–	–	–	2	–	20	–
–	–	38	154	80	250	41
–	–	–	–	–	–	–
–	–	38	154	80	250	41
–	–	–	–	–	–	–
–	–	–	–	–	–	10
–	–	–	–	–	–	–
–	**250**	**338**	**80**	**150**	**400**	**29**
–	–	–	–	–	–	–
–	–	–	–	–	300	–
–	–	–	–	–	–	–
–	250	338	80	150	90	20
–	–	–	–	–	10	9
–	–	–	–	–	–	–
–	–	–	–	–	–	–
–	–	–	–	–	–	–
60	**120**	**534**	**–**	**–**	**–**	**–**
60	120	534	–	–	–	–
–	–	–	–	–	–	–
–	–	–	–	–	–	–
–	–	–	–	–	–	–
–	–	–	–	–	–	–
–	–	–	–	–	–	–

12－26 医院诊疗

Number of

指　　标	Item	机构数(个) Number of Institutions (unit)	诊疗人次数(万人次) Total Number of Patients Treate (10000 person－times)
总　　计	**Total**	**4691**	**12170.06**
一、医院	**Number of Hospitals**	**277**	**6406.91**
1.综合医院	General Hospitals	131	3931.17
2.中医医院	Hospitals of Chinese Medicine	35	1017.04
3.中西医结合医院	Chinese Therapeutics with Western	6	449.83
4.专科医院	Specialized Hospitals	93	1004.38
#口腔医院	Hospitals for Mouth	13	130.69
眼科医院	Hospitals for Eye	6	130.69
耳鼻喉科医院	ENT Hospitals	－	－
肿瘤医院	Tumor Hospitals	3	63.38
心血管病医院	Cardiovascular Hospitals	2	47.66
胸科医院	Chest Hospitals	－	－
血液病医院	Blood Diseases Hospitals	－	－
妇产(科)医院	Hospitals for Pregnant Woman	12	224.48
儿童医院	Children Hospitals	3	304.06
精神病医院	Mental Hospitals	7	4.17
传染病医院	Hospitals for Infectious Diseases	1	62.17
皮肤病医院	Dermatology Hospital	3	19.95
结核病医院	Tuberculosis Hospitals	－	－
麻风病医院	Leprosy Hospitals	－	－
职业病医院	Occupational Disease Hospitals	－	－
骨科医院	Orthopaedics Hospitals	8	34.60
康复医院	Healing Hospitals	14	11.73
整型外科医院	Plastic Hospitals	1	5.27
美容医院	Beauty Hospitals	10	25.40
其他专科医院	Other Special Hospitals	10	14.92
5.护理院	Nursing Centers	12	4.49
二、基层医疗卫生机构	**Community Medical Institutions**	**4313**	**5539.68**
1.社区卫生服务中心(站)	Health Service Centers for Community	1275	3575.80
#社区卫生服务中心	Health Service Centers	134	3485.85
社区卫生服务站	Health Service Stations	1141	89.95
2.卫生院	Health Service Centers	88	450.65
#乡镇卫生院	Rural Township Hospitals in Country	88	450.65
3.村卫生室	Health Offices in Village	917	204.52
4.门诊部	Clinics	517	821.19
5.诊所、卫生所、医务室	Other Health Care Institutions	1515	48.75
三、专业公共卫生机构	**Professional Public Health Institutions**	**60**	**209.28**
专科疾病防治院(所、站)	Specialized Centers for Disease Prevention and Control(stations)	2	7.74
妇幼保健院(所、站)	Maternity and Child Care Centers(stations)	9	190.31
四、其他机构	**Other Institutions**	**41**	**14.18**
疗养院	Sanatoriums	8	14.18

次数和入院人数（2016 年）
Hospital Patients(2016)

门、急诊人次数(万人次) Out - Patients and Emergency Patients (10000 person - times)	入院人数 (万人) Hospital Admissions(10000 person)	每百门急诊次入院人数(人) Hospital Admissions Per 100 Patient - time (person)
11839.85	**205.91**	**1.74**
6385.64	**195.87**	**3.07**
3921.94	121.48	3.10
1011.73	22.80	2.25
449.83	11.13	2.47
999.18	39.74	3.98
130.69	0.12	0.09
18.19	0.77	4.21
-	-	-
63.38	10.63	16.77
44.34	1.36	3.06
-	-	-
-	-	-
224.06	10.17	4.54
304.06	7.81	2.57
41.68	2.08	4.99
61.61	2.32	3.77
19.95	0.01	0.04
-	-	-
-	-	-
-	-	-
34.60	1.71	4.94
11.66	1.07	9.19
5.27	0.40	7.60
25.26	0.73	2.87
14.42	0.56	3.88
2.97	0.72	24.32
5232.44	**1.88**	**0.05**
3427.46	1.24	0.04
3337.94	1.22	0.04
89.52	0.02	0.02
439.12	0.64	0.15
439.12	0.64	0.15
197.20	-	-
688.24	-	-
480.43	-	-
209.28	**5.49**	**2.77**
7.74	0.07	0.92
190.31	5.42	2.85
12.49	**2.68**	**21.42**
12.49	2.68	21.42

12－27 全市

Total Number of

单位:人

指　标	Item	全　市 Total	市　区 Urban District
总　计	**Total**	**123642**	**107691**
一、卫生技术人员	Number of Medical Technical Personnel	101194	88076
1. 执业(助理)医师	Registered (Assistant) Doctor	38172	33344
#执业医师	Registered Doctor	35361	31286
2. 注册护士	Registered Nurse	42011	37154
3. 药剂师	Druggist	6618	5540
4. 技师人员	Checking Member	5909	5183
#检验师	Docimaster	4315	3780
5. 其他	Others	8484	6855
二、其他技术人员	Other Medical Technical Personnel	5379	4828
三、管理人员	Managerial Personnel	5110	4584
四、工勤人员	Logistics Worker	11190	9956

卫生事业人员数(2016 年末)
Medical Technical Personnel(End of 2016)

(person)

萧山区 Xiaoshan	余杭区 Yuhang	富阳区 Fuyang	桐庐县 Tonglu	淳安县 Chun'an	建德市 Jiande	临安市 Lin'an
14769	**10309**	**6045**	**4352**	**2825**	**4133**	**4641**
12159	8607	4980	3596	2344	3354	3824
4298	3217	2025	1187	950	1160	1531
3705	2847	1725	985	801	972	1317
4890	3338	1765	1291	847	1358	1361
885	603	275	314	187	277	300
581	518	249	197	123	197	209
418	375	161	149	92	148	146
1505	931	666	607	237	362	423
455	285	231	138	73	82	258
516	374	196	183	58	160	125
1506	1043	524	413	180	321	320

12 - 28 卫生技术人员(1978 - 2016 年)

Number of Medical Technical Personnel(1978 - 2016)

单位:人 (person)

年份 Year	全市 Total	执业(助理)医师 Number of Registered (Assistant) Doctors	注册护士 Registered Nurses	市区 Urban District	执业(助理)医师 Number of Registered (Assistant) Doctors	注册护士 Registered Nurses
1978	19059	7375	3483	10867	4346	2510
1979	20060	7539	3536	11779	4733	2632
1980	21110	8311	3885	12376	5179	2804
1981	22737	9284	4139	13697	5946	3032
1982	23558	9883	4369	14221	6204	3193
1983	24914	10833	4562	15213	6990	3352
1984	25648	11291	4817	15807	7393	3487
1985	25593	11503	5071	15840	7644	3705
1986	26489	12623	5391	16543	8239	3940
1987	27663	12369	5805	17361	8329	4156
1988	28676	13674	6938	18022	8710	4801
1989	29791	14177	7348	18619	9146	5085
1990	30990	14483	7822	19231	9374	5397
1991	32169	14858	8153	19630	9494	5610
1992	32628	14842	8417	19690	9373	5736
1993	33172	15181	8643	19708	9499	5797
1994	33964	15465	8979	19907	9472	5940
1995	34245	16465	9531	19943	9607	6249
1996	34946	16789	9794	20695	9889	6508
1997	35423	17112	10019	20728	9902	6571
1998	35857	16022	10577	21035	9452	6788
1999	35256	16668	10587	20519	9610	6856
2000	35487	16317	11186	20344	9050	7300
2001	36643	16994	11576	28293	12968	9343
2002	37193	16092	11922	28818	12332	9653
2003	39019	16614	12460	30299	12731	10161
2004	39816	16770	13248	30886	12894	10840
2005	42353	17833	14514	33206	13802	12034
2006	45375	18831	15557	35904	14689	12986
2007	49780	20701	17455	39860	16290	14601
2008	52379	21223	18702	42015	16747	15556
2009	56270	22753	20997	45219	17996	17530
2010	61117	24345	23418	49232	19414	19481
2011	65869	25773	25231	53008	20566	20949
2012	71618	27369	28382	57971	22004	23760
2013	78340	29686	30996	63359	23886	25808
2014	85614	31977	34724	74064	27675	30528
2015	93036	34832	38182	80799	30316	33672
2016	101194	38172	42011	88076	33344	37154

12 - 29 体育运动情况(2013 - 2016 年)
Basic Statistics on Sports Activities(2013 - 2016)

单位:人 (person)

指 标	Item	2013 年	2014 年	2015 年	2016 年
一、年末体委工作人员数	**Workers in Sports Commissions at Year - end**	**923**	**685**	**695**	**705**
#教练员	#Full - time Coaches	140	131	151	152
二、等级裁判员发展人数	**Number of Referees in Grades**	**417**	**520**	**266**	**78**
#女	#Female	140	157	66	44
一级裁判员	First Grade Referees	89	55	34	28
二级裁判员	Second Grade Referees	328	465	232	50
三级裁判员	Third Grade Referees	-	-	-	-
三、等级运动员发展人数	**Number of Athletes in Grades**	**385**	**425**	**349**	**469**
#女	#Female	149	183	149	182
一级运动员	First Grade Athlete	47	124	64	78
二级运动员	Second Grade Athlete	338	301	285	391
三级运动员	Third Grade Athlete	-	-	-	-

主要统计指标解释

文化事业机构 指从事专业文化工作和为专业文化工作服务的独立建制的单独核算的单位。不包括这些单位另外举办独立核算的其他机构和各部门的业余文化组织。

艺术表演团体 指从事戏曲、音乐、舞蹈、杂技等专业艺术表演,有独立帐户,实行单独核算的团体。不包括半工半艺、半农半艺和民间职业剧团。

普通高等学校 指按照国家规定的设置标准和审批程序批准举办,通过国家统一招生考试,招收高中毕业生为主要培养对象,实施高等教育的全日制大学、独立设置的学院和高等专科学校、短期职业大学。

成人高等学校 指按照国家有关规定审批,招收通过全国成人高教统一招生考试的具有高中毕业或同等学历的在职从业人员利用脱产、半脱产、业余或函授等多种形式对其实施高等学历教育,培养高等教育专科或本科毕业水平的专门人才,修业年限、课程设置和总学时数均按高等学历教育要求付诸实施的学校。包括广播电视大学、职工高等学校、农民高等学校、管理干部学院、教育学院、独立设置的函授学院等。

小学学龄儿童入学率 指调查范围内已入小学学习的学龄儿童占校内外学龄儿童总数(包括弱智儿童在内,但不包括盲聋哑儿童)的比重。计算公式:

$$小学学龄儿童入学率=\frac{已入学的小学学龄儿童数}{校内外小学学龄儿童总数}*100\%$$

等级运动员人数 指经考核正式批准授予等级运动员称号的人数。运动员等级分为国际级运动健将、运动健将、一级运动员、二级运动员、三级运动员、少年级运动员。

等级裁判员人数 指经考核正式批准授予等级裁判员称号的人数。裁判员等级分为国际裁判、国家级裁判、一级裁判、二级裁判、三级裁判。

卫生机构 卫生机构是指从卫生行政部门取得《医疗机构执业许可证》,或从民政、工商行政、机构编制管理部门取得法人单位登记证书,为社会提供医疗保健、疾病控制、卫生监督等服务或从事医学科研、医学教育等卫生单位和卫生社会团体。不包括卫生行政机构、香港和澳门特别行政区以及台湾所属卫生机构。

卫生技术人员 卫生技术人员包括执业(助理)医师、注册护士、药剂人员、检验和影像技师(士、员)等卫生专业人员。

执业(助理)医师、执业(中)药师和注册护士 执业(助理)医师、执业(中)药师和注册护士是指领取医师、药师执业证书和注册护士证书的人员。不包括从事管理工作的医师、药师和护士。

Explanatory Notes on Main Statistical Indicators

Cultural Institutions refer to units which have their own organizational system and independent accounting system and specialize in or serve cultural development. They exclude other establishments run by these cultural institutions and amateur cultural groups established by various departments.

Art Troupe refers to the troupe which is engaged in drama, opera, music, dance, acrobatics or other art performance, opens independent accounts with banks and has self – supporting accounting system; excluding the troupes which are engaged partly in industrial or agricultural activities, partly in art performance and the professional troupes organized by the people.

Regular Institutions of Higher Learning refer to educational establishments set up according to the government evaluation and approval procedures, enrolling graduates from senior secondary schools and providing higher education courses and training for senior professionals, They include full – time universities, colleges, high professional schools and short – term professional universities.

Institutions of Higher Learning for Adults refer to educational establishments, set up in line with relevant rules approved by the government, enrolling staff and workers with senior secondary school or equivalent education, and providing higher education courses in many forms of full – time, part – time, space – time, or correspondence for adults. Professionals thus trained receive a qualification equivalent to graduates studying regular courses at regular universities, colleges and professional colleges. Institutions of higher learning for adults include Radio and TV universities, schools of high education for staff and workers and peasants, colleges for management cadres, pedagogical colleges, independent correspondence colleges.

Enrollment Rate of Primary School – age Children refer to the proportion of school – age children enrolled at schools to the total number of school – age children both in and outside schools (including retarded children, but excluding blind, deaf and mute children). The formula is:

$$\text{Enrollment Rate of Primary School – age Children} = \frac{\text{Total primary School – age Children at Schools}}{\text{Total Primary School – age Children Both at and Outside Schools}}$$

Number of Athletes in Grades refers to the number of athletes who have been given titles through examination. The titles of athletes include international masters of sports, masters of sports, first – grade, second – grade and third – grade sportsmen and young athletes.

Number of Referees in Grades refers to the number of referees who have been given titles after examination. They are classified as international referees, national referees and referees of the first, second and third grades.

Health Institutions refers to the Institutions and Society organization that get the registered license of health and medical institution from the health adiministration department, or get the registered license of units from civil administration department, industry and business administration and organization management department, and offers medical treatment, controlling of disease, supervision of sanitation. Health institution excludes health administration department and Institutions of Hong Kong, Macao, and Taiwan.

Medical Technical Personnel include registered (Assistant) doctor, registered nurse, druggist, checking members and photo artificer.

Registered (Assistant) Doctor, Registered Druggist and Registered Nurse refers to the personnel who get the licence of doctor, druggist and nurse, the management staff excluded.

十三、人民生活 物价、民政

PEOPLE’ S LIVELIHOOD, PRICE INDICES AND CIVIL ADMINISTRATION

13 人民生活、物价、民政
People's Livelihood, Price Indices and Civil Administration

主要统计指标
Major Statistical Indicators

非私营单位就业人员工资总额	Total Wages of Employed Persons of Non-private Units	2417.60	亿元	(100 million yuan)
非私营单位就业人员平均工资	Annual Average Wages of Employed Persons of Non-private Units	85022	元	(yuan)
全体居民人均可支配收入	Per Capita Disposable Income of Urban and Rural Residents	46116	元	(yuan)
为上年	As Compared with the Preceding Year	108.1	%	(%)
城镇常住居民人均可支配收入	Per Capita Disposable Income of Permanent Urban Residents	52185	元	(yuan)
为上年	As Compared with the Preceding Year	108.0	%	(%)
农村常住居民人均可支配收入	Per Capita Disposable Income of Permanent Rural Residents	27908	元	(yuan)
为上年	As Compared with the Preceding Year	108.5	%	(%)
市区居民消费价格指数	Consume Price Index of Urban District	102.6	上年=100	(Preceding Year=100)
市区商品零售价格指数	Commodity Retail Price Index of Urban District	101.5	上年=100	(Preceding Year=100)
工业生产者出厂价格指数	Producer Price Indices for Industrial Products	99.2	上年=100	(Preceding Year=100)

13－01　居民家庭人均收入支出(2014－2016年)

Per Capita Income and Expenditure of Households(2014－2016)

单位:元　　　　(yuan)

项　目 Item	全体居民 Urban and Rural Residents			城镇常住居民 Permanent Urban Residents			农村常住居民 Permanent Rural Residents		
	2016	2015	2014	2016	2015	2014	2016	2015	2014
一、可支配收入 Disposable Income	46116	42642	39237	52185	48316	44632	27908	25719	23555
工资性收入 Icome from Wages	26832	25619	24354	30090	28891	27638	17059	15860	14809
经营净收入 Income of Staff & workers in Other－owned Units	5232	5036	4789	4607	4502	4365	7108	6628	6021
财产净收入 Property Income	6214	5377	4719	7906	6851	6039	1137	982	879
转移净收入 Transfer Income	7838	6610	5375	9582	8072	6590	2604	2249	1846
二、消费支出 Expenditure	31905	30181	28492	35686	33818	32165	20563	19334	17816
食品烟酒 Food alcohol and tobacco	8948	8194	7767	9945	9171	8688	5957	5358	5091
衣着 Clothing	2034	1906	1912	2302	2157	2193	1228	1157	1094
居住 Residence	8588	8076	7534	9685	9111	8565	5297	4990	4539
生活用品及服务 Daily necessities and services	1646	1468	1491	1841	1622	1683	1062	1008	933
交通通信 Transportation and Communication	4721	5254	4835	5050	5707	5364	3735	3904	3299
教育文化娱乐 Education, Cultural and Recreation Service	3302	2731	2605	3815	3141	2990	1762	1507	1485
医疗保健 Medicine and Medical Service	1898	1764	1540	2143	2002	1708	1163	1055	1052
其他用品及服务 Other Supplies and Services	768	788	808	905	907	974	359	355	323

注:2014－2016年为城乡住户一体化改革后新口径数据。

a) The data in this table are calculated at new rage by the results of integrated survey of urban households and rural households since 2014.

13－02　城镇住户调查情况(1978－2016年)

Basic Conditions of Urban Households (1978－2016)

年　份 Year	调查户数 (户) Number of Households Surveyed (household)	平均每户人口 (人) Average Household Size (person)	平均每户就业人数(人) Average Number of Employed Persons Per Household(person)	年人均可支配收入(元) Per Capita Annual Disposable Income (yuan)	年人均消费支出(元) Per Capita Annual Consumption Expenditure(yuan)	人均住房建筑面积 (平方米) Per Capita Living Space in City Areas (sq. m)
1978	28	4.20	2.89	338	301	
1979	28	4.19	2.77	396	365	
1980	28	4.18	2.79	521	491	
1981	100	3.97	2.37	540	513	
1982	100	3.90	2.35	532	532	
1983	100	3.90	2.42	578	535	11.7
1984	100	3.90	2.36	729	679	12.4
1985	150	3.53	2.26	1026	908	12.9
1986	150	3.49	2.27	1169	1072	13.2
1987	150	3.42	2.25	1260	1118	14.1
1988	200	3.41	2.16	1565	1515	14.1
1989	200	3.40	2.15	1764	1615	14.1
1990	200	3.37	2.15	1985	1685	14.5
1991	200	3.40	2.20	2128	1894	14.4
1992	200	3.28	2.14	2580	2296	14.8
1993	200	3.21	2.10	3525	3183	14.9
1994	200	3.31	2.10	5249	4559	15.9
1995	200	3.20	2.05	6301	5559	15.6
1996	200	3.20	2.00	7206	6095	15.9
1997	200	3.14	1.99	7896	6766	16.5
1998	300	3.12	1.93	8465	7235	18.8
1999	300	3.11	1.92	9085	7424	19.5
2000	300	3.10	1.83	9668	7790	19.9
2001	440	2.98	1.72	10896	8968	20.7
2002	500	2.93	1.53	11778	9215	21.7
2003	500	2.92	1.51	12898	9950	22.9
2004	500	2.92	1.48	14565	11213	23.7
2005	600	2.84	1.42	16601	13438	27.6
2006	600	2.81	1.44	19027	14472	28.0
2007	600	2.72	1.45	21689	14896	28.8
2008	600	2.75	1.29	24104	16719	29.9
2009	600	2.68	1.25	26864	18595	30.8
2010	600	2.70	1.25	30035	20219	30.9
2011	600	2.71	1.32	34065	22642	33.7
2012	600	2.69	1.31	37511	22800	34.4
2013	1920	2.79	1.51	40925	30659	34.9
2014	1920	2.79	1.53	44632	32165	35.1
2015	1920	2.79	1.48	48316	33818	35.5
2016	1920	2.80	1.49	52185	35686	35.8

注:2000年及以前为主城区数据;2001－2012年为包括萧山区和余杭区在内的市区数据;2013－2016年为包括所有区、县(市)城乡住户一体化改革后新口径数据。

a) The data on the table include the main urban districts before 2000; The data include Xiaoshan district and Yuhang district in 2001－2012; The date include all districts and counties since 2013; The data in this table are calculated at new rage by the results of integrated survey of urban households and rural households sine 2013.

13－03 城镇居民家庭平均每百户耐用消费品拥有量(主要年份)
Number of Major Durable Consumer Goods Owned Per 100 Urban Households(Main Years)

项目 Item	1995	2000	2005	2010	2011	2012	2013	2014	2015	2016
家用汽车 Family Car (辆)(unit)		0.7	12.8	22.8	31.2	34.3	40.2	45.4	48.7	52.3
摩托车 Motorcycle (辆)(unit)	1.5	3.6	11.0	4.5	4.1	4.0	6.6	6.8	5.4	5.0
电冰箱 Refrigerator (台)(unit)	103.5	101.7	100.0	102.3	102.5	102.5	88.0	92.3	92.2	97.6
洗衣机 Washing Machine (台)(unit)	93.5	96.3	94.2	96.2	96.3	96.6	82.6	86.8	86.9	92.6
热水器 Water Heater (台)(unit)	43.5	81.3	92.3	99.4	103.4	105.4	89.4	93.7	95.5	101.4
空调器 Air Conditioner (台)(unit)	43.0	104.0	183.3	214.6	212.0	214.7	189.6	201.5	207.3	226.6
彩色电视机 Color TV Set (台)(unit)	102.3	146.7	182.7	179.2	176.9	178.4	166.4	174.0	174.1	183.1
摄像机 Video Recorder (架)(unit)		3.3	7.5	11.1	11.6	12.4	10.0	10.5	10.5	10.3
照相机 Camera (架)(unit)	54.0	64.7	59.0	54.8	62.1	63.5	50.6	54.4	51.5	48.4
计算机 Computer (台)(unit)		23.0	74.5	99.0	109.7	112.2	103.7	110.6	110.1	112.0
#接入互联网的计算机 of which: Internet－connected computer (台)(unit)				78.7	92.3	98.6	92.5	100.2	99.8	100.8
固定电话 Telephone (部)(set)		95.0	99.8	89.6	84.7	83.6	51.6	54.2	50.7	47.3
移动电话 Mobile Phone (部)(set)		19.0	178.7	193.6	211.0	213.1	217.4	227.9	229.9	242.1
#接入互联网的移动电话 of which: Internet－connected Mobile Phone (部)(set)							125.1	140.8	155.8	175.3

注:2000 年及以前为主城区数据;2001－2012 年为包括萧山区和余杭区在内的市区数据;2013－2016 年为包括所有区、县(市)城乡住户一体化改革后新口径数据。

a) The data on the table include the main urban districts before 2000; The data include Xiaoshan district and Yuhang district in 2001－2012; The date include all districts and counties since 2013; The data in this table are calculated at new rage by the results of integrated survey of urban households and rural households sine 2013.

13-04 全市农村住户调查情况(1978-2016年)

Basic Conditions of Whole Municipality Rural Households(1978-2016)

年份 Year	调查户数(户) Number of Households Surveyed (household)	平均每户人口(人) Average Number of Residents per Household (person)	平均每户就业人数(人) Average Number of Employed Persons Per Household (person)	人均可支配收入(元) Per Capita Annual Net Income of Rural Households (yuan)	人均消费支出(元) Per Capita Annual Consumption Expenditure (yuan)	人均住房建筑面积(平方米) Per Capita Floor Space (sq. m)
1978				162		
1979				204		
1980	60	4.72	2.93	250	287	23.3
1981	60	4.60	2.70	333	294	25.2
1982	60	4.43	2.73	405	328	26.3
1983	170	4.55	2.85	395	355	29.9
1984	170	4.44	2.81	510	416	31.7
1985	420	4.40	2.88	624	542	29.9
1986	620	4.39	2.88	675	601	31.3
1987	620	4.34	2.86	820	714	33.1
1988	620	4.26	2.87	996	925	35.5
1989	620	4.17	2.85	1117	1011	36.8
1990	620	4.16	2.89	1171	923	39.6
1991	620	4.03	2.81	1308	1018	38.0
1992	620	4.01	2.81	1493	1129	37.5
1993	540	3.91	2.76	1748	1276	37.1
1994	630	3.85	2.35	2267	1884	37.8
1995	630	3.87	2.30	3012	2373	40.5
1996	630	3.81	2.77	3482	2772	42.2
1997	630	3.87	2.86	3785	2762	42.0
1998	630	3.87	2.88	4006	2858	46.2
1999	630	3.80	2.80	4209	2851	48.0
2000	630	3.61	2.59	4894	3393	49.0
2001	630	3.57	2.53	5330	3909	52.0
2002	630	3.53	2.53	5708	4444	52.7
2003	670	3.48	2.53	6250	5142	54.7
2004	670	3.48	2.54	6950	5608	58.9
2005	1100	3.34	2.34	7655	6004	66.0
2006	1100	3.63	2.52	8515	6901	66.5
2007	1100	3.60	2.61	9549	7568	68.0
2008	1100	3.56	2.58	10692	8446	69.7
2009	1100	3.57	2.59	11822	9065	70.7
2010	1100	3.58	2.59	13186	10267	71.2
2011	1100	3.46	2.49	15245	12125	72.5
2012	1100	3.45	2.50	17017	13612	71.0
2013	1280	3.38	2.03	21208	16021	66.9
2014	1280	3.35	2.05	23555	17816	67.9
2015	1280	3.36	2.02	25719	19334	68.8
2016	1280	3.38	2.04	27908	20563	69.9

注:2013-2016年为城乡住户一体化改革后新口径数据。

a) The data in this table are calculated at new rage by the results of integrated survey of urban households and rural households sine 2013.

13－05　农村居民家庭平均每百户耐用消费品拥有量(主要年份)

Number of Major Durable Consumer Goods Owned Per 100 Rural Households(Main Years)

项　　目	Item	2000	2005	2010	2011	2012	2013	2014	2015	2016
家用汽车　(辆)	Family Car　(Unit)		4.0	15.7	21.6	27.5	28.8	34.3	38.2	42.4
摩托车　(辆)	Motorcycle　(Unit)	38.0	73.0	66.2	40.8	42.6	33.5	32.7	30.7	26.0
电冰箱　(台)	Refrigerator　(Unit)	46.0	72.0	98.1	93.3	101.8	93.8	99.5	103.9	109.0
洗衣机　(台)	Washing Machine　(Unit)	34.0	62.0	85.1	78.2	87.8	78.3	82.7	86.4	92.5
热水器　(台)	Water Heater　(Unit)			84.5	80.7	90.9	79.3	85.9	93.2	103.2
空调机　(台)	Air Conditioner　(Unit)	8.0	12.0	111.2	120.3	143.3	122.9	135.9	147.6	168.2
彩色电视机(台)	Color TV Set　(Unit)	86.0	141.0	186.3	192.5	210.6	186.0	196.1	202.0	213.5
摄像机　(架)	Video Recorder　(Unit)			2.0	1.3	1.8	2.3	2.5	2.9	2.4
照相机　(架)	Camera　(Unit)	7.0	14.0	22.6	21.7	26.5	21.1	21.1	19.6	19.8
计算机　(台)	Personal Computer　(Unit)	1.0	12.0	44.2	51.3	60.4	59.3	67.3	69.6	75.0
#接入互联网的计算机　(台)	of which: Internet－connected computer　(Unit)				44.6	51.8	51.5	59.8	64.2	68.5
固定电话　(部)	Telephone　(Set)						49.6	52.7	46.4	35.0
移动电话　(部)	Mobile Phone　(Set)	17.0	125.0	212.9	230.4	253.1	235.5	244.6	253.8	265.2
#接入互联网的移动电话　(部)	of which: Internet－connected Mobile Phone　(Set)						106.0	121.2	141.7	172.2

注:2013－2016 年为城乡住户一体化改革后新口径数据。

a) The data in this table are calculated at new rage by the results of integrated survey of urban households and rural households since 2013.

13－06　全市就业人员工资总额(1978－2016年)
Total Wages of Employed Persons(1978－2016)

单位:万元　　(10000 yuan)

年　份 Year	全市(非私营及规上私营) Total (includes private units above designated size)	非私营单位 Non－private	市区(非私营及规上私营) Urban District (includes private units above designated size)	非私营单位 Non－private
1978		43775		28256
1979		52127		34318
1980		67918		45574
1981		72896		48809
1982		75584		50959
1983		78336		52909
1984		102223		69135
1985		130114		87774
1986		157471		105995
1987		180077		121003
1988		230868		152859
1989		253956		167055
1990		277910		182985
1991		313906		209052
1992		377614		253653
1993		534537		359041
1994		772236		521669
1995		890488		615450
1996		973592		683244
1997		1073862		762957
1998		1112718		803264
1999		1180947		864418
2000		1267524		949872
2001		1481659		1279749
2002		1614676		1398222
2003		1867776		1617504
2004	2844691	2188159	2313930	1859164
2005	3711915	2970200	3112937	2584779
2006	4526841	3811735	3830043	3338568
2007	6233799	4954813	5256791	4317965
2008	8592198	6416424	7338932	5679543
2009	9909330	7549145	8475547	6665279
2010	12305726	9330552	10531483	8238017
2011	15012179	11222834	12934215	9954506
2012	19540005	14839012	17115217	13217453
2013	23604682	17582336	20762852	15820468
2014	26630950	19822713	24629017	18551986
2015	28884146	21523984	26718242	20179320
2016	32370091	24176045	29918514	22617274

注:口径范围,1997年及以前为全市全部职工,1998－2012为在岗职工,2013年起为就业人员。2004年起包含规模以上私营单位。

a) Data on this table refer to wages of all employees before 1997, that refer to all staff and workers in 1998－2012, and refer to employed persons since 2013. Data on this bill includes Private units above designated size since 2004.

13－07 全市就业人员年平均工资(1978－2016年)

Average Annual Wages of Employed Persons(1978－2016)

单位:元 (yuan)

年份 Year	全市(非私营及规上私营) Total (includes private units above designated size)	非私营单位 Non－private	市区(非私营及规上私营) Urban District (includes private units above designated size)	非私营单位 Non－private	市区全社会在岗职工 The Fully Employed Persons in Urban Districts
1978		597		642	
1979		643		692	
1980		777		814	
1981		783		810	
1982		791		809	
1983		813		835	
1984		1036		1071	
1985		1266		1316	
1986		1469		1536	
1987		1616		1690	
1988		1986		2073	
1989		2173		2261	
1990		2382		2486	
1991		2586		2706	
1992		3071		3233	
1993		4220		4561	
1994		6118		6597	
1995		7156		7786	
1996		7966		7851	
1997		9108		10048	
1998		10555		11512	
1999		12187		13225	
2000		14257		15454	
2001		18319		18962	18205
2002		21418		22091	19749
2003		24668		25535	20113
2004	21879	28891	24204	30719	22235
2005	24685	31069	26366	32166	22645
2006	27620	32791	29397	33967	23581
2007	29864	36496	31625	37991	25489
2008	32513	40193	34107	41501	27863
2009	35638	43947	37270	45149	30480
2010	39772	48772	41303	49938	34330
2011	45775	54408	47695	55958	38837
2012	51077	56417	52610	57548	42493
2013	55124	63664	56857	64941	46831
2014	60904	69209	61924	70034	51449
2015	66322	76073	67569	77061	55908
2016	73390	85022	74589	85767	61174

注:口径范围,1997年及以前为全市全部职工,1998－2012为在岗职工,2013年起为就业人员。2004年起包含规模以上私营单位。

a) Data on this table refer to wages of all employees before 1997, that refer to all staff and workers in 1998－2012, and refer to employed persons since 2013. Data on this bill includes Private units above designated size since 2004.

13－08　全市非私营及规上私营单位就业人员工资总额(2016年)

Total Wages of Employed Persons Including Private Units Above Designated Size(2016)

单位：万元　　　　(10000 yuan)

项　目 Item		就业人员工资总额 Total Wages of Employed Persons	非私营 Non－private	在岗职工工资总额 Total Wages of Fully Employed Staff and Workers	非私营 Non－private	其他就业人员工资总额 Total Wages of Other Employed Persons	非私营 Non－private
全市总计	**Whole city Total**	**32370091**	**24176045**	**30597509**	**23184590**	**1772582**	**991455**
市区总计	Urban District	29918514	22617274	28236456	21677301	1682058	939972
#上城区	Shangcheng	2251257	1910370	2075573	1811631	175684	98739
下城区	Xiacheng	2678809	2460384	2551902	2364882	126907	95502
江干区	Jianggan	3342006	2098102	2713138	1859536	628869	238566
拱墅区	Gongshu	2037729	1197136	1929232	1114220	108497	82916
西湖区	Xihu	4531811	3914661	4282218	3754883	249593	159779
高新(滨江)区	Hi－Tech(Binjiang)	3405144	2909192	3374923	2889427	30221	19765
萧山区	Xiaoshan	5072949	3364190	4927711	3275949	145237	88241
大江东产业集聚区	Dajiangdong Industry Cluster District	700429	474560	685535	464037	14894	10523
余杭区	Yuhang	3461731	2353554	3377525	2299698	84206	53856
富阳区	Fuyang	1331259	822899	1279768	795513	51491	27385
经济技术开发区	Economic and Technological Development Zone	1615162	1406838	1566099	1363772	49064	43066
西湖风景名胜区	The West Lake Scenic Zone	190658	179948	158369	147789	32289	32159
桐庐县	Tonglu	629747	343324	609081	331358	20666	11966
淳安县	Chun'an	425892	290560	401468	280851	24424	9709
建德市	Jiande	472048	316641	450145	305510	21903	11131
临安市	Lin'an	923890	608247	900359	589571	23531	18676

单位:万元　　　　13－08　续表　continued　　　　(10000 yuan)

项　目 Item	就业人员工资总额 Total Wages of Employed Persons	非私营 Non－private	在岗职工工资总额 Total Wages of Fully Employed Staff and Workers	非私营 Non－private	其他就业人员工资总额 Total Wages of Other Employed Persons	非私营 Non－private
按国民经济行业分组 **Grouped by Sector**						
农、林、牧、渔业 Farming, Forestry, Animal Husbandry & Fishery	4639	4621	4470	4453	169	169
采矿业 Mining	13977	5829	13519	5448	458	381
制造业 Manufacturing	6952629	4808462	6843538	4727833	109091	80629
电力、热力、燃气及水生产和供应业 Production & Supply of Electricity, Heat, Gas & Water	233310	224318	231167	222252	2143	2066
建筑业 Construction	7880605	3967250	6880453	3653916	1000152	313334
批发和零售业 Wholesale & Retail Trades	1882999	1355648	1828218	1310309	54781	45339
交通运输、仓储和邮政业 Transportation, Storage and Post	1244861	1046334	1225640	1036364	19220	9969
住宿和餐饮业 Hotels and Catering Services	443405	311256	418839	291278	24567	19979
信息传输、软件和信息技术服务业 Information Transmission, Software and Information Technology	2460233	2078631	2452826	2073060	7407	5571
金融业 Financial Intermediation	2046112	2040142	1864376	1858615	181736	181528
房地产业 Real Estate	970707	785575	928001	747652	42705	37923
租赁和商务服务业 Leasing and Business Services	1074012	766472	1028516	733315	45497	33157
科学研究、技术服务业 Scientific Research, Technical Services	1266851	1110498	1223621	1076640	43230	33858
水利、环境和公共设施管理业 Management of Water Conservancy, Environment and Public Facilities	286659	191165	276226	183553	10433	7612
居民服务、修理和其他服务业 Service to Honseholds, Repair and Other Services	117185	59005	109438	57759	7748	1246
教育 Education	1976501	1955261	1917532	1896781	58969	58481
卫生和社会工作 Health Care and Social Work	1497553	1463694	1403529	1373366	94024	90328
文化、体育和娱乐业 Culture, Sports and Entertainment	288383	272414	256494	240893	31889	31521
公共管理、社会保障和社会组织 Public Management, Social Security and Social Organizations	1729470	1729470	1691105	1691105	38365	38365

13－09　全市非私营及规上私营单位就业人员平均工资(2016 年)

Average Annual Wages of Employed Persons Including Private Units Above Designated Size(2016)

单位:元　　(yuan)

项目	Item	就业人员 Total employment	非私营单位 Non－private	在岗职工 Staff and Workers	非私营单位 Non－private
全市	**Total**	**73390**	**85022**	**75137**	**87153**
市区	Urban District	74589	85767	76430	87921
#上城区	Shangcheng	92058	104878	94454	107044
下城区	Xiacheng	100501	109735	104871	113275
江干区	Jianggan	71485	89178	74864	90568
拱墅区	Gongshu	63386	75225	65069	79936
西湖区	Xihu	70637	73130	73070	75836
高新(滨江)区	Hi－Tech(Binjiang)	104722	114281	105632	115139
萧山区	Xiaoshan	60646	68039	61127	68501
大江东产业集聚区	Dajiangdong Industry Cluster District	62281	70959	63379	72297
余杭区	Yuhang	75728	95860	76988	98447
富阳区	Fuyang	59196	70274	60348	72443
经济技术开发区	Economic and Technological Development Zone	82325	86728	82609	86777
西湖风景名胜区	The West Lake Scenic Zone	64418	66294	77731	82343
桐庐县	Tonglu	59054	75802	59786	77638
淳安县	Chun'an	65467	80686	67803	83038
建德市	Jiande	61122	74814	63264	77578
临安市	Lin'an	61324	73448	61846	74838

项 目 Item	就业人员 Total employment	非私营单位 Non－private	在岗职工 Staff and Workers	非私营单位 Non－private
按国民经济行业分组 Grouped by Sector				
农、林、牧、渔业 Farming, Forestry, Animal Husbandry & Fishery	55089	55280	57602	57829
采矿业 Mining	56932	55513	57799	55994
制造业 Manufacturing	64633	73528	64538	73346
电力、热力、燃气及水生产和供应业 Production & Supply of Electricity, Heat, Gas & Water	117578	122198	118681	123384
建筑业 Construction	50593	52269	50712	52806
批发和零售业 Wholesale & Retail Trades	68961	77434	69784	78824
交通运输、仓储和邮政业 Transportation, Storage and Post	87296	93112	88681	94247
住宿和餐饮业 Hotels and Catering Services	44921	47311	47828	52116
信息传输、软件和信息技术服务业 Information Transmission, Software and Information Technology	149412	167795	150172	168559
金融业 Financial Intermediation	177748	178136	202590	202983
房地产业 Real Estate	73172	74339	75383	76878
租赁和商务服务业 Leasing and Business Services	67305	68748	69461	70931
科学研究、技术服务业 Scientific Research, Technical Services	93004	98496	94294	99448
水利、环境和公共设施管理业 Management of Water Conservancy, Environment and Public Facilities	68521	71758	70115	74046
居民服务、修理和其他服务业 Service to Honseholds, Repair and Other Services	46947	55001	46941	55166
教育 Education	106750	108395	112364	114272
卫生和社会工业 Health Care and Social Work	129441	132804	133469	136965
文化、体育和娱乐业 Culture, Sports and Entertainment	105184	112424	117842	128510
公共管理、社会保障和社会组织 Public Management, Social Security and Social Organizations	126655	126655	131994	131994

13－10 市区消费价格指数(1978－2016年)

Consumer Price Indices in Urban District(1978－2016)

(上年＝100)　　(Preceding Year＝100)

年　份 Year	居民消费价格指数 Consumer Price Index	商品零售价格指数 Retail Price Index
1978	100.1	100.1
1979	100.4	100.9
1980	100.8	109.3
1981	102.0	102.0
1982	102.0	102.3
1983	102.1	102.3
1984	103.1	103.1
1985	117.2	117.5
1986	106.0	106.1
1987	110.5	111.3
1988	121.9	123.4
1989	117.8	118.2
1990	104.6	104.4
1991	107.5	106.9
1992	110.4	110.2
1993	121.4	117.3
1994	121.5	118.8
1995	116.5	113.3
1996	110.5	107.2
1997	106.7	102.4
1998	101.8	99.8
1999	100.4	98.2
2000	100.8	98.3
2001	99.5	95.3
2002	98.8	97.9
2003	99.5	98.1
2004	102.5	101.6
2005	101.7	100.3
2006	101.2	100.2
2007	103.5	103.1
2008	104.9	106.0
2009	98.6	98.6
2010	103.9	103.7
2011	104.8	104.4
2012	102.5	101.9
2013	102.5	101.5
2014	102.0	100.8
2015	101.8	100.2
2016	102.6	101.5

13－11　市区居民消费价格分类指数(2016年)

Consumer Price Indices by Category in Urban District(2016)

(上年＝100)　　(Preceding Year＝100)

项目	Item	2016
居民消费价格总指数	**Consumer Price Index**	**102.6**
一、食品烟酒	**Food, Tobacco and Liquor**	**106.0**
1.食品	Food	106.2
(1)粮食	Grain	100.5
(2)薯类	Tubers	103.8
(3)豆类	Beans	98.9
(4)食用油	Edible Oil and Fats	98.9
(5)菜	Vegetables	115.4
(6)畜肉类	Meat of Livestock	113.5
(7)禽肉类	Meat of Poultry	103.5
(8)水产品	Aquatic Products	105.4
(9)蛋类	Eggs	97.4
(10)奶类	Milk	100.3
(11)干鲜瓜果类	Dried and Fresh Melons and Fruits	100.9
(12)糖果糕点类	Candy and Cake	103.2
(13)调味品	Flavoring	104.3
(14)其他食品类	Other Foods	100.6
2.茶及饮料	Tea and Beverages	101.0
3.烟酒	Tobacco and Liquor	103.2
4.在外餐饮	Dining Out	106.9
二、衣着	**Clothing**	**100.3**
1.服装	Garments	100.8
2.服装材料	Garments Material	104.3
3.其他衣着及配件	Other Clothing and Parts	99.7
4.衣着加工服务费	Clothing Manufacturing Services	107.0

项　目	Item	2016
5. 鞋类	Footwear	97.8
三、居住	**Residence**	**102.2**
1. 租赁房房租	Rent of Rental Housing	101.9
2. 住房保养维修及管理	Housing Maintenance and Management	103.0
3. 水电燃料	Water, Electricity and Fuels	101.5
4. 自有住房	Private Housing	102.2
四、生活用品及服务	**Articles for Daily Use and Services**	**99.6**
1. 家具及室内装饰品	Furniture and Interior Decorations	99.8
2. 家用器具	Home Appliances	98.4
3. 家用纺织品	Home Textiles	95.3
4. 家庭日用杂品	Daily Use Household Articles	99.8
5. 个人护理用品	Personal - care Supplies	101.6
6. 家庭服务	Household Services	103.9
五、交通和通信	**Transport and Communications**	**99.0**
1. 交通	Transport	99.6
2. 通信	Communications	97.7
六、教育文化和娱乐	**Education, Culture and Recreation**	**103.7**
1. 教育	Education	106.9
2. 文化娱乐	Cultural and Recreation	100.0
七、医疗保健	**Health Care**	**100.8**
1. 药品及医疗器具	Medicine and Medical Instrument	102.1
2. 医疗服务	Medical Services	100.0
八、其他用品和服务	**Other Articles and Services**	**102.7**
1. 其他用品类	Other Articles	106.1
2. 其他服务类	Other Services	100.5

13-12 市区零售价格分类指数(2016年)
Retail Price Indices by Category in Urban District(2016)

(上年=100) (Preceding Year=100)

项目	Item	2016
商品零售价格指数	**Retail Price Index**	**101.5**
一、食品	**Food**	**106.1**
1. 粮食	Grain	100.5
2. 薯类	Tubers	103.8
3. 豆类	Beans	98.9
4. 食用油	Edible Oil and Fats	98.9
5. 菜	Vegetables	115.4
6. 畜肉类	Meat of Livestock	113.5
7. 禽肉类	Meat of Poultry	103.5
8. 水产品	Aquatic Products	105.3
9. 蛋类	Eggs	97.4
10. 奶类	Milk	100.3
11. 干鲜瓜果类	Dried and Fresh Melons and Fruits	100.9
12. 糖果糕点类	Candy and Cake	103.2
13. 调味品	Flavoring	104.1
14. 其他食品类	Other Foods	100.6
15. 在外餐饮	Dining out	106.9
二、饮料、烟酒	**Beverages,Tobacco and Liquor**	**102.6**
1. 茶及饮料	Tea and Beverages	101.0
2. 烟草	Tobacco	104.0
3. 酒类	Liquor	101.4
三、服装、鞋帽	**Garments,Shoes and Hats**	**100.1**
1. 服装	Garments	100.8
2. 鞋帽袜	Footgear and Hat	98.1
3. 其他衣着配件	Other Clothing and Parts	97.9
四、纺织品	**Textiles**	**97.3**
1. 服装材料	Garments Material	104.3
2. 床上用品	Bedding	94.8
五、家用电器及音像器材	**Household Appliances, Music and Video Equipment**	**97.3**
1. 家庭设备	Household Equipment	98.1
2. 文娱用耐用消费品	Durable Consumer Goods for Entertainment	95.4

项目	Item	2016
3. 专业音像器材	Audio and Video Equipment	97.6
六、文化办公用品	**Cultural and office Appliances**	**97.3**
七、日用品	**Articles for Daily Use**	**99.7**
1. 日用百货	General Merchandise for Daily Use	98.9
2. 厨具餐具茶具	Kitchen Ware, Table Ware, Tea Set	98.6
3. 清洗用品	Cleaning Supplies	100.9
4. 其他日用品	Other Articles for Daily Use	100.6
八、体育娱乐用品	**Sports and Recreation Articles**	**98.5**
1. 体育户外用品	Sports Outdoor Products	100.6
2. 娱乐用品	Recreation Articles	97.7
九、交通、通信用品	**Transportation and Communication Appliances**	**97.8**
1. 交通运输机械	Transportation Vehicles	99.8
2. 通信器材	Equipment of Communication	89.2
十、家具	**Furniture**	**99.9**
十一、化妆品	**Cosmetics**	**101.9**
十二、金银饰品	**Gold and Silver Ornaments**	**109.9**
十三、中西药品及医疗保健用品	**Traditional Chinese and Western Medicine and Health Care Articles**	**102.3**
1. 医疗卫生器具	Medical Instruments and Articles	98.3
2. 中药	Traditional Chinese Medicines	105.0
3. 西药	Western Medicines	100.1
4. 保健器具及用品	Articles for Health Care	105.2
十四、书报杂志及电子出版物	**Books, Newspapers, Magazines and Electronic Publications**	**105.6**
1. 教材及参考书	Teaching Materials and Reference Books	98.7
2. 书报杂志	Books, Newspapers and Magazines	100.0
3. 计算机办公软件	Computer Office Software	130.6
十五、燃料	**Fuels**	**102.5**
1. 煤炭及制品	Coal and Coal Products	111.4
2. 石油及制品	Oil and Oil Products	101.6
十六、建筑材料及五金电料	**Building Materials and Hardware**	**101.2**
1. 建筑装璜材料	Building Decoration Materials	101.6
2. 五金水暖	Hardware	100.1

13－13　工业生产者出厂价格指数(主要年份)
Producer Price Indices for Industrial Products(Main Years)

(上年＝100)　(Preceding Year＝100)

项　目 Item	2000	2005	2010	2011	2012	2013	2014	2015	2016
工业生产者出厂价格总指数 Total Producer Price Indices for Industrial Products	**100.3**	**103.5**	**104.9**	**104.7**	**97.2**	**98.5**	**98.6**	**96.5**	**99.2**
一、按轻重工业分 Grouped by Industries									
轻工业 Light Industry	**99.3**	**101.8**	**105.0**	**105.5**	**98.1**	**99.9**	**99.2**	**97.4**	**99.8**
以农产品为原料 Made from Agricultural Products	99.9	102.0	103.9	104.6	99.4	100.8	99.9	98.5	99.8
以非农产品为原料 Made from Non－agricultural Products	98.0	101.7	106.0	106.8	96.1	98.4	98.2	95.8	99.8
重工业 Heavy Industry	**101.1**	**105.6**	**104.7**	**104.2**	**96.5**	**97.5**	**98.2**	**95.8**	**98.7**
采掘 Mining & Quarrying Industry	99.5	103.0	114.0	116.6	101.3	101.0	104.2	94.9	97.3
原料 Raw Materials Industry	104.4	107.7	110.7	108.7	96.9	97.5	96.7	92.5	96.4
加工 Manufacturing Industry	98.9	104.3	102.5	102.8	96.4	97.5	98.5	96.7	99.4
二、按二大部类分 Grouped by Means of Producting and Consumer Goods									
生产资料 Means of Production	**101.9**	**104.8**	**106.2**	**105.1**	**95.5**	**97.8**	**98.0**	**95.3**	**98.8**
采掘 Mining	99.6	103.0	114.0	116.6	101.3	101.0	104.2	94.9	97.3
原料 Raw Materials	103.8	110.7	114.5	110.6	92.6	96.5	95.7	91.0	96.1
加工 Manufacture	100.3	101.6	103.9	103.3	96.4	98.2	98.7	96.6	99.6
生活资料 Consumer Goods	**97.5**	**101.2**	**101.0**	**103.7**	**102.6**	**100.6**	**100.6**	**100.1**	**100.1**
食品 Foods	96.4	101.6	100.1	104.3	101.8	101.0	101.1	100.9	100.0
衣着 Clothing	101.1	101.4	102.4	104.5	104.6	102.0	100.1	100.1	101.1
一般日用品 Articles for Daily Use	97.8	101.7	100.8	103.9	102.3	99.8	100.7	99.9	100.5
耐用消费品 Durable Consumer Goods	94.5	99.5	100.9	101.5	102.0	99.6	100.0	99.2	99.1

（上年＝100） 13－13 续表 continued （Preceding Year＝100）

项目 Item	2000	2005	2010	2011	2012	2013	2014	2015	2016
三、按工业部门分 Grouped by Industrial Sector									
冶金工业 Metallurgical Industry	104.0	104.8	108.0	107.1	93.3	95.4	96.2	93.2	101.7
电力工业 Power Industry	96.0	106.2	105.2	102.0	101.7	99.1	99.6	98.2	97.8
煤炭及炼焦工业 Coal and Coking Industry	107.9	102.1		–					
石油工业 Petroleum Industry	131.6	124.7	117.0	110.4	103.0	100.5	100.5	92.4	87.7
化学工业 Chemical Industry	101.1	106.0	111.9	109.3	93.8	97.3	95.8	92.7	97.3
机械工业 Machine Building Industry	96.7	102.9	100.8	101.3	97.6	98.1	98.9	97.6	99.4
建材材料工业 Building Materials Industry	103.0	91.7	109.3	109.8	94.0	97.3	103.0	94.0	96.3
森林工业 Timber Industry	96.9	101.4	101.6	102.0	100.7	101.0	101.3	99.9	98.9
食品工业 Food Industry	95.8	100.6	100.1	105.1	102.0	101.2	100.5	100.2	100.2
纺织工业 Textile Industry	107.3	103.4	107.5	105.1	95.5	101.1	98.9	96.3	100.1
缝纫工业 Tailoring Industry	100.5	101.5	102.2	105.6	104.6	102.6	100.5	99.8	99.6
皮革工业 Leather Industry	98.0	101.4	102.9	101.9	103.4	101.1	101.0	100.4	100.5
造纸工业 Paper Industry	102.9	100.3	104.6	102.0	96.7	96.3	99.7	98.5	98.9
文教艺术用品工业 Cultural, Educational & Handicrafts Articles	98.7	99.7	97.3	100.9	100.1	100.0	98.8	98.9	99.5
其它工业 Others	103.6	102.2	104.7	109.0	103.9	101.3	104.6	102.9	105.5

13-14 工业生产者购进价格指数(主要年份)

Purchasing Price Indices for Industrial Producers(Main Years)

(上年=100) (Preceding Year=100)

项目 Item	2000	2005	2010	2011	2012	2013	2014	2015	2016
工业生产者购进价格指数 Purchasing Price Index for Industrial Producers	**107.4**	**106.9**	**112.1**	**110.8**	**94.6**	**97.3**	**97.3**	**92.9**	**98.9**
燃料动力类 Fuel and Power	108.0	116.4	111.3	110.6	98.2	96.9	99.0	95.1	93.6
黑色金属材料类 Ferrous and Metals	102.7	105.2	108.6	107.0	88.7	95.0	92.4	85.9	100.9
1. 钢材 Rolled -steel	103.2	104.9	108.2	106.6	88.5	95.4	92.5	86.3	101.0
2. 其他 Other	101.0	105.7	113.0	113.1	91.2	90.1	90.3	80.5	98.2
有色金属材料及电线类 Non-ferrous Metals and Electric Wire	108.0	111.2	129.3	113.4	93.1	93.7	94.5	92.2	101.3
化工原料类 Chemical Raw Materials	111.0	110.1	113.3	114.3	94.2	97.0	97.7	91.7	100.8
木材及纸浆类 Wood and Paper Pulps	104.5	101.0	106.4	104.0	97.7	98.8	98.5	98.5	99.8
建筑材料及非金属类 Building Materials	100.6	102.3	108.8	116.8	99.5	99.4	105.7	96.9	99.0
农副产品类 Farm and Sideline Products	104.0	103.9	114.1	112.8	97.2	98.4	100.4	99.3	99.3
其他工业原材料及半成品类 Other Industrial Raw Materials and Semi-products	111.0	103.6	109.8	107.2	99.1	97.8	98.9	96.7	98.8
纺织原料类 Textile Raw Materials	104.7	99.9	110.4	110.5	96.3	101.9	99.9	97.1	98.8

13-15 住宅销售价格指数(2016年)
Sales Price Indices of Houses(2016)

月份 Month	新建住宅 New Residential Building		新建商品住宅 New Residential Commodities Building		二手住宅 The Second-hand House	
	上月=100	上年同期=100 Preceding Year =100	上月=100	上年同期=100 Preceding Year =100	上月=100	上年同期=100 Preceding Year =100
一月 January	100.9	107	100.9	107.1	100.5	104.4
二月 February	101.3	108.8	101.3	108.9	101.1	105.9
三月 March	102.3	111.8	102.3	111.9	102	108.2
四月 April	103	114.7	103	114.8	101.8	109.9
五月 May	102.5	116.9	102.5	117	101.3	111.1
六月 June	101.6	117.2	101.6	117.4	101.2	111.7
七月 July	102.3	119	102.4	119.1	102.3	113.6
八月 August	103.3	122	103.3	122.2	102.8	116.2
九月 September	105.5	128	105.5	128.2	104.5	121
十月 October	103.1	131.3	103.2	131.5	102.5	123.9
十一月 November	99.7	129.9	99.6	130.1	100	123.1
十二月 December	100	128.4	100	128.6	99.9	121.7

13－16 分地区社会办福利院情况(2016年末)

Basic Statistics on Welfare Homes by Region(End of 2016)

地区 Region	单位(个) Homes (unit)	职工(人) Staff and Workers (person)	床位数(张) Beds (bed)	在院人数(人) Persons Housed (person)	老人(人) Seniors(person)
全市 Total	**333**	**4921**	**67293**	**25077**	**24088**
市区 Urban District	211	4288	50933	18846	17923
#萧山区 Xiaoshan	46	1759	11011	3158	3087
余杭区 Yuhang	33	405	8349	2383	2345
富阳区 Fuyang	31	230	4656	1302	1281
桐庐县 Tonglu	26	192	3556	994	977
淳安县 Chun'an	31	133	3932	1182	1177
建德市 Jiande	33	149	4313	1646	1636
临安市 Lin'an	32	159	4559	2409	2375

13－17 分地区优抚对象

Number of Persons Enjoying

单位：人

指 标 Item	全 市 Total	市 区 Urban District	上城区 Shangcheng	下城区 Xiacheng	江干区 Jianggan
享受定期抚恤金人数 Number of Persons Receiving Periodical Commiseration	563	276	10	4	6
烈属 Number of Martyr Kinsfolk	288	108	5	2	1
牺牲军人家属 Number of the Sacrifice Soldiers	96	63	–	2	–
病故军人家属 Number of Kinsfolks of the Illness－died Soldiers	179	105	5	–	5
享受定期补助人数 Number of Persons Enjoying Regular Subsidies	37822	21416	301	322	602
在乡复员军人 Rural Demobilized Soldier	1978	963	5	10	11
抗日 The War of Resistance Against Japan	19	8	2	3	–
优待优抚对象带病回乡退伍军人 Number of Rural Veterans with Illness Receiving Subsiders	2828	1476	1	2	14
优待优抚对象户数 Number of Households Receiving Subsiders	36779	19727	176	177	544

人员情况(2016 年)
Public Subsidies by Region(2016)

(person)

拱墅区 Gongshu	西湖区 Xihu	高新(滨江)区 Hi - Tech (Binjiang)	萧山区 Xiaoshan	余杭区 Yuhang	富阳区 Fuyang	桐庐县 Tonglu	淳安县 Chun'an	建德市 Jiande	临安市 Lin'an
7	19	3	64	53	110	82	83	65	57
5	8	3	21	24	39	47	54	39	40
1	8	–	9	10	33	15	5	9	4
1	3	–	34	19	38	20	24	17	13
154	1231	88	8772	4819	5127	4654	2459	4228	5065
16	37	23	295	284	282	265	223	229	298
1	–	–	1	1	–	7	–	–	4
1	18	11	407	195	827	718	140	339	155
379	1248	173	8109	4700	4221	4992	2669	4139	5252

13－18 市、县级社会

Basic Statistics on Institutions and

单位：个

指标	Item	全市 Total	市区 Urban District	萧山区 Xiaoshan
合计	**Total**	**2906**	**2105**	**269**
按活动区域分	**Grouped by Region**			
地级社团	City－level Societies	742	742	－
县级社团	County－level Societies	2164	1363	269
按性质分	**Grouped by Category**			
科技与研究	Technology and Research	233	182	20
生态环境	Ecological Envirenment	22	14	3
教育	Education	34	27	2
卫生	Health	102	86	11
社会服务	Social Services	197	144	21
文化	Culture	230	188	28
体育	Sport	287	231	24
法律	Law	7	6	3
工商业服务	Industry and Business Services	698	522	84
宗教	Religion	42	26	4
农业及农村发展	Agricure and Rural Development	155	80	21
职业及从业组织	Vocational and Business Organizations	353	158	28
国际及涉外组织	International and Foreign Organizations	－	－	－
其他	Other	546	441	20

团体机构情况(2016年)

Organizations at County Level(2016)

(unit)

余杭区 Yuhang	富阳区 Fuyang	桐庐县 Tonglu	淳安县 Chun'an	建德市 Jiande	临安市 Lin'an
249	**216**	**217**	**226**	**132**	**226**
–	–	–	–	–	–
249	216	217	226	132	226
18	9	21	7	16	7
1	1	1	3	1	3
1	3	2	2	1	2
12	6	6	3	4	3
13	14	16	12	13	12
20	26	23	3	13	3
25	30	19	13	11	13
1	1	1	–	–	–
84	56	72	45	14	45
5	3	5	4	3	4
10	29	31	12	20	12
49	13	10	81	23	81
–	–	–	–	–	–
10	25	10	41	13	41

13－19　社会保障情况(主要年份)

Social Security(Main Years)

单位:万人　　　　(10000 persons)

项目 Item	2005	2010	2011	2012	2013	2014	2015	2016
城镇登记失业人员 Number of the Registered Unemployed Persons in Urban	6.09	4.85	4.40	3.97	4.60	4.03	3.67	3.72
城镇登记失业率(%) The Registered Rate of Unemployment in Urban (%)	3.71	2.19	1.86	1.63	1.85	1.84	1.74	1.72
失业人员再就业 The Re－employed Persons of Unemployment	13.09	15.54	13.17	13.29	13.13	13.50	14.22	11.48
职工基本养老保险参保人数 Number of Persons in the Basic Pension Program in Urban	227.58	383.97	428.12	492.62	530.70	559.48	569.09	575.98
失业保险参保人数 Number of Persons in the Unemployment Insurance Program	118.36	243.98	277.53	299.78	316.36	331.83	349.42	374.16
职工基本医疗保险参保人数 Number of Persons in the Basic Medical Insurance Program	187.71	345.24	386.33	425.82	448.35	469.40	500.21	529.32
工伤保险参保人数 Number of Persons in the Work－injure Insurance Program	111.03	314.95	355.28	382.21	394.82	406.65	418.17	428.41
生育保险参保人数 Number of Persons in the Bear Insurance Program	96.41	228.53	254.38	277.11	292.01	309.23	324.59	349.33
城乡居民养老保险(障)人数 Number of Persons in the Urban and Rural old－age Security	－	106.30	112.35	112.98	106.40	103.97	99.45	95.51
城乡居民参加医疗保险人数 Number of urban and rural residents participated in medical insurance	350.60	408.32	392.69	378.99	373.93	370.81	370.50	368.21

13－20 分地区社会保障情况(2016 年末)

Social Security by Region(End of 2016)

单位:人 (persons)

指标 Item	职工基本养老保险参保人数 Number of Employed Persons in the Basic Pension Program	职工基本医疗保险参保人数 Number of Persons in the Basic Medical Insurance Program	工伤保险参保人数 Number of Persons in the Work－injure Insurance Program	生育保险参保人数 Number of Persons in the Bear Insurance Program	失业保险参保人数 Number of Persons in the Unemployment Insurance Program
全 市 Total	**5759791**	**5293163**	**4284143**	**3493291**	**3741601**
市 区 Urban District	5069152	4728878	3829159	3190115	3443279
#萧山区 Xiaoshan	933292	763712	483811	476822	482114
余杭区 Yuhang	721590	615763	539315	420402	429830
富阳区 Fuyang	399701	284081	278449	173577	192040
桐庐县 Tonglu	168732	148221	123885	87542	68839
淳安县 Chun'an	97163	97313	88375	46242	48835
建德市 Jiande	180295	128315	84122	73756	76824
临安市 Lin'an	244449	190436	158602	95636	103824

主要统计指标解释

就业人员劳动报酬 指各单位在一定时期内直接支付给本单位全部就业人员的劳动报酬总额。

在岗职工工资总额 指各单位在一定时期内直接支付给本单位全部在岗职工的劳动报酬总额。

工资总额的计算原则应以直接支付给职工的全部劳动报酬为根据。各单位支付给本单位全部职工的劳动报酬,不论是计入成本的还是不计入成本的,不论是以货币形式支付还是以实物形式支付的,不论是单位自筹的资金还是上级(或政府财政部门)下拨的资金,不论是厂级单位筹集的资金还是下属车间(科室)及附属经营单位筹集的资金,均应列入工资总额计算的范围。

在岗职工平均工资 指各单位的在岗职工在一定时期内平均每人所得的工资额。它表明一定时期内在岗职工工资收入的高低程度,是反映在岗职工工资水平的主要指标。计算公式为:

$$在岗职工平均工资=\frac{报告期实际支付的全部在岗职工工资总额}{报告期全部在岗职工平均人数}$$

全社会单位 包括独立核算的机关、事业单位,非私营企业和私营企业,但不含个体工商户。

离休、退休、退职人员 指正式办理了离休、退休、退职手续,并享受相应的离休、退休、退职待遇的人员。

保险福利费用 指企业、事业、机关单位在工资以外实际支付给职工和离休、退休、退职人员个人以及用于集体的劳动保险和福利费用。

社会福利事业单位 指集中收养社会孤、老、残、幼的机构。包括由民政部门管理的社会福利院、儿童福利院、精神病人福利院和城镇集体办的福利院,以及农村集体举办的敬老院。

社会福利事业单位收养人数 包括民政部门管理和城镇及农村集体举办的社会福利事业单位中收养的老人,少年儿童,缺乏生活自理能力的残疾人员和精神病人。

商品零售价格指数 是反映城乡商品零售价格变动趋势的一种经济指数。零售物价的调整变动直接影响到城乡居民的生活支出和国家的财政收入,影响居民购买力和市场供需平衡,影响消费与积累的比例。因此,计算零售价格指数,可以从一个侧面对上述经济活动进行观察和分析。

居民消费价格指数 是反映一定时期内城乡居民所购买的生活消费品价格和服务项目价格变动趋势和程度的相对数。是综合了城市居民消费价格指数和农民消费价格指数计算取得。利用居民消费价格指数,可以观察和分析消费品的零售价格和服务价格变动对城乡居民实际生活支出的影响程度。

工业生产者出厂价格指数 是反映全部工业产品出厂价格总水平的变动趋势和程度的相对数。其中除包括工业企业售给商业、外贸、物资部门的产品外,还包括售给工业和其他部门的生产资料以及直接售给居民的生活消费品。通过工业生产价格指数能观察出厂价格变动对工业总产值的影响。

Explanatory Notes on Main Statistical Indicators

Labour Remuneration refers to total payment by various units to their employees during a certain period of time, including total wage bill of permanent workers and staff and remuneration payment to other employees.

Total Wages of Fully Employed Staff and Workers refer to the total remuneration payment to fully employed staff and workers in various units during a certain period of time. The calculation of total wages is based on the total remuneration payment to the staff and workers. Therefore, all the wages and salaries and other payments to staff and workers are included in the total wages regardless of their sources, category, and forms (in kind or cash). (Total wages of staff and workers in this yearbook include only total wages of fully employed staff and workers, excluding the living allowances distributed to those who have left their working units while keeping their labour contract/employment relation unchanged).

Average Wage of Fully Employed Staff and Workers refers to the average wage per person during a certain period of time for fully employed staff and workers in enterprises, institutions, and government agencies, which reflects the general level of wage income during a certain period of time and is calculated as follows:

$$\text{Average Wage of Fully Employed Staff and Workers} = \frac{\text{Total wages of Fully employed staff and workers in Reference Period}}{\text{Average Number of Fully employed Staff and workers in Reference period}}$$

Units of Whole Society refers to independent accounting units of government organizations and institutions, non – private and private enterprises, but excluding individual business.

Retired and Resigned Person refers to the persons who have form ally gone through the formalities for their retirement or quitting work and enjoy the corresponding treatments.

Insurance and welfare Funds refers to labour insurance and welf are funds paid by enterprises, organizations and institutions to their staff and workers as well as retired and resigned persons in addition to their wages and salaries.

Social Welfare Institutions refer to institutions taking care of old people without children, handicapped people and orphans. They include social welfare institutions run by civil affairs departments, children welfare institutions, social welfare institutions for mental patients, and collective – owned old people's home in rural areas.

Number of People Taken in by social welfare Institutions refers to the number of old people, children, totally dependent handicapped people and mental patients taken in by social welfare institutions run by civil affairs departments and those run by collective units in urban and rural areas.

Retail price Index reflects the general change in retail prices of commodities. The change and adjustment in retail prices directly affect the living expenditure of urban and rural residents, government revenue, purchasing power of residents and the equilibrium of market supply and demand, and the ratio of consumption to accumulation. Therefore, the calculation of retail price index is useful to analyze the changes of the above economic activities.

Consumer Price Index reflects the trend and degree of changes in prices of consumer goods and services purchased by urban and rural residents, and is a composite index derived from the urban consumer price index and the rural consumer price index. Consumer price index can be used to analyze the impact of consumer price change on actual expenditure for living cost of urban and rural residents.

Ex – factory price index of Industrial Products reflects the trend and degree of changes in general ex – factory prices of all industrial products, including sales of industrial products by and industrial enterprise to all units outside the enterprise, as well as sales of consumer goods to residents. It can be used to analyze the impact of ex – factory prices on gross industrial output value.

中国统计出版社最新图书简目

（仅供参考，以实际出版为准）

统计资料

中国统计年鉴	中国统计摘要	中国发展报告
中国经济普查年鉴	国际统计年鉴	金砖国家联合统计手册
中国—东盟国家统计手册	中国农村统计年鉴	中国县域统计年鉴
中国城市统计年鉴	中国对外直接投资统计公报	中国地区经济监测报告
中国贸易外经统计年鉴	中国零售和餐饮连锁企业统计年鉴	中国商品交易市场统计年鉴
大中型批发零售和住宿餐饮企业统计年鉴	中国农产品价格调查年鉴	中国住户调查年鉴
中国价格统计年鉴	中国能源统计年鉴	全国农产品成本收益资料汇编
中国环境统计年鉴	中国建筑业统计年鉴	国外资源、能源和环境统计资料汇编
中国工业统计年鉴	中国城乡建设统计年鉴	中国县城建设统计年鉴
中国城市建设统计年鉴	中国科技统计年鉴	中国房地产统计年鉴
中国证券期货统计年鉴	中国劳动统计年鉴	中国第三产业统计年鉴
工业企业科技活动资料	中国社会统计年鉴	中国高技术产业统计年鉴
中国人才资源统计报告	中国教育统计年鉴	中国人口和就业统计年鉴
文化及相关产业统计概览	中国文化及相关产业统计年鉴	中国教育经费统计年鉴
中国民族统计年鉴	中国残疾人事业统计年鉴	中国民政统计年鉴
中国乡镇街道行政区域简册	中国基本单位统计年鉴	中国妇女儿童状况统计资料（英）

省级综合统计年鉴系列

北京 天津 河北 山西 内蒙古 辽宁 吉林 黑龙江 上海 江苏 浙江 安徽 福建 江西 山东 河南 湖北 湖南 广东 广西 海南 重庆 四川 贵州 云南 西藏 陕西 甘肃 青海 宁夏 新疆 新疆生产建设兵团

市（县）级综合统计年鉴系列

滨海新区 石家庄 唐山 邯郸 保定 沧州 邢台 廊坊 承德 衡水 秦皇岛 张家口 太原 大同 阳泉 长治 晋城 朔州 晋中 运城 忻州 临汾 吕梁 呼和浩特 呼和浩特新城区 鄂尔多斯 包头 沈阳 大连 长春 吉林 延吉 四平 通化 松原 哈尔滨 齐齐哈尔 黑龙江垦区 上海浦东新区 南京 无锡 徐州 常州 苏州 南通 连云港 淮安 盐城 扬州 镇江 泰州 宿迁 江阴 丹阳 海门 杭州 宁波 温州 嘉兴 湖州 绍兴 金华 衢州 舟山 台州 丽水 合肥 安庆 马鞍山 福州 厦门 宁德 漳州 龙岩 南昌 九江 上饶 新余 抚州 萍乡 赣州 吉安 景德镇 济南 青岛 潍坊 枣庄 日照 滕州 郑州 洛阳 平顶山 三门峡 商丘 信阳 济源 汝州 武汉 十堰 荆州 宜昌 荆门 咸宁 长沙 广州 深圳 惠州 东莞 汕尾 南宁 柳州 桂林 来宾 河池 防城港 海口 三亚 成都 贵阳 黔南 毕节 昆明 西安 咸阳 延安 宝鸡 安康 铜川 汉中 榆林 兰州 庆阳 银川 乌鲁木齐 兵团一师 兵团十师

调查年鉴系列

天津 山西 内蒙古 辽宁 吉林 上海 福建 江西 河南 湖北 湖南 广西 重庆 四川 云南 甘肃 宁夏 新疆

统计方法应用/实用手册

实用 SAS 统计分析教程	马克威统计分析与数据挖掘应用案例	统计公文知识问答
乡镇统计人员岗位知识培训系列教材：	辅助调查员岗位基础知识	乡镇统计人员岗位基础知识
县级统计人员岗位知识培训系列教材：	Excel 在统计工作中的应用	简明统计分析
地市级统计人员岗位知识培训系列教材：	统计报告与演示	Excel 在统计工作中的应用

统计通俗读物/统计科普图书

国家统计局核心统计指标变迁	货架上的统计	账本里的统计

重点图书

砥砺奋进的五年——从十八大到十九大	新编英汉汉英统计大词典	中华医学统计百科全书
新常态下的中国服务业：理论与实践	新动能新产业发展报告—2017	
挑大学选专业 2018—考研择校指南	挑大学选专业 2018—高考志愿填报指南	

中国统计出版社发行部电话：（010）63376907 63376908 同榫行书店电话：68783171 68783172

地址：北京市丰台区西三环南路甲 6 号 邮政编码：100073 网址：http://www.zgtjcbs.com